All About Child Care and Early Education

A Comprehensive Resource for Child Care Professionals

Marilyn Segal

Betty Bardige

Mary Jean Woika

Jesse Leinfelder

Nova Southeastern University,
Mailman Segal Institute for Early Childhood Studies

PEARSON

Boston   New York   San Francisco
Mexico City   Montreal   Toronto   London   Madrid   Munich   Paris
Hong Kong   Singapore   Tokyo   Cape Town   Sydney

Series Editor: Traci Mueller
Series Editorial Assistant: James P. Neal, III
Senior Marketing Manager: Krista Clark
Production Editor: Annette Joseph
Editorial Production Service: Communicáto, Ltd.
Composition Buyer: Linda Cox
Manufacturing Buyer: Andrew Turso
Electronic Composition: Denise Hoffman
Interior Design: Denise Hoffman
Photo Researcher: Katharine S. Cook
Cover Administrator: Joel Gendron

For related titles and support materials, visit our online catalog at www.ablongman.com.

Between the time website information is gathered and then published, it is not unusual for some sites to have closed. Also, the transcription of URLs can result in typographical errors. The publisher would appreciate notification where these errors occur so that they may be corrected in subsequent editions.

Many of the designations used by manufacturers and sellers to distinguish their products are claimed as trademarks. Where those designations appear in this book and Allyn and Bacon was aware of a trademark claim, the designations have been printed in caps or initial caps.

ISBN 0-205-45789-4

Printed in the United States of America

10 9 8 7 6 5 4 3 2 1   WEB   09 08 07 06 05

Contents

Section III   On Stage: Supporting Physical and Intellectual Development   103

Chapter 4 • Physical Development   113

Chapter 5 • Cognitive Development   131

Chapter 6 ● Communication   157

Introduction

All About Child Care and Early Education is a comprehensive resource book for child care professionals, including teachers, caregivers, family child care providers, administrators, and directors. It provides practical suggestions for setting up classrooms; for developing curriculums for infants, toddlers, and preschoolers; for meeting children's social/emotional needs; and for working effectively with parents and staff. Child Development Associate (CDA) candidates and other students preparing for roles as early childhood educators can use *All About Child Care and Early Education* as a primary text. Students are also encouraged to use the *Trainee's Manual* that accompanies this text, and instructors may refer to the *Instructor's Guide.* These three books comprise the *All About Child Care and Early Education* series.

> *The early years are a critical time for learning and character formation.*

Research increasingly confirms what parents and caregivers have always known: The early years are a critical time for learning and for character formation. Those who teach and care for young children have an awesome responsibility. Their work requires skill and training, creativity and intelligence, and a lot of energy. Working with young children is also a great adventure. Each day, you share the wonder and delight of children who are discovering things for the first time.

Come along! Let us show you the wonders of a child's world and share the behind-the-scenes techniques and activities that can help you make a wonderful world for children.

Plan for the Text

All About Child Care and Early Education is divided into these five sections:

- *Section I, A Child Care Revue*, provides a brief history of child care and early education and describes the major theories of child development and selected curriculum models. The future challenges for the field are addressed, as well.
- *Section II, Setting the Stage*, describes developmentally appropriate indoor and outdoor learning environments. Individual chapters cover the CDA Functional Areas of Safe, Healthy, and Learning Environment.
- *Section III, On Stage*, provides broad developmental overviews of infants, toddlers, and preschoolers. Then, in separate chapters, it describes the typical sequences of development in particular domains and suggests methods of enhancing development at each stage. The CDA Functional Areas of Physical, Cognitive, Communication, and Creative are covered in individual chapters.

- *Section IV, The Performers*, focuses on emotional and social development. It covers the CDA Functional Areas of Self, Social, and Guidance.
- *Section V, Behind the Scenes*, addresses the underlying relationships and practices of adults that produce good outcomes for children. Individual chapters cover the CDA Functional Areas of Families, Program Management, and Professionalism.

All About Child Care and Early Education combines the broad perspective of an early childhood professor and policy expert with the practical know-how of a practitioner who works with children on a daily basis. All of the curriculums, activities, and suggestions for classroom management have been field tested in child care centers that serve children from a wide spectrum of ethnic and socioeconomic backgrounds. And in the interest of gender neutrality, the text has been written to alternate between the use of *he* and *she* where a general example refers to one individual—say, one child, parent, or teacher. Thus, some of the children are referred to as *he*'s and some are referred to as *she*'s. This usage is not intended to imply that the discussion refers only to someone of that gender but rather is an effort at making the language straightforward and clear.

Acknowledgments

We would like to thank several individuals for their help in preparing this book:

Charlene Swanson, Director of Child Care Training at the Institute for Early Childhood Studies of Nova Southeastern University, is a guru on health and safety and a stickler for creating learning materials that take into account the characteristics of adult learners. Dr. Swanson helped eliminate jargon and flagged passages that needed clarification.

Kori Bardige, an early childhood special educator, read our drafts with a teacher's eyes, and provided many practical suggestions, tricks of the trade, and tips for beginning teachers. We are grateful for her good ideas and good sense and for her unfailingly cheerful assistance.

Christine DiSilvestro, administrative assistant, caught our typos, suggested improvements, and integrated our multiple revisions into a properly formatted manuscript.

We would also like to acknowledge the A. L. Mailman Family Foundation for its ongoing support of the NSU Mailman Segal Institute for Early Childhood Studies and of this book.

We would like to thank the following reviewers, who read through the manuscript and offered useful suggestions: Jeanne W. Barker, Tallahassee Community College; Suzanne George, Southwest Missouri State University; and Kathleen Ludlow, Northern Virginia Community College.

About the Authors

Marilyn Segal, Ph.D., a noted developmental psychologist, educator, and researcher specializing in early childhood education, founded the Mailman Segal Institute for Early Childhood Studies at Nova Southeastern University in the early 1970s. The Institute offers a variety of early child care and education programs, parent/child classes, and professional development opportunities. Dr. Segal has developed and implemented training programs for Head Start teachers, infant/toddler caregivers, family support workers, and Child Development Associate (CDA) candidates. She has also created three comprehensive early childhood curriculums and is the author or co-author of sixteen books on early childhood development, including the popular *Your Child at Play* series.

Betty Bardige, Ed.D., is an early childhood policy and program consultant and chairs a national foundation on early childhood. She pioneered the development of educational software for preschoolers and developed related reading and math curriculums. She has written books for parents about supporting early development, books for teachers on early literacy, and books on national early care policies.

Mary Jean Woika, M.Ed., is the director of Nova Southeastern University's CDA program. She designed the active learning curriculum for the CDA course series at NSU and teaches a variety of classes for early childhood practitioners. She draws on her teaching experience, her experience as a child care center director, as well as her work with children with special needs in inclusive settings.

Jesse Leinfelder, Ed.D., a specialist in adult learning and training-of-trainer approaches, is Associate Director of Professional Development at the Mailman Segal Institute for Early Childhood Studies at NSU. She has worked at all levels of early child care and education in a variety of settings. She lectures nationally about strategies for resolving the cost/quality crisis facing child care, focusing on building infrastructure and investment to support quality enhancement through professional development.

Section I

A Child Care Revue

Miss Go-with-the-Flow had just enrolled in a Child Development Associate (CDA) course. She and some fellow students were looking through the textbook they were using for the course.

Miss Go-with-the-Flow: "Why do textbooks always start out with history and theories? I've been a preschool teacher for eight years, and believe me, nothing that goes on in my class has anything to do with theory! As far as I'm concerned, all you need to be a good teacher is a good dose of common sense."

Miss Clock-Watcher: "I couldn't agree with you more. I sure don't know any theory, and my kids don't give me any trouble. I know that kids love routine, and I keep to a strict schedule. Every day, we start out writing in our daybooks; then comes circle time, learning games, bathroom time, snack, outdoor play, bathroom, lunch, rest, free choice, circle time, and dismissal. When it's time to make a transition, I just flick the lights and the children automatically go to the next activity."

Miss Go-with-the-Flow: "Well, the kids I work with don't like to be scheduled. They are free spirits, just like me. They choose what they want to do, and if they're really into something—like building a block structure, putting on a puppet show, or playing 'doctor'—I am not about to stop them because it's bathroom time." ●

Although Miss Go-with-the-Flow and Miss Clock-Watcher both insist that you don't need to know theory to teach a class of preschoolers, these two seasoned teachers have very different ideas about the best way to operate a preschool classroom. Despite their insistence that their teaching techniques are based on common sense and not on theory, it is obvious that these teachers are making different assumptions about what is good for children. Although they do not realize it, these teachers are taking opposite sides on a theoretical issue.

This section provides a brief history of child care in the United States, gives a quick overview of the theories of child development that have shaped early childhood curriculums and instructional philosophies, and discusses some of the challenges faced by our field as we look to the future. Our hope is that this overview will help you to recognize the impact of theory on practice and will inspire you to play an active role in shaping the future of early childhood care and education.

Changing Perspectives: The American Scene
History of Child Care and Early Education

Child care, meaning care for children by someone other than their parents and family members, has a long history in the United States. Through the years, as the status and roles of women have changed and as more women have joined the workforce, there has been an increased recognition that providing quality child care for young children must be a national as well as a family concern. As we trace the history of child care in the United States, we recognize the close connections among the history of child care, the prevailing economic and social conditions, and the history of women in the workforce.

1828   The Boston Infant School is founded with the goals of providing a positive environment for children and facilitating the entrance of women into the workforce. Children from the age of 18 months to school age are accepted.

> *The provision of quality child care for young children must be a national as well as a family concern.*

1860   The first kindergarten is started in Boston. In contrast to the Boston Infant School, which emphasized physical care, the kindergarten emphasizes education for young children.

1880–1890   The day nursery movement begins in response to rapid urbanization and industrialization in the Northeast. The goals of these nurseries are to provide child care for children and training and employment for their parents.

1920   The professionalism of child care providers becomes a major issue. Trained teachers place an emphasis on education, de-emphasizing support to parents.

1933   Government support for child care begins, with the goal of providing jobs for preschool teachers during the Great Depression.

1940–1945   Extensive government support is given to child care, so that women can take jobs in defense factories during World War II. Much of the support is discontinued when the war ends.

1950–1960   The prevailing philosophy of the time pegs mothers as socially deviant if their children are enrolled in child care for more than two to three hours per day. The mother's place is considered to be in the home.

1965   Head Start is initiated as a key piece of the Johnson administration's so-called war on poverty. It provides education and health services for lower-income children and leadership and employment opportunities for their parents. The goal is to give these children a boost so that they will be ready to start school on a par with their more privileged peers.

The Child Development Associate (CDA) training system was founded during the early years of Head Start.

1970–1980   Child care is increasingly recognized as being potentially beneficial for children, regardless of whether they are living in poverty. This change in thinking is brought about by the women's movement, by new research demonstrating the benefits of quality child care, and by the fact that many women want to seek the economic benefits of returning to work while their children are still young.

1980–1990   With an increasing number of women with infants and young children joining the workforce, the shortage of available, affordable, and quality child care reaches crisis proportions.

1990–2000   An overriding concern in this decade is the severe shortage of accessible and affordable child care. This shortage is exacerbated by welfare reform, which forces welfare parents with young children to join the workforce.

An equally pressing concern is related to the quality of early child care. This concern is prompted by studies of the quality of child care in the United States and by what came to be known as the "brain research." Well-designed studies of child care quality, based on a broad sampling of child care centers and family child care homes, found that the quality of most child care in the country ranged from mediocre to downright dangerous. Programs for infants and toddlers received the lowest ratings. During the same period, research studies on brain development pointed out the important role of early experiences in shaping the structure and chemistry of the brain. According to this research, the early years provide special windows of opportunity for the enhancement of social, emotional, and intellectual development.

2000–2010   The National Academy of Sciences publishes *From Neurons to Neighborhoods: The Science of Early Childhood Development* in 2000 and *Eager to Learn: Educating Our Preschoolers* in 2001. Based on comprehensive reviews of research, both of these reports highlight the importance of nurturing relationships and learning opportunities in the early years (including infancy and toddlerhood) and stress the need for thorough preparation and support of caregivers and teachers.

As policymakers grow concerned about assuring "school readiness" for all children, there are new emphases on literacy and on numeracy (or math skills). Assessment of both children and programs is a major issue, as policymakers demand accountability and early educators insist that any testing must take into account the unique characteristics of young children and be driven by the best interests of the children and their families. In many states, there is a push for universal prekindergarten programs that would offer publicly funded preschools in a range of public and private settings. At the same time, the growing diversity of the United States is prompting new attention to the role of culture and to the importance of sustaining home language, supporting cultural identity, and building relationships with families and their communities.

In tracing the history of child care in the United States, we should recognize that many of the child care issues we must grapple with in this millennium are, in fact, older issues revisited: Is child care a benefit for children or simply a necessity for parents? Should child care be primarily caregiving or primarily educational? Should infants be enrolled in child care? Should the government be responsible for supporting or subsidizing child care? Are child care workers a part of a professional community? How can high-quality child care be made available to all children, regardless of family income?

Recurring Themes: Theories of Child Development and Learning

While economic and social conditions have influenced the popularity of child care over the past century, the philosophical foundations of child care have been determined by psychological theory. The theoretical writings of several major psychologists and educators over the past century have been responsible for the development of different models and practices.

The major theorists that will be described in this introduction have provided us with a basic framework for understanding child development. They have enabled us to recognize the expected sequence of developmental events and, at the same time, have provided the rationale for individual differences. Most important, these theorists have provided guidelines for child development practitioners who seek to enhance children's well-being, knowledge, and competence.

Maria Montessori

Maria Montessori was an Italian physician who developed an interest in education in a somewhat round-about way. As a young physician, she was appointed as director of a state-supported school for children with mental deficiencies. In this position, she had the opportunity to take a close look at children's learning processes and to see how play materials could facilitate children's learning. When Dr. Montessori was appointed in 1902 to direct a "children's house" for the children of Italian laborers, she was able to put her ideas into practice.

Here are some of Montessori's ideas that have influenced child care practices:

- The early years are ideal for learning.
- Children learn best by manipulating real materials.
- Materials can be designed to promote learning of a specific concept.
- Educational programs for young children should be organized so that activities and objectives for learning move from less complex to more complex and demanding.
- Children need a variety of sensory experiences—including touch, taste, and smell—to develop their full capacities.
- Children appreciate beauty and order. With guidance and encouragement, they will learn to maintain a beautiful and orderly environment.
- Children are intrinsically motivated to learn and are capable of taking an increasingly more active role in planning and supervising their own learning.
- Parents are very important and should be involved in their child's education.

Arnold Gesell

The work of Arnold Gesell provided the theoretical case for preschool programs in the United States during the middle years of the twentieth century. Dr. Gesell, a physician, believed that patterns of behavior unfold automatically during the course of a child's development in the same way as a child's physical growth and motor development. Gesell was one of the early leaders in the United States in the systematic study of young children's behavior. He and his colleagues at Yale University spent many years observing and recording the behavior of infants and young children.

Gesell's work has provided teachers, parents, and psychologists with an outline of what to expect of normal children during the course of development. His writings have influenced child care practices in the United States in several important ways, including the following:

- Children develop according to their own natural timetables. Attempts to speed up their maturation, such as teaching a baby to walk early, are a waste of time.

- Children should be provided with enriching experiences that are appropriate for their own level of development.

- Teachers should become familiar with developmental sequences so that they can provide individual children with appropriate experiences.

- Observing children at play is the most valid way of gathering information about their development.

Jean Piaget

Jean Piaget was a Swiss psychologist who began the systematic study of children's behavior in the 1920s. And even though Piaget's teachings have had a dramatic effect on educational theory, his focus was not on education but on the development of intelligence. Piaget described and elaborated the following basic concepts:

- All children, beginning from infancy, pass through an orderly succession of developmental stages and substages. Their current stage of development determines the way they interpret experiences, structure problems, and seek solutions.

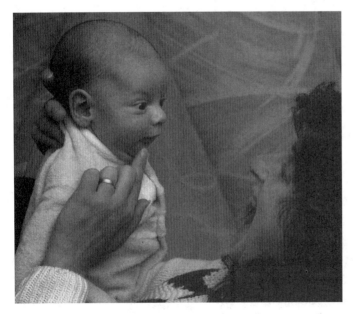

- The infant is in the *sensorimotor stage* of development. He understands the world by the actions he performs. The preschool child is in the *preoperational stage* of development. In contrast to the infant, the preschool child recognizes that objects exist even when he does not touch them. The preschooler has developed his own system of symbols (images, props, and words) to represent objects in the real world.

- Learning takes place by the processes of *assimilation* and *accommodation*. When a child is introduced to a new phenomenon, she tries to understand it by assimilating it, or associating it with things that she already knows. As the child gains experience with the new phenomenon, her way of thinking changes, or accommodates, to take into account the characteristics of the new phenomenon. This implies that children should be introduced to new experiences that are related to experiences they have already had but that also challenge their thinking in some way.

- Children are innately curious and motivated to learn, whether or not they receive external rewards and encouragement.

Piaget's Stages of Intellectual Development

Approximate Age	Stage	Accomplishments
Birth to 2 Years	Sensorimotor Stage	Knowing the world through action and observation
• 0–1 month	Substage 1: Reflexes	Inborn responses to external stimulation, such as light, sound, and touch
• 1–4 months	Substage 2: Repeating Motions (Primary Circular Reactions)	Recognizing sights and sounds that go together; noticing consequences of actions (e.g., that a mobile moves when batted); repeating actions with interesting consequences
• 4–8 months	Substage 3: Development of Schemes or Action Patterns (Secondary Circular Reactions)	Coordination of simple actions into *schema*, or patterns, such as reaching and grasping, bringing a toy to the mouth and chewing it; exploring objects by shaking, banging, turning over, poking, and pushing
• 8–12 months	Substage 4: Using Tools (Coordination of Secondary Circular Reactions)	Covering and uncovering objects; developing *object permanence* (out of sight is no longer out of mind); using one object, such as a stick or blanket, to move or retrieve another; coordinating actions in order to accomplish a purpose
• 12–18 months	Substage 5: "Little Scientist" (Tertiary Circular Reactions)	Repeating and varying actions (e.g., dropping or throwing a toy from a height) in order to see the results; exploring and testing
• 18–24 months	Substage 6: Mental Representation	Labeling objects and events with words; imitating sequences of actions; beginnings of pretending
2 to 6 or 7 Years	Preoperational Stage (Intuitive Operations)	Use of symbols and language; imaginative play
7 to 11 or 12 Years	Concrete Operations	Categorizing in two dimensions (e.g., color and shape); understanding that size can be held constant as shape changes; developing number concepts and arithmetic; playing by rules that are the same for all players
11 Years or Older through Adulthood	Formal Operations	Making logical inferences and abstract reasoning; doing mathematical proofs; understanding the scientific method and theories; understanding disciplines such as philosophy, history, and literary criticism

Based on this system of beliefs, preschools that ascribe to the Piagetian philosophy carry out the following practices:

- The teacher is seen as a facilitator. She arranges the environment and prepares activities and experiences appropriate to the developmental level of the children in the class.

- Recognizing that the child learns by actively organizing and constructing the environment, the teacher provides real materials for the child to sort, order, and arrange.

- Concrete experiences are introduced before abstract concepts. For example, a child is given ample experience with objects floating and sinking before being taught scientific concepts such as density and displacement.

- Imaginative play is encouraged. Pretending is viewed as a way of developing a system of symbols to stand for real events and as a way of learning to take different points of view.

- The child is given many opportunities to experiment with different media, including water, sand, paint, clay, and play dough. Through manipulation, the child will make her own discoveries about the nature of reality.

- No external rewards are offered for the accomplishment of a task, and children are permitted to make choices about what they are going to do.

- Repetition of a task is encouraged, if this is what the child wants.

B. F. Skinner

B. F. Skinner was a behavioral psychologist who had a major influence on both therapeutic and educational practices. Skinner recognized that patterns of behavior are influenced by their consequences. Children who are rewarded, or *positively reinforced*, for behaving in a particular way will increase the frequency of that behavior.

Children can learn new behaviors by *successive approximation*. By breaking a learning task into small segments and by carefully using rewards, a skilled adult can accelerate a child's learning. Negative behaviors that interfere with learning can also be brought under control by appropriate reinforcement. While punishment is ineffective because it creates anxiety, maladaptive behaviors can be reduced by not providing positive reinforcement or by reinforcing incompatible behaviors.

The ideas generated by B. F. Skinner that have influenced practices in child care include the following:

- Learning is an observable and measurable change in behavior.
- Learning can be facilitated by breaking tasks down into small segments.
- Learning can be strengthened by repetition.
- It is more effective to reinforce good behavior than to punish negative behavior.
- Negative behavior is learned and can therefore be unlearned.

- The teacher who is concerned about a child's negative behavior needs to take into account what happens after the negative behavior occurs. Is the child being rewarded in some way? For example, is she getting extra attention or avoiding having to do something she doesn't like?
- Negative behaviors can be eliminated by changing their consequences.

Erik Erikson

Erik Erikson has not had a direct influence on the development of early childhood curriculum and practices. Nonetheless, his focus on development as a lifelong process and his recognition of the importance of social interaction within each developmental stage have had a profound impact on our understanding of children and their parents.

Erikson described eight sequential stages of psychosocial development. At each stage, children are faced with challenges or issues that need to be resolved. Children who successfully meet these predictable challenges develop emotional resources that help them master the challenges of later stages.

The young child experiences three psychosocial stages:

1. Basic trust versus mistrust
2. Autonomy versus shame and doubt
3. Initiative versus guilt

The first psychosocial stage involves the development of trust. Babies who are loved and well cared for develop a sense of trust in the people who love them. This feeling of trust is also associated with feelings of self-worth and confidence. The trusting infant becomes an exploratory toddler.

The second psychosocial stage characterizes the toddler between 1 and 3 years old. The major issue the toddler faces is developing autonomy and overcoming shame and doubt. Toddlers who master self-care tasks and who have had opportunities to make choices and explore new territory develop confidence in their own abilities. They learn the basics of self-control and overcome the feelings of doubt and shame that they experience when they are told "no."

Preschool children between 3 and 6 years old are in the third psychosocial stage and facing the crisis of initiative versus guilt. As they interact with each other, they learn how to take initiative without being hurtful. Similarly, they gradually learn that the scary or mean things they imagine don't come true just because they think them. Children who have learned to be good playmates are ready for the challenges of the school-age years.

Lev Vygotsky

Lev Vygotsky was a Russian psychologist who asserted that the course of development is shaped by a child's interactions with a social environment. Like Piaget, Vygotsky recognized that children actively interpret the world around them and construct explanations that make sense to them. Vygotsky also recognized that children learn from experiences that challenge their current understandings and capacities—but not too much. He referred to the area of moderate challenge as the *zone of proximal* (nearby or next to) *development*.

Unlike Piaget, however, Vygotsky recognized that children are not just individuals trying to make sense of a world whose laws they deduce from experimentation and experience. They are also social beings, and much of their learning occurs through the use of language, nonverbal communication, and shared meaning making. As children share their insights, discoveries, questions, and observations with other people, they jointly construct symbols, explanations, and stories. Vygotsky stressed that children learn through interaction with peers as well as with adults. He urged teachers to *scaffold* children's learning by providing hints, images, intermediate steps, and frameworks that would help them to communicate what they know and to move from one level of understanding to another.

The Constructivists

The *constructivist* position incorporates both Piaget's theory that knowledge is constructed through hands-on experiences in the physical environment and Vygotsky's assertion that knowledge is constructed through social interaction. In other words, the child's level of cognitive development is determined both by the opportunities he is given to learn by doing and the opportunities he has to interact with responsive adults and peers. Individual differences are attributed to children's different experiences with both the physical and social environments. New knowledge is best taught by taking into account children's different starting points and allowing them to learn together by discussing hands-on experiences with each other.

The major theorists described in this introduction have provided us with a basic framework for understanding child development. They have enabled us to recognize the expected sequence of developmental events and, at the same time, have provided the rationale for individual differences. Most important, these theorists have provided guidelines that we, as child development practitioners, can use to enhance children's well-being, knowledge, and competence.

Selected Curriculum Models

The proliferation of early childhood curriculums based on different developmental theories illustrates the impact of theory on practice. In this section, we feature several curriculum models that are used extensively throughout the United States.

High/Scope

The High/Scope curriculum is based on Piaget's concept that children are active learners who construct their knowledge base through playing and experimenting with hands-on materials. High/Scope is a curriculum framework that describes educational ideas and strategies but does not rely on a specific set of materials.

A High/Scope classroom is set up with learning centers that invite children to explore the materials and engage in developmentally appropriate activities. The classroom schedule follows a *plan, do, and reflect* sequence, beginning with a group time in which children are helped to plan their day. Following the planning session, children disperse to the different leaning centers, where they engage in self-initiated or group activities. The day ends with another whole-group gathering, in which children have the opportunity to discuss what they did and reflect on what they learned.

The teacher is responsible for setting up the environment and developing the daily schedule. The schedule allots time for small-group and large-group activities. These activities are built around *key experiences*, designed to promote the development of rational thinking within each curriculum area. The teacher is also responsible for assessing the development of each child and assuring that each child engages in activities that promote his continuing growth.

High/Scope places a major emphasis on teacher training. This training is designed to help teachers understand the rationale of key experiences and to plan for their incorporation into each child's daily schedule. Ongoing in-service training hones the teacher's skills and provides him with new and creative curriculum ideas.

A special feature of High/Scope is its emphasis on *cultural relevance*. Each High/Scope program is expected to reflect the cultural and linguistic background of the children it serves and of their families. Children also are given opportunities to learn about other cultures and to appreciate diversity.

The Bank Street Model

The Bank Street model also reflects the point of view of the constructivists, with a special emphasis on the social aspect of learning. Its core beliefs are that children learn best when they like what they are doing and that children who feel confident and competent are motivated to learn and primed for intellectual growth. Children are encouraged to work in groups and to solve problems together.

Like High/Scope classrooms, classrooms that adopt the Bank Street model are organized in interest centers, and the teacher's role is to set up a variety of interesting experiences and to facilitate children's exploration, discussion, and reflection. Unlike High/Scope, however, Bank Street has no set curriculum or set of key experiences. Instead, teachers draw from a wide variety of sources to create classroom and community experiences that motivate children to ask questions, communicate ideas, and get excited about learning.

A distinct feature of the Bank Street approach is the emphasis it places on social studies. Children learn about people from different cultures and are encouraged to ask questions and find out more about other people. Inevitably, children begin to think about the ways in which the families they study are both alike and different from their own families. Motivated by their own curiosity, children broaden their understanding of the world in which they live. Their concrete experiences enable them to engage in higher-level thinking.

The Creative Curriculum

The Creative Curriculum is a system developed by Teaching Strategies, Inc. It began in the 1970s as a project in the Washington, DC, Model Cities Centers, and it now has a preschool as well as an infant/toddler curriculum. Recent publication of the *Developmental Continuum,* a tool for observing children's progress in relation to the objectives of the curriculum, gives coherence to the curriculum.

The Creative Curriculum is built on a base of theory and research about how children grow and learn. The curriculum has five branches, shown as sides of a pentagram:

1. How children develop and learn
2. The learning environment
3. What children learn
4. The teacher's role
5. The family's role

Each of these components is essential to a child's well-being, and together they make up the important conceptual parts of a good early childhood program.

The curriculum framework comes to life in 11 activity areas:

- Blocks
- Dramatic play
- Toys and games
- Art
- Library
- Discovery
- Sand and water
- Music and movement
- Cooking
- Computers
- Outdoors

The Creative Curriculum provides descriptions of these activity areas, lists of important materials to include in each area, and definitions of what children learn while working and playing with the materials. This approach focuses on how teachers can enhance learning and teaching in these 11 areas and how teachers can guide and assess children's learning. There is also a focus on the ways that families can support children's learning at the center and at home.

The Reggio Emilia Approach

The Reggio Emilia approach originated in a town in northern Italy shortly after World War II. Like High/Scope and Bank Street, it embraces the constructivist philosophy. Several features, however, distinguish it from the other constructivist models.

The Reggio Emilia approach stresses the importance of respecting children and discovering their amazing capacities. This begins with an emphasis on *relationships*. Children stay with the same teacher for several years, and the teacher, parents, and other family members work together to nurture children's relationships within the classroom, the school, and the larger community.

Respecting children also means being genuinely interested in their ideas. Rather than being preplanned by the teacher, the Reggio Emilia curriculum, also known as the *project approach*, emerges from the children's interests and questions. The teacher carefully observes the children's spontaneous work and play and brings in objects and experiences that she thinks will intrigue them. Together, the teacher and children conduct long-term projects or investigations that bring forth and stretch the children's ideas. Children are encouraged to ask new questions, to discover the answers through active exploration, and to express their ideas in many different media.

Central to the Reggio Emilia approach is the teacher's role, first and foremost, as a learner. Through careful observation and documentation of each child's work, the teacher gains insights into children's unique ways of thinking and knowing. Teachers become increasingly more effective as they learn from the children they teach.

The teacher's role as a facilitator is also central to the Reggio Emilia approach. The teacher asks questions, makes comments, and encourages the children to question. She challenges the children to explore their own ideas and carry out experiments. She also helps the children become close observers of their environment, paying special attention to different perspectives and details. In addition, the teacher encourages the children to represent their knowledge and ideas in spoken and written language, their own symbolic notation, drawing and painting, dance and pantomime, and various kinds of three-dimensional modeling. As an art coach, the teacher helps children learn new techniques, critique their own work, and redo their work as their thinking develops.

The teacher finds creative ways of displaying the children's products so that they can appreciate their own and each other's work and so that parents and community visitors can know and appreciate what they have been doing. Children often work together to create classroom displays and collective art projects that showcase their work and learning.

The concern with art and design goes beyond the children's work. The Reggio Emilia approach is also concerned with the way space is designed. It recognizes the importance of creating environments that are in harmony with nature and that give children an appreciation of order and beauty. Interior spaces are carefully crafted to encourage creative expression. Each type of environment is furnished with intriguing natural and recycled objects, which are carefully chosen and displayed to encourage children to create and experiment.

Direct Instruction

Although few people believe that young children should spend their day sitting at desks, listening to teachers lecture, and filling out worksheets as instructed, many preschool teachers do give lessons for at least part of the day. Recognizing that young children enjoy and learn from imitation, teachers may show them how to perform simple tasks, such as setting the table and chanting the alphabet, as well as more complex feats, such as stringing beads in elaborate patterns, writing their names, making counting books, and spelling words.

Often, teachers draw on their own or the children's cultural traditions as they plan and carry out lessons. For example, they may use a *call-and-response method*, derived from African American or African Caribbean culture, to teach a color name or arithmetic fact or to engage the children in a familiar story—for instance, "The Big, Bad Wolf said, 'I'll huff, and I'll puff, and I'll blow your house down.' What did he say, children? 'I'll huff, and I'll puff, and I'll blow your house down.'" This method is often used to reinforce important health, safety, and behavioral lessons: "What do we do when we feel angry? We use our words!"

Teachers who use *direct instruction* often follow a pattern of teach, repeat, and reward. The individual child or group is praised for repeating the teacher's lesson or following her instructions correctly. Individual children may also be rewarded with gold stars or "smiley faces" on their hands or on their work.

When young children play "school," they often use a direct instruction approach, even if their own classroom relies predominantly on other methods. They call their class to order and tell their pupils what to do. They quiz them to see if they remember what they have been taught and write new lessons on the board. They may even assign homework and give out stickers for good behavior.

Developmentally Appropriate Practice

Developmentally appropriate practice is the term used by the National Association for the Education of Young Children (NAEYC) to describe ways of teaching and organizing children's experiences that take into account the age and capabilities of each child. All of the methods described in the previous sections can be developmentally appropriate or not, depending on how they are implemented.

For example, it would not be appropriate to ask a group of 2-year-olds in a High/Scope classroom to plan a whole morning or to spend a long time reflecting on what they learned from playing in the sand. It would be appropriate, however, to let the children choose between sand and block play and to talk with them about what they are doing or how the sand feels. Similarly, it would usually be considered inappropriate to give 3-year-olds formal lessons in how to read, whereas it would be considered inappropriate *not* to give these lessons to 5- and 6-year-olds who are interested in books but cannot yet read on their own.

Curriculum Packages

Many teachers and family child care providers use *curriculum packages* that provide suggested activities and materials. A curriculum package may be based on a particular instructional method or framework, such as High/Scope, or it may incorporate a combination of approaches.

Challenges Ahead

This is an exciting and challenging time to be an early childhood educator and care provider, for many reasons:

- More and more mothers are going back to work, so child care is becoming more of a necessity and less of an option. In particular, more and more mothers of infants and toddlers are going back to work, making infant/toddler child care a priority need.
- More and more parents are becoming knowledgeable about child care curriculums and the intellectual potential of young children.
- Parents are continuing to ask for a warm, safe, supportive climate for their children, but they are also asking for intellectual stimulation.
- More and more government agencies are taking a hard look at standards, training, and licensing requirements. The larger the use of child care facilities, the greater the need for regulation.
- More and more corporations are recognizing that providing child care benefits for their employees is in their own self-interest.
- More and more public schools are assuming responsibility for children under 5.
- More and more educators are recognizing that there is no true distinction between quality child care and early childhood education. Quality child care uses developmentally appropriate practices and supports the teaching of young children.
- More and more research regarding the effectiveness of quality child care is being published and distributed.

Child care providers have become increasingly more aware of their status as professionals. They are asking questions like these of their supervisors and of themselves:

- What are my duties and responsibilities as a child care provider?
- What knowledge and skills do I need in my present position?
- What kinds of resources are available to help me acquire this knowledge and these skills?
- What kinds of career opportunities are open to me?
- What will the children in my care enjoy learning?
- How can I make sure that they will be ready to succeed in school?
- What kind of parent involvement should I encourage?
- How can I achieve this involvement?
- How can I, as a child care provider, serve as an advocate for children?

Goals for the Future

In the best of all possible worlds, access to high-quality care and education, beginning at birth, would be the entitlement of every child. In order to achieve this goal, we need to develop policies that will enhance the quality of child care as well as policies that will ensure an adequate supply of accessible and affordable child care options.

> *In the best of all possible worlds, access to high-quality care and education, beginning at birth, would be the entitlement of every child.*

Policies and Practices That Promote Teacher Competency

- Enact licensing laws that require at least 30 hours of prescribed preservice training for all teachers, assistant teachers, and personnel who do not have early childhood degrees or certification. This preservice training must include units on child growth and development, child abuse, and cultural competency.
- Provide scholarships for all early childhood teachers seeking CDAs or advanced early childhood degrees.
- Provide all teachers and assistants with ongoing learning opportunities, including exposure to new research and curriculum ideas, reflection on their own practice, sharing of strategies with colleagues, and formal coursework.

Policies and Practices That Support and Retain Good Teachers

- Provide worthy wages and benefits to child care personnel at every level.
- Develop career lattices that are open to all child care personnel.
- Provide free training and educational programs that enable child care personnel to make lateral or upward moves within the early childhood field.
- Incorporate mentorship as a component of in-service education.

Policies and Practices That Upgrade the Skills of Child Care Directors

- Develop director credentialing systems in every state.
- Include director credentialing in the licensing code of every state.
- Develop national credentialing systems for child care directors.
- Develop a system for recognizing child care directors who complete advanced levels of training.
- Develop training programs for directors that focus on mentoring staff and continually upgrading their skills.

Policies and Practices That Assure the Quality of Programs

- Enact national or state licensing laws that restrict group size and maintain professionally recommended teacher/child ratios.
- Provide an incentive system within each state that rewards centers and homes that have been accredited by a system that meets or exceeds the standards set by the National Association for the Education of Young Children (NAEYC) and by the National Association for Family Child Care (NAFCC).
- Involve parents in envisioning what they want for children and helping professionals to design and maintain appropriate programs.

Family-Friendly Policies and Practices

- Provide child care options that parents can select in accordance with their needs and preferences.
- Expand child care subsidies and scholarships to make high-quality child care affordable to all families.
- Provide all parents with information on child care, including a description of the kinds of child care programs available to their children and a set of guidelines on how to find and select a high-quality early childhood program.
- Provide parents with opportunities to serve on policy committees with decision-making power.
- Enact national or state legislation that provides every child with medical and dental insurance.

Policies That Protect the Rights of Children

- Develop programs within each state to provide developmental screening for every child.
- Provide assessment services for children identified through screening tests, and ensure their access to early intervention programs or services.
- Develop systems within each state for determining school readiness, and use the results as a way of improving preschool and early intervention programs.
- Involve parents in assessing programs and services and in determining which ones are right for their children.

The United States is largely a nation of immigrants, and its racial, cultural, and linguistic diversity continues to increase. By the year 2020, white children whose first language is English will no longer be in the majority in the nation's public schools. Many forecasters also expect that the gap between the lifestyles of children from high and low income levels will continue to widen. Moreover, new jobs in a new high-tech, global economy will demand new skills and higher levels of education. With these developments, the role of the early childhood teacher will continue to become more important and more challenging.

Think about these questions:

- What challenges do you see in your community or in your work and relationships with young children and their families?
- What new policies might be needed at the local, state, and national levels to meet these challenges?

Additional Resources about Early Childhood Education

Berk, L., & Winsler, A. (1995). *Scaffolding children's learning: Vygotsky and early childhood education.* Washington, DC: NAEYC.

Bredekamp, S., & Copple, C. (1997). *Developmentally appropriate practice in early childhood programs* (Rev ed). Washington, DC: NAEYC.

DeVries, R., & Kohlberg, L. (1987). *Constructivist early education: Overview and comparison with other programs.* Washington, DC: NAEYC.

Dodge, D., Colker, L., & Heroman, C. (2002). *The creative curriculum for preschool* (4th ed.). Washington, DC: Teaching Strategies.

Edwards, C., Gandini, L., & Forman, G. (Eds.). (1998). *The hundred languages of children: The Reggio Emilia approach.* Greenwich, CT: Ablex.

Hohman, M., & Weikart, D. (1995). *Educating young children: Active learning practices for preschool and child care programs.* Ypsilanti, MI: High/Scope Press.

National Association for the Education of Young Children. (1998). *Guide to accreditation.* Washington, DC: Author.

Roopnarine, J., & Johnson, J. (Eds.). (2005). *Approaches to early childhood education.* Upper Saddle River, NJ: Prentice-Hall.

Setting the Stage

Ensuring a Safe, Healthy, and Appropriate Learning Environment

Miss Disgruntled was talking with her colleague, Ms. Cool-Headed.

Miss Disgruntled: *"What a day! I feel like going home tonight and never coming back."*

Ms. Cool-Headed: *"You sound pretty upset. What's the matter?"*

Miss Disgruntled: *"What's the matter? Everything is the matter. Ever since we got our new director, she's given me nothing but trouble. Yesterday, she came into my room with this whole long list of complaints. My cribs were too close together, and I was endangering the health of the babies. My diapering supplies weren't close enough to the changing table. I had too much stuff on my shelves, and I couldn't possibly keep them all sterile. A couple of boxes were in front of the doors, and if there happened to be a fire, I couldn't get the kids out fast enough."*

Ms. Cool-Headed: *"I know what you mean. Ms. Striver is a real stickler when it comes to health and safety. Did you fix up the room?"*

Miss Disgruntled: *"I worked so hard. I stayed here until 8 o'clock last night rearranging the cribs, taking the toys off the shelves, throwing out the trash, and clearing off the shelf by the diaper area to make room for the diaper supplies."*

Ms. Cool-Headed: *"Ms. Striver must have been happy when she saw your room in the morning."*

Miss Disgruntled: *"Happy? Not one word of thanks or 'You did a good job.' All she said was that now if I wanted my room to be a safe and healthy place for children, I'd better make it more attractive. Now what does making a room attractive have to do with health and safety?"*

Ms. Cool-Headed knew perfectly well what the director was trying to tell Miss Disgruntled, but she also knew that this was not the time to talk about it. Instead, she said, "Go home and get a good rest, and I'll help you with the room tomorrow."

Both Ms. Cool-Headed and Ms. Striver recognize that a room that is uninviting might very well be a safety hazard for young children. All young children need to be in an environment that is attractive and homelike. They need large spaces for active play and smaller, more intimate places for quiet play. In a well-designed classroom, the noise level is controlled and age-appropriate toys are in reach and displayed in an organized fashion. There are places where children can gather in small groups and places where children can be alone or with one other friend. A well-designed classroom is a safe and healthy place where children can play and learn.

Safety

Chapter 1

Overview

Safety involves preventing the injury of children and adults.

Rationale

Following the old adage "Safety first" is especially important for those who are responsible for young children. Young children depend on adults to keep them safe; they do not yet have the knowledge, skills, or judgment to keep themselves out of danger. Therefore, it is the teacher's responsibility to create and maintain a safe environment while also helping children to learn safety skills.

Although as jobs go, caring for young children is relatively safe, teachers do need to be conscious of their own safety as well as the children's. Even a minor accident, resulting in a wrenched back or twisted ankle, can prevent a teacher from doing her job.

Objectives

1. To learn how to plan safe activities by taking into account children's developmental levels and likely behaviors

2. To learn how to create and maintain safe classroom and playground environments

3. To review what to do in case of a medical emergency

4. To learn safe practices for taking children on field trips

5. To develop and model good safety habits

6. To learn how to involve preschool children in developing safety rules for their classroom

7. To learn how to develop a safety curriculum

8. To learn how to set up a safe environment for children with special needs

Providing a Safe Learning Environment

Miss Carefree felt good about the safety record of her classroom. "Since the beginning of the year," she boasted, "not one child in my class has gotten hurt. Keeping children safe is no big deal," she went on. "All you have to do is keep a good eye on the kids." ●

While good supervision is certainly the most important safety rule, if we are really committed to keeping children safe, we cannot rely on supervision alone. In this chapter, we describe how teachers demonstrate their commitment to safety.

1 To learn how to plan safe activities by taking into account children's developmental levels and likely behaviors

Miss Full-of-Energy had been chided by the director, who told her that her classroom was out of control. "My classroom was not out of control," Miss Full-of-Energy insisted. "When you came into the room, they were playing Follow-the-Leader. It was just too bad that Kimberly bumped her head when she tried to jump off the chair, but she really didn't get hurt." ●

Miss Full-of-Energy should be commended for wanting her class to have fun. At the same time, she should realize that a rowdy, chair-climbing game of Follow-the-Leader is not appropriate for 2-year-olds. Two-year-olds are great imitators. When one child performs a feat like jumping off a chair, the other children will want to do the same thing, even if they don't have the skills to do it safely.

The first rule of safety is *prevention*. A safety-minded teacher must be aware of age-related norms and characteristics (see the Developmental Picture feature). She must also be aware of the characteristic behaviors of individual children. Kimberly was a daring child, although not physically adept. When another child performed a physical feat, Kimberly was bound to follow suit. Her fall from the chair was an accident waiting to happen.

> *The first rule of safety is prevention.*

Developmental Picture

The young infant (0–9 months):
- Is developing new skills day by day, such as rolling over, reaching, putting things in her mouth, pulling on things, and scooting

The caregiver:
- Childproofs the areas used by infants
- Never leaves infants unattended
- Provides a clean, protected floor space where infants can lay down, push up, roll over, and crawl
- Provides safe toys infants can touch and mouth

The older infant (9–14 months):
- Is learning new motor skills at a very fast rate, such as scooting, creeping, pulling up, climbing, and toddling from place to place

The caregiver:
- Cleans and childproofs the areas and supervises closely
- Provides safe, low, and sturdy structures for babies to pull up on and climb on
- Provides appropriate outdoor surfaces for crawling and toddling, such as blankets, clean sand, and outdoor carpeting

The young toddler (14–24 months):
- Is likely to develop a special interest in opening and shutting doors and drawers, picking up and mouthing small toys and objects, standing on top of things, and crawling into spaces that are hard to get out of

The caregiver:
- Safetyproofs indoor and outdoor areas, making sure there are no dangers that children can get into (thumb tacks, glass, sharp table edges, shelf units that can topple, loose rugs, etc.)

The older toddler (2 years):
- Is developing new motor skills, such as walking and going down stairs
- Is apt to run or dart from place to place but is not good at stopping
- Is curious and unable to identify dangers
- Is likely to imitate the feats of older children even when they are beyond his ability
- May be impulsive and dash into new places
- Investigates and experiments with throwing hard objects or hitting with sticks

(continued)

The caregiver:
- Makes sure that there are no places in the classroom or on the playground where a child cannot be seen or can escape from
- Makes sure that the 2-year-old has no opportunity to explore or play with dangerous things like matches, pills, poisonous plants, and cleaning fluids
- Recognizes that electric fans, balloons, and plastic bags are potentially dangerous

The preschooler (3–5 years):
- Is frequently a risk taker, especially with large-muscle activities
- Is gaining the ability to consider safety and is ready to learn safety rules
- Learns safe practices through experiences
- Is insistent about doing things for herself and does not like to hold hands while crossing a road, put on a safety belt, or let an adult help when she is climbing down or jumping

The caregiver:
- Provides a safe environment with careful supervision
- Teaches safe practices and safety concepts

Think about the young children you know, or skip ahead to the developmental overviews at the beginning of Section III (pages 105–112). Based on your observations or these descriptions, think about the following:

- Which of the activities listed below would be safe for preschoolers but not for younger children?
- Which would be safe for toddlers but not for infants?
- Which would be safe for children of all ages?
- Which would not be safe for children under 6?
- What conditions or child characteristics would make these activities safe or unsafe?

Activities

- Blowing and watching soap bubbles
- Dodge ball
- Tricycle races
- A game of chase or tag involving 10 children
- Drawing with chalk on a sidewalk
- A game of musical chairs
- Finger painting with shaving cream

Objective 2
To learn how to create and maintain safe classroom and playground environments

Mrs. Happy-Go-Lucky was in great spirits. She had just made a tour of the infant/toddler room, and it looked beautiful. There were pictures tacked up on all the walls at eye level for the children. There were hanging plants with textured leaves that even babies could touch. There was a floor fan in the infant area that made the mobiles spin. There were jars of marbles on the table near the window that reflected the rays of the sun. There were pillows in the shapes of turtles in all of the infant cribs. ●

As you can imagine, Mrs. Happy-Go-Lucky was not so happy after her supervisor inspected the classroom. Can you find five potential hazards that need to be removed?

A good beginning for thinking about the safety of a classroom or a playground is to identify the kinds of accidents that are likely to occur. In a classroom, children can get hurt by falling down, by having something fall on them, by bumping into something sharp, by getting an electric shock, by ingesting something harmful, by getting fingers pinched in doors or drawers, by getting cut with something sharp, by getting burned, or by being hit or poked by another child. Infants can suffocate on a surface that is too soft, if they roll onto their stomachs and then can't turn their faces to get a breath. (That is why parents and caregivers are taught to put infants to sleep on their backs and to provide firm surfaces for infants to lie on when they are awake.) On the playground, children can get hurt by falling off something high, by falling on something sharp or hard, by colliding with something, by getting hit by something, by getting a part of their body caught or pinched, by eating or touching a poisonous plant, or by getting a splinter.

No matter how careful we are, we cannot prevent all accidents. But by looking at the kinds of accidents that can happen, we can recognize ways to reduce the risks.

Safety in the Classroom

Once you have thought about the kinds of accidents that can happen, take a close look at the classroom you work in and see if you can answer the following questions:

- Are all potentially dangerous materials safely out of reach of children, even children who can climb? (This includes cleaning materials, medicines, poisonous plants, sharp scissors or knives, electric cords, hot drinks, and so on.)
- Are all electrical outlets covered?
- Are there no sharp edges on tables or ledges that children could run into?
- Is the floor clear of obstacles, loose rugs, and wet spots that could cause a child to trip or slip?
- Have any dangling cords been removed or secured, so that a child cannot get tangled in them or pull on them and cause something to fall?
- Are heavy pieces of furniture—including bookshelves, highchairs, and folding tables—secure and stable, so that they cannot be tipped over by children who climb, push, pull, or swing?
- Do you know where the fire extinguisher is and how to use it, and are you sure it works?
- Are all the toys in good repair and safe for the developmental ages of the children in the group?

- Have objects that can be swallowed or have small parts been removed, if there are children under 3?
- Are the room dividers low enough so that you can see all the children at any one time?
- Are there appropriate precautions and adaptations for children with allergies, physical limitations, and other special health needs?

Safety on the Playground

Now it is time to go out to the playground and ask a second set of questions:

- Is the playground area securely fenced off, with safety locks on all gates?
- Is the playground clear of broken glass and other debris?
- Are there railings and walk spaces on the tops of slides to prevent falls?
- Are the S-hooks tightly closed on all the swings? Are all the chains and ropes holding the swings in good condition?
- Is the framework of the swings securely mounted by being set in cement?
- Are the swings made of soft, lightweight material, so that a child who walks into an empty moving swing will not be hurt?
- Is there a minimum of 6 (and preferably 8) inches of sand, mulch, or grass under all climbing structures and swing sets?
- Is all equipment free of splinters, cracks, rusted areas, and loose screws and bolts?

- Is metal equipment in the shade, so that children cannot get burned?
- Is the playground surface smooth, with no holes or protruding objects?
- Are the riding paths wide, gently curved, and marked for one-way traffic?
- Has all broken equipment been removed?
- Has the playground been checked for poisonous plants?
- Is all play equipment anchored well in the ground and placed in an area with a safety gate around it? (Barriers to younger, inexperienced children should be placed around dangerous climbing structures, reserving them for only those children who are capable of getting around the barriers. Swings should be placed in an easily supervised area that is isolated from other playground traffic.)
- Are there appropriate precautions and adaptations for children with allergies, physical limitations, and other special health needs?

Complying with Safety Standards

Mrs. Cautious was visiting different child care centers. She wanted to find a center where she could be sure her son would be safe. When she entered the classroom where her child would be placed, she heard the director talking to the teacher. "Please move those boxes, Miss Rule-Bender. They are blocking the exit." Miss Rule-Bender immediately apologized. "I'll move them right after class," she promised. "I completely forgot that the fire department is coming tomorrow morning." Mrs. Cautious decided she would find a different place for her son. ●

Every state establishes minimum safety standards for licensing child care establishments. Although the stringency of these standards differs among states, all states require that child care establishments adhere to fire safety standards and are monitored by the fire department on a regular basis. The purpose of standards is to protect children from harm. No one expects that there will be a fire in a child care center, and the chances of it happening are certainly slim. Unfortunately, even slim chances do happen, and when we are responsible for children's safety, even the slimmest chance is too great a risk.

Every family child care home and child care center needs to have an evacuation plan in case of a fire or other emergency. This plan should include routes out of the building, what to bring along, and what to do before leaving. The plan should be posted in a public place and practiced through regular fire drills.

To review what to do in case of a medical emergency

If you are working with young children, you should have up-to-date training and certification in first aid and cardiopulmonary resuscitation (CPR). Since recommendations change frequently in response to new research, it is important to keep your certification current.

Your center or family child care home should have policies in place so that everyone can respond promptly in case of a medical emergency—for instance:

- Emergency supplies should be stored in a place that is accessible to adults but not to children.
- Contact information for all families, as well as information on children's known allergies and other special medical needs, should be kept in a secure and readily accessible place.
- *In an emergency, first call 911.* Then call the child's parents or emergency contact. When you call 911, be sure to state the problem briefly and clearly, including the age of the child. Give your program's full address and telephone number. (This information should be posted on or near each telephone.)

First Aid Guidelines

Locate and become familiar with sources of up-to-date information about first aid practices. On the website of the Mayo Clinic are guidelines that reflect the recommendations of specialists, adapted from their Medi-Smart First Aid Guidelines (2004). To access these guidelines, go to www.medi-smart.com/fa-mayo.htm.

To learn safe practices for taking children on field trips

Field trips can be great fun or absolutely disastrous. The outcome depends less on chance than on careful planning. The most important thing to plan for is the safety of the children. Use these points as a checklist to help take the risks out of field trips:

- Visit the field trip site in person ahead of time.
- Get a signed permission slip for each child.
- Recruit parents to help you on the field trip.
- Prepare the children for the field trip by reviewing where they are going, how they will get there, and what safety rules they will need to follow. Be sure to teach them the name of their center or program, in case they get separated from the group.
- Dress the children in matching tee-shirts, preferably ones imprinted with the center's or program's name and address.
- If you are going by car, make sure that there is a seatbelt for every person in the car and a car seat for each child under 3 (or whatever your state requires).
- Bring along the permission slips, a first aid kit, and the emergency phone numbers of all the children.
- Make sure that each child is paired with a buddy.
- Use the travel time to sing songs and tell stories.
- Count the children at least once every 15 minutes and before moving to a new area.

To develop and model good safety habits

After a good two hours of extra work, Mrs. Happy-Go-Lucky completed the job of childproofing her classroom. She was standing on a little chair, putting away the marbles, when her supervisor returned to the room. "Get down from that chair this minute!" her supervisor insisted. "That's a good way to break a leg!" Poor Mrs. Happy-Go-Lucky! She wasn't allowed to leave the center until she had studied the safe practices list. ●

Keeping Yourself Safe

Maintaining safe patterns of behavior includes much more than keeping your classroom and playground free of hazards. It also involves keeping yourself safe.

28

Here is an adult safety checklist that one center compiled after keeping track of the kinds of accidents that had occurred there over the past several years:

- Bend your knees and use your legs, rather than your back, to lift heavy objects and children.
- Don't carry more than one child at a time.
- Use a stepladder for reaching high shelves.
- Dry the floor after washing it or after mopping up a wet spill.
- When using a sharp knife or tool, make sure that you will not be bumped or distracted by active children. If children are nearby, ask them to sit down and watch you or give them jobs of their own.
- Do not use or demonstrate child-sized furniture or equipment that is not designed to support an adult.
- Use common sense, and don't take risks.
- Do not hesitate to ask another adult for help.

Keeping Children Safe

Young children are notoriously unpredictable. Safety-conscious teachers know that they cannot eliminate every danger or intercept every fall. But they can practice some basic safety habits and teach children to behave safely. Teachers can demonstrate their commitment to safety by doing the following:

- Supervise the children at all times.
- Count the children whenever you move to a new area to be sure that none are left behind.
- Keep the door to your classroom closed but not latched. (You can put a bell or chime on the door to alert you when someone is leaving or entering.)
- Model safe behavior.
- Show children the safe way to climb up or down, sit on a swing, carry something heavy or awkward, knock down a block tower, handle a tool, or use playground equipment.
- Don't give children foods that may cause choking, including popcorn, whole grapes, ice cubes, nuts, seeds, raw carrot rounds, hard candy, and corn chips.
- Plan and practice fire drills.
- Release children only to those who are authorized to pick them up; check the IDs of unfamiliar parents.

Helping Parents Follow Good Safety Practices

Many of the accidents and emergencies that occur at preschools involve parents and occur during busy drop-off and pick-up times. For instance, a child may run into the traffic lane while his parent is talking to a friend or strapping a younger sibling into a car seat. A rushed parent may accidentally lock a child in a car or give in to his pleas to sit in the front seat or stay out of the car seat. A child may wander into an unsupervised area while her parent is gathering her belongings.

To avoid these mishaps, you may want to make a safety discussion part of an early parent meeting, send home a safety flyer, or post reminder notices on the parent bulletin board or in other appropriate spots. Here are some points to cover:

- Young children should always ride in the back seat of a car in a safety-approved car seat that has been installed correctly. (You might invite a parent volunteer or police officer to do a safety check, if parents have questions.)
- Children should be carried or held by the hand when entering or leaving the center.
- Everyone should take care to close the door slowly and firmly upon entering or leaving the center.
- Children can only be released to authorized persons.
- Drivers should follow a clearly marked, one-way traffic pattern, if possible.
- Extra caution should be used when backing out of parking spaces.
- Parents are responsible for supervising their children if they use the playground when the center is not officially open.

If parents and staff feel it is necessary, you can station a staff person or parent volunteer outside during drop-off and pick-up times.

In addition, you will want to share general child safety information with parents. Parents of infants should be reminded of the "Back to Sleep" campaign to reduce sudden infant death syndrome (SIDS) by having babies sleep on their backs. All parents should be given information about local safety and first aid courses and product recalls. They should be reminded of the dangers of second-hand smoke and of having guns in the home. Parents should have opportunities to bring up any concerns that they may have, as well.

Finally, you will want to help parents talk with their children about safety issues, especially if there has been an accident or a scare in your neighborhood. Brainstorm ways of reassuring the children and of teaching commonsense precautions without inducing fear.

To learn how to involve preschool children in developing safety rules for their classroom

Mr. Nose-to-the-Grindstone dropped into his daughter's prekindergarten classroom during morning circle time. The children were helping the teacher draw up a list of safety rules for the classroom. The red-headed boy suggested "No hitting or kicking." The class agreed that that was a good rule, and it was added to the list. Next, the girl with the ponytail shouted out that she knew one: "Nobody should drop their juice pop on the floor." The boy beside her chimed in, "That's a dumb rule. I don't ever eat juice pops. They are yucky." The teacher asked the group if it was all right to drop any kind of food on the floor. One child said, "Maybe you can't help it if you drop something on the floor. Like it could be an accident." The girl with the ponytail agreed. "Maybe we should say if you drop food or something on the floor, you should clean it up." "And you shouldn't throw blocks at people," the boy in the red shirt added. "Good thinking," the teacher commented, as she wrote down the two new rules.

Mr. Nose-to-the-Grindstone left the room and went right to the director. "You've got to have a talk with that teacher," he told the director. "Instead of teaching these kids something, she has them sitting in a circle making up safety rules." ●

Despite Mr. Nose-to-the-Grindstone's assertion, the teacher was teaching the class something. First, she was helping the children think about behaviors that could cause someone to get hurt. Second, she was teaching them that creating a safety rule is a way of preventing an accident. Third and most important, the teacher recognized that older preschool children are likely to follow rules that they have helped to create.

> *Children are likely to follow rules that they have helped to create.*

As you read the following lists of rules that were developed by a class of 4-year-olds, think about which of them would be appropriate for your classroom and what other rules you would add.

Safety Rules for the Classroom
(In the words of 4-year-olds)

- No running.
- Sit on chairs but don't stand on chairs or on tables either.
- You shouldn't point things at people, like scissors.
- You don't leave the classroom unless your teacher says it's okay.
- You don't fool around with electric outlets or things like that.

Safety Rules for the Playground
(Also in the words of 4-year-olds)

- You have to sit in the middle of the swing and you can't stand up and you stop it before you get off.
- One at a time on the slide and you have to go down frontwards.
- You don't bump into people when you ride your tricycles.
- You don't say "Ha-ha, Scaredy-cat" if somebody is scared to go on the jungle gym.

Objective 7
To learn how to develop a safety curriculum

In addition to childproofing the classroom, modeling safe behavior, and developing safety rules, teachers can help children become safety conscious by including safety lessons in their lesson plans. Here are some ideas for activities.

Activities for Improving Safety

Go on a Safety Walk

Objective: To teach children to recognize and talk about potential hazards

Procedure: Give each child a red circle sticker. Ask the children to walk around the classroom (or the playground) and put their red stickers on things that could be dangerous. In circle time, ask children where they put their stickers and what the dangers are.

Play a Freeze! Game

Objective: To teach children to respond immediately to the word *stop*

Procedure: Make two parallel lines on the playground using crepe paper or yarn. Line the children up on the starting line. When you say "Go," ask the children to begin walking toward the finish line. When you say "Stop," all the children must stop on the spot. If the children keep moving when you say "Stop," they must go back to start. Add an element of cooperation by having the children walk in pairs.

Read a Story

Objective: To teach children about safety

Procedure: Read children a safety story in circle time. Allow them to talk about experiences in which they have had to practice good safety.

"Fire Station" Pretend Play

Objective: To teach children to dial 911 in case of a fire

Procedure: Turn your pretend play area into a fire station and encourage the children to play "fire station." For props, use a telephone, fire hats (which you could make as a craft), a bell, a length of hose, whistles, and some blankets. Help the children play out a scenario in which someone sees smoke and dials 911. The call is received in the "fire station." Someone rings the bell, and the children get out the hose, rush to the fire, and put it out.

Safety Walk

Objective: To teach traffic safety

Procedure: Take the children for a safety walk on the playground. Pretend the path is a busy street. (If you do not have a path on your playground, make a path out of rope or mark one with chalk.) Use a yardstick with red on one end and green on the other as a signal. Teach the children to walk to the end of the road, wait until the light turns green, look both ways, and say "All clear" before they cross.

Safety Crafts

Objective: To reinforce awareness of safety

Procedure: Children can make all sorts of pretend play props: fire hats, safety badges, 911 signs to put by the phone, and even a working traffic light (with green, red, and yellow paper covering holes cut in a milk carton that they can shine a flashlight through). As children incorporate these crafts in their play, you can talk together about safe practices.

Field Trip

Objective: To increase safety consciousness

Procedure: Take a trip to a fire station or police station, or invite a police officer or fire marshal to come to your center. Encourage the children to ask questions. After the trip or visit, help children work together to make a list of things they learned or to draw pictures for a class book about safety.

To learn how to set up a safe environment for children with special needs

Prior to the opening day, the director of Open Arms Nursery School was telling the staff about the new children who were enrolled in their classes. "There are three children in your class who were not in the school last year," she told Mrs. Keep Safe. "There's Jim, who is Cornelia's younger brother; Jacques, whose family recently immigrated from Haiti; and Madeline, who is quite a self-sufficient child, although she is legally blind."

Mrs. Keep Safe turned pale. "I would be happy to have Jim and Jacques, but I must admit I am worried about having a blind child in my class. You know the children in my class are quite active, and I feel a blind child might get hurt. As far as I am concerned, my first obligation is to keep the children safe."

"You worry too much," the director responded. "I used to teach in a school where almost half of the children in the class had some sort of disability, and we had a perfect safety record. As a matter of fact, I just read an article about how children with disabilities in an inclusive school are less likely to get hurt than typically developing children. The article went on to say that typically developing preschool children are protective of children with special needs and are careful not to hurt them."

"Well, okay," Mrs. Keep Safe agreed. "I guess I'll give it a try." ●

The director of Open Arms Nursery School is absolutely right. Children with special needs are less likely to get hurt in a preschool setting than are typically developing children. Nevertheless, teachers and caregivers of children with special needs must remain continually vigilant and anticipate the kinds of accidents related to children's disabilities that could occur and take preventive measures.

Setting Up a Safe Indoor Environment

The kinds of modifications needed to make the classroom safe for a child with a disability depends very much on the nature of the disability. Many children with conditions such as mild retardation and language delays do not require any special room arrangements. Children with physical or sensory limitations, however, may benefit from some adaptations. Modifications needed in the classroom may include raising or lowering a table, making a bathroom wheelchair accessible, and being extra careful to ensure that there are no sharp corners on tables or shelves and that doorways are barrier free.

> *Children with special needs are less likely to get hurt in a preschool setting than are typically developing children.*

In addition to the room arrangement, children with special needs may need special equipment and materials. Children who are visually impaired may need a braille computer, large-print books, or a magnifying glass. Children who are hearing impaired may need a hearing aid or language board. Children who are physically challenged may need a wheelchair, standing table, or chair with special supports. Children with learning problems may need materials such as puzzles or pegboards that are likely to be used with younger children.

Setting Up a Safe Outdoor Environment

Like all children, children with special needs benefit from active play. Again, some modifications will be needed. The kinds of modifications that you make on the playground will depend on the nature of the child's disablity and the recommendation of the parent or therapist. Children who are physically challenged may need to have a balance beam set in the ground, so that they can practice balance without getting hurt, or a tricycle with foot holders that make it easier to pedal.

With a visually impaired child, you may also need to cordon off the area behind the swings or to provide soft Nerf balls for playing circle games. Children who are hearing impaired do not need special equipment, but you may want to use hand signals to give them directions.

Additional Resources about Safety

Caring for Our Children—National health and safety performance standards: Guidelines for out of home child care programs (2nd ed). (2002). Washington, DC: NAEYC. (Updated standards issued jointly by the American Academy of Pediatrics, American Public Health Association, and the National Resource Center for Health and Safety in Child Care)

Health

Chapter 2

Overview

Often, we think of *health* as simply meaning the absence of disease. It is true that we can't stay healthy unless we learn good health habits that protect our bodies from illness, but we need to think of health in a larger sense. Being healthy means feeling fit and fine. It means having the internal resources to fight off illness and overcome the effects of physical insult; it also means having the energy and stamina to lead a productive life.

Rationale

Health is an important aspect of learning and development. Children who are healthy have the vigor they need for play, learning, and across-the-board development. Also, the more scientists learn about health, the more they become aware of the importance of behavior. Eating right, exercising, avoiding risks, practicing good hygiene and sanitation, and managing stress all contribute to long-term health. The habits acquired in early childhood tend to persist, so it is important to begin early with health education. In addition, nutritional deficits and toxic exposure in early childhood can cause wide-ranging, lifelong problems.

The early childhood teacher promotes health within the classroom by doing these things:

- Observing good health practices
- Conforming to the health rules and regulations of her center
- Recognizing the signs and symptoms of illness
- Developing a program of health education that teaches children to value good health and to follow the routines that maintain it

Objectives

1. To develop a sound knowledge base regarding health, nutrition, and oral hygiene

2. To carry out routine practices that will prevent illness and promote good health and nutrition

3. To establish guidelines/policies regarding how to handle health issues, including a record-keeping system

4. To incorporate activities that teach children and their families about health, oral/dental hygiene, and nutrition

5. To recognize indicators of abuse and/or neglect and follow the reporting policy mandated by the state

6. To keep oneself healthy and model appropriate wellness behaviors for children and their parents

Providing a Healthy Learning Environment

Mrs. Good-Care was washing out the bathroom sink when her assistant came into the room. "What are you doing?" she asked. "Just cleaning up the bathroom," Mrs. Good-Care explained. "The janitor didn't come in this morning." "That's ridiculous!" the assistant insisted. "Cleaning the bathroom is not part of your job description." ●

Like any good early childhood teacher, Mrs. Good-Care did not consult her job description before she cleaned the bathroom. She realized that she was responsible for the well-being of the children in her class, and she wasn't going to let a job description keep her from protecting their health.

In this chapter, we look at different ways in which classroom teachers safeguard the health of the children in their classes by updating their own health knowledge, maintaining a healthy environment, teaching children about health and nutrition, and recognizing and reporting child abuse and/or neglect.

To develop a sound knowledge base regarding health, nutrition, and oral hygiene

While classroom teachers are not expected to be physicians, they do need to know some fundamental concepts about health and nutrition. Most important, in order to safeguard the health and well-being of the children in your class, you need to be able to share information with parents. Your knowledge base should include the signs and symptoms of illness, recommended immunization timetables, and the daily nutritional needs of children under 6.

Before you focus on the knowledge about health issues related to child care, it is important to recognize the sequence of development relating to health and wellness (see the Developmental Picture below).

Developmental Picture

The young infant (0–9 months):

- Is dependent on others for meeting all basic needs
- Is likely to be alert and interactive during feeding and diapering
- Mouths objects to explore them

The caregiver:

- Helps infants establish a comfortable individual rhythm of sleeping, eating, waking, and playing
- Uses feeding and diapering times as opportunities to play and interact with babies
- Maintains routines for sanitary diapering, disinfecting mouthed toys, and washing bedding and clothing

The older infant (9–14 months):

- Is developing food preferences related to taste and texture and may push a spoon away
- Is interested in feeding himself and playing with food or throwing food on the floor
- Is learning from adult models
- Explores objects by touching, mouthing, and chewing on them

The caregiver:

- Provides time and support for practicing self-care tasks
- Provides finger foods and encourages children to feed themselves
- Is careful to offer nutritious food but not to force food
- Routinely cleans floors, equipment, and mouthed items
- Maintains sanitary diapering routines

The young toddler (14–24 months):

- Is not usually ready to be toilet trained
- Is likely to enjoy handwashing
- May be insistent about self-feeding
- Continues to explore objects with all senses, including taste

The caregiver:

- Does not expect toileting skills and maintains sanitary diapering routines
- Washes mouthed objects and maintains clean floors and play spaces
- Helps children wash their hands frequently
- Provides nutritious foods the child can eat easily with fingers or spoons in a relaxed atmosphere
- Does not force foods or insist that a child eat

(continued)

The older toddler (2 years):

- Is at a good age for toilet learning but may have accidents even when such learning has been achieved
- Enjoys being able to eat with a fork or spoon, wash her own hands, and brush her teeth with help
- Is anxious to do things all by himself
- Becomes listless or cranky and whiny when coming down with an illness

The caregiver:

- Makes toileting a routine activity for children who have begun toilet learning
- Makes sure every child has a change of clothes available
- Maintains a clean environment and washes toys after a child has mouthed them
- Recognizes signs of illness and separates the ill child from classmates

The preschool child (3–5 years):

- Is mastering self-care
- Is capable of learning good health habits
- Accomplishes independent eating, handwashing, toileting, toothbrushing, and nose wiping
- Is likely to be frightened of going to the doctor

The caregiver:

- Provides ample opportunities to develop body image, to practice self-care, and to develop good health habits
- Ensures children have nutritious foods, outdoor exercise, regular rest time, and a clean environment
- Isolates and sends home children with contagious diseases

Knowing the Signs and Symptoms of Illness

Some signs of illness, such as having a high fever and vomiting, are unmistakable, while other signs are more subtle and may be attributed to other causes. These signs and symptoms should be attended to:

Listlessness	Poor appetite
Inactivity	Urinating frequently
Moodiness	Tiring easily
Paleness	Deep circles under eyes
Excessive thirst	Chronic cough or runny nose
Difficulty with vision or hearing	Pink eyes
Hoarse voice	Nausea, vomiting, diarrhea
Skin rashes, crustiness, blotches	Complaints of headache, stiff neck, or other pain
Difficulty breathing	

Knowing about Contagious Diseases

Parents sometimes expect teachers to be all knowing. Although it is impossible to meet this kind of expectation, teachers should have a basic knowledge of the most common contagious diseases. They should also know how to obtain updated information from the local public health department, a pediatrician who consults to the center, and the Centers for Disease Control (www.cdc.gov).

Use the following chart to help you answer questions that parents might ask, like these:

"My child was exposed to the measles last Saturday. If she is going to come down with the measles, when would she first show symptoms?"

Common Contagious Diseases

Disease	Incubation Period	When It Is "Catching"	Symptoms	Rash	Length of Illness	Prevention
Chicken pox	4–21 days	1 day before rash and 6 days after rash	Fever Rash Itching	Individual spots begin as water blisters, spread over whole body, form crusts by fourth day	7–10 days	Varicella
German measles	14–21 days	2 days before symptoms and 3 days after	Fever Slight cold Enlarged glands	First day: reddish-purple; Second day: Scarlet	3–5 days	M.M.R. vaccine
Measles	10–14 days	1 day before fever and until rash disappears	Fever Cough Conjunctivitis	Reddish-purple spots running into each other, from head downward	7–10 days	M.M.R. vaccine
Mumps	12–24 days	1 day before swelling and as long as swelling lasts	Fever Swelling under jaws	None	7–10 days	M.M.R. vaccine
Scarlet fever	2–7 days	From first symptoms until 7 days later	Fever Sore throat Headache Vomiting	Pinpoint scarlet rash on body, not on face	7–10 days	None
Whooping cough	7–14 days	From beginning of cough for 3–4 weeks	Cold Whooping cough Vomiting	None	4–6 weeks	D.P.T. vaccine

"My child has just had chicken pox. He's all better except for a couple of crusted-over spots on his forehead. Can he come back to school?"

"My child has a couple of red spots on her foot. Could that be the beginning of chicken pox?"

Use the next chart to help you answer the following questions that parents might ask about immunization:

"I went through the whole bit with shots and vaccinations when Theresa was a baby. She is turning 4 pretty soon. I don't need to do anything else, do I?"

"I think Marvin has had all of his shots. At least, they said he did at the health clinic when he was 6 months old. He's 18 months now. We just got back from a year in Uruguay. Does he need any kind of booster shots, or am I too late?"

Centers for Disease Control Immunization Guidelines (2004)

Disease and Vaccine	First Dose	Second Dose	Third Dose	Fourth Dose/ Boosters
Hepatitis B	At birth, if mother has been exposed; otherwise, 2–4 weeks	1–6 months	6–18 months	—
Diphtheria, Tetanus, Pertussis (DPT)	2 months	4 months	6 months	15–18 months, 4–6 years, then TD at 11–12 years and every 10 years thereafter
H. Influenza type B (HIB)	2 months	4 months	—	12 months or older
Polio (IPV)	2 months	4 months	6–18 months	4–6 years
Measles, Mumps, Rubella	12 months	4–6 years	—	—
Varicella (Chicken pox)	12 months if no history of chicken pox	—	—	—
Hepatitis A	2–12 years but only in high-risk geographic areas	—	—	—

Note: Any dose not given at the recommended age should be given as a catch-up immunization at any visit when indicated and feasible.

Source: www.cdc.gov. Approved by the Advisory Committee on Immunization Practices, the American Academy of Pediatrics, and the American Academy of Family Physicians. Note that the guidelines are reviewed every six months, so be sure to check for updates.

Conditions and Diseases That Are Common in a Child Care Setting

Additional information about the following diseases and conditions, as well as many others, can be found on the website of the national Centers for Disease Control (www.cdc.gov).

Head Lice

Signs and Symptoms: Intense itching. Nits are most often found in the hair at the nape of the neck and over the ears.

Incubation Period: Retreatment is generally recommended 7–10 days after the first application due to the hatching of more nits.

Treatment: A special shampoo, available over the counter or by a doctor's prescription. Removal of the nits with the use of a fine-toothed comb.

Mode of Transmission: A parasite that is passed from person to person via personal items such as hats and combs.

Prevention: Do not allow children to share items that touch the hair, such as hats and combs. Clean rugs and bedding frequently.

Pink Eye (Conjunctivitis)

Signs and Symptoms: Red, watery eyes, discharge, crusty eyes, sensitivity to light.

Incubation Period: Usually 24–72 hours.

Treatment: Antibiotic (through a doctor's prescription).

Mode of Transmission: Through contact with eye discharge.

Prevention: Avoid touching the eyes. Practice frequent handwashing. Wash towels and bedding. Avoid sharing of these items.

Impetigo

Signs and Symptoms: Flat, yellow, crusty, or weeping patch on the skin.

Incubation Period: 5 days.

Treatment: Washing of infected areas with mild soap and water. Doctor may prescribe an antibiotic or ointment.

Mode of Transmission: The infected person can easily spread the infection to other parts of his own body and to others by direct contact.

Prevention: Bathe daily with a mild soap. Keep hands and fingernails clean. Practice frequent handwashing.

Pin Worms (Seat Worms)

Signs and Symptoms: Tiny, white worms that cause itching and irritation of the anus.

Incubation Period: After swallowing the eggs, it takes from 15–28 days for the worms to mature.

Treatment: Consult a physician.

Mode of Transmission: The eggs are passed from the anus to the mouth. Children scratch the affected area where the eggs are, and the eggs then lodge under the fingernails.

Prevention: Practice frequent handwashing and proper diapering and toileting procedures.

Common Cold

Signs and Symptoms: Runny nose, watery eyes, sore throat, chills and malaise (blah feeling). Usually no fever unless complication has developed.

Incubation Period: 12–72 hours. Usually 24 hours.

Treatment: No specific treatment. Treat the symptoms to make the infected person feel better. Rest. Drink plenty of fluids.

Mode of Transmission: Through direct contact with coughs and sneezes and indirectly through contaminated surfaces, hands, and articles such as tissues.

Prevention: Wash hands. Cover coughs and sneezes. Dispose of tissues properly. Wash surfaces and toys frequently.

Ear Infection (Otitis-Media)

Signs and Symptoms: Pain, drainage from the ears, red ears, fever, tugging at the ears, irritability.

Incubation Period: Several days to several months.

Treatment: Consult a physician. Chronic infections may be treated with the surgical placement of tubes so that the ears can drain.

Mode of Transmission: Virus or bacterial infection. Upper-respiratory infections are usually spread by coughs and sneezes. Sometimes antibiotics are given. Some doctors have a wait-and-see attitude.

Prevention: Cover sneezes and coughs. Practice frequent handwashing and disinfecting of surfaces and toys.

Respiratory Syncytial Virus (RSV)

Signs and Symptoms: Similar to common cold. May result in lower-respiratory tract infections or otitis-media. Especially seen in toddlers younger than 18 months.

Incubation Period: Contagious before symptoms appear to 1–3 weeks after symptoms subside.

Treatment: Symptoms are treated. Severe cases may require hospitalization.

Mode of Transmission: Spread through direct contact with infectious secretions.

Prevention: Practice frequent handwashing, cleaning, and disinfecting of surfaces and toys.

Diarrhea (Rotavirus)

Signs and Symptoms: Loose, watery stools, abdominal cramps, sometimes a runny nose and cough.

Incubation Period: 2 days.

Treatment: Rest and a bland diet, avoidance of dairy products, plenty of fluids to reduce the chance of dehydration.

Mode of Transmission: Through the fecal/oral route.

Prevention: Practice frequent handwashing. Disinfect surfaces and toys.

Salmonella

Signs and Symptoms: Diarrhea, flulike symptoms, stomach cramping, vomiting.

Incubation Period: Several days to several months.

Treatment: Usually no specific treatment. Severe cases should seek a doctor's advice.

Mode of Transmission: Eating of infected foods, cross-contamination of foods, handling of reptiles such as iguanas and turtles.

Prevention: Ensure the proper preparation, cooking, handling, and storage of food. Practice proper handwashing after handling reptiles and other pets.

Fifth Disease

Signs and Symptoms: A "slapped face" rash. Fever and flulike symptoms. The rash spreads to the trunk and extremities and may cause itching.

Incubation Period: Usually 4–14 days but can be as long as 20 days. Most contagious before symptoms appear.

Treatment: No specific treatment.

Mode of Transmission: By direct contact with respiratory secretions and airborne droplets.

Prevention: Wash hands after touching any secretions from the nose or mouth.

Hand–Foot–Mouth Disease (Coxsackie Virus)

Signs and Symptoms: Canker sore–like sores in the mouth and a rash on the bottoms of the feet, the palms of the hands, and sometimes the buttocks. A sore throat and mild fever.

Incubation Period: Usually 3–6 days. Most infectious for 7 days after development of the rash.

Treatment: No specific treatment.

Mode of Transmission: Through the fecal/oral route or through respiratory secretions.

Prevention: Practice frequent handwashing and good personal hygiene.

Hepatitis B (HBV)

Signs and Symptoms: Fatigue, loss of appetite, jaundice, dark urine, light stools, nausea, vomiting, abdominal pain.

Incubation Period: Around 3 months.

Treatment: No specific treatment.

Mode of Transmission: Infected mother to newborn through blood exposure at birth, or through exposure of cuts or mucous membranes to contaminated blood.

Prevention: Practice frequent handwashing. Clean up and disinfect blood spills immediately, and wear gloves. Do not share toothbrushes.

Strep Throat

Signs and Symptoms: Sore throat, sometimes a fever and tiredness. A rash may also appear. Swollen tonsils and lymph glands.

Incubation Period: 1–3 days.

Treatment: Doctor's prescription of antibiotics.

Mode of Transmission: Contact with infected person.

Prevention: Isolation of infected person for at least 24 hours after starting antibiotics.

Chicken Pox

Signs and Symptoms: Virus and a slight fever. Blisters that first appear on the face, the back, under the arms, and the "hot spots" on the body.

Incubation Period: 2–3 weeks. No longer contagious as soon as all of the lesions have crusted over and the sores are not wet or weeping.

Treatment: There is a vaccine for chicken pox. If children do get chicken pox, a fever-reducing medicine is usually suggested by a physician. Do *not* give aspirin, which can cause Reyes syndrome.

Mode of Transmission: Respiratory. Contact with an infected person. Hands and surfaces that are contaminated through sneezing and coughing discharges, as well as airborne germs through the same transmission.

Prevention: Again, there is a vaccine. An infected person should be isolated for at least 24 hours after starting medicine.

Bottle Mouth

Signs and Symptoms: Tooth decay.

Treatment: See a dentist.

Mode of Transmission: Infants' and toddlers' teeth are exposed to surgery liquids, formula, milk, and juices.

Prevention: Do not let an infant/toddler go to sleep with a bottle in his or her mouth; wean from bottle at 12 months. Do not let an infant/toddler carry a bottle around in his or her mouth.

Knowing about Nutrition

Mrs. Easy-Going was talking with her 4-year-old's teacher. "My Melissa is a very fussy eater," she explained. "Like most 4-year-olds, she hates fruits and vegetables. She also hates meat, milk, cheese, yogurt, and cereal. But don't worry if she doesn't eat lunch at school. I always stop on the way to school to buy her hash browns, and we get a big bag of french fries on the way home. She's perfectly healthy, and I don't want to make a big deal about food." "Is she allergic to anything?" the teacher asked. "No," said Mrs. Easy-Going, "she has no allergies. She just knows what she likes and what she hates."

Melissa's teacher assured Mrs. Easy-Going that she would not force Melissa to eat anything she did not want. True to her word, Melissa's teacher did not make a fuss over Melissa's lunch. She served Melissa a small portion of the school lunch every day and explained to Melissa that she could eat as much or as little as she wanted. When Mrs. Easy-Going came to visit her daughter at lunch one day, she was surprised to find her eating a cheeseburger with a glass of milk. "I thought you hated cheeseburgers," Mrs. Easy-Going commented to Melissa. "I do," Melissa replied, "except I like the way they make them at school."

Melissa's teacher was concerned about providing her preschool children with a well-balanced and nutritional meal. At the same time, she respected Mrs. Easy-Going's child-rearing philosophy and agreed not to pressure Melissa into eating. She served Melissa a small portion of a well-balanced lunch on a daily basis and gradually introduced new foods to her.

Meeting Young Children's Nutritional Needs

Proper nutrition is very important for young children. They are growing rapidly, and they need adequate amounts of protein, carbohydrates, fats, vitamins, and minerals in order to stay healthy. Vitamin C, iron, protein, and calcium are especially important, and some children do not get adequate amounts of these essential nutrients.

Foods rich in Vitamin C include tomatoes, broccoli, cabbage, peppers, strawberries, kiwi fruit, cantaloupe, and citrus fruits, such as oranges, tangerines, and grapefruit. High-protein foods include soy, lean meats, beans and other legumes, nuts, eggs, and fish. Dairy foods are high in both protein and calcium. Foods rich in iron include meat, eggs, legumes, spinach and other leafy greens, dried fruits (e.g., prunes, apricots, and raisins), and whole-grain and cereal products that have been enriched with iron.

The toddler and preschool years are also the time when eating habits are established. Although all children develop personal likes and dislikes, they also take cues from those around them. If a toddler sees others enjoying vegetables, she is likely to think they are tasty. If junk food is the norm at the child's home and child care setting, he may develop poor habits that are hard to break.

The U.S. Department of Agriculture (USDA) provides food guides to help Americans set nutritional goals and to promote overall health. These guidelines cover such issues as how much protein should be consumed each day; how much fat or sugar is too much; what counts as a serving of fruits, vegetables, whole grains, or dairy; and how many servings of each are recommended. The guidelines are revised every five years to reflect new research and to make sure that they are clear and easy to follow. The most recent dietary guidelines describe a healthy diet as one with these characteristics:

- Emphasizes fruits, vegetables, whole grains, and low-fat milk products
- Includes lean meats, poultry, fish, beans, eggs, and nuts
- Is low in saturated fats, trans fats, cholesterol, salt, and added sugars

Food groups are defined to help people determine what goes into a balanced diet. They include the following:

- *Breads and other cereals*—breads, pasta, rice, cereals
- *Fruits*—apples, pears, oranges, peaches, bananas, pineapples
- *Vegetables*—peas, carrots, broccoli, collard greens, sweet potatoes, beans, corn
- *Meats and other proteins*—beef, poultry, fish, dry beans, eggs, nuts
- *Milk products*—milk, yogurt, cheese
- *Fats, oils, sweets*—butter, soy margarine, chocolate, candies, sodas

The USDA also publishes materials for specific populations, such as guides for young children, vegetarians, people with particular religious requirements or cultural preferences, and people with food allergies and other special dietary needs.

The most up-to-date information can be found on the USDA website (www.usda.gov/FoodAndNutrition). Kid-friendly recipes for nutritious meals and snacks, tips for cooking with young children, age-appropriate teaching activities, and other resources can be found at www.nal.usda.gov/childcare.

The USDA also operates several programs to help low-income individuals and families meet their nutritional needs. As a teacher or caregiver of young children, you should be informed about two such programs in particular:

- The Special Supplemental Nutrition Program for Women, Infants, and Children, better known as the *WIC Program*, helps to safeguard the health of low-income women, infants, and children up to age 5 by providing nutritious foods to supplement their diets, information on healthy eating, and referrals to health care. See www.fns.usda.gov/wic for information on how families can access these services.

- The Child and Adult Care Food Program (CACFP) is funded by the federal government and administered by state agencies. It helps child care providers—including centers, Head Start programs, family child care homes, and school-age programs—to purchase nutritious meals. Providers can receive various levels of reimbursement for meal purchases, depending on the percentage of children they serve whose family incomes make them eligible for free or reduced lunch or other federal subsidies. For agency contacts in your state, see www.fns.usda.gov/cnd/Contacts/StateDirectory.htm.

Providing a Pleasant Environment during Meals and Snacks

- Bottle feeding provides a special opportunity to hold a child in your lap and encourage closeness. Never prop the bottle.
- In some child care centers, family-style serving (having the children select from serving bowls) is preferred. In other centers, particularly those where children bring in their own meals, each child is served individually. Family style extends the time it takes to have a meal and, at the same time, provides opportunities to use utensils and to have the children talk about the food with their caregivers.
- Have a comfortable conversation with the children as they are having their meal.
- Try not to rush the children or leave them at the table too long.

Presenting Meals to Children That Take into Account Their Age and Readiness

- Mealtime provides an opportunity to help children develop self-help skills.
- Encourage children to use the appropriate utensils and cups.
- Young toddlers can learn to use a spoon and drink from a "tippy" cup.
- Older toddlers can learn to use a fork with rounded tines and to drink from a cup with handles.
- Preschool-age children can learn to use a dull knife and to drink from a glass.
- Provide activities that allow children to help with simple food preparation. Some examples include helping to set the table, pouring their drinks from small pitchers, and spreading cream cheese, hummus, or salsa on a bagel, pita, or tortilla.

Avoiding Foods That Could Endanger Children's Health

- Avoid foods that could cause choking. Children 5 years old and under should not be given foods that they could choke on, such as hotdogs, undiced carrots, and whole grapes.
- Avoid foods that could be aspirated or sucked into the lungs. Children 5 years old and under should not be given foods such as popcorn and nuts.

Recognizing That Some Children May Have Food Allergies or Sensitivities

- Maintain a list of children with food allergies and other allergies.
- As you plan menus and cooking projects, consult the food allergy list.
- Know how each individual child's allergy manifests itself and what to do in case of accidental exposure.

Involving Parents in Nutrition

- If parents provide snacks and/or meals, provide a list of suggestions to help them select nutritious foods.
- Provide parents with a list of appropriate and inappropriate foods to bring into the classroom for special events.
- Provide parents with a list of healthy snacks that they can give their children, such as the following:

Cheese	Bananas
Cooked carrot rounds	Whole-wheat crackers
Orange sections	Cheerios
Cooked or frozen peas	Yogurt
String cheese	Rice pudding
Cottage cheese	Quesadillas
Cut-up grapes	Cherry tomato halves
Hard-boiled eggs	Tofu squares
Thinly sliced or diced apples, pears, or peaches	

Promoting Good Oral Hygiene

Oral hygiene is another important health topic:

- Provide healthy foods for teeth, including calcium-rich foods like milk and crunchy foods like apples.
- Limit the amounts of sugary, sweet, and sticky foods.
- Explain to parents that leaving a bottle in an infant's crib while she is falling asleep is likely to produce "bottle mouth," or rot a baby's teeth.

To carry out routine practices that will prevent illness and promote good health and nutrition

The health practices that are most important for controlling the spread of disease in a classroom include the following:

- Following universal precautions
- Washing hands
- Washing and disinfecting surfaces
- Following appropriate procedures when changing diapers
- Maintaining a healthy indoor environment

Following Universal Precautions

Universal precautions is the term used to identify a set of strategies designed to protect people from infections that are spread through contact with blood and other bodily fluids. These guidelines should be followed without exception in child care settings, both for the protection of the caregiver and for the protection of the children:

- Avoid direct contact with bodily fluids, including blood, urine, feces, vomit, saliva, and nasal/eye discharge.
- Use disposable gloves in these situations:
  - When handling body fluids
  - When handling food
  - When helping a child in the bathroom
  - When changing a diaper
- Clean up and disinfect any bodily fluid spills immediately.
- Avoid any contact with sources of bodily fluids, such as the eyes, nose, mouth, and open sores.
- Discard contaminated material in a tightly secured plastic bag.

Using Appropriate Handwashing Procedures

Staff in child care centers should wash their hands in these situations using the sequence outlined in the box on page 50:

- When arriving at work
- Before leaving for the day
- Before preparing and/or serving food or bottles
- Before and after diapering a child or helping a child in the bathroom
- After cleaning up body fluids
- After wiping a child's nose
- When coming in from the playground
- After handling pets
- After tying shoes
- When hands look dirty
- After coughing or sneezing
- After personal toileting

Handwashing Sequence

- Gather all of the materials necessary.
- Remove jewelry. (When possible, avoid wearing jewelry when working with children.)
- Use soap and running water.
- Rub hands vigorously as you wash them.
- Wash the backs of the hands, the palms, the wrists, between the fingers, and under the fingernails.
- Rinse your hands well and leave the water running.
- Dry your hands with a paper or single-use towel.
- Turn off the water by using a paper towel, not your bare hands.

Activities for Engaging Children in Handwashing

The procedure for washing hands for children and adults is the same. The problem is that children aren't very good at judging how long to keep their hands under the water in order to rinse well. It also takes children time and practice to remember the sequence for washing hands.

The following activities provide ways of helping children learn handwashing techniques:

Handwashing Song   Sing this handwashing song with the appropriate motions (to the tune of "All around the Mulberry Bush").

This is the way I turn on the faucet,
Turn on the faucet, turn on the faucet.
This is the way I turn on the faucet,
Early in the morning.

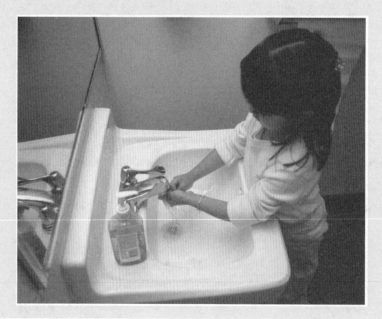

This is the way I lather my hands, etc.
This is the way I scrub my hands, etc.
This is the way I rinse my hands, etc.
This is the way I dry my hands, etc.
This is the way I turn off the faucet, etc.

"Oops—I Forgot!" Game Pantomime the sequence on handwashing. Leave out one step, and see if the children can tell you what is missing.

Sequence Cards Buy or create your own set of sequence cards on handwashing. Let children arrange the cards in order, or put the cards in the wrong order and let the children correct your mistake. Omit one card, and see if the children can tell you what is missing. Put up handwashing sequence cards in the bathroom to serve as a reminder.

Doll Bath Set up a doll bath in the classroom. Then give a doll a bath in front of the children. Talk to the doll about the importance of washing its face first or making sure that you wash between the toes and so on. Give the children a chance to wash the doll, praising them for remembering the correct order and for making sure all parts get cleaned.

Cleaning and Disinfecting the Room and Materials

The director of Safeguard Child Care Center was taking new parents around to see the facility. "What makes our school so special," the director explained, "is the professionalism of our staff. We are very proud of the fact that our teachers are given job descriptions that recognize that teaching children is a full-time job. We have a secretary to manage the office, a bus driver to drive the bus, a cook to make the meals, and a custodian who comes in after school to clean up the classroom. Our teachers are not expected to wipe down the shelves or wash off toys that babies have used."

The director was sure that all the parents on her tour would be impressed with her personnel policies. However, several of the parents were upset by her comments and began asking questions:

- *What happens if a child messes up the floor in the middle of the day when the custodian isn't around?*
- *What happens if babies put toys in their mouths?*
- *Who is responsible for cleaning off the tables before and after snack-time?*

Although the director thought that she was just being considerate of her staff when she relieved them of clean-up duty, it was easy for the parents to recognize that the children were being placed at risk.

Cleaning up in an early childhood classroom is an ongoing responsibility that everyone must share. Messes must be cleaned up when they are made. Toys must be cleaned after they have been mouthed.

Here is a short poem about cleaning that will help you to remember the quick and easy solution to the clean-up problems you will face during a normal day:

Keep out germs. Cut down on pollution.
Spray every day with a fresh bleach solution.
Mix water (1 gallon) with bleach (¼ cup).
The sick rate will go down and attendance will go up!

Here are more guidelines for cleaning solutions:

- Make a fresh bleach solution every day (¼ cup bleach to 1 gallon water).
- Dispense the bleach solution from a spray bottle.
- On a daily basis, disinfect all tabletops and toys that have been mouthed.

Practicing Appropriate Diapering Procedures

Using appropriate diapering procedures, as described in the box below, is another important health practice.

Diapering Sequence

- Have needed supplies ready, including a clean diaper, clothing, towelettes, and any creams or lotions that you are using with the child.
- Be sure that the diaper-changing surface is washable and nonporous.
- Place a fresh piece of paper on the changing area. It is important to change the paper after each diaper change.
- Put on gloves.
- Place the child on the changing table. Remember to keep one hand on the child at all times.

Use diapering time to carry on a playful conversation with the child.

- Remove the soiled diaper.
- Clean the child with towelettes, wiping from front to back.
- Dispose of the soiled diaper and towelettes in a plastic-lined container.
- Remove your gloves and dispose of them in the container.
- Put on a clean diaper and dress the child.
- Wash the child's hands.
- Return the child to a safe area.
- Place any soiled clothing in a plastic bag to give to the parent.
- Remove the changing table paper and discard it, remembering to only touch clean areas of the paper.
- Clean and disinfect the diaper-changing area.
- Wash your hands thoroughly with soap and hot water, using appropriate handwashing techniques.

Maintaining a Healthy Indoor Environment

Follow these suggestions for providing a healthy indoor environment:

- Keep the air in the room fresh by opening windows, if possible.
- Make outdoor activities part of the daily schedule.
- Alternate quiet times and physical activity to keep children active, alert, and healthy and to provide a time for children to rest or sleep.
- Provide space between children's mats, cots, and cribs to reduce the spread of respiratory infections.
- Check state and local rules and regulations for additional requirements, such as lead-free certification, ventilation requirements, and pest-control guidelines.

To establish guidelines/policies regarding how to handle health issues, including a record-keeping system

Establishing guidelines and keeping accurate records is also important to ensuring a healthy environment.

Maintaining Health and Immunization Records for Every Child

- The Centers for Disease Control (CDC) publishes annually a recommended immunization chart that lists the types of immunizations required by law and the ages when initial immunization and booster shots are required. You should have verification of up-to-date immunization for every child or a note from a physician stating the reason that the child has not been vaccinated.
- Require that verification of physicals be updated, as required by the state and local enforcement agencies.
- Develop a system for maintaining physical and immunization records for children and a system of informing parents when they need to update immunizations and/or physicals.
- Maintain a health record for each child that includes comments from the daily health check, any unusual incidences or concerns, height and weight, alternative food plans, and allergic reactions.

Knowing the Guidelines Set By Your Center for Excusing Children from Child Care Due to Illness

Centers need to develop policies indicating when mildly ill children can and cannot attend child care. Many children with mild illnesses can safely attend the center. Be sure to share these guidelines with parents. Also, know when to report communicable diseases and other conditions to the health department.

To incorporate activities that teach children and families about health, oral/dental hygiene, and nutrition

When we think about all the different things we would like young children to know about health and nutrition, it is difficult to know what to emphasize or even where to begin. One possible way to start is to make a list of some of the basic concepts you would like children to learn in the course of the year. Next, develop lesson plans devoted to these concepts. You might want to do a theme or unit near the beginning of the year or offer brief lessons on a weekly basis.

Basic Concepts about Health and Wellness Appropriate for Preschool Children

- Our bodies get strong when we get to sleep on time, get a lot of fresh air, and eat healthy foods.
- Germs make us sick. When we wash our hands before we eat and after we go to the bathroom, we get rid of germs.
- Germs spread when we sneeze or cough. That's why we need to cover our mouths with our hands when we sneeze or cough and then wash our hands.
- Cigarettes are not good for our bodies.
- We brush our teeth at least twice a day to keep them clean and healthy.

Basic Concepts about Nutrition

- Eating the right kinds of food makes us strong and healthy.
- Foods like candy and sweetened cereal are bad for our teeth.

- Foods that are high in protein—such as meat, fish, beans, and cheese—make us strong and give us energy.
- Eating a lot of fruits and vegetables gives us vitamins that keep us feeling well.

Activities for Learning about Nutrition

Pretend Play

Objective: To teach children to recognize healthy foods

Procedure: Set up a "restaurant" in your classroom. Provide appropriate props, such as chef hats, aprons, menus, trays, pads and pencils, pretend food, napkins, place settings, and a cash register. Join the play as the "waitress" or the "parent," so that you can talk about ordering healthy foods.

Food Books

Objective: To teach children about the different food groups

Procedure: Help children construct their own food books by cutting pictures of foods out of newspapers and magazines or using labels from food packaging. Make separate pages or books for breads and cereals, dairy products, meats and other proteins, fruits, and vegetables.

Basic Concepts about Dental Care

- Brushing our teeth after every meal keeps them strong and healthy.
- The dentist is a special kind of doctor who helps us take care of our teeth.

Activity for Learning about Dental Care

No-Cavities Collages

Objective: To teach children oral hygiene

Procedure: Draw a smiling face on one piece of tagboard and a sad face on another. Ask children to bring in magazine pictures and wrappers that represent foods that are good for your teeth and foods that are not good for your teeth. Let the children paste things that are good for your teeth on the "happy face" tagboard, such as a picture of an orange, and things that are bad for your teeth on the "sad face" tagboard, such as a candy wrapper or the top from a box of highly sugared cereal.

To recognize indicators of abuse and/or neglect and follow the reporting policy mandated by the state

Child abuse and neglect is a national problem. Maltreatment, according to long-term studies, is associated with dropping out of school, committing violent crimes, and being unemployed. There is also evidence that children who have been abused are at risk for becoming child abusers when they become parents.

Every child care provider is required by state law to report suspected abuse. If you suspect that a child in your center has been abused, follow the procedures for reporting set by your center. If you are a family child care provider, report directly to the abuse hotline in your state. Familiarize yourself with the indicators of abuse described in the following child maltreatment chart.

Types of Child Maltreatment

Type of Abuse or Neglect	Physical Indicators	Behavioral Indicators
Physical abuse	• Unexplained bruises, welts, burns, fractures, lacerations, and abrasions	• Afraid of adults • Afraid of parents and/or to go home • Anxious about routine activities, like sleeping, eating, and toileting • Can be either aggressive or withdrawn
Emotional abuse	• Failure to thrive • Lags behind other children in physical development • Developmental delays	• Habit disorders (sucking, biting, rocking) • Withdrawn or aggressive • Poor peer relations
Sexual abuse	• Difficulty walking or sitting • Bloody underclothes • Bruises or bleeding in genitalia, vaginal, or rectal areas • Venereal disease or pregnancy (with teens) • Wears clothing and/or makeup beyond his or her years	• Unwilling to take off clothing • Unusual sexual behavior or knowledge of sexual behavior beyond what children his or her age should know • Poor peer and adult relations
Neglect	• Poor hygiene • Inappropriate dress • Medical needs are not met • Lack of supervision • Abandonment • Always hungry	• Begging, stealing food, or taking food from the trash • Asks to take food home • Arrives early and is picked up late • Constant fatigue or falls asleep in class • Withdrawn

Objective 6 To keep oneself healthy and model appropriate wellness behaviors for children and their parents

Miss It's-My-Business was called into the office by the director of the center.

Director: "I heard that you had a great meeting last night with your parent volunteer group."

Miss It's-My-Business: "They're a fabulous group of parents, and we made some really exciting plans."

Director: "There is just one thing that concerns me. One of the parents said that when you went out for coffee after the meeting, you were smoking nonstop and—"

Miss It's-My-Business (interrupting): "I never smoke at school, and I don't appreciate your telling me what I should do after school! If I want to ruin my health, I'll do what I please. It's my health."

Director: "I wasn't trying to interfere with what you do in your spare time. It's just that I would like to see you take better care of yourself. Remember, last year, you had three attacks of bronchitis."

Although Miss It's-My-Business was miffed when the director commented on her smoking, the director made a valid point. It is important for all child caregivers to maintain their own health.

Most of us are fully aware of how to take care of our health:

- Eat nutritious meals.
- Maintain the weight level recommended for your height and body build.
- Get an annual physical and regular dental check-ups.
- Get prenatal care in the first trimester of pregnancy.
- Get enough rest and exercise, and avoid getting overstressed.
- Abstain from smoking, abusing alcohol, and taking illegal drugs.
- Make sure your immunizations are up to date. Also ask your health provider if an annual flu shot is advisable.

> *Unfortunately, the easy part is knowing how to stay healthy. The hard part is making a commitment to wellness and living up to that commitment.*

Unfortunately, the easy part is *knowing* how to stay healthy. The hard part is making a commitment to wellness and living up to that commitment.

One way to convert your good intentions for maintaining a healthy lifestyle into commitment is to recognize the benefits that desirable health practices provide:

- When we feel good, we are happier, more energetic, and better at coping with minor problems.
- If we "practice what we preach," we are good models for children and parents. When Miss It's-My-Business smoked in a coffeehouse with parents from her center, she was sending a message that it is okay for adults to smoke when they are not in the child care facility.
- When we are committed to wellness, we are more likely to have a better attendance record at work. If we ever want to change jobs or advance our careers, letters of recommendation that include a good record of attendance are bound to be helpful.
- Staying healthy is cost effective. The cost of medical care continues to rise, so in a very literal sense, it pays to stay healthy.

You should have health insurance. If you are an independent provider or if your center does not offer insurance coverage, investigate state programs. Your local child care professional organization, union, or resource and referral agency may be able to help you locate resources for obtaining medical insurance.

Additional Resources about Health

Aronson, S. (2002). *Healthy young children: A manual for programs* (4th ed.). Washington, DC: NAEYC.

Caring for Our Children—National health and safety performance standards: Guidelines for out of home child care programs (2nd ed). (2002). Washington, DC: NAEYC. (Updated standards issued jointly by the American Academy of Pediatrics, American Public Health Association, and the National Resource Center for Health and Safety in Child Care)

Centers for Disease Control (CDC). www.cdc.gov.

Learning Environments

Chapter 3

Overview

A learning environment for preschool children is a place that is conducive to learning and appropriate for the developmental levels and learning characteristics of the children.

Rationale

The arrangement of a classroom or family child care setting sets the tone for learning. The selection and setup of play materials, the pictures on the walls, and even the way the room is divided all support beliefs about what and how children should learn. For example, placing puzzles and sorting toys on low shelves invites children to learn mathematical concepts through play. Creating a pretend play area that can become a "fire station," "circus tent," or "café" invites children to learn about their world by playing together. On the other hand, setting desks in rows and keeping materials on high shelves suggest that learning is controlled by the teacher and that children should not explore on their own or learn from each other.

Preschoolers need an environment that is safe and welcoming, intriguing but not overwhelming. In a well-planned environment, babies will spend less time crying and more time exploring. Older children will spend less time wandering, fidgeting, and fighting and more time asking questions, working together, and mastering new skills.

Objectives

1. To set up an environment that takes into account the behavioral characteristics, needs, and interests of infants at different stages (0–14 months)

2. To set up an environment that takes into account the behavioral characteristics, needs, and interests of young toddlers (14–24 months)

3. To set up an environment that takes into account the behavioral characteristics, needs, and interests of older toddlers (2 years)

4. To organize and equip a preschool classroom that promotes different kinds of play and learning experiences and that reflects the interests, needs, ability levels, and family backgrounds of the children (3–5 years)

5. To organize and equip a learning environment for a multiage or family child care setting that includes children ages birth through 5

6. To develop a well-balanced daily schedule

7. To set up an outdoor play and learning environment

8. To ensure that the learning environment works for adults as well as for children

Providing a Developmentally Appropriate Learning Environment

The chair of the parent advisory board from the Key to Growth Child Care Center arrived in the director's office full of excitement. "I just received the most wonderful news," the chair reported. "The Tot Toy Factory has agreed to give us the most fabulous contribution. They are giving us their complete display of oversized cardboard Sesame Street characters. This place will look great with a giant Muppet in every classroom!"

The director of the center was in a quandary. On the one hand, she wanted to be gracious and accept this gift with enthusiasm. On the other hand, she wasn't so sure that her teachers would welcome the giant Muppets. They were too big to fit into a classroom without rearranging the learning centers. Thinking quickly, she came up with a perfect solution. "I am so appreciative of all that you have done for this center. You are always thinking of us. Instead of putting one Muppet in each classroom, why don't we line them all up on the way out to the playground? They'll be a real conversation piece for the children." ●

The director didn't want to give up either her belief in the importance of parent participation or her belief in setting up an environment that expressed the philosophy of active learning that was so important to her and to her teachers. Fortunately, she found a quick solution that was consistent with both.

To set up an environment that takes into account the behavioral characteristics, needs, and interests of infants at different stages (0–14 months)

Ms. Shipshape had the infant room just the way she liked it. The cribs were lined up in a row on one side. The rattles were in a box that she could reach without stooping. The floor was clear. The walls were gleaming white. There wasn't a pillow in sight. Everything had been disinfected.

"This is no place for a baby," said Mrs. Earthmother when she came to visit. "It's too sterile!" ●

Ms. Shipshape and Mrs. Earthmother each have a point. Babies do need an environment that is easy to keep sanitary. They also need to be in a space that is cozy, that looks and feels like home, and that provides them with interesting things to look at and inviting places to explore. As described in the Developmental Picture on page 62, infants have specific interests as well as needs.

Basic Considerations for Setting Up an Infant Room

Consider the following in deciding how to set up an infant room:

- *Infants spend much of the day sleeping.* The infant room should have a sleeping room or area with a crib for every child.

- *During their periods of wakefulness, infants learn best from their interactions with adults.* The infant room should have well-equipped areas for changing and feeding that encourage adult/infant interaction.

- *During their wakeful periods, infants learn from playing with a variety of toys.* Teachers should be sure that every infant, when awake, has age-appropriate toys to play with.

- *Infants as young as 6 months old enjoy interaction with other infants.* The infant room should have a safe and easily cleaned area where two or three infants can play together.

- *The needs and schedules for an infant may change on a daily basis.* Every infant room should have a bulletin board where emergency telephone numbers, schedules, and instructions from parents are posted.

- *Infants are vulnerable to contagious illnesses and to overstimulation.* If there are more than 8 to 10 children in a room, it should be divided into two or more areas so that there are never more than 10 bodies in a room together.

Equipping the Infant Room

Sleeping Area

An infant room must have one crib for every infant, but finding room for cribs can be a challenge. Some people solve the problem by putting the cribs on wheels and moving them aside when they are not in use. Others use the spaces under cribs for storage.

When in use, cribs should be at least 18 inches apart and should be arranged so that the supervisor has full view of every infant. See-through cribs let caregivers look in and babies look out.

Generally, infants should have a separate area for sleeping, where the light and noise levels can be kept low. When a separate space is not available, use room dividers to create a quiet corner. A rocking chair in the sleeping area is useful for comforting fussy babies.

Developmental Picture

The young infant (0–9 months):

- Is limited in mobility
- Is attracted to interesting sights, sounds, and objects and enjoys watching people
- Has individual needs for sleeping and eating
- Is likely to be startled or overstimulated by a sudden noise or a room that is noisy, very bright, or filled with activity
- May "tune out," fuss, fall asleep, or be unable to sleep when overstimulated
- May fuss or cry when bored
- Needs to spend some playtime on his stomach on a firm surface to learn to roll over, crawl, and get into a sitting position

The caregiver:

- Provides a variety of perspectives by moving the infant about
- Brings experiences to the infant to look at, listen to, and touch
- Recognizes that infants have different levels of tolerance in terms of sound and visual stimulation and reads each child's cues
- Separates young infants from more active playmates
- Provides a quiet sleeping area
- Follows the infant's feeding and sleeping schedule, moving toward a regular rhythm

The older infant (9–14 months):

- Is creeping, cruising, and learning to walk and may be practicing walking and climbing skills
- Has favorite toys and is interested in selecting her own toys
- Enjoys emptying and filling and holding soft cuddly things
- Is interested in exploring new spaces
- Can suddenly become overtired and/or overstimulated

The caregiver:

- Provides space and equipment for active movement indoors and outdoors
- Divides the space so that infants can play in small groups
- Keeps toys on low, sturdy shelves within reach
- Stores small items in see-through boxes
- Creates interesting obstacle courses for babies who are learning to crawl, cruise, walk, and climb
- Provides a reliable rhythm that meets babies' needs for frequent eating and resting

Changing Area

The changing table should be waist high for adults' comfort and have a washable surface. Changing supplies, a sink with hot and cold running water, and a covered trash container should be in easy reach. Having a nonbreakable mirror behind the changing table is fun for babies.

The changing table needs to be set up with the caregiver in mind. Items should be easy to reach and well organized to minimize the chance of skipping steps in proper diapering and handwashing procedures.

Feeding Areas

The infant room should include places to warm bottles and to sit comfortably while bottle feeding a baby. A quiet corner with a rocking chair is ideal. There should also be a comfortable, private space for nursing mothers.

Babies between 9 and 14 months are also eating solid food and may enjoy having mealtimes at the table, especially if this is what they are used to at home. You can use highchairs, table-height feeding chairs, or seats that attach to a regular table. Make sure the chairs have seatbelts that can restrain a baby who suddenly learns to stand and that they are sturdy enough so that they can't be tipped over by a cruising toddler. In many programs, older babies eat their meals at small tables with sturdy chairs they can climb in and out of.

Bouncy Chairs and Swings (Caution!)

While bouncy chairs and swings give children the opportunity of seeing the world from a sitting position, they need to be selected carefully and used with caution. Bouncy chairs and swings should have safety belts and should not be placed in doorways where they may block emergency access. Confining babies in chairs or swings for too long a period deprives them of opportunities to learn new motor skills, such as rolling over, sitting, and crawling. Walkers with wheels should never be used in an early childhood setting. There is too much of a danger of colliding with another child, rolling over someone's fingers, tipping over, or getting stuck.

Storage Areas for Infant Supplies

Infants come with lots of supplies! You'll need places to store clean diapers, extra clothes, food, and perhaps even car seats for each child.

Play Areas

An infant room should have safe, easily cleaned areas where infants can play together. Low shelves, foam dividers, couches, a play yard or corral, and an empty wading pool can all be used to define intimate spaces and provide support for pulling up and cruising. Mirrors, "busy boxes," and laminated pictures can be mounted at different heights to intrigue babies who are learning to sit, crawl, stand, and walk.

Peep holes, hiding places (visible to an adult), crawling tunnels, large vinyl blocks, low windows, and different colors and textures on the floor help make spaces interesting for babies who are just learning to get around.

Put a sheet on the carpeted play area so that you can wash it daily.

63

Selecting Learning Materials

Shelf Toys

No infant should be left during a wakeful period without access to age-appropriate toys. Keep some of the toys where babies can get them themselves—on low shelves, in play areas and crawl spaces, or mounted on the walls or on the backs of shelf units.

Here are some toys that are appropriate for babies in the following age groups:

- *3 to 6 months:* rattles, soft squeak toys, cradle gyms, musical toys, washable dolls, animals
- *6 to 9 months:* toy telephones, roly-poly toys, pop-up toys, colorful wheel toys, unbreakable mirrors, washable cuddle toys
- *9 to 14 months:* "busy boards," fill and dump toys, rolling toys, push and pull toys, large balls, soft blocks, cloth or cardboard blocks

Crib Toys

Although the amount of awake time that infants spend in their cribs should be minimized, age-appropriate toys should be placed in every crib:

> *Although the amount of awake time that infants spend in their cribs should be minimized, age-appropriate toys should be placed in every crib.*

- *3 months and under:* crib mobiles that attach to the side of the crib or hang from the ceiling, wind chimes, musical mobiles, see-through crib bumpers
- *4 to 7 months:* cradle gyms, see-through rattles, clutch balls, teething rings
- *8 to 14 months:* "busy boxes," squeak toys, rattles, soft cloth dolls, clutch balls, pop-up toys, and mirror toys

Sensory Bin

Infants enjoy a variety of sensory experiences, such as splashing water, finger painting with pudding, and rubbing their hands in wet cornstarch. A large dishpan is ideal for this kind of play. You can put it and the babies into an empty plastic wading pool to help contain the mess.

Music Area

A cassette recorder, CD player, or record player is a must in an infant play area. "Easy-listening" music, lullabies, nursery rhymes, and classical music provide satisfying listening experiences for infants and their caregivers. You might also encourage parents to record and share the songs or chants that they use with their babies.

Arranging the Infant Room

The way an infant room is arranged depends on how large the room is, how many infants there are, how many staff members are in the room at any one time, the age and mobility of the infants, and whether the room is single purpose (sleeping, eating, or playing) or multipurpose. Looking at the room with a "baby's-eye view," you may see things you want to change as the babies develop new capabilities and interests.

In every situation, however, there are some prime considerations for setting up an infant environment. Arrange the room or rooms according to these guidelines:

- Provide a separation between awake and sleeping babies.
- Make sure that changing tables and feeding areas can be accessed easily from both the sleeping and play areas.
- Provide easy access to running water, refrigeration, covered waste disposal cans, and some type of food warmer.
- Designate an adult "lookout spot" with full visibility.
- Carpet the floor of the crib area for quiet and easy clean-up.
- Enclose the play area and make sure that it has a soft but washable surface.
- Arrange toys and books on shelves and group similar items.
- Make sure the CD, cassette, or record player is in easy reach for adults but out of reach of children.
- Allow a 2-foot-wide walkway at all exits. Keep exits clear in accordance with fire safety laws.
- Make sure the arrangement works for the babies and for you.

> *Looking at the room with a "baby's-eye view," you may see things you want to change as the babies develop new capabilities and interests.*

Objective 2

To set up an environment that takes into account the behavioral characteristics, needs, and interests of young toddlers (14–24 months)

Consider these qualities of young toddlers in setting up a room for them:

- *Young toddlers spend long stretches of time in active play.* Cots can be stacked, except during naptime, and the same room can be used for sleep and play.
- *Young toddlers are developing their large-muscle skills and need opportunities to practice running, climbing, throwing, pushing, pulling, and carrying things around.* The young toddler classroom should provide indoor slides, indoor climbing structures, riding toys, and rocking boats.
- *Young toddler need different kinds of spaces—large, open spaces that let them explore space and small, cozy places that make them feel comfortable and secure.* Create both a large, open space and cozy, crawl-in spaces, such as playhouses, cartons, and corners.
- *Young toddlers are just learning to say "It's mine" and for the most part have not learned about sharing.* They cannot understand why some things, like toys, have to be shared while other things, like lunches and shoes, cannot be shared. Make sure that most of the toys and equipment in the classroom are

65

conducive to group play. The presence of very attractive one-of-a-kind toys can initiate power struggles.

- *Young toddlers are delighted with rhythm, music, pictures, and books.* Your classroom should have a CD or tape player, a collection of CDs or tapes, attractive pictures at the child's level, and a library corner with indestructible books.

- *Young toddlers tend to be exuberant and excitable and can quickly make a shambles of a classroom.* Simplify the task of cleaning up. Limit the number of small, loose toys that are kept within reach of children. Provide attractive containers for toys that make cleaning up fun. A carton "cage" or Noah's ark can be used as a container for toy animals. A corner of the classroom with lines drawn on the floor or marked on the carpet can be a "parking lot" for wheel toys. Colorful plastic laundry baskets make great storage containers for balls and beanbags.

- *Young toddlers are active and can be very noisy.* With the exception of areas that are used for eating, art, and water play, the room for young toddlers should be carpeted. Also, if possible, there should be acoustic tiles on the ceiling to absorb sound.

- *Young toddlers learn through active exploration.* Provide areas in the classroom where toddlers can finger paint, play with water and clay, experience different textures, and create different sounds. Create a texture wall where the children can feel different surfaces (hard, soft, smooth, rough, furry, slippery, bumpy) or a sound wall where the children can ring a bell, toot a horn, squeak a rubber animal, or beat a drum.

- *Young toddlers are creatures of habit and thus disturbed by too many changes in their environment.* Once you have created an attractive and orderly classroom, change the basic layout as little as possible. Young toddlers gain a sense of security by finding everything in its place. It is especially important for them to have their own special private space (a cubby or a shelf) that is never changed or disturbed.

For more information on the characteristics of young toddlers, see the Developmental Picture.

Equipping a Young Toddler Room

Tables and Chairs

One- to two-year-olds enjoy sitting at tables and chairs, not only for eating but also for sensory experiences, puzzle play, and art activities. Tables should be toddler size (16 to 18 inches high).

Highchairs

By age 1½, most children can eat comfortably at a low table-and-chair combination. For younger children who are still learning to feed themselves, however, it is best to have highchairs or table-height feeding chairs. By using individualized eating schedules, a room only needs a couple of highchairs, not one for every child.

Developmental Picture

The older infant (9–14 months):

- Is creeping, cruising, and learning to walk and may be practicing walking and climbing skills
- Has favorite toys and is interested in selecting her own toys
- Enjoys emptying and filling containers and holding soft, cuddly things
- Is interested in exploring new spaces
- Can suddenly become overtired and/or overstimulated

The caregiver:

- Provides space and equipment for active movement indoors and out
- Divides the space so that infants can play in small groups
- Keeps toys on low, sturdy shelves within reach
- Stores small items in see-through boxes
- Creates interesting obstacle courses for babies who are learning to crawl, cruise, walk, and climb
- Provides a reliable rhythm that meets babies' needs for frequent eating and resting

The young toddler (14–24 months):

- Is practicing large-muscle skills and may be an active climber
- Enjoys emptying filling, dumping, and pouring
- Enjoys sensory play using materials such as water, rice, sand, and shaving cream
- Likes to play alongside others with matching toys
- Enjoys pretend play
- Is developing a sense of where things belong
- Becomes overstimulated by active activities and is calmed by quiet activities

The caregiver:

- Provides space and equipment for active play both indoors and out, such as push, pull, and scooting toys; slides and climbers; and large, lightweight blocks
- Provides duplicates of favorite items
- Provides simple materials for pretend play, such as purses, scarves, brooms, sponges, telephones, plastic dishes, and cooking pots
- Stores toys on low shelves
- Outdoors, separates the wheeled toy area from the climbing area
- Provides a separate area for eating, with low tables and right-sized chairs
- Maintains a consistent daily rhythm that alternates quiet and active activities and that provides toddlers with a sense of order and time

Arranging the Young Toddler Room

The young toddler room combines some of the features of the infant room with some of the features of the older toddler room. Like infants, young toddlers need a place to sleep, a place to eat, and a place to play, and their caregivers need a place for changing diapers.

Like older toddlers, younger toddlers need larger places for active play; a place for imaginative play; a quiet place for reading a book, playing with manipulatives, and playing alone or with a friend; and a place for sensory play.

Before you can decide where to put the different areas, you first need to look at the "givens" in your room.

- Windows provide light and views but also take up wall space. You may want to put tables for eating and art activities in front of the windows, saving your walls for other activities.
- Doors need to be kept clear as emergency exits. Closet doors that open out create dead spaces in the room when clearances are allowed.
- Carpeted areas are best for active play, circle time activities, and other activities in which children sit on the floor. Tiled areas provide easy clean-up for feeding, sensory play, and art activities.
- The locations of electrical outlets will determine where you put the CD or tape player, bottle warmer, refrigerator, and microwave oven.
- Corners are ideal for quiet play.
- Built-in furnishings will determine the locations of storage spaces. Since you want to limit the number of toys available in the room at the same time, you will need plenty of storage for toys, art materials, and other equipment. Remember to provide storage for your personal belongings, as well as for the children's.
- Use high wall space for the parent information board and for posting emergency plans and phone numbers. Use child-level wall space for sound and texture boards, mirrors, photos of the children and their families, and a flannelboard for displaying the children's creations.

Next, make a rough diagram that indicates the placement of major furnishings and equipment, taking into account all of these fixed features.

Setting Up and Equipping Activity Centers

Your room should include the following basic areas or activity centers.

Greeting Area

The greeting area should include a place where children can store their personal belongings, such as cubbies. Parent boards also are most visible in this area, as are teacher boards.

Eating, Sensory Play, and Creative Art Area

This area will include toddler-sized tables and chairs, highchairs if needed, storage for art and craft supplies, and at least one chair that you can sit on comfortably. Ideally, the eating area should also include a small refrigerator, a microwave oven, running water with disposable paper towels, and a covered garbage can.

Toileting/Diapering Area

Most children under 2 are still in diapers, so you should include a changing table, a diaper bin, and a storage unit for clean diapers and supplies. Access to hot and cold running water is a must. You will also need potty chairs if you do not have access to small toilets for those children who are ready to give up diapers.

Pretend Play Area

Early pretending is very simple and has a strong imitative quality. Children replay experiences that are familiar to them, such as driving, sleeping, cooking, and eating. Having a toddler-sized stove, sink, and table and a doll-sized highchair and crib will encourage early pretending. Make sure, too, that there are places for dishes, cooking utensils, play food, and, of course, ethnically appropriate dolls. Nice additions to the pretend area also include an unbreakable mirror; dress-up jewelry, ties, scarves, purses, and carry-alls; and a "steering wheel" chair to serve as a pretend vehicle.

Active Play Area

Climbing Structures Because young toddlers spend much of their day practicing their motor skills, the choice of climbing structures is critical. The size and number of climbing structures that are placed in the room depends on several factors:

- How much space you have
- How many children are using the space
- How well equipped your playground is
- How much outdoor time the weather permits

Desirable climbing structures include the following:

- *Slides:* A slide is an important piece of basic equipment. A good indoor slide has a crawl space underneath and is designed so that the stairs are easy to mount.
- *Rocking boat:* A rocking boat that converts to a staircase is a particularly desirable structure. It provides opportunities to practice different motor skills and at the same time encourages cooperative play.
- *Special structures:* Ramps, wedges, tunnels, and platforms can provide further practice in motor skills. Again, it is important to remember that young toddlers need room to move around. A desirable climbing structure that takes up too much space is really not desirable.

Blocks Blocks can be either large cardboard bricks, large nesting blocks, or vinyl-covered shapes.

Push/Ride-On Toys Young toddlers are also on the move. Cars and trucks that can be ridden, pushed, and pulled will keep them busy.

Music Every young toddler room should include a cassette tape recorder, CD player, or record player. This should be placed on a relatively high shelf along with the tapes, CDs, or records, and if the equipment is not battery operated, it should be located near an electric outlet. One- to two-years-olds should not have access to this equipment. Rhythm instruments also require a storage bin out of reach of the children so that their use can be controlled.

Quiet Play Areas

Cuddle-Up Structures Young toddlers need closed, protected, quiet spaces just as much as they need spaces to move around in. Cushions wedged in a corner, foam forms, beanbag chairs, and large cardboard boxes with cut-out "windows" are some ideas for creating private spaces.

Reading Corner Cuddle-up spaces can also double as reading corners. Place cuddly stuffed animals in the cuddle-up area and a small book display rack within easy reach.

To set up an environment that takes into account the behavioral characteristics, needs, and interests of older toddlers (2 years)

Mr. By-the-Book had just read a book on setting up a toddler environment. He loved the book's suggestions on creating open spaces and interest centers and decided to set up his room exactly like the diagram in the book. When he completed the task, he asked the director to come in and admire it.

The director was at a loss for words. She congratulated him on his hard work and told him the room looked great, but there was one small problem: She didn't see the cots.

Mr. By-the-Book explained that he had put the cots in the empty room across the hall. "I arranged the room exactly like the diagram in the book you lent me," he told her proudly. "I didn't have room for everything, so I decided I would just put the cots down the hall and bring them back for naptime."

"You need to put the cots back in the classroom," the director explained gently. "Unfortunately, our toddler room isn't nearly as large as the one in the book, and you can't simply follow a diagram. Try rearranging the room, leaving space for the cots." ●

As you read about the suggested layout for a toddler room, you will undoubtedly have the same problems as Mr. By-the-Book. If you do not have enough room to follow all of our recommendations, you will have to make compromises. Keep the essential furnishings in the room and work around them. And remember: Not all things have to be available all of the time. Although some basics should remain constant, your room can change over time as the children develop new interests and capabilities.

Characteristics and Interests of Older Toddlers

Older toddlers are about 2 years old and have these characteristics and interests:

- *Older toddlers are practicing emerging motor skills and enjoy running, jumping, twirling, and marching to music.* The classroom needs open spaces where children can engage in active circle time activities.
- *Older toddlers are interested in exploring different kinds of spaces.* The classroom should include a variety of different space experiences, such as a tunnel, a pit, a platform, a bridge, a two-level townhouse, and/or an indoor climbing structure.
- *Older toddlers enjoy quiet, cozy spaces.* The classroom should include a comfortable hideaway spot. It may be a corner with cushions and bolsters, a carton to crawl into, a playhouse, or a hideaway reading corner.
- *Older toddlers are beginning to learn about sharing and turn taking.* The classroom should include some toys for side-by-side play and some toys like blocks and wagons that encourage cooperation.
- *Older toddlers enjoy constructive play.* The classroom should have a carpeted block area, where children have easy access to a variety of plastic and cardboard blocks.
- *Older toddlers are interested in creating with different kinds of materials.* The classroom should have access to fluid and pliable materials, such as water, sand, easel paint, clay, and crayons.
- *Older toddlers are becoming more sophisticated in their pretend play.* The classroom should contain play structures, props, and dress-up material for involved types of pretending and small representational objects, such as toy animals, vehicles, and dolls, for more simple pretending.
- *Older toddlers are experiencing a rapid growth in language skills.* The classroom should be well stocked with culturally and thematically appropriate picture books, tapes, prints, and photos that encourage receptive and expressive language.

See the following Developmental Picture (page 72) for more on the interests and activities of older toddlers.

Developmental Picture

The older toddler (2-year-old):

- Pushes, pulls, and carries things around
- Enjoys practicing motor skills
- Is interested in simple dress-up clothes and pretend play
- Pulls toys off the shelves
- Enjoys choosing books, toys, and puzzles
- Recognizes where things belong

The caregiver:

- Provides an area for imaginative play and an area for motor activities
- Recognizes that children will mix toys from different areas as they combine them in play
- Keeps a variety of toys within easy reach
- Maintains an orderly classroom and a consistent but flexible routine
- Provides ample time for activities and care routines so the atmosphere can be relaxed

Equipping the Room for Older Toddlers

A room for older toddlers should contain the following equipment.

Tables and Chairs

Older toddlers enjoy sitting at tables for snacks, mealtimes, arts and craft activities, and manipulative play. Follow these specifications in choosing tables and chairs:

- *Size:* The tables for older toddlers should be approximately 18 inches high; the chairs should fit under the tables, allowing enough space for leg room.

- *Number:* Because older toddlers enjoy meal- and snacktimes together, it is important to have a chair and room at a table for each child.

- *Shape:* The shape and size of the tables depends on how the classroom is arranged. If the same tables are used for snacktime, art projects, and manipulative activities, it is important to have small tables that can be moved. Rectangular or trapezoidal tables work better than round ones for arts and crafts and can be put together in different configurations and then taken apart.

Structures

Toddlers love to climb and explore, both alone and together. A loft with a ladder serves several purposes. It challenges toddlers to climb up, gives them a bird's-eye view, and provides spaces above and below where two or three friends can have private playtime. At the same time, it presents endless possibilities for pretend play. Add a blanket, and it becomes a tent for going camping or giving a circus performance. Add a steering wheel, and it's a car, a truck, an airplane, a boat, or a rocket ship. Make sure the loft is sturdy enough and the railings high enough to support jumping toddlers.

Shelves and Room Dividers

Because older toddlers enjoy a room that is organized into play centers, it is important to have enough shelving, book racks, and room dividers to section off the classroom.

Selecting Materials and Toys

Pretend Play Props and Equipment

The amounts and types of pretend play equipment depend both on budget constraints and the size of the classroom. A well-equipped older toddler classroom will include six types of pretend play equipment:

1. Equipment for "kitchen" play, including a stove, refrigerator, sink, highchair, mop or broom, and table and chairs

2. Equipment for "store" or puppet play, including a puppet stage that converts into a grocery store, post office, or bank

3. Equipment for doll play, including a variety of ethnic dolls plus a crib, a carriage, blankets, and a box with doll clothes

4. Dress-up play equipment, including a mirror and appropriate storage for costumes, shoes, purses, and jewelry

5. Equipment for "driver" play, such as a shopping cart or doll carriage, a riding toy or steering wheel, chairs that can be lined up to make a train, and a large box or laundry basket the children can climb into and use as a boat, racing car, or jeep

6. An assortment of miniature play sets, such as a farm, zoo, restaurant, dollhouse, garage, train, and fire station, with the accompanying props and miniature characters

To organize and equip a preschool classroom that promotes different kinds of play and learning experiences and that reflects the interests, needs, ability levels, and family backgrounds of the children (3–5 years)

Two preschool teachers from different schools were having dinner together. Miss Free Thinker, who worked in the Creative Workshop Preschool, began the conversation:

Miss Free Thinker: "Boy, am I glad it's Friday. School begins on Monday, and I spent most of the week moving furniture and arranging shelves. I do feel it was worth it, though. I needed to add a pretend play area and a science discovery area. Now, the room looks great."

Miss Discontented: "Well, you know I took a job at the College Prep Preschool, and we never have to change the room arrangement. The teacher sits at the desk in front of the room and the children sit at tables, two children per table, facing the teacher's desk."

73

Miss Free Thinker: "Do you like that arrangement?"

Miss Discontented: "Personally, I hate it, but it goes along with the philosophy of the school. The director believes that the best way to get children ready for success in school is to teach them academics, and so you should arrange the room like an elementary classroom. It sets the right tone."

Miss Free Thinker: "Do you agree?"

Miss Discontented: "I told you, I hate it, but that's the way the director wants it, and the parents are all right there behind her. So, as long as I stay in the school, I am not going to rock the boat." ●

This book is built on the philosophy that children are active learners who do best in environments that encourage exploration, imagination, and creativity. The suggestions for organizing learning environments provided in this chapter are a reflection of that philosophy.

Characteristics and Interests of Preschool Children

Just as infant and toddler classrooms are designed to meet the special needs of very young children, preschool classrooms must take into account the social, emotional, and intellectual characteristics of 3-, 4-, and 5-year-olds and the cultural backgrounds of these children. Consider the following:

- *The preschool child appreciates a beautiful classroom.* The preschool classroom should be inviting and attractive. If there is a choice, the walls should be painted a neutral or light pastel color, and pictures and materials should be added to provide the color. Shelves are critical. Even the best-equipped classrooms are often short of shelf space. Shelves serve the double function of dividing space into discrete areas and providing a place where toys and learning materials are accessible to children.

- *The preschool child enjoys an orderly classroom.* Materials should be arranged and coded so that everything in the classroom has its appropriate place. An ideal plan is to color code or picture code the shelves and materials so that it is easy to remember where everything belongs.

- *The preschool child needs a variety of social experiences with large-group, small-group, and individual activities.* The classroom should provide a variety of spaces for each, which may include the following:
  - *Large-group space:* A circle on the carpet, individual mats that can be placed in a circle on a carpet, and round or trapezoid tables all facilitate large-group interaction.
  - *Small-group space:* Interesting areas where the space is defined by lofts or corner enclosures encourage children to interact in small groups.
  - *Individual space:* Private, "all-by-myself" time can be provided by a reading corner with large pillows or beanbag chairs, a telephone booth structure, or even a large carton with a fuzzy rug on the bottom.

- *The preschool child likes to feel at home.* Make the children feel that the classroom is an extension of their home and a part of their neighborhood by providing a careful selection of family photos on the walls, materials such as play foods that are familiar to them, dress-up clothes that resemble the clothes the adults they know are likely to wear, dolls that look like the children in the classroom, and rhythm instruments that are used in the ceremonies they attend.

- *Preschool children need help to learn to be considerate of each other.* A classroom should be arranged to make it easy for children to be considerate. Noisy areas for music, block play, and pretend play should be separated from quiet areas, such as the library corner or problem-solving areas. Shelves should be used to control the traffic flow so that children won't upset each other's work.

- *Preschool children are ready to make activity selections.* Whether a preschool classroom is large or small, it should be organized into learning or interest centers. Both the number and the types of interest centers depend on the size and configuration of the classroom, the objectives of the curriculum, the staffing pattern, and the ages and characteristics of the children.

- *Preschool children enjoy working at tables.* Tables and chairs should be placed in the art and snack area and in some of the work areas. Children may enjoy using tables for practicing writing, putting puzzles together, setting up scenes with miniature figures, and playing math or language games.

- *The preschool child needs opportunities to pretend.* Every preschool classroom should provide spaces and equipment for imaginative play. Housekeeping equipment, a dress-up corner, a mirror, a telephone, dolls, and dishes are basic requirements. Other items can be added to reflect the children's interests, home cultures, and favorite stories as well as the themes that the teacher has introduced.

- *The preschool child must have experience with music and art.* The classroom should be equipped with a CD, tape, or record player; a variety of music, including marches, folk songs, and nursery rhymes; simple musical instruments; and a place where children can sit or march in a circle. For art, there should be tables and chairs, a sink, a noncarpeted floor area, and plenty of eye-level wall space where the children's work can be attractively displayed. Easels, drying racks, and whiteboards are desirable, as well.

- *Preschool children need opportunities to play with blocks and to work with a variety of construction toys.* Every preschool classroom should have a block area where children can learn to construct. Block play helps children develop their imagination and creativity and, at the same time, teaches mathematical and spatial concepts. Providing miniature figures, toy animals, cars and trucks, and small balls encourages children to build pretend worlds and raceways.

- *Preschool children are developing their language and communication skills.* A preschool classroom should provide spaces and materials that encourage language development. Picture books, display counters, eye-level wall treatments, puppet stages, elevated platforms, mirrors, cameras, and tape recorders can all be used to encourage language development.

75

- *Preschool children are ready and eager to learn new concepts.* A preschool classroom should include spaces and materials for manipulative play, problem solving, and science exploration. The traditional preschool science and discovery corner should not be simply a display area; rather, it should provide opportunities for hands-on experiences, including the following:

  —*Science and discovery:* pets (check with the local health department), plants, sink-and-float activities, magnet challenges, shells and rocks that can be classified, a scale, prisms, magnifying glasses, color paddles, and a sand table

  —*Manipulative play and problem solving:* a variety of materials that encourage sorting, ordering, number skill development, and pattern making, such as number puzzles, pegboards, table blocks, picture puzzles, counting games, stacking toys, color and shape games, sequencing boards, beads, and sewing cards

The Development Picture below provides additional information about the interests and abilities of preschoolers.

Arranging the Preschool Classroom

In order to meet the specific needs of the preschool child, it is important to take a broad look at the way the space is utilized—that is, to see the "big picture." To begin, we need to consider three factors:

Developmental Picture

The preschool child (3–5 years):
- Is an active learner
- Is developing a sense of self
- Is learning to play with others
- Can put toys away in the right places
- Recognizes and can choose a special interest area
- Learns through playing with dramatic play materials, blocks, manipulatives, art materials, and books
- Is likely to want some choices about what to do and when

The caregiver:
- Provides a rich variety of experiences and materials
- Defines activity areas, such as pretend play, science/discovery, art, language, blocks, and manipulative play
- Encourages choices
- Provides symbols or color codes to help children put toys away in the appropriate places
- Provides a daily routine that balances active/quiet, individual/group, and indoor/outdoor activities

- How can we use space to control group size?
- How can we separate noisy and quiet spaces?
- How can we control traffic flow?

Using Space to Control Group Size

We have said that children need opportunities to spend time in large groups, in small groups, and by themselves. A carefully engineered classroom provides areas that invite different-sized groups. A circle in the middle of the floor is an invitation to form a large group. A table for two or three, an interest area set off by bookshelves, a loft, or a playhouse invites children to cluster in small groups. "All-by-myself" places can be created in a book corner with a rocking chair, a small carton "house," and a beanbag chair that faces the wall.

Separating Noisy and Quiet Areas

In a well-designed classroom, there is a separation of noisy and quiet activities. Activities that require concentration, such as reading, problem solving, and practicing language skills, are on one side of the classroom. Noisy activities, like block building, climbing, and music, are on the other side. Art and imaginative play, which are relatively quiet activities that do not require excessive concentration, can be done in areas that serve as buffers.

Controlling Traffic Flow

The placement of furniture can be used to discourage Follow-the-Leader games and to encourage the formation of small groups. The placement of furniture also can be used to discourage children from interfering with each other. A block area that is arranged as an interest area, with only one space for exiting and entering, provides a safe place to build a structure.

Other Factors to Consider

Other factors should also be considered in arranging a successful space for 3- to 5-year-olds:

- What kind of floor covering to use
- What kinds of work and play surfaces work best
- How to make the best use of wall space
- How to create interest centers

Floor Covering

Floor covering is an important consideration in designing a preschool setting. A low-pile carpet is great for most of the classroom, but a vinyl-type floor covering is best for the "messy activity" areas. The sink area, snack area, art corner, and science and discovery area should be set over vinyl or similar floor covering to allow for quick, easy clean-up. Smaller pieces of carpet can be used to define specific playing areas, where a child can take an activity and be on his own private "island." Alternatively, if the entire floor is carpeted, vinyl remnants can be placed in messy areas.

77

Work and Play Surfaces

Thought should be given to providing open-space areas (versus tables) near display units. Some activities work better at tables than on the floor and vice versa. Table work is often approached more seriously by children and should be encouraged with activities requiring concentration and problem solving.

To direct traffic to a table or floor space, simply place a table close to shelves displaying table work activities and leave open floor space near other activities. Don't be too concerned about separating table from floor activities. Children will often make this distinction according to their own set of rules. Keep in mind that a good use of space allows 35 square feet (about the size of a king-sized bed) of unencumbered space per child.

Wall Space

In most classrooms, wall space is at a premium. Walls are taken up by sinks, doors, windows, shelves, and storage units. This means that all available display wall space has to be used wisely.

Here are some suggestions:

- Make sure that you have posted all items required by the licensing bureau, which are likely to include the following:
  —A fire escape plan
  —Emergency telephone numbers
  —A daily schedule
- A high priority in using wall space is to display children's products. Make sure that the products are hung at the child's eye level in an attractive arrangement.
- Use some accessible walls for conversation starters. These can be posters, photographs taken on field trips, interesting things that children have said, and displays relating to what the children are investigating.
- If your classroom is divided into interest centers, tie in the wall decoration with the purpose of an interest center. The housekeeping wall could have a mock window with an outdoor scene, or when it changes to a "doctor's office" or "veterinary hospital," post a sign saying "The doctor is in."
- Display photos of children and their families in places where children can point to and talk about them.
- Put up words. Put children's names on their cubbies, family photos, and artwork. Label each interest center with its current theme. Post appropriate reminders, such as "Close door gently."

Setting Up Interest Centers

An *interest center* is a defined classroom area that can accommodate three to six children. Some interest centers, like a block area or an art table, remain the same throughout the year. Others, like a "firehouse," puppet stage, or "science museum" may change with the curriculum units and the children's interests. Some areas, such as a wood-working center or cooking center, may be open only when you have extra help.

The following sections describe some interest centers that work well in most preschool classrooms. You, the children, and their families will certainly add others.

Imaginative Play Center

Type of Space Semienclosed. Carpeted. Child-sized furniture. Shelving for play materials. A mirror and clothes storage. A loft or other play structure adds space and flexibility.

Pretend Play Area

Type of Play	Benefits	Equipment and Materials
Doll play	• Consolidates experiences • Encourages care and empathy	Multicultural dolls, doll bed, stroller, highchair, blankets, clothes, bathing tub, diaper set, feeding items like bottles, bibs
Kitchen play	• Encourages cooperative play • Provides practice in playing a grown-up role • Encourages helping behavior	Telephone, stove, sink, refrigerator, small table and chairs, dishes, tableware, pots and pans, tablecloth, placemats, pot holders, oven mitt, baking utensils, toaster
Cleaning and housekeeping	• Encourages helping behavior • Provides practice in playing a grown-up role • Develops new skills	Brooms, mops, dustpans, carpet sweepers, scrub brushes, feather dusters
"Store"	• Creates a feeling of power • Invites cooperative play • Develops number skills	Cash register, balance scale, paper bags, play money, stamps, empty cans, boxes, play food
"Doctor/Nurse"	• Helps children cope with fears • Gives children a feeling of power • Encourages cooperation	Play stethoscope and thermometer, Band-Aids, gauze and tape, sling, diploma, eye chart, blood pressure cuff, flashlight, doctor and nurse uniforms, empty medicine bottles, spoons, prescription pad, play syringe

Dress-Up Play Area

Type of Play	Benefits	Equipment and Materials
Dress-up	• Provides practice in role-playing • Encourages creativity • Builds self-confidence • Provides practice in dressing and undressing	Firefighter and police hats, masks, mirrors, purses, wallets, keys, "credit cards," suitcases, clothing racks Clothing: shirts, dresses, capes, vests, shawls, scarves, robes, ties, belts Footwear: slippers, boots, shoes

Constructive Play Area

Type of Play	Benefits	Equipment and Materials
Constructive	• Encourages creativity • Promotes cooperation • Develops numerical concepts • Improves small-muscle development • Promotes language	Blocks of various types and sizes: unit blocks, large plastic interlocking or stacking blocks, small fit-together blocks like large Legos, bristle blocks, giant dominos Accessories such as vehicles, people, zoo and farm animals

Move-and-Grow Center

Type of Space   Large and open; relatively noisy. Carpeted. Storage space for large equipment and rhythm instruments. CD, tape, or record player.

Movement Area

Type of Play	Benefits	Equipment and Materials
Large muscle	• Develops large-muscle skills • Provides an outlet for energy • Provides opportunities for group play	Tumbling mat, walking board, balance beam, Hop Scotch or number line, skipping rope, beanbags, large sit-on trucks, train

A carefully engineered classroom provides areas that invite different-sized groups.

Music Area

Type of Play	Benefits	Equipment and Materials
Music	• Develops an appreciation of music • Improves coordination and rhythm • Develops listening skills • Provides opportunities for self-expression	Rhythm instruments; CD, tape, or record player; CDs, tapes, or records; scarves, songbooks

Create and Discover Center

Type of Space Large and noisy. Uncarpeted. Sink, tables and chairs, shelves for craft materials, table for science and discovery displays, sand and water tables, hot plate.

Science and Discovery Area

Type of Play	Benefits	Equipment and Materials
Sorting and classifying	• Develops observation and discrimination skills	Rocks, shells, beans, nuts, seeds, small containers, magnifying glass, mystery boxes, labels
Encouraging investigation	• Helps children use their senses for investigation	Water table with sieves, basters, funnels, pitchers, bottles, measuring cups, egg beaters
Manipulation	• Provides opportunities for sensory play and investigation	Sand table with sifter, different-shaped containers, scoops, shovels, spoons
Discovery	• Develops problem solving	Magnets and metal objects, sink-and-float tub, lab book
Sharpening of senses	• Develops observation and use of senses	Kaleidoscope, color paddles, sound-and-smell containers, prisms
Growth center	• Develops observation and nurturance	Pots, seeds, shovels, ruler, graph paper
Pet center	• Develops nurturance and responsibility	Goldfish, hamster, ant farm, guinea pig, pet care books, notebook

The traditional preschool science and discovery corner should not be simply a display area but should provide opportunities for hands-on experiences.

Cooking Area

Type of Play	Benefits	Equipment and Materials
Cooking	• Provides opportunities to use all the senses • Helps children to learn about food and nutrition • Develops small-muscle coordination • Stimulates language and concept • Helps children learn to follow directions	Heat source: stove, hotplate, or electric pan Refrigerator and sink (ideal but not essential) Other kitchen equipment: table and chairs, pots and pans, cooking utensils, recipe board, chef hats and smocks, cleaning materials, food and recipes, large paper for displaying recipes

Arts and Crafts Area

Type of Play	Benefits	Equipment and Materials
Painting	• Encourages expression	Easels, brushes, paper, rollers, paints, drying rack or clothes line
Crafts	• Develops artistic sense • Develops a sense of personal accomplishment • Encourages exploration in a variety of media	Clay, scissors, scrap materials, paste, tape, wallpaper, books, markers, crayons, colored tissues, cookie cutters, chenille stems, stamps and inkpads, sponges, screen, toothbrushes, hole punches, craft sticks
Weaving	• Encourages exploration with materials	Weaving loom, yarn
Collage	• Encourages exploration with materials	Cloth and carpet samples, wallpaper, books, ribbons, scraps of paper, buttons and beads, feathers, old magazines and catalogs, recycled items (berry baskets, meat trays, egg cartons, boxes, paper towel rolls)
Wood working	• Provides experiences with unusual materials and tools	Scrap pieces of soft wood, safety glasses, wood glue, hammer and nails, vise, sandpaper, paints, patterns and diagrams

Circle Activity Area

Type of Play	Benefits	Equipment and Materials
Circle activity	• Provides a place for daily opening and closing activities • Develops language and listening • Provides opportunities for participating in large-group activities	Carpet squares for the children to define individual spaces, flannelboard for language activities, chartpaper for recording experience stories

Play and Learn Center

Type of Space   Relatively quiet. Carpeted. Shelving for materials, small table and chairs. Computer (optional).

Reading and Writing Readiness

Type of Play	Benefits	Equipment and Materials
Visual skills	• Develops visual skills related to reading	Inset puzzles, beads to string, blocks and pattern-matching cards, picture dominos, Lotto games, block design sets, sequence puzzles
Auditory skills	• Develops listening skills related to reading	Rhyming cards and letter/sound games
Learning the alphabet	• Encourages working alone and completing a task	Tactile letter board, alphabet puzzles, alphabet cards, magnetic letter board
Writing readiness	• Practices motor skills for writing • Develops concepts of print and symbol correspondence • Learns to use simple computer programs	Writing utensils, templates, stencils, chalk and chalkboards, pencils, paper and crayons Wooden tool sets, sewing cards, lacing shoes, geo-form boards, dressing frames, lock boxes Computers with word-processing and picture-making software
Reading	• Develops an appreciation for stories and pictures	A collection of different books from an appropriate bibliography, including "big books," multicultural, teacher-made and child-made books, cassette tapes or CDs with read-along books A quiet corner with comfortable pillows, child-sized couches or easy chairs, camera and film, pictures, posters, puppets

Language and Concept Development

Type of Play	Benefits	Equipment and Materials
Vocabulary development	• Increases vocabulary • Learns classification skills	Picture cards, occupation match-up cards, Lotto games, classification games, category cards, touch-and-match sets, feel tablets, color boards, color tablets, computer stories, storytelling software

(continued)

Type of Play	Benefits	Equipment and Materials
Pattern relationships	• Learns about patterns and relationships	Spatial relationship cards, play tile sets, parquetry blocks, pegboards
Problem-solving skills	• Develops problem-solving skills	"What's missing" games, puzzles, attribute blocks, computer-based treasure hunts

Number Readiness

Type of Play	Benefits	Equipment and Materials
Counting	• Develops concepts of number and sets that prepare the child for learning	Cubes, buttons, counting frame, abacus, bead-o-graph, color and object sorting materials, Montessori beads, computer and board games
Learning sets and numbers	• Helps children make discriminations on the basis of shape, weight, and size	Number cards, peg numbers, Unifix cubes, magnetic numerals and boards, dominos
Learning about shape and size	• Introduces the basic numerical concepts of measurement and quantity	Geometric shapes, fit-a-shape sets, nesting toys, stacking squares, Montessori cylinders, pink tower, long stair, broad stair
Learning about measurement, time, and money	• Introduces tools for measuring size, weight, and time • Provides experiences with money	Balance scale, play money, see-through clock, yardstick, rulers, tape measure, nesting measuring cups

Use low furniture to define areas.

Interest Center Dividers

Use low furniture to define areas. Make sure that the furniture is sturdy. In some areas, it is useful to have double-sided bookcases, which will be accessible to interest areas on both sides.

Other Essentials

For Health and Safety

- A place for toothbrushes and drinking cups
- A fire extinguisher
- A place to post the fire evacuation plan
- A place to keep health records and emergency numbers
- A place for tissues and paper towels
- Wastepaper baskets
- An out-of-reach place for cleaning products
- A locked cabinet for medication

For Personal Possessions

- A special cubby for each child
- A place for you to keep plans, records, and personal items
- A place for cots, mats, and blankets
- A drinking fountain at the children's height or a water bottle for each child
- Some private hideaways or soft spaces where children can be alone

From the Drawing Board to the Classroom

Whether you are arranging a classroom for the first time or simply rearranging an existing classroom, begin your task with a paper and pencil. (It is much easier to erase a line than to move a shelf.) Do these things:

- Draw the outline of your room, putting in doors, windows, fixed furniture and partitions, electrical outlets, sinks, closets, and the like.
- Using circles, lay out your classroom areas, remembering to do the following:
  - Put the art area on a noncarpeted floor near the sink.
  - Put the music center or any interest center requiring electrical power near an electrical outlet.
  - Separate quiet and noisy areas.
- Walk through your classroom with your fingers. Are there any problems with traffic flow?
- Make an inventory of the materials to go in each interest area. Is the area the right size? Is the needed storage available?
- Finally, put down the paper and actually move the furniture and equipment. Make changes and adjustments until things work well.

To organize and equip a learning environment for a multiage or family child care setting that includes children ages birth through 5

Spring had sprung at Growing Together Family Day Care, and the children couldn't wait to get outside. "Here's your coat, Jomo," said 4-year-old Luis to his 2-year-old friend. "Let me help you put it on."

Outside on the playground, Luis and Jomo turned over rocks together, looking for bugs and sprouts. Luis drew an "L" in the damp earth and then showed Jomo how to make a "J." "That gives me an idea," said their teacher. "Let's go to the sandbox and draw shapes and write messages." ●

Today, many parents are choosing family child care because they like its homelike atmosphere. They like the idea that brothers and sisters can be together and that their children will have playmates of different ages. Many centers are also experimenting with *multiage grouping*. They put infants, toddlers, and even preschoolers together,

> *Today, many parents are choosing family child care because they like its homelike atmosphere.*

as they would be in a family, so that the younger children can learn from the older ones and the older children can experience the joy of helping to take care of the younger ones.

Multiage grouping presents the teacher with unique challenges, however. How can she set up a room to accommodate such a range of developmental needs? How can she structure the environment to get the most benefit from multiage grouping?

One way to begin planning for a multiage environment is to block out some key areas:

- A gathering place for the whole group
- A cubby or personal storage space for each child
- Sleeping spaces
- Protected floor space for babies and young toddlers, with sturdy furniture for cruising and climbing
- An active play area for older toddlers and preschoolers
- Some places in lofts and on tables where older children can draw, build, display collections, and work with puzzles and games without interference from the babies
- Spaces for cooking, eating, music, pretending, reading, and looking after pets that everyone can share

Also add some special spaces where children can be alone or spend time with one or two friends—a cardboard box "house," a quiet corner with a beanbag chair or soft pillows, a rocking boat, or a loft. Don't forget about the adults' needs: a rocking chair, places for planning and record keeping, comfortable seating, and safe and efficient setups for diaper changing, food preparation, and (in a home) daily chores and maintenance.

Next, make sure that each area is furnished appropriately, with safe toys that the children can reach. Young babies like to watch older children, so make sure you have an easy way of moving them from place to place, and keep some of their toys within reach. Toddlers like to imitate, so make sure there are items they can use for "cooking," building, reading, art, active sports, and other activities that the older children will be involved in.

Stock up on items with broad age appeal, such as balls, soap bubbles, rubber animals, sensory play and art materials, dolls, and riding toys such as wagons that children of different ages can use together. Store some of the toys in bins, baskets, and other containers so that you can rotate them easily to maintain children's interest. Keep popular toys where children can get at them and put them away easily. You might set up appealing storage spaces, such as a "garage" for cars and trucks under a small table, a basket for balls or beanbags, or a doll "house" on a shelf for miniature figures.

Finally, assess each room or area from different heights. What interesting things can a baby see from an infant seat or from the floor? Where can a crawler go, and what can she get to play with? Where can a young toddler pull up to a stand? What is within his reach? What will stimulate conversations among the older children and encourage them to play together? Will the younger children be able to participate in the older children's games and activities? Is the area safe for all of the children who will use it?

To develop a well-balanced daily schedule

With more parents in the workforce, children's time has become more scheduled. For many children, weekdays involve getting up early, going to one or more child care placements, and returning home late in the day. Most child care centers and family child care homes now operate 10 to 13 hours a day; some have evening and/or weekend hours, as well.

When children are spending significant portions of their waking hours in a child care facility, it is important to establish a daily routine that meets their developmental needs. Although activities will change from day to day, there needs to be a basic schedule that is flexible but predictable.

Planning the Infant's Day

Mrs. Davis was looking for a child care center for her 6-month-old baby. She found the Wee Care Center in the telephone book and made an appointment to visit.

Mrs. Carer (the child care provider): "Oh, yes. We have a fine staff here. We feed our babies on demand and keep them dry and clean at all times."

Mrs. Davis: "That sounds like just what I'm looking for. What sorts of activities do you have for the babies when they are awake?"

Mrs. Carer: "Activities? I told you already that we feed our babies on demand and keep them clean and dry at all times. Oh, I know you might have read about infant curriculums in some of those fancy books, but you can bet your bottom dollar that the people who wrote those books never changed a baby's diaper! If you want to run a real good nursery, you sure don't have time for fun and games!"

Mrs. Carer has obviously not been reading the "fancy books" she complains about, nor has she kept up with the research on infants' brain development. If she has no time for "fun and games," she may be caring for too many babies. In any case, she needs to rethink her schedule so that she has time to talk and play with each baby and engage all the babies in simple activities. Much of the "fun and games," of course, will take place during routine care. As she changes diapers, gets babies up from their naps, feeds and soothes them, and puts them to sleep, Mrs. Carer can take the time to talk with the babies, tickle their tummies, play simple body awareness games, help them pull up into a sitting or standing position, point out interesting sights, and sing songs.

Setting up a simple, basic schedule and spending some time planning for each day could help Mrs. Carer make the time she needs for other activities.

Some Hints on Planning the Day for Infants

Routine and Flexibility Within a child care setting, as at home, it is important to let young infants follow their own feeding and sleeping schedules. At the same time, babies will be more playful and less fussy when their schedules are somewhat predictable. Dividing the day into segments that follow a consistent pattern helps young infants to develop more regular eating and sleeping patterns. Older infants will tend to be more flexible and can begin to adjust to a common eating and sleeping schedule. Infants should be assigned to a specific caregiver so they can establish a relationship with one significant person who knows their schedule and can read their cues.

> *Infants should be assigned to a specific caregiver so they can establish a relationship with one significant person who can read their cues.*

Indoors and Out Infants enjoy spending time each day outside, as long as the weather permits. Riding toys, pull and push toys that need space, and small climbing structures are appropriate for the 12- to 18-month group. Infants who are not walking can be placed outdoors on quilts along with their toys. A patio area covered with tile or indoor/outdoor carpet provides a nice play area. Messy sensory experiences—such as playing with water, soap bubbles, or wet cornstarch—can be conducted outside to minimize clean up.

Quiet and Active Balance quiet times (playing soothing music, rocking, or reading) with more active periods.

Special Times Set aside a special time every day for a sensory activity.

Movement/Music Time Have a regularly planned time so that infants are exposed to music each day.

Books and Language Activities Set aside a quiet time for looking at books and doing language activities to ensure this important area is not neglected.

For more information on planning the day for infants, see the schedule on the following page.

Planning the Day for Toddlers

Young toddlers are very busy trying out new motor and language skills. Given this, they need a lot of watching as they learn to walk, run, and climb and a lot of individual attention as they try to make their wants and discoveries understood with grunts, gestures, and newly learned words. Participation in group activities, such as circle time, is likely to be sporadic and brief. Still, a regular schedule, with a good deal of repetition of favorite activities, provides a comforting rhythm to the day. Rituals like singing "hello" and "good-bye" songs help young toddlers mark time and place and provide a sense of security.

A Basic Schedule for Infants

Arrival Time

Caregivers exchange information with parents and help each baby get comfortable.

Midmorning Playtime (on floor)

Sensory activities, reading, singing, and music/movement. Playing with toys and with caregiver.

Outdoor Time

Outdoor play and sensory activities.

Lunch

For infants who are on solid food; individualized feedings for young infants.

Naptime

For older infants; individualized sleeping for young infants.

Midafternoon Playtime (on floor)

Sensory activities, reading, singing, and music/movement. Playing with toys and with caregiver.

Afternoon Walk

Or time outdoors.

Late Afternoon

Start to organize each infant's belongings for the trip home. Complete the daily report.

Departure

Parents arrive to pick up the infants. Time for communication between caregivers and parents.

Older toddlers also do best with a predictable schedule, and they enjoy learning routines. Rituals at the beginning and end of the day help them feel secure and in control. A comfortable, predictable balance of active and quiet activities helps keep their natural energy and exuberance within bounds. With their short attention span and insatiable curiosity, 2-year-olds tend to flit from one activity to another. At the same time, they may resist transitions that they do not initiate. You can play music or sing special songs to help the children know when it is time to join the circle, clean up, eat, take a nap, or get ready to say good-bye.

A regular schedule, with a lot of repetition of favorite activities, provides a comforting rhythm to the day.

Most toddlers will be able to follow a common schedule when it comes to eating and naptimes (see the box on page 90). But they will still be on their own schedules when it comes to getting drinks of water, diaper changing, and, for some, learning to use the toilet.

A Basic Schedule for Toddlers

Arrival Time

Caregivers exchange information with parents and help each toddler get comfortable.

"Hello" Song

Short circle time (for children who are interested).

Morning Snack or Breakfast

Midmorning Playtime

Music and movement experiences, reading to individual or small groups of children, playing in activity centers; special planned activity for small group.

Outdoor Time

Lunch

Naptime

Midafternoon Playtime

Music and movement experiences, reading to individual or small groups of children, playing in activity centers.

Outdoor Time

Late Afternoon

Start to organize the children's belongings for the trip home. Complete the daily report.

Departure

Parents arrive to pick up the children. Time for communication between caregivers and parents.

Developing a Daily Schedule for Preschoolers

Mrs. Curtis came to visit a child care center. The director brought her to a classroom and invited her to go in and spend some time. She found the teacher, Mrs. Owens, sitting with a small group of children reading a rainbow story. In the center of the room, four children were sitting in a rocking boat singing "Row, Row, Row Your Boat." Several children were trying on old clothes at the far end of the room. In another corner, a boy was working alone building a giant block tower. When Mrs. Owens spotted the visitor, she finished the rainbow story and suggested that the children go to the drawing table and color their own rainbows. When the children she had been reading to got settled making drawings, Mrs. Owens welcomed her guest to the classroom.

Mrs. Curtis looked amazed. "How do you ever do it?" she asked. "You have twelve children in this classroom, and every child seems busy and happy. I've got three kids at home and my house is always in a state of turmoil."

"I've been at it for some time," Mrs. Owens replied modestly.

Although Mrs. Owens made light of her accomplishment, keeping a room of 3-year-olds productively involved in a variety of tasks is not easy. It requires a teacher who is confident, well organized, and adept at engineering a classroom. Let us look at some of the ingredients of good classroom management:

- Developing a daily schedule
- Implementing a daily schedule
- Planning for a "rainy day"
- Transition time

Whether you are a family child care provider taking care of four children or a child care center teacher with a class of twelve, the place to begin good management is with a daily schedule. A schedule is not a curriculum or a daily plan. It does not describe the crafts, lessons, or activities that have been scheduled for the day. It does, however, describe the timetable that you follow on a daily basis throughout the year.

Criteria for Developing an Effective Daily Schedule

A daily schedule must take into account the philosophy of the program, the ages of the children you are working with, the size of the group, the length of the day, the children's patterns of arrival and departure, and the physical setup of the child care facility.

Philosophy

A daily schedule is a reflection of the philosophy of the center. A program that stresses academics will set aside large blocks of time for structured lessons and for play-based activities that promote academic skills. A program that stresses the development of creativity in art, music, and movement will provide time slots in the daily schedule for these activities. A program with a religious orientation may block out time for prayer or religious teaching. A program with a major focus on physical health and nutrition may provide blocks of time for health checks, personal care, and the preparation and serving of nutritious snacks.

Ages of the Children

All preschool children, whether they are 3 years old or 5 years old, are still developing their ideas about time. Most cannot yet read a clock or even understand what is meant by the words *minutes* and *hours*. The best way for children to understand time is through routine events. Events that mark off the day include mealtime, snacktime, circle or whole-group meeting time, playground time, and naptime. Because children perceive time as passing at a much slower rate than adults do, for them a day is very long. Time markers help them to realize that a day goes by in an orderly way and that going-home time will come and can be counted on. The younger the children, the more important it is to have distinct and predictable time markers.

A second way in which a daily schedule takes into account the ages of the children is in the amount of time devoted to group activities. Very young children have a short attention span and cannot be expected to participate in a group experience for more than 10 or 15 minutes.

Length of the Day

A schedule for a full or extended program is necessarily quite different from one for a half-day program. For a short period of time, children and adults enjoy a fast-paced program, in which there are quick changes in activities and little time is spent in making transitions. For a full-day program, it is better to increase the duration of activities and take more time moving from one activity to the next. It is also critically important to provide a balanced day, alternating quiet activities with activities that are faced paced and active.

The two boxes below provide examples of preschool schedules.

A Basic Half-Day Schedule for Preschoolers

8:30 A.M.	Arrival, circle time
8:45 A.M.	Learning centers with small-group activities offered
10:00 A.M.	Snack with conversation
10:15 A.M.	Outdoor play
10:45 A.M.	Learning centers with small-group activities offered
11:30 A.M.	Clean-up
11:40 A.M.	Storytime, songs and games
11:55 A.M.	Prepare for departure

A Basic Full-Day Schedule for Preschoolers

Morning

7:30–9:00 A.M.	Arrival time; Learning centers; breakfast
9:00–9:15 A.M.	Circle time
9:15–10:30 A.M.	Learning centers with small-group activities offered
10:30–11:15 A.M.	Outdoor activities
11:15 A.M.	Wash up; storytime
11:45 A.M.	Lunch; wash up

Afternoon

12:30 P.M.	Look at books; get ready for resting/naps
2:30 P.M.	Snack; put nap items away
2:45 P.M.	Learning centers with small-group activities offered
3:30 P.M.	Outdoor time
4:15 P.M.	Wash up; storytime
4:30 P.M.	Learning centers; children are departing
6:30 P.M.	Closing

Implementing the Daily Schedule

Having a workable schedule posted on the wall is a good first step—but it is only that. By far, the greater challenge is making the schedule work. Here are some guidelines:

- Make sure to differentiate between setting up a *daily schedule* and developing a *daily plan*. A daily plan describes the curriculum to be implemented during the time slots indicated on the schedule.
- Make your daily plans at least a week in advance, so that you can make phone calls, purchase supplies, and prepare materials as needed.
- Read the plan for the next day before you leave the center, and make sure you have all the materials you need.
- Early in the day, build in time for talking with the children about what they are going to do; toward the end of the day, make time to go over with the children what they have done and to talk about plans for the next day. This can be done in small groups or individually.

Planning for a "Rainy Day"

No matter how carefully we plan and how well we have thought out our curriculum, there are always days when our greatest plans must be canceled or our favorite ideas must be scrapped. It rains for the picnic, or there is a three-alarm fire the day the firefighter is supposed to come to class. The bus for the field trip is late, lunch is taking longer to cook than usual, or the visitor you invited is stuck in traffic, and you find yourself with extra time on your hands and a group of restless children. Whatever the problem, it happens to all of us, and so we should be prepared.

The best quick-fix solution for an unexpected waiting time is to have a repertoire of familiar songs with appropriate variations. Some suggestions are provided in Chapter 7, Creativity.

Activities for a "Rainy Day"

While a song or finger play is appropriate for filling up a five-minute waiting space, there will inevitably be emergency situations with longer time slots to fill up. The best way to prepare for a "rainy day" is to have an emergency daily plan, with all the appropriate materials put away on the top shelf. These "surprise boxes" can turn a disappointing day into a special one.

Unbirthday Party
Materials: old greeting cards, stickers, glitter, old party hats, tissue paper or foil and ribbons (children can wrap toys from the classroom for the presents), birthday candles (can be stuck in clay, cheese, or Jell-O as well as real cakes or cupcakes).

(continued)

Activities continued

Procedure: Let the children help prepare an unbirthday party for the class. Sing "Happy Unbirthday."

Let's Go to the Beach

Materials: shells, pebbles, driftwood, picnic cloth or blanket, story books about sea animals, pails, shovels, and sand molds, "picnic basket" or "cooler."

Procedure: The children can set up a beach scene or make a sandcastle at the sand table, make sandcastles from play dough and decorate them with shells, draw or paint beach scenes and glue on real sand and shells, pack the cooler with pretend food, spread out the blanket, and listen to a beach story. For a change, you can serve lunch or a snack on the picnic blanket instead of at the table.

Edible Art

Materials: recipes and ingredients for chocolate syrup drawing or finger painting (on wax paper), alphabet pretzels, or edible faces (children can make these by decorating paper plates or buttered rice cakes with bits of fruit and vegetables, pieces of cereal, or small crackers).

Procedure: You don't have to save this activity for a "rainy day."

Old Favorites

Materials: toys, books, puzzles, and games that the children have seemed to be finished with.

Procedure: Children will enjoy rediscovering their old toys and will know just what to do with them.

Valentines

Materials: heart cutouts, doilies, stickers, rubber stamps, envelopes, glitter, gold and silver pens, mailbox.

Procedure: Any day can be Valentine's Day.

Train Ride

Materials: train book, engineer's cap, whistle, pictures of exotic places.

Procedure: Put on the cap, line up the chairs, blow the whistle, and call "All aboard." Sing some train songs. Let the children take turns suggesting places to go. Make some suggestions yourself. You might go to a baseball game, the zoo, a faraway or nearby city, or an imaginary place. Pretend to ride the train to the destination and then talk about what you see, or get out and pantomime the action.

Transition Times

Moving from one activity to the next needs special consideration. A typical crisis in a classroom occurs when the whole class is ready to go outside except for one child who hasn't put the last touches on a craft or the last piece in a puzzle. Here are some ways of avoiding problems with transition times:

- Sing a special song or ring a bell five minutes before the end of an activity so that the children have time to get ready.
- Make clean-up time fun by having everyone join in singing a clean-up song.
- Sing a marching song or play "train" (children place their hands on the shoulders of the child in front) when you go to the playground or to a different room.
- Don't insist on perfection when children line up. They are not very good at it.
- Find fun ways of moving in a line, such as tiptoeing, walking with hands in the air, putting hands on heads, or singing a counting song.
- Plan for one of the staff in the room to move with the children when most of them are ready and for another staff to come and move with the stragglers when they are ready.

Scheduling and Planning for a Multiage Group

In scheduling the day for a family child care home or a multiage group at a center, you should begin by asking several questions:

- How many children are present?
- How many caregivers will care for the children?
- What are the ages of the children in care?
- What are the hours that the children will be in care?

Having infants and toddlers in care will mean creating a schedule where children eat, are diapered, and nap on their own individual schedules, with scheduled times for outdoor play or stroller rides.

Having preschoolers in care will require scheduling of large blocks of time for child-directed play. Meals/snacks, outdoor play, and naps/rest times will be scheduled at approximately the same times everyday.

The schedule for a homogeneous group in family child care will look very similar to a center-based child care schedule.

For a mixed-aged group, whether in center-based or family care, the provider will schedule those activities that need to get done in the day according to the needs of the children. Those activities will include the following:

- *Activities associated with the arrival of children*
- *Preparing and having meals and snacks.* Older children can help with setting the table and some simple food preparation. At the end of the meal/snack, the children can assist in the clean-up. Bottle-fed babies will have individual schedules for feedings.

- *Preparing for and naps/rest times.* Children take naps or rest depending on their individual needs. Babies may be awake during this time, if they recently have awakened from a nap.

- *Providing time for pretend play and child-directed play.* Most of the day should provide for child-selected and -directed play. This will allow you to change activities when children seem to be flagging and to bring babies in and out of the older children's activities, as appropriate.

- *Providing for music and creative arts.* As part of the self-directed play or in small groups, music and other creative arts activities need to be considered for all ages. Music activities and art/sensory activities especially lend themselves to mixed-age groups, so try to schedule them when the older infants and toddlers will be awake.

- *Providing for reading and literacy promotion.* Daily experiences with books and other literature need to be planned for all age groups. These should occur several times in the day, depending on the group in care and the length of time in care.

- *Providing for projects with wide age appeal.* Allow for thematic explorations that may extend over a period of time, such as putting on a play or rhythm band concert, visiting a zoo or farm and creating a mural or setting up a mini-zoo, celebrating a holiday, or planting a garden.

- *Observing children for program planning.* Plan a time when caregivers can look at individual children and record notes.

- *Preparing for children's departure.* Soon before the scheduled departure of the children, allow time for the caregiver to prepare the children and gather their belongings.

- *Keeping records and performing other administrative duties.* Time to maintain records and complete other required administrative duties also must be allowed. These tasks could typically be done when the children are napping, after the children leave, or at a set time, if there is more than one child care provider.

- *Diapering and using the bathroom.* Diapering and toileting are taken care of as needed.

- *Giving individual attention to children.* Children of all ages need individual attention. Be sure to schedule time for private conversations with each child. Also try to find time when you can follow the child's lead as you play together.

Other considerations for planning and scheduling should include the following:

- Balancing active and quiet activities
- Balancing whole-group activities—such as story reading, outings, cooking, some pretend play and art/sensory activities, music, and parachute play—with age-specific activities—such as sports, puzzles, games, and lessons
- Making schedules dependable but flexible
- Providing time for the caregiver to share ideas with parents

To set up an outdoor play and learning environment

The amount of time devoted to outdoor play will depend in part both on the ages of the children and the daily weather conditions. Regardless, every child care center should provide opportunities for children to spend part of each day outdoors.

"Musts" for the outdoor play area are as follow:*

- Forty-five square feet of space for every child over 2 years
- A 5-foot fence that completely encloses the play area and that has childproof latches on the exits
- Adequate shade
- Safe play equipment
- Adequate space between pieces of play equipment
- Soft surfaces under the climbing structures

Creating an Outdoor Play Area for Infants and Toddlers

Infants enjoy spending a part of the day outdoors. They can be placed in carriages, strollers, baby swings, or oversized playpens. Spreading a blanket on the ground also can allow for sensory play outdoors for infants. Crawling around on the blanket, feeling the warm breeze, watching the world around them, and watching soap bubbles are all enjoyable activities for infants.

Toddlers love the opportunity to play outside, as well. Outdoor play provides a chance to release energy, initiate games, and practice emerging motor and social skills with other youngsters. A toddler play area should include the following types of play opportunities.

Wheel Toy Section

Wheel toy play is particularly desirable for toddlers because it combines opportunities to practice motor skills with opportunities for pretending. A wheel toy area works best when it comprises a circular path that children can ride around. It also is an excellent idea to include a "service station," where wheel toys can be washed, oiled, fixed, and filled with gas.

> *Wheel toy play is particularly desirable for toddlers because it combines opportunities to practice motor skills with opportunities for pretending.*

Climbing Structures

Climbing structures for toddlers should take into account the fact that children this age may not be fully aware of their own capabilities and limitations. In selecting toddler structures, we cannot assume that the children's natural fear will keep them out

*Please check the regulations for your particular state.

of danger. A toddler who is learning to climb may climb to the top of a structure without concern for getting back down again. Make sure, therefore, that the height and construction of each structure minimizes the danger of a fall. Also make sure that climbing structures are placed on soft surfaces that comply with licensing regulations.

Many climbing structures have swing sets attached. In general, this is not a good idea. If a swing set is included in the toddler area, it should be a reasonable distance from other structures. Toddlers do not recognize the danger of running behind someone on a swing. Finally, the swings should be made of soft material.

Sandboxes and Sand Tables

Although 1- to 3-year-olds enjoy playing and digging in a sandbox or a sand table, doing so poses some problems that require special supervision:

- Toddlers are likely to throw sand at each other and take a bite of a sand "cake."
- It's difficult to convince toddlers to keep the sand inside the sandbox or sand table.
- Sandboxes can be breeding grounds for pinworms. (Sand tables are unlikely to present this problem.)
- Sandboxes and sand tables must be covered when not in use.

Despite these disadvantages, sandboxes and sand tables provide young children marvelous opportunities to fill and empty, to sieve, to pour, to experiment, and to pretend. If you have enough staff to maintain a sandbox, it deserves a place on the toddler playground.

Creating an Outdoor Play Area for Children 3 to 5

In designing playgrounds for children between 3 and 5 years old, consider the kinds of play that these children will engage in. The three kinds of play that children of this age enjoy are play for mastering motor skills, construction play, and representational play.

Play for Mastering Motor Skills

Because of the need for space and noise tolerance, the playground is the most logical place for large-muscle activity. As children run, climb, swing, and balance, they are learning to control their bodies, to understand spatial relationships, and to master a host of important motor skills.

Providing the following structures and equipment can foster motor skill development:

Structures

Jungle gyms	Tunnels	Basketball hoops
Slides	See-saws	Balance beams
Swings and tire swings	Log walks	

Equipment

Balls	Tricycles	Riding toys
Hoops	Wagons	Nerf bats and balls

Construction Play

A second type of outdoor play that children enjoy is *construction play,* where children experiment and create with different media. Construction play can take place with liquid, semiliquid, or solid materials. The following structures and materials can be used creatively in many construction play activities:

For Creating and Exploring with Liquid and Semiliquid Materials

Water tables	Sandboxes	Clay/soil digging areas

For Creating and Constructing with Solid Materials

Large, hollow blocks	Planks	Plastic crates
Cardboard cartons		

Representational Play

A third type of play that occurs on the playground is *representational play,* which parallels the imaginative play of the indoor environment. Children can vent frustrations, express feelings, and work out problems as well as engage in social interaction with their peers (perhaps even more so in this wide-open environment). Although

99

children will use climbing structures and construction materials for imaginative play, their pretending can be enhanced by inclusion of some key props:

Climbing Area

Steering wheel on a "car"

Telephone

Row of tree stumps or plastic crates (for seats on a "train" or "bus")

Sandbox

Plastic animals and people

Empty containers

Cars, trucks, bulldozers, back-hoes, and boats (various sizes)

Shovels

Kitchen utensils, pots and pans

Water Play

Empty containers

Objects that float/sink

Baby dolls with soap

"Gasoline Station"

Clean, unused gas containers with spouts

Money box with plastic coins to pay for gas

Toy tools to repair cars

Playhouse

Children love child-sized spaces. A well-equipped playground for young children should include a playhouse with a telephone and a shed that can be used for both imaginative play and storage. Because eating is so important to young children, pretend routines often revolve around playhouse activity. A picnic table with tableware is an excellent playhouse prop for encouraging pretending.

Science and Discovery

The outdoors is the perfect setting for science and discovery. Children have a natural curiosity about nature and living things. Taking nature walks and listening to nature sounds can add to the sensory experience of the outdoors. Simple and portable equipment that can enhance this experience includes the following:

Magnifying glasses

Binoculars

Tools for digging and raking

Bug catchers or plastic jars

Butterfly nets

Also provide paper and writing instruments so that children can document their discoveries.

To ensure that the learning environment works for adults as well as for children

When asked what keeps them working in child care, most teachers and caregivers immediately say, "The children." Experienced professionals talk about the importance of their work. They enjoy watching young minds and personalities unfold and find that each day brings new discoveries and surprises. They know they are providing an important service to families and to society. Yet when pressed, these professionals often give another reason for staying in jobs that pay relatively low salaries: "I love the people I'm working with and the atmosphere of the workplace."

Child care centers and family child care homes can be special places for adults as well as for children. But this doesn't happen by itself. Conscious effort is needed to make spaces comfortable for child care workers and welcoming for parents.

Creating Spaces for Adults

Most child care centers have some spaces that are designed for adults: an office, a teachers' room and/or parents' room, adult-sized bathrooms, and a kitchen/work area that is off limits to the children. These spaces should be clean, bright, and cheerful, with comfortable furnishings, sufficient windows, attractive wall displays, plants, bulletin boards, and reading materials. An inviting place for adults to linger encourages communication. Having a few toys and children's books in these areas will help to welcome parents whose younger children are not in the center or who would like to spend some time with their child outside the classroom.

Although they are designed for children, classrooms also need to be set up with adults—teachers, parents, and classroom visitors—in mind. Each room should have these items:

- Comfortable seating for adults: a rocking chair in an infant or young toddler sleeping area, places to sit while feeding or eating with children, seating with back support for reading to children, and chairs that visitors can use

- A desk or other work and record-keeping station, conveniently located to allow simultaneous supervision of children who are playing or sleeping

- A secure place for the teacher's purse, briefcase, and other personal belongings

- Displays of children's work and words that let parents know what is happening in the classroom

- Pictures of the children's families and artifacts that represent their home cultures

- Pictures and artifacts that are meaningful to the teacher

- Inspirational posters, favorite quotes, and visionary messages that inspire adults who care for young children and reflect their wisdom

- Words in the children's home languages along with notes to parents in their home languages, when possible

- A bulletin board on which teachers and parents can post and exchange information
- A telephone

A learning environment for young children should be a place where their teachers, caregivers, and parents feel at home. The environment you create will be a reflection of who you are—your philosophy of teaching and learning, the things you love and want to share, and what you find beautiful, engaging, calming, and inspiring. It should be a place where you like spending time—a learning environment for adults as well as for children.

Additional Resources about Learning Environments

Bredekamp, S., & Copple, C. (Eds.). (1997). *Developmentally appropriate practice in early childhood programs* (Rev. ed.). Washington, DC: NAEYC.

Bronson, M. (1995). *The right stuff for children 0–8: Selecting play materials to support development.* Washington, DC: NAEYC.

Curtis, D., & Carter, M. (1996). *Reflecting children's lives: A handbook for planning child-centered curriculum.* St. Paul, MN: Redleaf Press.

Greenman, J. (1998). *Places for childhoods: Making quality happen in the real world.* Redmond, WA: Exchange Press.

Greenman, J. (1988). *Caring spaces, learning places: Children's environments that work.* Redmond, WA: Exchange Press.

Greenman, J., & Stonehouse, A. (1996). *Prime times: A handbook for excellence in infant and toddler programs.* St Paul, MN: Redleaf Press.

Harms, T., Clifford, R., & Cryer, D. (1998). *Early childhood environment rating scale–Revised.* New York: Teachers College Press.

Harms, T., Cryer, D., & Clifford, R. (2003). *Infant-toddler environment rating scale–Revised.* New York: Teachers College Press.

Hohman, M., & Weikart, D. (1995). *Educating young children.* Ypsilanti, MI: High/Scope Press.

Lally, R., Griffin, A., Fenichel, E., Segal, M., Szanton, E., & Weissbourd, B. (1995). *Caring for infants and toddlers in groups: Developmentally appropriate practice.* Washington, DC: Zero to Three.

On Stage

Supporting Physical and Intellectual Development

Mrs. Try-My-Best, a family child care provider, had the following discussion while having dinner at a restaurant with a friend:

Mrs. Try-My-Best: "Sorry about being late. I was talking to one of my parents about her baby, and she wouldn't let me go."

Friend: "Was she complaining about something?"

Mrs. Try-My-Best: "No, she is a very helpful parent, and she almost never complains. But she wanted me to tell her about her baby, and no matter what I told her, she kept asking me the same question."

Friend: "What was the question?"

Mrs. Try-My-Best: " 'How is my baby developing?' It was strange. I told her how well he was sitting by himself and how he had just learned to pass a toy from one hand to the other. But whatever I told her, she would say, 'That's great, but it's not what I'm asking. I just want you to tell me about my son's development.' " ●

Although Mrs. Try-My-Best could not figure out what this parent wanted to know, this parent's question is quite legitimate. Knowing how well a child is doing in several domains of development does not answer the question of how well that child is developing overall. Domains of development are interdependent. In order to master a task like picking up a spoon on demand, the child must have the language ability to understand what he is expected to do, the cognitive ability to recognize which object is a spoon, the physical ability to pick up the spoon, and the psychological motivation to do it. A child's *developmental level* refers to the total range of his capacities and resources at a particular point in time.

In this text, we describe several domains of development: physical, cognitive, language, imaginative or creative, emotional, and social. Each of these domains is described in its own chapter. The emotional and social domains are touched on in the first part of this section but described in more detail in the next.

This approach allows us to focus on the expected developmental sequences in each domain and to suggest activities to reinforce existing skills and to encourage the development of emerging skills at each stage. The downside of this approach is that it does not provide a wide-angled picture of the expected developmental status of children at different ages. In the developmental overviews that follow, we present a global picture of child development at age points from birth to 5 years.

Developmental Benchmarks

Benchmark age periods for children from birth to age 3 need to be considered through at least two lenses. Practitioners have become used to thinking of children in one-year increments: 0 to 12 months, 12 to 24 months, and 24 to 36 months. Moreover, child care licensing regulations in many states define specific adult/child ratios and group-size limits according to one-year increments. That practice has contributed to organizing the classrooms in many child care programs along lines of annual chronological age.

In contrast, some child development experts describe development during the months from birth to age 3 according to developmental benchmarks, rather than annual divisions. The following age groupings have been defined by Zero to Three and the CDA Council. (Contact information for these organizations is provided at the end of this section; see page 112.) Note that the descriptive terms used differ slightly, even though they describe the same general characteristics:

Age in Months	Zero to Three	CDA Council
0–8	The early months	Young infants
9–17 or 8–18	Crawlers and walkers	Mobile infants
18–36	Toddlers and 2-year-olds	Toddlers

This text generally uses these benchmark divisions. In the narrative sections and in the Developmental Picture features in each chapter, the following age indicators are used:

0–9 months	Young infants
9–14 months	Older infants
14–24 months	Young toddlers
24–36 months	Older toddlers/2-year-olds

Developmental Overviews

Infants

Following an infant's development is an exciting experience. Infants change from week to week, from day to day, and sometimes from minute to minute. Like busy scientists, they are continually seeking new information, performing experiments, and testing new ideas. Over time, infants discover new things about themselves, as well. They discover ways to kick with their legs, grasp with their hands, and make interesting sounds with their mouths. They discover that people are useful, that language is important, and that an object that is hidden from sight continues to exist. In fact, many behavioral scientists feel that the foundations for all later development—physical, psychological, intellectual, and social—are established within the first year of life. This means that the kinds of experiences we provide for babies are extremely important and can have a lifelong impact.

Before zeroing in on the kind of curriculum that would be appropriate for babies, let us look at the characteristics of babies at different ages so we know what to expect.

Young Infants

Birth to Three Months

Although we may think of a newborn baby as being fragile and helpless, he comes into this world with an impressive set of built-in reflexes and adaptive behaviors. He looks into his mother's eyes and attends to the sound of her voice. He closes his eyes in response to bright lights and reflexively grasps a finger when it is placed in his palm. Within the first three months, a baby will make connections among feelings, sights, and sounds. When he hears the sound of a rattle, he will search for it with his eyes. Upon seeing a smiling face, he will respond with a smile and a coo.

At first, babies respond more to what is happening *inside* them than to what is happening *outside* them. Then there is a gradual turning outward—an awakening to the world outside. A baby who is held, rocked, sung to, smiled at, and loved begins to make some early connections between the sound of a special person's voice and the smile on that person's face or the sensation of being rocked. A baby who is played with, cuddled, and soothed learns to associate the presence of a caregiver with a sense of well-being.

As caregivers, our goals and activities during these early months are designed to help the infant develop her emerging capacities. We help her to focus her eyes and follow moving targets. We encourage the baby to listen and respond to different sounds. We provide special exercises to help her relax and gain muscle tone. Alert caregivers recognize the infant's needs. There are times when infants need stimulation and times when soothing them is more appropriate. We must try to recognize and respond to each baby's rhythm and to adjust our activities and routines to her individual needs.

Three to Six Months

From 3 to 6 months old, infants are learning to explore the world with their hands as well as with their eyes. Learning to reach out is dependent on having something to reach for. If an interesting gym is strung across a baby's crib, she will bat at it, watch it move in response to the batting, and bat at it again. This tendency to repeat an action that creates an interesting effect shows the infant's first intuitive recognition of her own ability to affect her environment.

At about the same time babies are making discoveries about their emerging ability to make things happen, they are also discovering things about their social world. They have learned to smile and coo at a caregiver and to expect a cooing response, and they are developing their first conversational skills. With appropriate experience, a baby will learn to draw the caregiver into an interaction; to coo back and forth, taking turns with her partner; and to imitate simple cooing sounds.

During these next three months, infants become more responsive and less irritable. Their interest in environmental exploration increases. Important developments include social smiling, hand watching, hand play, the gradual development of increasingly precise reaching skills, interest in playing with toys, rolling over, and by the end of the sixth month, progress in learning to sit. This is an important time for face-to-face interaction between the infant and the caregiver.

Activities for caregivers during the 3- to 6-month period are designed to give the baby an opportunity to practice these new and emerging skills. Motor activities enhance balance and muscle strength in preparation for crawling and sitting. Activities with rattles and squeak toys encourage manipulation and hand/eye coordination. Language and cooing games encourage making new sounds and engaging in social interaction.

Six to Nine Months

By the age of 6 to 9 months, the baby has begun to drop things on purpose and then look for them, to bang objects on a hard surface, and to transfer things from hand to hand. He is beginning to have a crude notion of *object permanence* (something continues to exist even when we can't see it) and can imitate simple actions (like banging) that he has already learned. In the next three months, the infant's notions about objects will become more sophisticated, and by the end of the ninth month, he will begin to look for hidden objects.

At this age, the infant will add many more sounds to his vocabulary and will begin babbling ("Mamma," "Dadda," "babba"). He will start to respond to a few specific words, like his name and "Hi," and he may begin to show a wariness of strangers. During this time period, most babies prefer sitting up, and they begin to use some method of crawling. They can drink from a cup with help and will hold his own bottle.

Activities for caregivers during this period are designed to help infants become more sophisticated in their ability to manipulate objects. We provide the infant with a variety of toys that are different in shape, size, and texture and in the sounds they make. How many different things will an infant do with a toy? Does he know that a soft rubber toy is for squeaking and a rattle is for shaking? Do his hands work together when he plays with a toy? As we give infants experience with finger foods, we help to develop their grasping skills. Dropping games are useful as an aid in learning releasing skills. During this period, infants are learning to recognize the patterns and rhythms of language. We introduce songs and nursery rhymes to give infants exposure to the special qualities of language.

Older Infants

Nine to Fourteen Months

From 9 to 14 months is a time when we see many rapid developments. Older infants understand more and more specific words, such as "Mommy," "no," "bottle," and the like. They become interested in looking at books and may start pointing to specific objects. Their babbling starts to sound more like true speech; some babies during this time will start saying words.

Babies' imitative skills also improve, and they begin to imitate new actions. They learn to wave bye-bye and to play Pat-a-Cake. At first, these gestures are imitative—the caregiver waves and then the baby waves. But after a while, the baby responds to the verbal command. Babies at this age may also learn to imitate simple social actions, such as "making nice" to a doll and putting a hat on one's own head.

Older infants' interest in objects shifts from simple manipulation to performing tasks with the objects, like dropping them into a container and throwing or rolling them. Babies learn to use new methods of exploration, such as poking with a finger, and will begin to actively explore objects within reach. Babies perfect the *pincer grasp* (thumb/finger) and enjoy picking up small objects and finger foods.

Older infants are now really on the go. They creep quickly on all fours, pull themselves to a standing position, and cruise sideways along furniture. This new ability to move through space brings with it the potential danger of moving away from Mother or a trusted caregiver. Fortunately, a baby recognizes his caregiver's face, even from a distance, and is able to keep a close watch on that person's whereabouts. For the baby between 9 and 14 months, his mother or caregiver becomes the base of operations. The baby will explore freely as long as his caregiver is in sight.

Caregivers' activities during the 9- to 14-month period are designed to teach understanding of specific words, to encourage the development of object permanence, and to help in learning to imitate simple actions. We also work on developing simple self-help skills and on providing opportunities for infants to explore their rapidly developing motor capacities.

Young Toddlers

Between 14 and 24 months, babies develop at greatly varying rates. Each baby seems to have her own special strengths. Some babies are very social; they like to "talk" and interact a great deal. Others are more interested in their toys. Some babies are concentrating on learning to talk and are not in such a great hurry to run or climb. Others never have the time to stop to talk. They are always on the move—running, climbing, and manipulating.

During this time period, most babies will learn to walk steadily. They will attempt to run, and they will begin to walk up and down stairs. Self-help skills will improve. By 24 months, they should be able to use a cup and spoon fairly well and to help in the dressing process by pulling off their socks, raising their arms, and picking up their feet so their shoes can be put on.

In addition to practicing emerging motor skills, babies between 14 and 24 months have become interested in exploring and experimenting. They are continually searching for objects with moving parts, for things that fit into other things, and for things that can be poured, spilled, carried, or somehow transported. They enjoy toys that can be pushed, pulled, or wheeled around; toys that can be stacked, pounded, or lined up; and toys that respond to their manipulations by making interesting sounds.

At the same time that children show an interest in sound-making toys, they are also likely to expand their own sound-making repertoire. Sometime during the second year, expressive babbling language is converted to meaningful words. Most children by 18 months have a meaningful vocabulary of 15 words. By 2 years old, their vocabulary may include as many as 200 words.

More important, the young toddler is showing quantum leaps in *receptive language*, which is the understanding of spoken words. Babies this age can show you their eyes, nose, mouth, and ears; point to photos of different family members; and follow short, one-word commands. In the course of the second year, there will be a rapid expansion of receptive language and an emerging capacity to listen to a story, watch a video with a story line, and follow a two-step command.

Paralleling the emergence of receptive language is an emerging capacity to imitate behavioral sequences. Young toddlers will jabber on a toy telephone, wipe up a spill, place a key in a lock, smear their faces with makeup, sweep with a broom, and lap up the water from the cat's dish. This imitation of familiar actions is evidence of a child's capacity to think in symbols and is the precursor of pretend play.

Another important development in the second year of life is the emergence of self-awareness. The child is becoming increasingly aware of himself as an actor. If you laugh at something he does, he will promptly do it again to produce another laugh. He is also sensitive to the fact that some of the things that he wants to do are prohibited by adults. When an adult tries to curtail his explorations with a "No," he is likely to persist in what he is doing until he recognizes that he does not have a choice.

The fact that the baby can now choose between conforming and not conforming puts a new strain on the adult. Parents and caregivers are likely to be torn between encouraging exploration and independence and teaching caution, obedience, and responsibility. An overriding concern is that a baby who hears "No" too many times may lose interest in exploring, thus limiting his opportunities to learn.

Older Toddlers (Two-Year-Olds)

The period from 2 to 3 is sometimes known as the "terrible two's." The "No" of the toddler has become a convincing temper tantrum and the 2-year-old is often described as "ornery," "stubborn," and "impossible to live with."

Two-year-olds have, for the most part, earned their reputation. During this period, they are continually exerting authority. The "No's" of the 2-year-old are not simply a way of saying "I don't want it" or "I won't do it." The "No's" are a way of declaring her right to make decisions. Two-year-olds want to do things by themselves, even when that may not be in their best interest.

For the most part, the tantrums of the 2-year-old disappear as long as they are ignored. After all, it is not really worth having a tantrum if no one is going to pay attention. A few children at this age, however, have tantrums as a reaction to being tired, and leaving them alone doesn't change the behavior. For these children, it is usually a good idea to take them out of the situation, hold them quietly but firmly, and invite them back to play when they recover their composure.

Two-year-olds have learned to run and would much rather run than walk, even when they are tired. Although they can run forward at a good pace, most 2-year-olds have not learned how to negotiate a turn or to run around a corner. When 2-year-olds are running on the playground, some bumps and falls are to be expected. Emerging motor skills for 2-year-olds include jumping with their feet together, riding a tricycle, walking up and down stairs alternating feet, and sliding down a slide at an accelerated pace. Throwing and catching skills are just beginning to emerge.

An important development in 2-year-olds is the emergence of constructive play. They love to make castles and cakes out of sand, packing sand into a mold, turning the mold upside down, and marveling at their creations. They are also learning to build towers and rows of blocks, to scribble with a crayon, and to propel a wheel toy across the floor.

The most remarkable developmental phenomenon at 2 years old is gaining the capacity to think in symbols. This new capacity manifests itself both in the emergence of pretend play and in the mastery of language. The 2-year-old represents thoughts and ideas in imitative actions, pretend play routines, and a rapidly growing vocabulary. While their pretend play is largely imitative, 2-year-olds are quite capable of acting out assumed roles or talking for miniature characters.

Three-Year-Olds

Three-year-olds have broadened their view of the world. Their ideas of time and place have undergone interesting transformations. They are beginning to grasp the complexities of their social world and to recognize the difference between real and pretend. Typical questions include "Where do birds sleep at night?" "Were there dinosaurs when you were a baby?" and "Are the people on television real or pretend?"

For these children, the past is divided into the immediate past, yesterday, last week and last month, and a long time ago, such as when their parents were young. The future is divided into tomorrow, soon, and "when I get big." Although they may not know the names of the seasons, 3-year-olds are beginning to make the relevant associations. They might remember summer as when it's hot and you go on vacation and fall as when the trees turn color, when you go trick-or-treating, and when you watch football on television.

Space, like time, is also divided into categories. Some places are near and you can walk to them. Some places are too far to walk. Some places are really far away, like Africa and the moon. There are also categories of people, such as children, teenagers, people who are old and work at jobs, and people who are very old and don't do much at all. Things can be living or not living, people and animals can be alive or dead, and things can be real or pretend.

By age 3½, the turbulence of the "terrible two's" has passed and a quieter child emerges. The 3-year-old is able to focus on a task for several minutes and to interact in a positive way with other children. By 3 years, children have expanded their repertoire of emotional responses. They can be sad or pensive. They can be jealous, wary, or frightened. They can be contented, jolly, or exuberant. They are also more tuned in to the feelings of others. Pleasing adults is becoming increasingly more important, and receiving praise or affection is becoming a powerful reinforcer. Although 3-year-olds are less apt to throw temper tantrums than 2-year-olds, their behavior can disintegrate when they are tired or hungry.

Four-Year-Olds

Four-year-old children are becoming increasingly aware of themselves as members of a peer group. Much of their day is spent establishing and maintaining their position with peers. Children who are 4 years old use their growing facility with words to praise or to criticize and correct other children, to call attention to their own accomplishments, and to convince a group to adopt their ideas. Four-year-olds are interested in playing with other children and will use threats and promises to win a friend or gain entry into a group. Remarks like "I'll be your best friend" and "I won't be your friend" are frequently heard in a preschool.

Out on the playground, 4-year-olds require plenty of space. They enjoy all varieties of play and are particularly fond of "monster" and "superhero" play.

Although 4-year-olds are learning to take turns and share toys, arguments over possessions take place continually. Frequently, disputes that begin verbally end with a push, a punch, or a skirmish. For the most part, the children do not really hurt each other in these skirmishes, but providing adult supervision is an important safeguard.

Four-year-olds love to learn new things, like pumping a swing, naming all the dinosaurs, counting up to 20, and playing games on the computer. They believe in what they see, hear, and touch. If a 4-year-old thinks his glass looks like it contains less juice than a friend's, then the friend has more juice, even if the juice was poured from two same-sized cans. If a 4-year-old heard a monster make growling noises under the bed, then there is a monster under the bed, even though his father says it's just his imagination. Four-year-olds are very curious, and their favorite word is likely to be *why*.

Five-Year-Olds

Five-year-olds seem older than 4-year-olds in many ways. Like 4-year-olds, 5-year-olds love to learn new things, but they are likely to be more persistent about mastery. If they are drawing a rainbow, a house, or a self-portrait, they will work for quite a while until it's just the way they want it to look. Like 4-year-olds, 5-year-olds love to pretend, but their pretending is more elaborate. They gather props before the pretending begins, and when they act out a pretend scene, the events take place in a logical sequence. If they are putting on a performance, they will set the stage, make the tickets, and put on their costumes before the performance begins. The performance is likely to include an announcement of what is going to happen, some sort of act or acts, and an elaborate ending with many bows and the expectation of applause.

Five-year-olds are interested in using and interpreting symbols. While some 5-year-olds are faster than others in learning the mechanics of reading and writing, most are serious about wanting to learn. They like to choose from a menu in the restaurant, read the signs on the road, make lists of things they need to buy, and write their names on their books or their drawings. They can work out simple problems in their heads and can grasp the concepts of adding and subtracting, although they are likely to count on their fingers before they come up with the right answer.

Five-year-olds who have the opportunity to use a computer love interactive programs. They are able to understand and apply the rules of a game and enjoy reading, writing, and number activities where the computer lets them know if they have the right answer. Favorite computer activities include programs that have them solve problems, programs that have them arrange characters on the screen to create their own imaginative stories, and programs that help them make drawings, paintings, birthday cards, and invitations.

Children at this age are quite likely to make playground plans before the day begins. Their choice of friends is likely to be made on the basis of shared interests. Children who like active play will choose to play on the climbing equipment, engage in running and chasing games, play some sort of ball game, or race around the playground on a vehicle. Children who like quieter play are more likely to play in the sand, hunt for bugs or lizards, put on a performance, or huddle with a friend and just talk.

Resources about Child Development

Berk, L. (2001). *Infants and children: Prenatal through middle childhood* (4th ed.). Upper Saddle River, NJ: Prentice Hall.

CDA Council for Professional Recognition. www.cdacouncil.org.

Zero to Three. National Center for Infants, Toddlers, and Families. www.zerotothree.org.

Overview

Physical development refers to the development of gross-motor or large-muscle skills, such as crawling, walking, and batting, and of fine-motor or small-muscle skills, which are involved in tasks such as eating, writing, cutting, and drawing.

Rationale

Because young children are always on the go, parents and teachers are apt to relax about their physical development. You might hear a parent or teacher say "Just let them run around and play, and they'll get all the exercise they need."

It is true that every child has her own developmental timetable and will sit up and walk and run according to that timetable no matter how we arrange her environment. But physical development involves a lot more than learning how to walk and run. Physical development is an important facet of the whole developmental process. The child's mind and body work together. The development of motor skills contributes to the development of social and emotional skills, language skills, and problem-solving skills. The teacher plays an important role in supporting children's physical development by preparing the environment and by providing a variety of appropriate equipment, activities, and opportunities.

113

...nize expectable sequences in small- and large-muscle development ...ncy and describe materials and activities that will enhance this ...velopment

2. To recognize expectable sequences in small- and large-muscle development in young toddlers and describe materials and activities that will enhance this development

3. To recognize expectable sequences in small- and large- muscle development in older toddlers and describe materials and activities that will enhance this development

4. To recognize expectable sequences in small- and large-muscle development in preschoolers and describe materials and activities that will enhance this development

5. To identify materials and activities that will enhance the physical development of children with special needs

Supporting Physical Development

Ms. Braggart and Mr. Doubtful were both seated in the waiting room of their babies' pediatrician's office. Their babies, who were approximately the same age, were playing on the floor with some of the same kinds of toys. Mr. Doubtful noticed that his baby was not getting around as well as Ms. Braggart's baby and asked, "How long has your baby been crawling that well?" "About three weeks," answered Ms. Braggart. "My baby is very intelligent; he is almost pulling up to a standing position on the furniture. Soon, he will be walking all over the place."

Mr. Doubtful was very concerned about his baby because he was barely getting up onto his hands and knees to crawl. He thought to himself, "I will have to talk to the doctor about this. I hope my baby will be as smart as hers."

In the first four sections of this chapter on physical development, we describe the developmental sequences, environments, and activities that facilitate the development of infants (young infants, 0–9 months, and older infants, 9–14 months), young toddlers (14–24 months), older toddlers (2 years old), and preschoolers (3–5 years old). While reaching developmental milestones is a critical component of healthy development, there is no reason to assume that children who acquire motor skills at an accelerated rate will be equally advanced in other facets of development. Nor can we assume that children who are advanced in one area of physical development, such as growth, will be ahead of schedule in reaching motor milestones, such as walking.

To recognize expectable sequences in small- and large-muscle development in infancy and describe materials and activities that will enhance this development

During the first 14 months of life, the infant learns important motor skills. He learns to hold his head without support, to turn from side to side, to turn from stomach to back and back to stomach, to hold his head when he is pulled to a sitting position, to reach or grasp, to pull to a sitting position, to cruise holding onto furniture, and perhaps to walk.

Motor development occurs so quickly during the first year of life that observant caregivers see almost daily changes in the children in their care. The Developmental Picture describes how infants develop and how caregivers can support their development.

Developmental Picture

The young infant (0–9 months):
- Is born with all the basic movements
- Turns toward sounds
- Follows moving objects
- Practices movements such as lifting the head, supporting oneself with the arms, and then rolling over and sitting
- Increases the ability to explore and discover through mastery of small-muscle skills, such as bringing the hand to the mouth, reaching, swatting, grasping, raking, and using an immature pincer grasp to pick up small objects

The caregiver:
- Provides infants the opportunity to practice emerging skills in large- and small-muscle development
- Uses caregiving times as opportunities to encourage infants to practice motor skills
- Provides infants the opportunity to kick and move their arms while lying on their backs
- Allows infants to spend time on their abdomens so that they can practice lifting their heads and chests and watching moving objects
- Provides a variety of safe positions for practice that use all the muscles
- Provides appropriate toys and environments to encourage large- and small-muscle development

The older infant (9–14 months):
- Is learning to use motor skills to achieve desired goals
- Crawls, creeps, pulls to standing, cruises, walks with help, rides scooting toys, and walks alone in a predictable sequence
- Enjoys mastering motor skills and wants to share accomplishments
- Is always on the move
- Uses objects to hold, mouth, bang, drop, pick up, turn, and put together

The caregiver:
- Identifies the motor skill that the infant is trying to master
- Provides opportunities for each infant to practice her emerging skills
- Provides safe spaces, furniture, and equipment for large-muscle activity
- Provides many safe and interesting objects for manipulation and sensory exploration

Activities That Enhance Large-Muscle Development

Infants need to practice their new large-muscle skills. Caregivers must create barriers so that the space is safe and older infants are not tumbling onto the younger infants playing on the floor.

Birth to Three Months

Massage Gently rub the baby's arms, legs, and body.

Change Baby's Position Make sure the infant is sometimes placed on his back and sometimes on his stomach. At times, the infant can be propped up in an infant seat.

Rolling Over Help the infant learn to turn over by rolling him back and forth. Bend one knee and arm and gently roll the child.

Kicking Place a cradle "gym" over the infant's feet to encourage the development of reciprocal kicking.

Reaching Out Place the baby on his stomach and hold a toy a few inches in front of him to encourage stretching.

Three to Six Months

Reaching and Grasping Hold a rattle out for the baby to encourage reaching and grasping.

Turning from Side to Side Attach an attractive toy or mobile first to one side of the crib and then the other. The baby will turn from side to side in order to look at the toy.

Pull-Ups Pull the baby slowly to a sitting position, providing only as much head support as he needs.

Six to Nine Months

Come and Get It Hold a toy in front of the infant, and encourage him to retrieve it. Make sure the infant is allowed to be successful. To help a child get started crawling, let him push with his feet against your cupped hands.

Sitting Up Make sure the infant spends time sitting up, even if he has to be propped by pillows.

Nine to Fourteen Months

Pulling Up Provide low shelves and other items the infant can use to pull himself to a standing position.

Ball Games Roll a ball back and forth. Play retrieval games. Hang the ball on a string, and show the infant how to bat it.

Walking Give the beginning walker something that he can push and use as a walker. A riding toy with a raised handle works well.

Feeding Encourage the infant to use a cup and spoon.

Tunnel Crawl Encourage the infant to crawl through a tunnel.

"Walkers" in the Early Childhood Setting

Contrary to popular belief, infant "walkers" (either the moving type or the type with a stationary seat) do not promote the muscle development needed for walking. Moreover, they can be dangerous if the children placed in them can fall down the stairs or get to objects that are intended to be out of reach. "Walkers" also curtail children's ability to explore materials and limit the amount of time infants can practice cognitive skills.

Activities That Enhance Small-Muscle Development

Birth to Three Months
- Provide shake toys, such as rattles, with handles for holding. (Beginning rattles with handles are better than dumbbell-type rattles.)
- Provide toys and materials with different textures for feeling.

Three to Six Months
- Make available toys for handling and mouthing.
- Provide objects for visual tracking, such as mobiles, plate puppets, fish in a tank, soap bubbles, wind-up cars, and pendulums.

Six to Nine Months
- Develop hand strength with squeeze toys, like a rubber ducky.
- Activity boards require the infant to hold onto, poke at, and pull on things.
- Finger foods, such as dry cereal, bits of cheese, and macaroni, help infants develop the *raking motion*, or to pick up small objects by bringing the fingers to the palm.
- Provide stuffed animals and soft dolls to build hand strength.

Nine to Fourteen Months
- Engage in simple finger plays, like Pat-a-Cake and Where Is Thumbkin?
- Finger foods, such as dry cereal, bits of cheese, and macaroni, help infants develop the *pincer grasp*, or to pick up small objects by bringing the fingers to the thumb.
- Provide blocks and objects for filling and dumping from buckets.
- Provide sensory experiences like painting with pudding.

To recognize expectable sequences in small- and large-muscle development in young toddlers and describe materials and activities that will enhance this development

Young toddlers spend much of their waking time practicing their motor skills. When they accomplish a new feat—such as walking backward, climbing stairs, or doing a somersault—they not only perform it over and over again, but they also find new ways of making it more difficult. The young toddler who has learned to walk downstairs holding onto your hand will insist on walking down unassisted, carrying his teddy bear.

See the Developmental Picture below for an overview of the young toddler's interests and abilities.

Toys and Structures That Promote Motor Skills

The increase in large-motor skills between 14 and 24 months of age can be attributed in part to an improvement in balance. Emerging motor skills include stepping onto a stool, backing into a chair, going from sitting on the floor to standing without getting on one's hands and knees, propelling a riding toy, and going down a slide. Walking and running skills continue to improve in subtle ways. As hands are not needed for balance, the toddler is able to carry a large toy, lift a small suitcase, push a play

Developmental Picture

The young toddler (14–24 months):
- Is developing new skills, such as squatting, pushing, pulling, climbing, walking, and running
- Is able to drop toys into a bucket
- Enjoys bouncing up and down in time to music and tries to perform simple finger plays
- Enjoys rolling a ball back and forth
- Is practicing small-muscle skills, such as stacking blocks, turning the pages of a book, and putting large pegs in a pegboard
- Is building eye/hand coordination

The caregiver:
- Provides opportunities for each child to practice acquired skills and develop emerging skills
- Provides toys for practicing large-muscle skills, such as large balls, pull toys, riding toys, and sturdy push toys
- Provides toys for developing small-muscle skills, such as blocks, stacking toys, large pegboards, and pounding benches
- Engages in back and forth ball play
- Plays recorded music that encourages movement

vacuum cleaner or lawn mower, and control the pace of a pull toy by walking front-ward or backward.

Small-muscle skills, like large-muscle skills, are expanding rapidly for young toddlers. Children are learning to master cups, spoons, and forks with only a little spilling. They are also learning to turn a handle, pound with a hammer, use one finger to point and probe, zip a zipper, open and close doors, and turn dials on radios and television sets.

Activities to Encourage Large-Muscle Development

- Provide toys that encourage pushing, like corn poppers, carpet sweepers, and toy lawn mowers. For safety reasons, look for push toys that have knobs or handles.
- Provide sturdy riding toys, such as sit-on-top-of cars and trucks that children can propel with their feet.
- Provide rocking boats that convert to stairs to give children practice with balance and coordination.
- Provide toddler slides that allow children to practice climbing stairs and experience momentum.
- Provide movement and music activities that increase body awareness, encourage imitation, and provide motor skill practice.
- Provide safe places for toddlers to climb both in the classroom and outdoors. Toddlers will find unsafe places to climb if they are not offered safe places. Given that, it is a good idea to provide a small climbing structure inside the classroom so that toddlers will not climb on the cubbies and the tables.
- Children of this age enjoy picking up and carrying items around. Some of these items could include balls of different sizes and lightweight blocks.
- Tunnels for crawling through not only give children practice with motor skills but also give them a quiet place to go to when they need to be by themselves.

Activities to Encourage Small-Muscle Development

- Provide "busy boards," lock boards, and dressing frames for practicing small-muscle skills.
- Provide pounding benches that give children practice with wrist action and eye/hand coordination.
- Encourage children to play with toys that have cranks that turn, like a music box and a jack-in-the-box.
- Provide materials that help children strengthen their hands and fingers, like pop-beads and squeeze toys.
- Offer children drawing materials, such as paper and large crayons for scribbling.

To recognize expectable sequences in small- and large-muscle development in older toddlers and describe materials and activities that will enhance this development

Mrs. Overprotective was giving some last-minute instructions to her daughter Suzy's teacher: "And remember, I do not want Suzy out on the playground. Why, I can just see her climbing up on the jungle gym and getting hurt. My Suzy has never had so much as a scratch. Her dad and I see to that." ●

Although we can understand Mrs. Overprotective's desire to keep her daughter safe, keeping an active, healthy 2-year-old from practicing motor skills is not a good idea. It is far better to risk getting a few scratches and bruises than to tell a 2-year-old that she can't jump, can't run, can't climb, or can't scoot around on a riding toy.

See the Developmental Picture for more on 2-year-olds' motor development.

Developmental Picture

The older toddler (2 years):
- Is learning to go up and down the stairs
- Is proud of physical accomplishments and insists on being watched and praised
- Is likely to get wound up and overactive
- Is developing small-muscle skills
- Continues to build eye/hand coordination
- Tears paper, glues, scribbles with a crayon, and enjoys easel painting
- Enjoys big toys and equipment, such as slides, bounce toys, and wagons
- Experiments with throwing different objects, like balls, blocks, and puzzles

The caregiver:
- Provides toys and equipment that encourage children to play together
- Provides toys that encourage active play, such as big balls, hoops, and ride-on toys
- Provides toys and materials that develop small muscles, such as play dough for molding, large beads to string, pitchers for pouring, and paper for wadding and tearing
- Alternates quiet and active play so that the children are not overstimulated
- Supervises children closely during jumping, climbing, and going up and down stairs

---

Activities That Encourage Large-Muscle Development

Rope Train Two-year-olds love to run around the playground, but that running around can easily get out of control. To maintain control, tie two or three skipping ropes together and then tie ribbons or pieces of cloth at equal intervals along the rope about 1½ feet apart. With each child holding onto a section of the rope, lead them around the playground at a fast walk or a slow trot.

Obstacle Course Obstacle courses work well with 2-year-olds, so long as the obstacles are easy to master. One way to create an obstacle course is to lay a ladder flat on the ground.

Bullfrog Create a "pond" by making a circle with a long skipping rope. Have the children line up on the outside of the circle. When the "bullfrog" (teacher) says "Ribbit, ribbit," all of the little "frogs" (the children) have to jump over the rope and into the pond. When the "bullfrog" turns around, the children jump out of the pond.

Large-Motor Equipment Provide equipment like ride-on toys, push toys, and transportation vehicles as well as age-appropriate climbing structures and slides.

Outdoor Ball Play Provide large balls for kicking, throwing, catching, and trapping.

Music and Movement Children enjoy moving to recorded music while they play rhythm instruments.

Blocks and Construction Materials Children can build with a variety of blocks. Other construction materials, such as pieces of cardboard, paper towel spindles, and miniature props, can extend this play. For example, add animal and figures to the blocks and the children may build a "corral" or use the blocks as "hay" for the horse.

Activities That Encourage Small-Muscle Development

- Children this age are just beginning to really use manipulatives that can be put together and taken apart, like large put-together sets of building blocks.

- Children enjoy tearing paper that they can glue onto other sheets of paper. Other types of art materials that encourage small-muscle development include big crayons and paper, easels and large brushes, beginning scissors for snipping paper, and chalk for use on paper or outdoors on the sidewalk.

- Place the baby dolls in the water table with some sponges and washcloths. As children wring out the sponges and washcloths, they will develop their hand strength.

To recognize expectable sequences in small- and large-muscle development in preschoolers and describe materials and activities that will enhance this development

Mrs. Matthews had decided to place her son, Billy, in Little Follies Play School. She was just finishing an extended visit with Billy's teacher, Miss Janice, and was giving her some last-minute instructions. "And by the way," she continued, "I don't want Billy spending too much time outdoors playing. That playground looks very dusty, and I don't want to take chances with his allergies. Furthermore, I am against all the stress you people place on sports. I want my Billy to grow up with a good mind. I don't care a bit whether or not he grows up to be an athlete!"

The following day, Billy arrived at the school. Much to Miss Janice's surprise, Billy got along well with the other children. When playground time arrived, he ran out enthusiastically with a group of active boys and joined them in a "space explorers" game on the jungle gym. At the end of the playground period, he was red faced, dusty, and full of happy chatter.

When Billy's mother arrived to pick him up, her first words were, "Oh, I see you let him go out on the playground."

"Yes," Billy added with great gusto. "And I climbed on the jungle gym and I was Darth Vader and I jumped off the jungle gym and I . . ." Mrs. Matthews had a dark look in her eyes as her son talked on excitedly.

Miss Janice decided not to be defensive. She replied calmly, "Yes, Mrs. Matthews, I did let Billy go out on the playground. He had a very good time, and it did not bother his allergies. Billy is an extremely well-coordinated youngster, and he enjoys active play. You know that, contrary to what many people believe, bright children are usually healthier and more athletic than less-bright children. Intellectual development and physical development frequently go hand in hand."

Mrs. Matthews was now interested. All of a sudden, she forgot about Billy's allergies and dusty clothes.

Miss Janice was quite correct. The development of motor skills is a critical component of a good preschool curriculum. The very fact that children spend so much of their time practicing motor skills suggests the importance of physical development. Furthermore, children themselves attach great importance to motor skill achievements. Parents who accompany their preschoolers to the playground or the swimming pool are constantly bombarded with cries of "Watch me, Mommy" and "Look at me, Daddy." Each new motor achievement is a source of pride for young children.

> *Children, like adults, need variety and change of pace.*

In planning activities to develop large-muscle skills, it is important to remember that children, like adults, need variety and change of pace. They need to have free-play activities, in which there are opportunities to socialize and make up rules, as well as guided activities, in which they listen to and follow directions. They need to have slow-paced activities, in which their energy is channeled, and fast-paced activities, in which their energy is expended.

Motor skill development is important in the preschool for many reasons. As children learn to control their bodies in space and master motor feats along with their peers, they are doing the following:

- Developing body awareness
- Perfecting eye/hand coordination
- Improving balance
- Learning about position in space
- Improving throwing, catching, and jumping skills
- Engaging in imaginative activities that foster creativity while enhancing large-muscle skills

Developmental Picture

The preschool child (3–5 years old):

- Is proud of physical accomplishments and insists on being watched
- Is aware of the motor skills that other children are mastering
- Likes to jump and climb but is not aware of the risks of doing so
- Is learning new small-muscle skills, such as scribbling, pretend writing, cutting and gluing, coloring and painting
- Is perfecting eye/hand coordination
- Is learning new motor skills, including climbing, jumping, throwing and catching, peddling a tricycle, pumping a swing, hopping on one foot, and galloping
- May engage in competitive rough-and-tumble games involving sliding, racing, jumping, balancing, and swinging without regard for safety

The caregiver:

- Recognizes that preschool children like to be on the move and require large, open spaces to play
- Recognizes that stopping a movement or staying still is a major challenge for preschoolers and knows they may have trouble sitting still
- Recognizes that supervision is essential because most preschoolers are not safety conscious
- Provides children with a variety of opportunities for indoor and outdoor motor activities on a daily basis
- Provides opportunities to engage in quiet as well as active activities
- Provides many opportunities to develop small-muscle skills, such as scribbling, lacing, wadding and tearing paper, pasting/gluing, and cutting with scissors and with plastic knives

The Developmental Picture on page 123 provides more information about the motor skill development of preschoolers. In addition, the following sections describe the various categories of large-muscle skills developed in the preschool years.

Balance

- *Static nonmovement:* Activities that require standing or reaching while standing still
- *Dynamic movement:* Activities that require crawling, walking, running, marching, or climbing

Coordination

- *Expressive movement:* Typically seen in music and gymnastic-type activities, in which children make their own interpretation of a dance, musical, or gymnastic movement. The movement can express moods, feelings, or concepts.
- *Integration:* Following directions or putting together what you hear or see with what your body does. An example of this kind of activity is playing Simon Says.

Developing Body Awareness

A good way to develop body awareness is to lead the children in action songs. "This Old Man" is a good song to use:

> *This old man, he played one. He played nick-nack on my thumb, etc.*
> *This old man, he played two. He played nick-nack on my shoe, etc.*
> *This old man, he played three. He played nick-nack on my knee, etc.*
> *This old man, he turned red. He played nick-nack on my head, etc.*
> *This old man, he liked cheers. He played nick-nack on my ears, etc.*

See if the children can add any rhymes. Other action songs and rhymes include "Miss Polly Had a Dolly," "Simon Says," "Brown Girl in the Ring," "Skip to My Lou," and "Head and Shoulders."

Activities for Improving Balance

Cross Over the River Use carpet strips or pieces of tagboard as stepping stones. Play Follow the Leader across the river, cautioning the children about "getting wet."

Toe the Line Draw a chalk line or place masking tape on the floor, securing each end with masking tape. Ask the children to walk on the line like little mice. When the children have learned to walk forward on the line, vary the activity by walking backward, sideways, on tiptoes, or with eyes closed.

Walk the Plank Repeat the Toe the Line activity using a plank or balance board.

Activities for Learning about Position in Space

Obstacle Course Set up an obstacle course in the classroom by weaving a string in and out of the tables and over and under the chairs. Encourage the children to follow the course.

Formation Draw a circle out of chalk or make a circle out of strips of tape. Distribute red and yellow ribbons to the children, giving every other child the same color. Explain that when the music stops, the children with red ribbons are to take a giant step into the circle and those with yellow ribbons are to take a giant step out of the circle. When the music starts up again, everyone is to take a giant step back to the circle and walk around it. Make the activity more difficult by playing faster music.

Recorded Music and Musical Instruments Children will naturally start to move when they use musical instruments and hear marching music.

Activities for Improving Throwing, Catching, and Jumping Skills

Circle Game with a Large Ball Seat the children in a circle with their legs spread apart. Roll the ball to each child and encourage the child to roll the ball back to you. At first, roll the ball to the children going from left to right. When the children have become adept at catching and returning the ball, play the same game with the children standing in a circle.

Tether Ball Place a rubber ball or beach ball in a bag or net and hang it from the ceiling. Let the children bat at the ball with a Nerf bat.

Beanbag Toss Have the children toss a beanbag into a wastepaper basket or carton. When they become skilled at this, draw a clown with a large mouth on the side of a carton and have the children "feed the clown."

Crossing the Stream Give two children the task of holding the ends of a skipping rope. Have the children jump over the rope when it is on the floor. The gradually raise the height of the rope.

Activities for Enhancing Large-Muscle Skills

Encourage the children to play a variety of pretend motor activitiess:

- Jog in place
- Swim in place
- Hop like rabbits
- Roll over like a dog
- Do the bicycle on your back
- Pretend to fly a kite

- Play skating in a circle
- Fly around the room like birds
- Crawl like a baby
- Kick like a baby
- Kick a pretend football
- Pretend to catch a high ball

Activities That Encourage Body Awareness

All of the activities in this section are well suited to circle time:

Pass the Shoe   The children sit in a circle. Each child takes off one of his shoes for passing. The children then sing the following song as they pass their shoes to the right. When the children receive their own shoes back, they stand up and clap.

Sing these words to the tune of "London Bridge":

> *Pass the shoe from me to you, me to you, me to you:*
> *Pass the shoe from me to you, and do just as I do!*

Little Sally Walker   In this African American ring game, the children form a circle, with one child in the middle. "Sally" or "Sal" kneels in the center of the circle and acts out the words to the song. The other children in the circle walk around as the song is sung or chanted. "Sally" or "Sal" shakes toward the child that he or she chooses to be in the circle next.

Here are the words:

> *Little Sally Walker sittin' in a saucer.*
> *Rise, Sally, rise.*
> *Wipe your weeping eyes,*
> *Put your hands on your hips, and let your backbone slip.*
> *Ah. Shake it to the east. Ah. Shake it to the west.*
> *Ah. Shake it to the one that you love the best.*

We're Going to Kentucky, We're Going to the Fair   The children hold hands to make a big circle. Then they drop hands to find their space in the circle. One child is chosen to be in the center. The children sing the following song, and the child in the center performs the moves as directed in the song. During the last line in the song, the child in the middle closes her eyes and spins around. The person she stops on then has a turn in the center.

Here are the words:

> *We're going to Kentucky. We're going to the fair.*
> *To see the Senorita with flowers in her hair.*
> *Oh! Shake it, Shake it, Shake it.*
> *Shake it till you stop.*
> *Turn around and turn around until you make a stop.*

Activities for Enhancing Small-Muscle Skills

All of these small-muscle activities build eye/hand coordination:

- Activities that practice finger isolation and finger strength need materials such as beads, pegboards, geo-boards (rubber band boards), and lacing materials.

- Put a clothesline with clothespins in the dramatic play area. The children will be able to develop their pincer grasp and finger strength as they hang up clothes on the clothesline.

- Provide a basket with different-sized plastic jars and their lids. The children will develop their wrist swivel as they put the lids on the jars.

- Making play dough and then playing with it helps children to develop hand strength. Be sure to include a variety of objects that the children can use for rolling, shaping, cutting, molding, stamping, and poking into the play dough.

- Give the children tongs to pick up small objects and transfer them into a container. Some objects could include pom-poms and ping-pong balls.

- Provide materials that develop finger/thumb opposition, like pegboards.

Activities for Improving Motor Skills Outdoors

Playground Activities and Equipment

The playground is especially appropriate for large-muscle activities that require space, equipment, and climbing structures. The following types of equipment are especially desirable:

- Wheel toys and a riding path
- A climbing structure that is safe, provides space for several children, and encourages imaginative play
- Planks and large blocks that the children can use to create their own structures
- Small tires or spindles that can be rolled
- Larger tires that can be used for jumping
- Beach balls and playground balls
- Hula hoops
- Jump ropes
- Tire swings
- Tunnels
- Balance beams and log walks

(continued)

Activities continued

Organized Outdoor Activities

Red Light, Green Light The children form a line. When the caller says "Green light," they run forward. When the caller says "Red light," they stop.

Ring around the Rosy The children hold hands in a circle and dance around to the familiar chant. On the words "all fall down," they stop and sit down abruptly.

Freeze This game can be played with or without music. The players begin to move around a predesignated area. At the signal to "Freeze" or when the music stops, the players try to stay as still as possible. When the signal to "Go" is given or when the music is turned back on, the players begin to move around again.

Follow the Leader One child is chosen to be the leader. The other children line up behind the leader and follow her actions.

The Teacher's Role on the Playground

Playground time offers a good opportunity for teachers to work with children who have mild delays in motor skill development and need special instruction and/or encouragement. Children who are not well coordinated may shy away from active physical play.

To identify those children who could benefit from physical activities, look for the ones on the playground who seldom engage in active play. Then play a game like Monkey Say, Monkey Do, in which the children have to imitate your actions. First, ask the children that you have selected to imitate everything you do. Jump, bounce and catch a ball, balance on one leg, march heel to toe, or touch your toes. Give each child in the group an opportunity to choose a stunt that you and the group have to imitate.

Playground time offers a good opportunity for teachers to work with children who are mildly delayed in terms of motor skill development and need special instruction and/or encouragement.

When you return to the classroom, check off the names of the children who were in your selected group. Put a star beside the name of each child who had difficulty imitating the activities that you demonstrated. While the rest of the group may have selected quiet play because they prefer it, the children who have difficulty with motor skills could be selecting it to avoid active play out of a fear of failure. These children may need some special time on a daily basis to practice motor skills. Planned physical activities for the identified children should include activities that allow them to practice the skills they have already achieved and activities that help them develop new skills appropriate for their age. Use a checklist of physical skills to chart their progress.

Plan a daily outdoor activity that focuses on physical skills that need strengthening. Your list of activities may include the following:

- Walking on a board to improve balance
- Running games to improve skill and stamina
- Obstacle courses to improve coordination and motor control
- Climbing structure activities to improve coordination, balance, and upper-body strength
- Ball play to encourage eye/hand coordination, thrust, and aim
- Hula hoop games with the hula hoops on the ground to encourage jumping skills

 To identify materials and activities that will enhance the physical development of children with special needs

Mrs. Protect had come to school to observe her daughter, Merissa, who has cerebral palsy. It was midmorning and Mrs. Protect was surprised to find Merissa on the playground. The children were sitting in a circle on the ground, tossing a playground ball around the circle. Mrs. Protect was worried; Merissa wasn't good at catching and perhaps the ball would hit her in the face. Just as this concern came to mind, the ball hit Merissa's cheek. Mrs. Protect expected Merissa to burst into tears, but instead, she just started laughing and then all the children joined in. Needless to say, Mrs. Protect was proud of her daughter and delighted with the teacher.

An *individualized education plan (IEP)* determines the types of interventions that the classroom teacher is responsible for implementing for a child with a diagnosed disabling condition. However, it is up to the classroom teacher to modify the recommended activities for each child with special needs so that he can participate as much as possible in the group activities that the other children are enjoying.

Here are examples of some ways in which a teacher can include children with special needs in physical activities:

- If an infant or toddler has difficulty with sitting or balance, place her on the floor inside a rubber tube or swim ring so that she can join the other children in floor play.
- If a child is in a wheelchair, adjust the height of the table so that she can join the other children in craft or clay activities that encourage small-muscle development.

- If a child is on crutches, has poor balance, or is visually impaired, make sure that the furniture is not out of place so that she has a clear path to anywhere in the room.
- If a child is unable to stand, play movement games during circle time in which the children sit on the floor. This way, all the children can perform the arm and hand movements together.
- If a child has physical disabilities and cannot use the playground equipment, plan outdoor activities that he can participate in, like digging for "gold" (rocks) in the sandbox and catching bubbles.
- If a visually impaired child wants to play in a group game, try a three-legged race. Each child chooses a partner, and the teacher ties the left leg of one child to the right leg of his partner. Some visually impaired children do well in this game because they have had practice in trusting other children to take the lead.

Also encourage the other children to join you in supporting the children with special needs. Talk to them about ways to support their peers. Your first suggestion should be to provide assistance to someone with a disability only when he asks for help or seems to need it. Also suggest to the children that they should take special care when running, swinging, or riding wheel toys so they do not bump into a child who, for instance, has poor balance or cannot see them or hear them.

Fortunately, young children are usually quite trustworthy when they know that another child needs their help.

Additional Resources about Physical Development

Bredekamp, S., & Copple, C. (Eds.). (1997). *Developmentally appropriate practice in early childhood programs* (Rev. ed.). Washington, DC: NAEYC.

Sanders, S. (2002). *Active for life: Developmentally appropriate movement programs for young children.* Washington, DC: NAEYC. (Published in cooperation with Human Kinetics Publishers)

Torbert, M., & Schneider, L. (1993). *Follow me too: A handbook of movement activities for three- to five-year-olds.* New York: Addison-Wesley.

Cognitive Development

Chapter 5

Overview

Cognitive, or *intellectual*, *development* refers to the child's growing ability to give meaning to experience, to reason, to acquire knowledge, and to problem solve.

Rationale

As children interact with the environment, they discover how things work. As they interact with people, they acquire patterns, language, information, and ideas. As they try to make sense of their experiences, they develop new concepts and modify old ways of thinking.

Although what individual children learn is unique, the concepts that underlie their learning are developed in a predictable sequence. Each new step provides the foundation for the next.

Objectives

1. To recognize expectable sequences in cognitive development in infancy and describe materials and activities that will enhance this development

2. To recognize expectable sequences in cognitive development in young toddlers and describe materials and activities that will enhance this development

3. To recognize expectable sequences in cognitive development in older toddlers and describe materials and activities that will enhance this development

4. To recognize expectable sequences in cognitive development in preschool children and describe materials and activities that will enhance this development

5. To learn how to create a preschool environment that encourages exploration, curiosity, and critical thinking

6. To learn techniques for introducing meaningful themes into preschool classrooms

Supporting Cognitive Development

Ms. Get-Them-Ready was teaching her 4-year-olds a lesson on colors. She held up a card with a turquoise square on it. She said, "This color is turquoise. What color is it, class?" "Turquoise," they responded. She held up a second card and said, "And this is chartreuse. Can you say that?"

A parent who happened to be visiting the class asked Ms. Get-Them-Ready why she had chosen those particular colors to teach. "They're on the kindergarten readiness test," replied the teacher. "I want to make sure that all my kids get a perfect score."

Ms. Get-Them-Ready's concern about the kindergarten readiness test is understandable. In some communities, children who do poorly on such tests may be held back from entering kindergarten. In other communities, schools, programs, and even individual teachers may be penalized or stigmatized if the children don't do well. The pressure can be intense.

But research shows that prepping young children for tests is not the best way to prepare them for long-term success. If Ms. Get-Them-Ready really wants her students to be ready for kindergarten, she should worry less about the test and more about helping them develop their minds. For instance, to help them learn about colors, she should recognize that preschool children are naturally curious, and colors are just one of the things they notice about their environment. Choosing wallpaper for the dollhouse, comparing the colors of leaves collected on a nature walk, mixing paints, planting a garden, designing outfits for paper dolls, stringing beads in a pattern, making rainbows with a prism or hose, and playing sorting games all provide opportunities to talk about colors in a meaningful way. Activities like these build on children's interests, deepen their knowledge, and enhance their cognitive development.

Young children who are given opportunities to explore and investigate, solve problems, make discoveries, and develop new thinking skills will be primed for success both in school and in life.

To recognize expectable sequences in cognitive development in infancy and describe materials and activities that will enhance this development

Allison's mother agreed to take care of Allison's 6-month-old son when Allison went back to work. When Allison dropped her son off at her mother's on her first day back to work, she gave her a long list of instructions. One instruction was underlined in red: "After his 10 o'clock nap, spend 15 minutes showing Timothy flash cards of words. Begin by showing the flash card with cat, cake, *and* mouse.

Allison's mother looked over the list of instructions and then said, "I am delighted to take care of Timothy. But what is this about showing him flash cards? Six-month-old babies, no matter how bright they are, should not be taught how to read." At first, Allison was not at all sure that her mother was right about the flash cards. But then she had second thoughts. "Maybe my mother is right," she told her husband that night. "When we show Timothy the flash cards, he watches our faces and smiles, but he never looks down at the cards."

Babies are born with a built-in need to take in new information and make sense out of their world. In the beginning, an infant experiences sounds, sensations, sights, smells, and tastes as loosely connected experiences, and over time, she discovers connections between these experiences. For example, the infant recognizes that the sound of her own cries is followed by the appearance of her mother's face and the comfortable feeling of being held in her arms. The infant learns to anticipate sequences of sensations, and the world becomes more predictable. See the Developmental Picture for more information on infants' cognitive development.

> *Babies are born with a built-in need to take in new information and make sense out of their world.*

Developmental Picture

The young infant (0–9 months):

- Is unique in terms of temperament, coping ability, and developmental timetable
- Is working hard to make sense out of the world by listening, watching, and touching
- Is programmed from birth to engage in interactions with parents and/or caregivers
- By 4 or 5 months of age, can make interesting things happen again
- Puts together sensations and information from different senses
- Shows interest in new information
- Gets accustomed to familiar sights and sounds

133

(continued)

The caregiver:

- Recognizes and adapts to each infant's unique temperamental characteristics
- Discovers ways of enabling infants to experience sensations, sounds, feel, tastes, smells, and sights
- Responds to each infant in a predictable way
- Recognizes that different infants have different thresholds of responsiveness and responds to each infant's need for more or less stimulation

The older infant (9–14 months):

- Learns through exploration and discovery
- Anticipates new events based on past experiences
- Recognizes that people can affect objects and other people
- Imitates actions and expressions
- Empties and fills, opens and shuts, pushes and pulls, pokes and prods
- Points to an interesting object and expects the caregiver to look at it
- Looks at objects that the caregiver points to or looks at
- Uses simple tools, such as shovels, spoons, and drum sticks
- Demonstrates awareness that objects are there even if they are out of sight by playing Peek-a-Boo or finding toys covered by a blanket

The caregiver:

- Identifies and reinforces each infant's interests and capabilities
- Shares the joy and excitement of new learning and new discoveries
- Provides opportunities for infants to experiment with dropping objects into a container
- Plays games that the infant enjoys, such as Peek-a-Boo and Where Did Teddy Go?

Activities to Encourage Problem-Solving Skills

Birth to Three Months

Although babies spend much of their time sleeping in the first 3 months, they also have periods of quiet wakefulness when they are alert and ready to learn. Babies learn to put together information they receive from different senses. Within the first 3 months, they make connections between sounds they hear, sights they see, and sensations they feel. They learn to search with their eyes for the source of a sound and to respond to a smiling face with a smile and a coo.

Look and Stare Hold a brightly colored object in front of the infant, and see if he can focus his eyes on it.

Tracking Hold a bright toy 12 inches in front of the infant, slowly moving it from side to side. When the infant has mastered this, move the toy vertically and then in a circle.

Grasping Place a small article in the baby's hand, and allow her to grasp it. Then change to the other hand.

Sound Search Shake a bell or rattle behind and above the child's head. Give him time to turn his head to see what made the sound.

Three to Six Months

Between 3 and 6 months old, babies are learning to reach out and grasp for toys. They are making connections between actions and outcomes. They shake a rattle, hear its tinkle, and purposefully shake it again.

Rattle Shake Give the infant a rattle, and show him how to shake it to make a sound.

Wristband Make a wristband and put it on the baby to help him discover his hands.

Banging Give the infant a rattle to bang on a hard surface.

Reaching Activities Give the infant a lot of opportunities to reach. For instance, hold out objects, dangle objects on ribbons, or put a cradle "gym" within the infant's reach.

Kicking Activities Place a cradle "gym" near the baby's feet so he can make it move by kicking.

Peek-a-Boo Play a Peek-a-Boo game with the baby.

Toy Manipulation Give the infant a soft squeak toy.

Six to Nine Months

By now, babies are making fine discriminations relating to people and toys. They greet familiar people with smiles and babbles, and they turn away from strangers. They play with different toys in different ways, in accordance with their attributes. They test new toys in a variety of ways, looking at them from all sides, shaking or banging them, and even tasting them.

Squeaks Show the infant how to make a squeak toy work.

Cause-and-Effect Activity Give the baby a cause-and-effect toy, like a pop-up or musical toy that responds when he pushes down a key or lever.

Learning Scheme Give the baby a wooden spoon and a pie tin. Show him how to use the spoon to bang the tin and make an interesting sound.

Batting Give the infant a roly-poly clown toy to bat back and forth.

Hidden Object Partially hide a favorite toy, and see if the infant can find it.

Bell Ringing Give the infant a bell to ring.

Block Tower Build a block tower, and let the baby knock it down.

(continued)

Activities continued

Nine to Fourteen Months

During the 9- to 14-month period, babies develop a new repertoire of problem-solving skills. With increased memory power, they develop the ability to hold in mind the image of an object and to recognize that objects continue to exist even when they are out of sight and out of touch. Because they know that someone can be there even when they cannot see her, older infants will initiate a game of Peek-a-Boo by hiding under a blanket. When the caregiver hides a toy under a blanket, these infants will lift the blanket and joyfully recover the toy.

Dropping Games Give the older infant objects to drop into different-sized containers. Once the infant has mastered this, cut a round hole in the plastic lid of a coffee can and show him how to drop a Ping-Pong ball through the hole.

Ball Play Play a rolling game with the older infant. Say "I roll the ball to Baby, and Baby rolls it back to me."

Reaching Challenge Hold a plastic tray upright and hold a toy behind it. See if the baby tries to reach the toy by reaching around the tray or by trying to go through it.

Hidden Object Game Hide a toy under a small cloth, and let the older infant retrieve it. Next, use two and then three cloths. Try hiding the object in the infant's clothes and inside boxes.

Emptying Game Fill a box with interesting objects. Let the older infant empty the objects from the container.

Objective 2 To recognize expectable sequences in cognitive development in young toddlers and describe materials and activities that will enhance this development

Pedro and his wife, Rosita, shared the care of their daughter, Maria. Pedro was always telling people how easy it was to take care of a baby. But when Maria was 1 year old and walking, he began changing his mind. Maria would not stay in one place. All she wanted to do was toddle around the house, pulling at lamp cords, pulling books and magazines off the shelves, and turning the house upside down. By the time Rosita arrived home at noon to take over with the baby, Pedro was always exhausted. "She's a handful all right," he would admit to his wife as he hurried off to work. ●

Young toddlers are active and curious. They are continually on the go—prodding, exploring, and investigating. Although they often cannot communicate with words, they are curious about everything and trying to find out answers to questions like these:

- What sorts of things are inside Mommy's purse?
- What does the dog's water taste like?

136

- How many stuffed animals can fit inside the toilet?
- For how long can I keep pulling the tissues out of the box?
- What happens when I take the top off the perfume?
- What could I reach if I climbed up on the kitchen stool?

While parents and other caregivers can appreciate the scientific spirit of young toddlers, for the sake of safety and cost containment, their explorations must be limited. The challenge that caregivers face is to provide young toddlers with problem-solving activities that are age appropriate, safe, and feasible. See the Developmental Picture for ideas on how to do that.

The challenge that caregivers face is to provide young toddlers with problem-solving activities that are age appropriate, safe, and feasible.

Developmental Picture

The young toddler (14–24 months):

- Imitates actions that she sees caregivers do, like sweeping, stirring, and hugging a toy animal
- Is beginning to engage in pretend activities, such as going to sleep, eating a cookie, and talking on the phone
- Knows where to find a favorite toy even when it is not in sight
- Can help with simple tasks, such as putting toys away, passing out crackers, and wiping off the table
- Plays with toys in appropriate ways, like putting together a stacking toy, zooming a miniature car across the room, and using a stick to beat a drum or play a xylophone

The caregiver:

- Provides housekeeping materials like dishes, plates, spoons, play food, brooms, and mops that encourage simple pretending
- Initiates pretend play, such as going shopping and serving a pretend meal
- Places toys on shelves in categories—for instance, puts manipulative toys together, picture books together, cars and trucks together
- Asks children for help with simple tasks
- Provides toys that challenge each child

Activities That Encourage Problem Solving

- Play Hide-and-Seek games with objects and toys. Hide favorite toys under one or several hollow blocks, or hide a toy inside your pocket and let the children find it.
- Place large beads inside a large container. The children will have to tip over the container in order to retrieve the beads.

(continued)

Activities continued

- Provide a sloped board for wheel toys. Young toddlers will learn to let the wheel toys roll down the slope.

- Place toys in boxes with different kinds of lids. The children will learn to remove the lids in order to retrieve the toys.

- Give the children pots with lids to play with. See if they can put the right lid on each pot.

- Make a "house" from a large appliance box. Cut a door that the children can open and close and windows that they can peek in or out of.

- See if young toddlers can figure out how to climb into a large box or laundry basket and how to climb out.

- When a young toddler is sitting in a highchair, give her a toy with a ribbon attached to it. The child will toss the toy over the edge of the highchair and pull it up again with the ribbon.

- Demonstrate ways of using hollow blocks for stacking and nesting.

Objective 3

To recognize expectable sequences in cognitive development in older toddlers and describe materials and activities that will enhance this development

Jack, age 2½ years old, walked into his family day care home dragging a pink and black jump rope. "'Nake," he said, as soon as he saw his caregiver. "Oh," she responded. "I see you brought your snake. Is he hungry?" "Yes," said Jack. "Want s'ghetti." "Here's some spaghetti, Snake," the caregiver responded, feeding the snake from an imaginary bowl. "No," said Jack. "Me do it." ●

Older toddlers, like younger toddlers, are learning about their world through exploration. Their needs to explore, to find out, and to do things their own way and by themselves dominate their play activities (see the Developmental Picture on page 139). But despite the fact that 2-year-olds are self-willed and on the go, we can also see the beginning of task-oriented behaviors. The 2-year-old will systematically complete a simple puzzle, sort toys according to color, place a round ball in a shape box, or fill up a pegboard with pegs.

Developmental Picture

The older toddler (2 years):

- Is interested in sorting objects according to qualities such as color and shape
- Can string large beads, stack 3 to 4 blocks to make a tower, and complete an inset puzzle with 4 to 10 pieces
- Recognizes when something is out of place or doesn't belong
- Enjoys playing with toys that present a challenge
- Uses one object to represent a different object (e.g., pretends a block is a cookie)
- Enjoys playing with other children and copying their actions but is probably not ready to share toys

The caregiver:

- Encourages children to sort things into categories
- Encourages pretend play
- Color codes shelves so children can help with pick up
- Provides a variety of materials and toys that encourage exploration, manipulation, and problem solving

Activities That Encourage Problem Solving

Nature Corner Provide trays of shells, rocks, or pine cones of various shapes and sizes. Encourage children to name the objects, to talk about the likes and differences they notice, and to arrange the objects in pleasing ways. Increase the children's interest by adding magnifying glasses.

Exploring Textures Collect materials with a variety of textures, such as fabric swatches, pieces of wood, stones, sandpaper, sponges, jar tops, plastic, and bark. Ask the children to find things that are rough and smooth, heavy and light, hard and soft, thick and thin. The children will have fun finding matches and opposites.

Salt Tray Fill a shallow tray with salt. The children will enjoy drawing circles, lines, and eventually letters in the salt with their fingers.

Nature Walks Increase the fun of taking a nature walk by making nature bracelets. Put a piece of tape, facing sticky side out, around each child's wrist. During the walk, have him stick blades of grass, seeds, flowers, gravel, and bark on the tape. Also collect leaves, rocks, bark, and the like in a bucket. When you get back from the walk, sort the materials and make collages, paint rocks, or do leaf printing.

Sinking and Floating Experiments Put out a tray of objects and a bowl of water. Let each child pick up an object, guess whether it will sink or float in the water, and then try it out. Put all of the objects that sink on one tray and all of the objects that float on another.

(continued)

Activities continued

Color Paddles Using transparent colored paddles and colored gels will give children experience with mixing colors.

Planting Activities Plant seeds in dirt, sponges, or water. Talk about how they grow. Look at the roots, stems, and leaves. A fun toddler activity is to give each child a paper cup, have her punch holes in the bottom, and decorate it with markers or paste scraps of paper to it. Then have each child put dirt in her cup and plant seeds in it. (*Note:* Radish seeds and bean seeds are good choices because they sprout and grow quickly.)

Animals Although it requires extra effort, having classroom animals such as fish, rabbits, or gerbils helps children learn about animals' needs and the responsibility of caring for another living thing.

To recognize expectable sequences in cognitive development in preschool children and describe materials and activities that will enhance this development

Mrs. Push-and-Pull was visiting the Sunny-Isles child care center prior to enrolling her 3-year-old. After taking a tour of the center, in which she saw the art area, the dramatic playhouse, the music and rhythm room, and the block-building corner, Mrs. Push-and-Pull was very ambivalent. She told the center's director, "It's a beautiful center, and the children seem happy and all that, but I want my Angelica to learn academics. She's a very bright child, you realize. She already knows how to count to 10, and she can pick out all the letters in her name."

Mrs. Push-and-Pull is not very different from many parents. She wants her child to do well in school, but she doesn't realize that getting ready for school involves much more than being able to count by rote and to recognize the letters of the alphabet. Real understanding of letters and numbers rests on the understanding of key concepts and the development of thinking skills. See the Developmental Picture on page 141 for more information on the cognitive development of preschoolers.

Understanding Basic Properties of the Real World

Vanessa's grandmother bought her two beautiful new dresses for her third birthday. The day after her birthday, Vanessa wore one of the dresses to preschool. "What a beautiful dress!" her teacher commented as soon as Vanessa walked into the room. "Red dress," Vanessa repeated. "That's right," said the teacher. "It's a red dress. You are learning your colors."

140

Developmental Picture

The preschool child (3–5 years):

- Is eager and excited about learning new things and making new discoveries
- Is interested in finding out how things work, what things change into, and how they can be transformed
- Is interested in nature and natural phenomena
- Is discovering how things are alike and different and what things belong together
- Is interested and ready to learn about counting and creating sets of objects up to 10
- Is able to understand concepts and make generalizations and is ready for a thematic curriculum
- Enjoys sorting things and making collections
- Tries out different ways of making objects move, change, and fit together
- Learns from watching adults and other children and imitates what he sees
- Remembers things that happened in the past and anticipates what will happen in the future

The caregiver:

- Provides opportunities for children to learn through hands-on experience
- Provides children the time and space to manipulate, explore, and experiment
- Provides opportunities for children to learn about things outside their immediate experience
- Allows children to try things in their own ways, to make mistakes, and to try again
- Provides children with a variety of experiences with plants and animals
- Provides children with opportunities to learn about counting, measuring, and arranging items into sets by size and shape
- Introduces familiar themes, such as transportation, families, weather, and building things

The next day, Vanessa wore the other new dress to school. "Red dress," Vanessa repeated, as she proudly showed her dress to her teacher. "No, Vanessa," said her teacher. "It's not a red dress. This dress is blue." Vanessa was disappointed and confused. The last time she called a new dress "red," the teacher was happy. Today she called a new dress "red," and the teacher was sad. ●

Vanessa's problem with learning color names is a very common one. She can remember the word *red* and connect it with *dress*, but she does not know what aspect of the dress *red* stands for. The guess she made is perfectly logical from her point of view. The most special thing about her dress is its newness, so *red*, she decided, means "new."

Before children can name the color of an object, they have to figure out what is meant by the concept of color. Actually, color is a complicated concept involving several insights:

- *Red, green, blue,* and so on are all names of colors.
- Color is a property of objects, just as size and shape are properties of objects.

- The answer to "What color is it?" must be one of the color names. It cannot be a size name, such as *big*, or a shape name, such as *square.*
- Colors that look different sometimes have the same name (*light blue* and *dark blue*), while colors that look similar sometimes have different names (*dark blue* and *purple*).

Categorizing objects according to color is one of the many ways in which young children learn about real-world objects. In this section, we are concerned with the development of thinking skills that help children acquire concepts about the physical world. These skills include sorting objects into categories, placing objects in a logical sequence, learning about number relationships, discovering relationships, and learning concepts about science and social studies.

Sorting Objects into Categories

In a manner of speaking, even the very youngest infants categorize their experiences. Newborn infants are programmed to discriminate between voices and other sounds. By 6 weeks of age, they respond differently to voices, showing a preference for the sound of their mother's voice over the voice of a stranger. During the infancy period, these sorting skills become more sophisticated. Children learn to recognize familiar faces, a skill that requires comparing a new face with an earlier memory of a face.

Preschool children continue to develop more sophisticated sorting skills. As they play with objects and look at pictures, they put like objects together and discover pictures that match. Sometimes, this ability to recognize a match creates a problem in the family. The toddler may make a fuss if the cup he is drinking from doesn't match the other cups or if a sibling receives a present that does not exactly match his own present.

When children have become proficient in matching objects and pictures, they are ready to sort objects on the basis of their properties, such as color and shape. We see children group objects that are the same color but have different shapes, and we see them group objects like toy cars even though their colors and sizes are different. In performing a sorting task, children may start off with the notion of color or shape in mind but lose it as the task continues. In other words, children may begin by putting red objects in a pile but then add a green triangle because it looks like the red triangle that they just placed in the pile.

We have been talking so far about sorting objects according to the way they look. It is also possible to sort objects into nonvisual categories, such as where they belong, how they are used, and what they are called. Some toys belong in the house, and some toys have to stay outside. Some food goes on the shelf, and some food goes in the refrigerator. Some clothes are for cold days, and some clothes are for hot days. Some kinds of foods are called *fruits*, and some kinds of foods are called *vegetables.* Through everyday experience, children continually learn new ways of categorizing objects and events.

Activities to Develop Sorting Skills

Matching

Matching Objects

Materials: A cardboard tray with pairs of small objects (small cars, blocks, little people, balls).

Procedure: Pick up one object from the tray. Ask the child to find another object from the tray that is just the same. If the child selects an object that is different, say, "That one is not the same. I will help you find one that is just the same. Here it is. We found one that matches." To do this with a small group, give each child in the group one of a pair of like objects. Then, pass the tray around to the group. Let each child select an object that is the same as the one he or she already has.

Matching Pictures

Materials: Make pairs of matching cards by cutting out two pictures from two identical catalogs. (That is, cut out the same picture from each catalog.) Laminate or cover each card with clear contact paper.

Procedure: Follow the same procedure as in the previous activity. When several children have the concept of matching, place trays with sets of pictures or objects within reach on a shelf so that the children can play alone.

Sorting by Color

Activity 1

Materials: A pegboard with pegs of different colors.

Procedure: Let the children help you arrange the pegs so that each row is a different color. (If the 3-year-olds have difficulty with the idea of making a row, cover most of the pegboard so that only one row is visible at a time.) When the children have become adept at arranging pegs in color rows, play Guess What's Wrong and Guess What's Missing with individual children or small groups. In Guess What's Wrong, have the children close their eyes and then switch two of the pegs; have the children open their eyes and then guess which two have been moved. In Guess What's Missing, remove one of the pegs from one of the color rows and have the children guess what color the missing peg is.

Activity 2

Materials: Slip-on clothespins, a can or box, colored tape or construction paper.

Procedure: Cover a section of the rim of the can or box with different-colored materials, and then paint the clothespins to match. Have the children place the clothespins around the rim, matching the colors.

Activity 3

Materials: Counting bears, milk cartons or small boxes, construction paper.

Procedure: Make red, green, yellow, and blue 'houses" by covering small milk cartons or boxes with construction paper. Cut a door in each house. Have the children help the different-colored teddy bears find their "own" houses.

(continued)

Activities continued

Activity 4

Procedure: Take the children on a "color walk" through the classroom or outdoors. Have them point out and name all the things that are blue, all the things that are red, and so on.

Classification

Activity 1

Materials: Two sheets of tagboard, one cut in a circle and the other cut in a square. Catalog cutouts of round things and square things (plates, clocks, boxes, blocks).

Procedure: Give the children turns finding round things and square things to place on the circle and the square.

Activity 2

Materials: Cut out a large tagboard hand and foot. Cut out pictures from magazines of things that go on a hand (gloves, mittens, rings) and things that go on feet (socks, stockings, shoes, and boots).

Procedure: Let the children place the cutouts on the hand or the foot.

Activity 3

Materials: Plastic farm animals and zoo animals and a sandbox.

Procedure: Help the children build a "farm" on one side of the sandbox and a "zoo" on the other side. Let the children place each animal in either the zoo or the farm.

Activity 4

Materials: Make books that are shaped to represent concepts (a truck could stand for transportation, a fruit bowl could stand for fruit, and a suitcase could stand for clothes). Cut corresponding shapes from construction paper to create book covers. Bind the books by lacing them with yarn, by stapling them, or by using paper fasteners.

Procedure: Let the children sort through old magazines and catalogs to find pictures for their books.

Activity 5

Procedure: Make a classroom "museum" to display objects that the children have collected or made. These can be rocks, shells, leaves, seedpods, toy cars or toy animals, clay creations, photographs, jar tops, small balls, bead necklaces, or anything else that the children find intriguing. Have the children work together to arrange their objects in boxes or on shelves so that similar things are grouped together. Help the children label the displays.

Discovering Order and Sequence

At the same time that children are learning to put things into categories, they are also learning about order. A child who sorts a box of buttons into small buttons, medium buttons, and big buttons is also learning to put things in order according to size. When we think about ordering, we usually think about ordering in space according to size or ordering in time according to clock units or calendar units. Actually, any quality we can think of—any adjective we can use to modify a noun—implies the possibility of ordering. A heavy object can be *somewhat heavy*, *heavy*, or *very heavy*. A flower can be *pretty*, *very pretty*, or *beautiful*. An odor can be *mild*, *strong*, or *overpowering*.

When preschool children first place objects in order of size, their sorting may be accidental. For instance, they may push three blocks together in ascending order and decide that it looks like a staircase. Children are able to recognize order by the way something appears before they understand the logic behind it. Understanding the logic of order means being able to recognize that each element has more of a certain quality than the element that precedes it and less of the quality than the object that comes after it. Before children can understand the logic of order, they need to have many different opportunities to arrange objects according to different dimensions.

Activities to Develop Ordering Skills

Activity 1

Materials: Stacking blocks or a stack of cans. (Make sure there are no rough edges.)

Procedure: Demonstrate ways of stacking the blocks or cans, or make a tall tower by beginning with the largest block or can.

Activity 2

Materials: A set of stacking rings on a spindle.

Procedure: Demonstrate how to place the rings on the spindle so that the larger rings go on the bottom and the smaller rings go on the top.

Activity 3

Materials: Table blocks of varying length.

Procedure: Demonstrate several different ways of building a block staircase.

Activity 4

Materials: Objects that involve matching and ordering (sets of cups and saucers of different sizes, plastic bottles with lids, dolls of different sizes with doll clothes).

Procedure: Allow children to play freely with these objects. They will learn to recognize that the smallest cup fits on the smallest saucer, the next-sized cup fits on the next-sized saucer, and so on.

Activity 5

Materials: Buy or make puzzles that require sequencing of items according to size. You can make puzzles that require double sequencing. For example, use tagboard to create a puzzle with dolls and ladders. The smallest doll gets the highest ladder.

Procedure: Let the children complete the puzzle by trial and error. After a while, they will recognize the appropriate order of items.

Learning Number Skills

Johnny, a sturdy 3-year-old, stood up in the middle of the room and slowly looked around. Grandma and Grandpa smiled encouragingly. Mother nodded her head and said, "Go on, Johnny, let's hear you count." Johnny counted loudly to 10. When he finished, there were kisses, hugs, applause, and extravagant praise. Johnny laughed delightedly.

The next day at his child care classroom, Johnny had another counting experience. "That's right, Johnny: one, two, three," the teacher said as he pointed to each cookie on the plate. "You have three *cookies." Johnny picked up the cookie the teacher had labeled "three" and proudly carried it over to the table, repeating, "Three! Three!" "No, no, Johnny," the teacher added. "That is* one *cookie." Johnny was confused. He looked back and saw that cookie number "one" was still on the plate.* ●

> *Counting is an enormously complicated concept and thus takes a long time for children to master.*

Counting is an enormously complicated concept and thus takes a long time for children to master. When a child has learned to recite numbers (count by rote), he has taken the first of many steps. We have already talked about the ways in which young children develop concepts about the physical world by sorting and ordering. A numeral, such as *3*, has two meanings. On the one hand, it refers to a set of three items. This is called its *cardinal meaning*. On the other hand, it stands for the third item in a sequence. This is called its *ordinal meaning*.

When children learn to sort items into groups and order objects along a particular dimension, they are gaining the basic insights that will help them learn to count. In the story of Johnny and the cookies, we see how easy it is for a child to be confused about the ordinal and cardinal meanings of numbers. An even more common problem that children have is to move from counting by rote to actually counting objects. Counting by rote or learning a number chant is easy for children. It is a social game that adults enjoy playing with them. Counting objects, however, involves a critical concept that is difficult for children to grasp: one-to-one correspondence. *One-to-one correspondence* means that each object or item is counted once and only once. If the teacher has to help the child count by placing the child's finger on each item as it is counted, the child has not yet learned one-to-one correspondence.

Activities to Develop Number Skills

Learning to Count by Rote Singing number songs or counting as a group in the classroom teaches the child counting order. Until the child has learned the other counting skills, it is better not to teach him a counting rhyme or chant that goes beyond 10.

Learning One-to-One Correspondence Give children turns passing out cookies or napkins. Help them understand that each child gets one and only one cookie or napkin. Give children colored counting bears and colored blocks, and ask them to match one bear with one block.

Matching Numerals to Sets Cut out pictures that have several objects in them. Glue each picture on a large card. At the bottom of the card, make a circle and glue a washer on it. Make matching circles with numerals on them and magnets on the backs. Have the children count the objects and match the correct circle to each picture.

Number Puzzles To help children understand the ordinal meaning of numbers, give them practice by filling a bead counter. Provide one bead of one color, two of a second color, three of the third color, and so on. When children first start working with a bead stacker, you may want to paint the stacks to match the beads.

Match Up Begin a row of block "houses." Ask the children to put one roof on top of each house or one tree beside each house.

Creating Sets Let the children create books or posters based on sets. A book of the "two set" would include pictures of things that come in two's (two eyes, a pair of shoes, a cup and saucer, a set of twins).

Go Fishing Make a "fishing pole" from a dowel, a stick, or the small cardboard tube from a coat hanger. Make the line from string or yarn and the hook from a pipe cleaner. Glue a magnet on the hook. Make different colors of construction paper "fish," and put a staple or paper clip on each one. On the back of each fish, write a number. Have the children take turns "catching fish" and calling out the numbers of the fish they have caught. Then let each child place her fish on the correct counter in the "fish market." The "counter" is a piece of tagboard with pockets on the bottom that are color coded to match the fish. For example, if the fish with the numeral 3 on it is blue, then it is placed in the third pocket, which is also blue.

String Along Hang a clothesline low enough for the children to reach easily. Provide clothespins and 10 numbered cards (a different number on each card). Have the children hang up the cards in order from 1 to 10.

Take Your Share Pass around a tray of crackers or a basket of crayons. Ask each child to take, for instance, three crackers or four crayons.

Crowd Control Post a sign in each interest area or play center indicating the number of children who can play there—for example, a sign with the numeral 4 and four dots or stick figures.

Hide and Count Play guessing games with small groups of children. Put down five or more chips, and let the children count them. Then, have the children close their eyes and remove several chips. Ask them how many chips you are hiding in your hand. Give the children a chance to play the game with you as the guesser, and let them play the game with each other.

(continued)

Activities continued

Number Talk Use numbers and number concepts in everyday conversations with children. Talk about how many days are left until a special event, how many children are usually in the group and how many are missing on a particular day, how many places to set when guests are expected, the shapes and sizes of blocks and buildings, and how long a trip will take. Have the children help you count out crackers for snack, put the blocks away in order of size, pour in the right amount of each ingredient in a recipe, and measure an area for a new carpet or bulletin board.

Everyday Math Set up a play "store," "fast-food restaurant," "veterinary clinic," or "gas station." Include a cash register and appropriate measuring instruments, such as a scale, a yardstick, a tape measure, a thermometer, or a tire gauge. Introduce number concepts and problems when you join the children's play.

Sing-Along Make songs and finger plays about numbers part of your regular routine. When children have become proficient at counting, introduce rhymes that involve counting by 2, like "Two, four, six, eight, who do we appreciate?"

Pattern and Counting Books Include in your library counting books; books about size and shape; books with hidden, camouflaged, unusual, or out of place objects to find; and books with repeating or cumulative (add an element each time) patterns. Encourage the children to read these books with you and with each other, and have them make their own variants of favorite books.

Algebra 1 Teach children addition by giving them real-life problems to solve. For instance, at snacktime, when six children are sitting around the table, provide just four crackers. Ask the children if there are enough crackers. When the children say "No," ask them how many more crackers are needed. If they answer "2," then say, "You are right. We have six children, so we need six crackers. Four crackers plus two more crackers equals six crackers." If they answer "5," then take out one more cracker and pass out the five crackers. Then say, "Oops, I have *six* children. I need one more cracker. Four plus two equals six."

Discovering Relationships

The more experience children have with manipulating real-world objects, the more proficient they become at putting objects into categories. At the same time, manipulating real objects helps children recognize ways in which certain objects relate to other objects. For instance, a child playing with a toy car and a plank discovers that the speed at which the car rolls is affected by the angle of the plank. A child bouncing a ball discovers that the height of the rebound is related to the force of his downward throw.

Spatial Relationships

Children learn about spatial relationships by fitting things together and taking them apart. Puzzles, wooden blocks, interlocking blocks, and toys that come apart and fit back together are all useful materials for developing this concept. Here are some activities you can do:

- Provide materials in the house area that can be put together and taken apart—jars and lids, several sizes of plastic containers and tops, pots and pans with matching lids.

- As a class project, draw a large diagram of the room, building, or playground. The class should decide where to place cutouts representing furniture and equipment. During the discussion, use some of the following words: *next to, beside, between, in front of, behind, close to, far away, under, over, up, down.*

- As a small-group activity, give each child an empty milk carton or small box, a scissors, glue, and a tray of scraps to decorate with—fabric, construction paper, tissue paper, wallpaper, sandpaper, and so on. Let each child decorate his box as desired and then describe to the group what he has done. You may have to help by asking some questions, such as "Did you put anything inside?" and "What is next to the red paper?"

Science and Social Studies Concepts

We have talked so far about very concrete ways of sorting, ordering, and exploring spatial relationships. Performing these concrete activities lays the groundwork for more abstract thinking in such areas as science and social studies.

Sparking a Child's Interest in Science

Young children often develop intense interests in scientific information. For example, they may become interested in dinosaurs and want to learn all of their names, be fascinated with stars and planets, or want to learn all there is to know about snakes. It is a good idea to make available a variety of science picture books and nature guides in your classroom activity areas to spark and build on children's interests. Encourage children to learn by making direct observations and predictions as well as by looking at books. For example, the children might plant seeds, make drawings of what they think the plants will look like under and above the ground, and then make books of drawings showing how the plants look at different stages.

When we talk about *sorting*, *ordering*, and *counting*, we are describing the basic building blocks of a science curriculum. Scientists categorize plants, animals, minerals, and other physical phenomena according to shared attributes. They discover the order in which things happen in time or occur in space. They discover the ways in which one set of phenomena or events relates to another set of phenomena or events. As preschool children are given opportunities to sort and manipulate objects and materials, they are learning the basic skills of the scientist.

There is one aspect of scientific thinking that we have not yet mentioned: Scientists use what they know to discover what they do not know. They develop hypotheses and then carry out experiments to see if their hypotheses are correct. In other words, scientists continue to ask *if/then* kinds of questions. If/then questions are difficult for young children to ask in an abstract way, but they do ask these questions in a concrete way. The child who places the plank at more of an angle to see if the marble will slide down faster is asking an if/then kind of question. A scientific environment for young children provides many different opportunities for if/then investigations.

Suggested Materials to Invite Scientific Investigation

- A water table containing funnels, sieves, a water pump, see-through containers of different sizes and shapes, ladles, basters, clear plastic tubing, soap bubbles, food coloring, soda straws
- A balance scale with dishes of small objects that can be placed on the pans
- A standing magnifying glass with a basket next to it full of interesting materials to look at (shells, rocks, cones, bark, nuts, postage stamps)
- A large magnet with a basket of items—some that stick to the magnets and some that do not
- A water tub with a tray of objects—some that float and some that do not
- Different kinds of clay, play dough, and plaster—some that get hard and some that stay soft
- Toy cars and small balls; planks and tubes; blocks that can be used to raise one end of the track
- Different colors and kinds of paint
- Unusual materials to make like "oobleck" (cornstarch, water, and food coloring); soap-suds clay (beat ¾ cup soap powder and 1 tablespoon warm water with a hand mixer); and glue paint (Elmer's Glue mixed with water and food coloring)
- Books and pictures
- Live animals
- Shells, leaves, rocks, sticks, and birds' nests

Sparking a Child's Interest in Social Studies

Sometimes, when we think of *social studies*, we think of geography, history, and political science. Young children cannot think about things that are remote in time and space, nor can they think about things that involve abstract principles and systems. They are interested in the things that are happening and the people that are making things happen in their immediate world.

The social studies curriculum, like the science curriculum, must deal with the concrete and the immediate. It must provide children with opportunities to categorize people and events, to find out about the orders of things, and to discover relationships. It must build on students' knowledge of their own families and communities to teach them about other people, places, and times. Through song and celebration, social studies should help children appreciate their own heritages and those of others.

The following sections provide some sample themes and activities that can be included in a social studies curriculum.

Activities for a Family Unit

A child's family—no matter what its size or composition—is the most important thing in her life. Given that, a social studies unit on the family is always appropriate.

Create Family Albums Let children bring in pictures of different members of their families. Use them to create family albums in which different-colored pages are used to show different generations. Construct a family tree using family pictures.

Make Individual Books An *All About My Family* book can contain pictures of things the family does together (plays ball, eats dinner, watches TV). You can include holidays the family shares and places the family goes together (the supermarket, a restaurant, the beach).

Bring Families into the Classroom Place photographs of the children and their families where the children can study them. Ask families to bring in recipes for special foods as well as songs, nursery rhymes, games, and other elements of their heritages that they would like to share with the class.

Study Families around the World Collect pictures and books that show families from different cultures and different parts of the world. Choose pictures that show ordinary events, such as eating, sleeping, taking children to school, styling hair, washing clothes, and reading together. Have the children identify similarities and differences among the pictures. For example, you might have several pictures of a child helping a mother, each picture showing two people carrying food. The children might notice the differences in foods, containers, and clothing. If you use cutouts from calendars and magazines, the children can make books or bulletin board displays showing how families are alike and different.

Build a Multicultural Library Be sure that your library includes books that reflect the children's family heritages as well as books about families with different structures and cultures.

Activities for a Transportation Unit

Children are very interested in all kinds of vehicles, and so a unit on transportation will provide limitless opportunities for interesting activities.

Truck Day Invite people with different kinds of trucks to come to your school. Talk about ways in which the trucks differ from each other, and help the children discover reasons for the differences (e.g., some trucks have double sets of back wheels; some have attachments like snowplows, trailer hitches, and flashing lights).

Field Trips Take a bus ride, a trolley ride, or a train ride with the children. Visit an airport, a bus terminal, or a train station. Take a walk around the school, and see how many different kinds of transportation you see. Did you see bicycles, motor-cycles, buses, delivery trucks, moving vans, and garbage trucks?

Pretend Play Create an "airport" in the classroom in the imaginative play corner. Include as props a scale, suitcases, tickets, luggage tags, purses, wallets, money, and so on. You might also add a "plane" (which can be as simple as a row of chairs or pillows, with a joystick or steering wheel and painted control panel for the pilot), some tools for the mechanics, food and trays for the flight attendants, and a wagon to bring gas, luggage, and supplies to the plane. Read the children books about airplanes, and help them role-play airplane trips.

Music Time Sing songs about different kinds of transportation, such as "The Wheels on the Bus," "Row, Row, Row Your Boat," "I've Been Working on the Railroad," "Yankee Doodle," and "Jingle Bells."

Craft Time Make trucks out of cracker boxes by having the children glue on wheels, cut out or paste on windows, and make license plates. Construct a "train" in the classroom using large cardboard boxes. Put chairs in the boxes so children can sit on the train, and cut out windows the children can look out as they sing a train song or pretend to take a train ride.

Mural Cover a wall with large sheets of paper, and draw some roads on it. Have the children make or cut out pictures of vehicles, houses, stores, gas stations, and other places in the "city." Help them glue the pictures onto the mural.

Book Corner Make transportation books in which each child cuts out pictures of trucks, boats, airplanes, cars, and the like and glues them onto the pages. Or make trip books that show pictures of various places and the kinds of transportation you would take to get to them. Read these books along with library books about transportation, trips, and vehicles.

Other Ideas for Social Studies Units

The possibilities for developing social studies themes that are interesting and important to children are almost endless. Social studies themes may be developed around the following:

- The places people live
- The kinds of stores we have in our city
- The holidays we celebrate
- All kinds of machines
- What happens to a letter
- Pets and other animals

- The jobs people do
- Places we like to visit (the farm, the beach, the zoo, etc.)
- Babies
- Things that go up in the air
- Different kinds of clothes

Once you have decided to develop a theme for your classroom, invite the children and their parents to help you think of different ways of expanding it.

Objective 5 — To learn how to create a preschool environment that encourages exploration, curiosity, and critical thinking

Annabelle had just enrolled Amelia, her 6-month-old infant, in the College-Bound Academy for preschool children. Annabelle was excited about the school and couldn't wait for her husband to come home so she could tell him all about it. "It is an unbelievable place," she told her husband, Peter, as soon as he walked in the door. "Even the 3-year-olds can count to 100 and name every state in the union! It's so cute to see those little tots sitting quietly at their desks trying to copy a big 'A.'" But Peter was not impressed. "What happened to good old-fashioned play?" he asked.

When parents like Annabelle and Peter can't agree on the choice of a preschool, the problem may well be that they have different ideas about how children learn. Annabelle believes that her daughter should spend her time in preschool learning academic skills that are taught by the teacher. Peter believes that his daughter should be playing in school and discovering the world on her own.

> *The learning environment created in a preschool is a reflection of the school's philosophy.*

The learning environment created in a preschool is a reflection of the school's philosophy. A preschool with a *behavioral orientation* views children as consumers of knowledge. The teacher is responsible for presenting the children with carefully designed lessons in accordance with a preset curriculum. The room arrangement and the materials placed in the classroom also are determined by this curriculum. In contrast, a preschool with a *developmental* or *constructivist orientation* views children as active learners who construct knowledge through their own activities. The teacher designs a classroom environment that invites the children to explore, experiment, and make their own discoveries.

All About Child Care and Early Education is built on the philosophy that children are active learners who will be happier and learn more when they have many opportunities to explore materials with other children and to talk about concepts with teachers. Children who have had preschool experiences in which exploration and discovery are encouraged will do better when they enter first grade than children who have attended a preschool with a highly structured academic curriculum that allows little time for play.

However, simply having interesting materials to be engaged with does not ensure meaningful learning. You, as a teacher, have a critical part to play:

- Help the children think about what they are doing. Asking well-timed, open-ended questions can focus a child's observation or help make a concept understandable.

- Provide words while the children are exploring materials. You might describe what they are doing or name the items they are using. Doing so builds the vocabulary that supports a child's acquisition of concepts.

- Carefully select the materials that will be made available for exploration. For example, change the dramatic play area into an "office" by adding interesting props like file cabinets, folders, and briefcases; add office supplies to the writing area. When discarded office machinery (keyboards, etc.) is added to the science area, children can explore what it might be like to work in an office and gain that conceptual understanding.

Conducting planned small-group learning activities is another way to ensure opportunities for critical thinking and learning. During activity time, one teacher can offer a special learning activity for a small number of children. The type of small-group learning activity provided depends on the age of the children and the curriculum that underlies your program. Many ideas for small-group activities are presented throughout this book.

To learn techniques for introducing meaningful themes into preschool classrooms

Several teachers from the Wee Care Preschool were meeting informally after school. Their director had just distributed a list of themes that she wanted the teachers to introduce into all the preschool classrooms. She made it clear that she wanted them to incorporate these themes into all *the learning centers: reading, art, music and movement, science, manipulatives, blocks, and dramatic play. The list of themes included All About Me, Far-Away Places, Plants and Animals, My Five Senses, and Imagination.*

The teachers thought their director's notion about themes had merit, but when they tried to figure out how to apply it, they found themselves getting silly. "I have a great idea for teaching kids about smell!" one teacher exclaimed. "First, we'll spray each of the learning centers with different-scented spray bottles. Then we'll blindfold the children and let them smell their way to the learning center they decide to go to." "That idea," a second teacher commented, "absolutely stinks!" By this time, all the teachers were laughing so hard that they couldn't do any more work. ●

Educators have different opinions about the value of themes in a preschool classroom. Those who are strong proponents of themes give the following arguments:

- Teaching around a theme is a way to help children grasp a new concept.
- Using themes is a way to integrate the curriculum, as children are introduced to the same concept in different contexts or learning centers. The experiences they have in different learning centers build on each other, and the whole becomes greater than the sum of its parts.
- Using a theme is a way to introduce new materials and activities in each interest center.
- Themes provide a way to involve parents in the classroom and to strengthen the bonds between home and school.
- When learning is based on a theme, children can connect the experiences they have outside the classroom with those they have inside the classroom.
- Themes give teachers a way to express their own creativity.
- Children have fun with themes.

Educators who are opposed to themes give the following reasons:

- Using the same theme in every interest area is silly and restrictive. For instance, there is no good reason to believe that children are going to learn more about life on a farm because they are singing "Old MacDonald Had a Farm" or putting a cow puzzle together.
- Themes are usually selected by the teacher or the director, with no input from the children.
- Themes can interfere with learning. For instance, if the teacher has been using Montessori beads to teach a sequence of counting skills, changing from counting beads to counting miniature cows may be distracting rather than productive.
- The use of themes is likely to involve take-home craft projects in which the teacher does most of the work. Instead of engaging in process art, in which children are free to use art materials to express ideas and feelings, they are taught how to put a craft together that relates to the theme of the week.

Most early childhood educators do not take an all-or-nothing approach to the use of themes. Rather, they believe that themes make good sense as long as they are used properly. Here are some of the criteria that many teachers use in making decisions about themes:

- A theme should be built on the spontaneous interests of the children.
- The theme should not have a predetermined end date. The children should be allowed to investigate a theme for as long as their interest in it lasts.
- Themes should be applied only in those areas of the curriculum in which there is a natural fit.

Once a theme has been selected, it is up to the teacher to discover different ways in which it can be expanded. A theme like the wind, for instance, could lead to an investigation of what causes the wind to blow, a creative movement activity like pretending you are taking a walk with a strong wind blowing in your face, or an art activity such as drawing a picture of clothes on a line blowing in the wind. The children also could experiment with blowing soap bubbles, making waves in the water table by blowing through a tube, flying paper airplanes, throwing light scarves into the air, making wind with a fan, blowing into and across bottles of different sizes, making wind chimes, and watching clouds on still and windy days. Their investigations might lead to new themes about flight, weather, or musical instruments.

(Additional ideas for themes are suggested in the discussion of social studies units in Objective 4 of this chapter.)

Additional Resources about Cognitive Development

Bredekamp, S., & Copple, C. (Eds.). (1997). *Developmentally appropriate practice in early childhood programs* (Rev. ed.). Washington, DC: NAEYC.

Bronson, M. (1995). *The right stuff for children 0–8: Selecting play materials to support development.* Washington, DC: NAEYC.

Copley, J. (2000). *The young child and mathematics.* Washington, DC: NAEYC.

Curtis, D., & Carter, M. (1996). *Reflecting children's lives: A handbook for planning child-centered curriculum.* St. Paul, MN: Redleaf Press.

Hohman, M., & Weikart, D. (1995). *Educating young children.* Ypsilanti, MI: High/Scope Press.

Lally, R., Griffin, A., Fenichel, E., Segal, M., Szanton, E., & Weissbourd, B. (1995). *Caring for infants and toddlers in groups: Developmentally appropriate practice.* Washington, DC: Zero to Three.

Meisels, S., Marsden, D., & Stetson, C. (2000). *Winning ways to learn: 600 great ideas for children.* New York: Goddard Press.

Communication

Chapter 6

Overview

Communication is the sharing of thoughts, feelings, and ideas through language or through nonverbal means such as gestures, facial expressions, and art.

Rationale

Language, a uniquely human accomplishment, is the basis of much of our thinking as well as our communication. It is the primary way we receive the accumulated wisdom of humankind and communicate with people remote to us in space and time. Language also provides the way we communicate with ourselves, recalling past events, working out problems, planning ahead, and keeping our impulses in check. We urge children to think before they act, just as we urge children to "use their words" to control the behaviors of others. We think about school as the time when children learn reading, writing, and arithmetic. We can think about preschool as the time when children develop the language skills underlying these school-related achievements.

Language development begins at birth, as the baby and her caregivers communicate with gazes, sounds, and touches. Teachers and caregivers provide children with many opportunities to learn communication skills, to use verbal and nonverbal means to communicate their own ideas and feelings, and to understand the ideas and feelings of others.

Objectives

1. To recognize the relationship between language development and real-world experiences

2. To describe the expectable sequence of communication skills in infants and suggest ways to support their development

3. To describe the expectable sequence of communication skills in young toddlers and suggest ways to support their development

4. To describe the expectable sequence of language skills in older toddlers and suggest ways to support their development

5. To describe the expectable sequence of language skills in preschool children and suggest ways to support their development

6. To learn ways of reading to children that encourage active participation and engender a love of books

7. To describe early literacy skills and suggest activities that promote them

8. To describe the small-muscle skills that are used in writing and suggest activities that develop these skills and provide children with opportunities to practice writing

9. To select books that foster empathy, promote prosocial behavior, counteract bias, and support bilingualism

Supporting Communication and Language Development

Objective 1

To recognize the relationship between language development and real-world experiences

Three-year-old Jennifer was having a family dinner with her parents, grandparents, and great-grandparents and tuned in to the adults' conversation about the approaching hurricane. She heard the following comments: "If it doesn't change course, the eye will pass right over us." "But they say it might turn north and miss us completely." "We'd better stock up anyway." "Cheese is good for hurricanes."

All of the sudden, Jennifer began to cry. She sobbed, "I'm scared of the hurricane." "Do you know what a hurricane is?" her mother asked. "Yes," said Jennifer with conviction. "It's a one-eyed monster that eats cheese and doesn't know where it's going!" ●

Having no experience with hurricanes, Jennifer put together a logical explanation based on her prior knowledge. Like a typical preschooler, she interpreted words literally and personified the storm.

The hardest part of learning language is not learning how to repeat a word but learning the connection between the spoken word and a real-world object or event. The toddler learns to say *dog* when the family dog licks his face or takes a biscuit from him. After a while, the toddler will use the word *dog* to stand for any member of a category of animals that have some of the features of his dog. He may use the word *dog* to label all the four-legged animals he sees, whether they are dogs, horses, or elephants. Later, he will refine this category and reserve the label *dog* for animals that have four legs, bark, and wag their tails.

> *The hardest part of learning language is not learning how to repeat a word but learning the connection between the spoken word and a real-world object or event.*

In order to learn a language, a child must first grasp the concept that a word can stand for a particular object, person, or action or for a category of objects, people, or actions. In "toddlerspeak," *car* can stand for Daddy's car, any car, or any vehicle with wheels. *Daddy* can stand for his father or for every other man, whether or not he is somebody's father. *Down* can stand for "put me down" or where the ball went after it rolled off the highchair. Children can also learn ways of refining a category by using descriptive words. A child might use *big dog* to label a dog that is bigger than his own dog or a four-legged animal that is bigger than a dog. He might say *box juice* for juice that comes in boxes or *Mommy paper* for papers he is not supposed to touch.

By the time a child is 2 years old, he is likely to speak in short sentences that describe a relationship between a familiar object and action or between a person, object, and action or location, such as *Baby crying* and *Daddy bye-bye car.* Before long, the child will acquire a much larger vocabulary that includes nouns, verbs, pronouns, adjectives, adverbs, and prepositions. He will also learn to use language for many different purposes: to request, direct, ask questions, describe, joke, talk to himself, or invite interaction. But throughout the preschool years, the language a child uses and the concepts he is able to grasp are built on what he sees and experiences in real life, in picture books, and in stories that he can imagine and visualize.

Objective 2

To describe the expectable sequence of communication skills in infants and suggest ways to support their development

> *Gina, a teenage mother, had just dropped her baby off at the Cuddle and Croon Child Care Center and was talking to her friend Gilda. "Gilda, you'd never believe it," Gina muttered. "You know that child care center where I drop my kid? Well, they're a little touched in the head. There are two old ladies who sit there holding the little babies in their laps and talking to them. 'How are you today, sweetie pie? Should we play a little game of Patty-Cake?' I bet they think those babies understand them. Just listening to them is a blast!"* ●

Despite Gina's uncomplimentary remarks, the caregivers at Cuddle and Croon have a very good understanding of language development in young children. They realize that infants, from the moment of birth, tune in and attend to language. They know that even before babies can understand words, they can be soothed or excited by different tones of voice. They know that the high-pitched "baby talk" or "parentese" that adults tend to use with babies is especially engaging. They recognize that in the first year of life, infants are developing critical communication skills—distinguishing and repeating the sounds of their language, carrying on babble-type conversations, and recognizing the difference between a playful tone and a serious tone that means "Stop." They realize that in the second and third year, babies who have been involved in a lot of back and forth conversation will burst into language, understand single words and phrases, and speak in one-word, two-word, and finally three- or four-word sentences.

> *Even before babies understand words, they can be soothed or excited by different tones of voice.*

Beginning at birth, infants have a real repertoire of communication skills, both verbal and nonverbal. Infants communicate through cries, coos, facial expressions, movements, and autonomic signs. Caregivers who know an infant well can read the messages in the baby's cries. They can differentiate between the rhythmic, intense cry that means "I'm hungry," the sharp cry that means "I'm in pain," and the whiney cry that means "I'm not comfortable." They can also read a baby's autonomic signs. They know that when a baby hiccups, tenses her body, tightens her lips, screws up her face, stiffens her body, or curls her toes, the baby is saying "I am overstimulated or overwhelmed and need to be soothed." During the first year, the baby will learn ways of communicating through purposeful nonverbal signs. The baby will lift her arms to signal "Pick me up," push away your hands to signal "I don't want that," point with one finger to tell you to look at something, or turn or shake her head to refuse what you are offering. As caregivers interpret and respond to a baby's signs, the baby learns the value of conversational exchanges (see the Developmental Picture).

Developmental Picture

The young infant (0–9 months):

- From the moment of birth, seeks and responds to human contact
- Is capable of communicating feelings, wants, and needs through smiles, cries, and gestures
- Initiates "conversations" with others in a back and forth manner, using looks and babbling sounds
- Signals the need for a break from the conversation by turning or looking away
- Enjoys cooing, babbling, and changing pitch and loudness
- Recognizes familiar voices by looking toward the speaker or quieting and seeking eye contact
- Has different-sounding cries that indicate hunger, distress, and other needs and wants
- Is soothed by a quiet, comforting voice and alerted by a playful voice

The caregiver:

- Provides every infant with many opportunities to engage in face-to-face conversational exchanges
- Recognizes that a high-pitched voice alerts the infant and that a lullaby calms her

- Recognizes and responds appropriately to the infant's cries and calls
- Uses caregiving routines as opportunities to talk with the infant in a calm voice, close to the baby's ear
- Mimics the sounds that an infant makes and recognizes and responds to the ways in which an infant signals "pause time"

The older infant (9–14 months):

- Tunes in to words and phrases such as *bye-bye, uh-oh, Patty Cake,* and *up*
- By 12 or 13 months, begins to use recognizable words, such as *wa-wa, Ma-ma, Da-da, down,* and *ba-ba*
- Uses recognizable words and strings of sounds that sound like talking
- Recognizes the difference between playful and soothing words and words that signal disapproval and may stop what she is doing upon hearing *No* or *Hot*
- Uses language to initiate and maintain contact with parents and caregivers

The caregiver:

- Communicates individually with every child at every opportunity
- Maintains eye contact during conversations
- Responds to children's interests in objects and events using words and gestures
- Engages children's interest in objects and events using words and gestures

Activities to Encourage Language and Imitation

> *Caregivers need to provide opportunities for infants to hear language as part of every daily routine.*

Language learning is not confined just to special times and special activities. Language is a part of our daily experience. Caregivers need to provide opportunities for infants to hear language as part of every daily routine, including diapering, rocking, feeding, and playing. When you are with an infant, describe what is happening, what you are doing, and what the infant is doing. Speak slowly and in short sentences, varying your pitch and sound level. In addition, find time to engage with the baby in purposeful activities that promote her language development.

Birth to Three Months

Talk with Baby Talk softly to the baby as you hold or feed him.

Sing a Lullaby Sing a lullaby as you put the infant to sleep.

Three to Six Months

Face-to-Face Interaction Hold the baby directly in front of you. Talk to him and encourage him to coo back. Follow this pattern: Talk–pause–talk–pause. Try making the same cooing sounds as the baby. If the baby looks away, it may not mean that he wants to end the conversation. Most babies need to take breaks when they are engaged in a cooing conversation.

Picture Show Let the infant explore and touch large pictures from sturdy story books, magazines, calendars, and the like.

(continued)

Activities continued

Six to Nine Months

Let's Babble Make some of the sounds you know the baby can make, and see if she will imitate you.

Imitating Banging Begin banging with your hands on a hard surface, and see if the infant will bang with you. When she does, say "Bang, bang, bang." Once the infant has mastered this activity, see if she will imitate you when you bang with a spoon.

Clapping Clap your hands and encourage the infant to do the same. Once she can imitate clapping, see if she will clap when given a verbal command to do so.

Waving Substitute waving for clapping in the previous activity.

Body Parts Using a large doll with clear features, show the baby how to point to the eyes, ears, nose, and mouth. Next, teach her to point to her own body.

Blowing Blow on the baby's tummy. Let the baby watch your face, and see if she will pucker her lips.

Smelling Pick up a flower, sniff it, smile, and then hold it in front of the baby.

Nine to Fourteen Months

Object Show Place two objects in front of the baby, such as a shoe and a plate. Say "Show me the shoe" and "Show me the plate." Later, add more objects and ask similar questions.

Look at a Picture Book Ask the infant to point to specific pictures.

Songs, Chants, and Nursery Rhymes Songs, nursery rhymes, and chants give infants the opportunity to hear language. Repetition at this age is important, and hearing songs helps infants become more aware of the rhythms, patterns, and inflections of a particular language.

Family Album Ask parents to put together books of family pictures. See if the baby can point to her family members when you say their names.

To describe the expectable sequence of communication skills in young toddlers and suggest ways to support their development

Between 14 and 24 months of age, children are learning to communicate with words. At first, a single word will stand for a whole sentence, and the caregiver will know from the context what that one word means. For instance, *cookie* may mean "I want a cookie" or "My cookie fell on the floor." After a while, the toddler will put together two words and the meaning will be easier to interpret: *Gimme cookie* or *That a cookie.*

While learning to use *expressive language* is an important development, it is only one aspect of the language skills that toddlers are learning. A second aspect of language learning is *receptive language,* or the ability to assign meanings to words and sentences. Both expressive and receptive language are based on the recognition that a word is a symbol that stands for something else.

Toddlers who enjoy pretend play often invent their own symbols. When a toddler who is pretending to cook takes a bite of a block, he is creating his own symbol. The block, like the word *cookie*, becomes the symbol of the object cookie. By supporting pretend play, we are fostering language development. (See the Developmental Picture for more on toddlers' language development.)

> *Both expressive and receptive language are based on the recognition that a word is a symbol that stands for something else.*

Developmental Picture

The young toddler (14–24 months):
- Is developing a single-word vocabulary that usually ranges from 50 to 100 words
- Enjoys picture books about familiar things
- Is learning to make the sounds of pets and farm animals
- Puts together two-word phrases, such as *Baby cookie, Mommy home,* and *Daddy push*
- Can follow a one-step command, such as *Bring me the keys* or *Give Nana a kiss*

The caregiver:
- Responds appropriately to toddlers' requests
- Provides opportunities for toddlers to follow simple directions
- Recognizes that toddlers learn language at different rates
- "Reads" picture books by naming the pictures or talking about the pictures in her own words
- Repeats and expands the child's language—for example, when a toddler says "Mommy bye-bye," the caregiver says "Yes, Mommy went bye-bye"
- Provides toddlers with many experiences that match objects with their names

Activities to Encourage Language and Imitation

Picture Books Read often with young toddlers. Help them point out and label familiar pictures and items. Don't worry about finishing the story. Let the children touch the pages, hold the books, and carry the books around with them as they play.

Picture Games Play games involving pointing to and labeling specific pictures and objects.

Doll Games Give the young toddler a doll (or a stuffed animal) and the appropriate props. Ask him to hug the doll, kiss the doll, put the doll to sleep, wipe the doll's nose, rock the doll, feed her, and put her to bed. Show him how to brush the doll's hair and give the doll a bath.

Picture Albums Make picture albums with pictures of familiar toys, objects, and people.

Retrieval Games Send the children on "errands"—for instance, say "Get the doll," "Bring me the ball," and so forth.

(continued)

Activities continued

Puppets Introduce puppets. Show the children how to make them "talk."

Picture Matching Games Between 20 and 24 months, many children like to match pictures. They also like to match an object with a picture of the object.

Sensory Games Playing games with water and ice cubes, bubbles, shaving cream, and crinkly paper invites children to explore their senses and at the same time provides opportunities to learn and practice new words.

Telephone Games Encourage two-way conversation by talking with a child as she plays with a toy telephone.

Nursery Rhymes, Songs, and Chants Give toddlers many opportunities to participate in music experiences.

Pretending Encourage pretending by introducing simple props, such as a doll or stuffed animal; doll-sized pots, dishes, and utensils; a wallet or old purse; a small brush; and a play telephone. Also join the children in pretend play.

Objective 4   To describe the expectable sequence of language skills in older toddlers and suggest ways to support their development

Although most children learn language upon hearing it spoken, learning language involves much more than the imitation of adult speech. The foundation of language is real-world experience. Babies associate names with the most important people in their lives (*Mama, Dada, Nana, Papa,* siblings' names), the most important objects in their lives (*cookie, blankie, car*), and the most important actions or experiences in their lives (*bye-bye, up, hot*). As soon as toddlers master the concept that a spoken word can stand for an experience, they are poised for a second discovery: that putting two words together is a way of describing a relationship. *Big ball* can mean that "The ball is big" or "I want the big ball." *Daddy car* can mean that "The car belongs to Daddy" or "Daddy is in the car."

When older toddlers advance from the two-word stage to the three-word stage, their language becomes much less ambiguous. *That a big ball* means "That is a big ball." *Gimme big ball* means "I want you to give me the big

> As toddlers expand their vocabulary, their language becomes more than a tool for talking about real-world experiences. It also becomes a tool for expanding their knowledge.

164

ball." *That Daddy car* means "The car belongs to Daddy." *Daddy bye-bye car* means "Daddy drove away in the car."

When toddlers can use three-word sentences, they can carry on conversations. They can also ask questions, give orders, describe feelings, provide information, and play with words. As toddlers expand their vocabulary, become more fluent, and speak in longer sentences, their language becomes more than a tool for talking about real-world experiences. It also becomes a tool for expanding their knowledge of the world beyond their direct experiences (see the Developmental Picture below).

The understanding of language and the ability to communicate ideas, feelings, and needs is an evolving process. During these early years, children need many opportunities to hear language and to practice using it. At 2 years old, most children understand simple commands and can put a few words together. By age 3, they have learned to speak in sentences (maybe even paragraphs) and can understand simple stories.

> *Every area should provide many opportunities for children to hear language and to practice emerging language skills.*

While preschools may have a special time of the day and a special area of the classroom set aside for language, language learning is an ongoing activity. It takes place in the classroom, on the playground, in the bathroom, and at the lunch table. Every area should provide many opportunities for children to hear language and to practice emerging language skills.

Materials That Encourage Language Development

Provide materials such as the following to encourage toddlers' language development:

- Books: books with hard cardboard pages, as well as simple story and picture books
- Picture cards: purchased picture cards, homemade cards, matching cards made from catalogs, and cutout pictures or stickers placed on index cards

Developmental Picture

The older toddler (2 years):

- Is rapidly expanding her vocabulary
- Enjoys rhymes, picture books, and books with repetition
- Speaks in two- and three-word sentences
- Can follow a simple two-part command, such as "Go to the table and bring me a napkin"
- Uses words to communicate wants and needs, to share interests, and to initiate interactions
- Asks *where* and *what's that* questions

The caregiver:

- Repeats with brief expansion when children begin to communicate with words
- Provides opportunities for children to hear nursery rhymes and songs
- Reads books with children that have a simple and familiar story line
- Names and describes objects and experiences to develop children's vocabulary

- Common objects: small animals; miniature cars, trucks, and trains; small dishes and dolls; and so on. Make an object box and continually change the objects inside it.
- Puzzles with pictures of common objects
- Old typewriters and computer keyboards
- Printing stamps: a transportation set, a food set, and the like
- Lotto games: present one card at a time for a simple matching activity
- A puppet theater
- Wall posters with interesting pictures
- A Polaroid camera
- Writing materials: markers and crayons, paper, envelopes, stickers, postcards, old greeting cards, index cards, scrap paper, a chalkboard or whiteboard

Activities to Encourage Language Learning

Although language occurs in every area of the classroom, it is helpful to devote a special area to language learning. It is also important to recognize conversational techniques that encourage language learning and to initiate activities in the classroom that increase children's understanding, production, and appreciation of language. Here are some activities and techniques that work well with 2-year-olds.

Everyday Conversation Make a special point of carrying on a conversation with every child at least three times a day. Before beginning the conversation, position yourself so that you are on the same level as the child and then establish eye contact. Remember that it is only considered a *conversation* if you and the child are sharing information and there is a back and forth exchange of ideas—for example:

> *Teacher:* "Look at that! You have a new pair of sneakers."
>
> *Child:* "New shoes."
>
> *Teacher:* "Yes, you have new shoes. I'll bet you can run really fast with your new shoes on."
>
> *Child:* "Bobby runs fast."
>
> *Teacher:* "Oh, your brother Bobby is a fast runner. Did he get new shoes, too?"

Farm Animal Game Hold a toy farm animal behind your back, and engage one or more children in a guessing game. Tell them, "I am holding an animal behind my back that says 'moo.' It is a _____." As the children fill in the word *cow*, show them the miniature cow. Repeat the game with a pig, horse, lamb, chicken, and so on. Let the children have a turn picking up the animal, making its sound, and letting you or the other children say its name.

Let's Go Shopping Game Put play foods on a tray and give each child a paper bag. Have each child take a turn choosing an item, such as a play banana, cookie, hotdog, apple, pizza, or tomato. Have the child name the item as she places it in her bag. If she can't name the item, let the other children help her. (This game works best with two to four children.)

Describing Your Actions Talk about what you are doing as you prepare for an activity. "We are going to play with play dough. I am going to give each of you a ball of dough: a ball for Pedro, a ball for Kirsten . . ."

Describing Their Actions Increase children's understanding of language and build vocabulary by describing what they are doing. "You have made a block tower. Oh, you're putting the yellow block on the top."

Object Boxes Use object boxes as story starters in circle time. Have each child choose an object from the box—a toothbrush, a shoelace, a toy car, a Band-Aid, or the like. As the child selects an item, ask him to say something about it. Some children may just name the object, while others may tell a short story about it.

Puppets Introduce puppets in a variety of ways. Use them to talk to the children, or let the children talk for the puppets.

Taking Pictures Take photos of field trips, special days, and even routine events. Encourage the children to sequence the photos and retell the events.

Sharing Books Look at picture books with the children. Good books for 2-year-olds have these qualities:

- They are simple and repetitive. Books with rhymes, repetition, and choruses are particularly appropriate.
- They are filled with high-quality illustrations that have clear details and bright colors.
- They have themes that are familiar to children.
- They can be retold by the children by looking at the pictures.

Two-year-olds also like books that contain a lot of things they can learn the names of, like all kinds of cars, trucks, machines, or animals (such as Richard Scary's books). They also like books in which you have to find something hiding (such as the *Spot* books) and books that have clear photographs of a variety of different objects. The children can learn many details that can then be incorporated into pretend play. Here's an example:

> *Two-year-olds like books that contain a lot of things they can learn the names of.*

> *Miss Love-the-Kids took the children on a field trip to a nearby park. Several children were climbing on the toy train. "What kind of train is this?" Miss Love-the-Kids asked. "Big 'team engine," said Jacob, who insisted that Miss Love-the-Kids read his favorite train book nearly every day. "See tender?" he said, pointing to the car attached to the engine. "I'm glad we have a tender to carry fuel for our steam engine," said the teacher. "We need coal to keep the fire hot." "I get coal," said Maisha, as she scooped up a handful of grass and sprinkled it on the "tender." "Go fast." Ralph grabbed the wheel and turned it vigorously back and forth. "Me engineer," he said proudly. "All aboard!"*

At the age of 2, children learn new words eagerly and easily, perhaps more so than at any other time in their lives. As they expand their vocabulary, they are building a firm

> *At the age of 2, children learn new words eagerly and easily, perhaps more so than at any other time in their lives.*

foundation for reading. In fact, many researchers believe that helping children develop a rich vocabulary at age 2, 3, and 4 is one of the most important things we can do to promote their success in reading and in school.

Here are some other things you can do to help 2-year-olds build a foundation for literacy:

- Provide children with many opportunities to see you read and write and to imitate reading and writing in their play. They might use tickets or menus, ask you to write their names or other words on their drawings, "write" (with scribbles) a card or letter and "read" it aloud, play "office," or follow along as you point out the title of a favorite book or their names on their cubbies.

- Encourage children to handle books and to "read" on their own. As they imitate your reading, the children will practice holding a book right side up and turning pages from front to back. They may even point to words as they read, if they have seen you do this.

- Let the children choose their favorite books for storytime. It is surprising how many 2-year-olds can recognize their favorite books, cereal boxes, videos, and even signs. They notice how words look long before they can read.

- Help children act out simple stories they have heard or special experiences they have had, or play them out with miniature figures and props. Ask questions to expand the play or to move it forward.

- Engage in word play with children. For example, they might enjoy making up nonsense words and repeating rhymes like "Anna banana" or simple tongue-twisters like "Peter, Peter, pumpkin eater" and "Peter Piper picked peppers."

To describe the expectable sequence of language skills in preschool children and suggest ways to support their development

Just before a recent election, Jamie, age 4½, explained how the process works:

"Well, you see, there are these two people. They are going to have a race, and the one that wins gets to live in Washington in a white house. It's not a race in cars; it's just a running race." •

This anecdote points out two aspects of children's language: First, it shows how much in tune children are with the language that is spoken around them. Obviously, Jamie does not understand what an *election* is, but he has picked up some key words and is able to repeat them. Second, the anecdote shows how children interpret the language they hear in a very concrete way. Jamie did not recognize the metaphorical interpretation of either *running a race* or *living in the White House*. (See the following Developmental Picture for more on preschoolers' language development.)

168

Developmental Picture

The preschool child (3–5 years):

- Is bursting with language
- Is learning the rules of language as well as the meaning
- Has mastered the basic vocabulary, rules, and sounds of language by 6 years of age
- Asks questions using *when, where, why,* and *how*
- Has the capacity to master more than one language but learns best in her first language

The caregiver:

- Provides opportunities to use language in a variety of ways
- Recognizes the level of each child's expressive language and uses repetition and expansion to increase the child's proficiency
- Recognizes that children construct the rules of language and provides children with good language models but does not correct their grammar
- Maintains a language-rich environment
- Creates a loving and trusting environment, in which children feel comfortable asking questions and sharing information
- Engages in frequent conversations with children, asking open-ended questions and avoiding known-answer questions
- Reads books to children daily, including books with multicultural themes, rhymes, prose, repetition, and high-quality illustrations

Helping Preschoolers Enhance Their Spontaneous Language

Psycholinguists, who study the stages of speech development in young children, have identified several facets of early speech that are important to parents and caregivers to understand:

- Children do not merely parrot back the words they hear. Their language is an original creation or construction.
- Children have their own grammar or consistent word order that is not the same as that of adults.
- When children listen to adult speech, they tune into its meaning and not its form.

Correcting children's grammar does not make sense because they are focused on the communication and do not recognize that there are correct and incorrect ways of expressing the same meaning. The same thing is true about correcting pronunciation. Children attend to the meaning of a sentence, not to the way it sounds. Correcting a child's pronunciation is completely ineffective, as shown by this example of a conversation between a mother and a preschool child:

> *Abbie:* "Mommy! Mommy! My pasgetee keeps slipping off my fork."
> *Mommy:* "Abbie, you mean your *spaghetti* keeps slipping off your fork."
> *Abbie:* "That's what I said. It keeps slipping. See?"
> *Mommy:* "Say 'spa.'"
> *Abbie:* "Spa."

Mommy: "Now say 'get.' "

Abbie: "Get."

Mommy: "Now say 'tee.' "

Abbie: "Tee."

Mommy: "Now say 'spa-get-tee.' "

Abbie: "Spa-get-tee."

Mommy: "Very good! You said it perfectly."

Abbie: "But Mommy, my pasgetee falled off again. Can I use my fingers?"

Although adults cannot improve children's pronunciation or grammar by correcting their speech, adults do play a critical role in helping children develop language:

- Adults provide children with real-world experiences, which are the basis of language development. These experiences include opportunities for the following:

  To manipulate objects   To experience a variety of sights and sounds

  To practice motor skills   To visit new people and see new places

  To see and create pictures   To hear stories, poems, and songs

- Adults use words in meaningful contexts so that children can discover that words stand for real-world things and events.

- Adult serve as good speech models, exposing children to correct grammar and pronunciation.

If we accept children's language and avoid the pitfalls of correcting their pronunciation and grammar, they will in time learn to speak correctly. It seems that children have an innate ability to abstract the rules of grammar and articulation and to apply them to their own original sentences. When Abbie complained because her "pasgetee falled off" the fork, her use of the word *falled* demonstrated how much she already knew about language. Abbie recognized that the *-ed* sound at the end of a word was a way of indicating that something happened in the past. She made this kind of connection: "I *kick* the ball today. I *kicked* the ball yesterday. I *fall* down today. I *falled* down yesterday." Abbie had never heard her parents use the word *falled*. Rather, her use of the word was a logical application of a rule. It will take several years for Abbie to realize that there are exceptions to rules, however, and to know when they apply.

> *Although adults cannot improve children's pronunciation or grammar by correcting their speech, adults do play a critical role in helping children develop language.*

Adults model not only the forms of language for children but also the uses of language. As children listen to adults use language in a variety of ways, they learn that language is used in many ways:

  To give commands and directions   To greet people

  To ask questions   To express how you feel

  To provide information   To tell jokes and stories

  To describe things that happen   To sing songs and have fun

170

Finally and most important, adults serve as good listeners and good audiences. They provide an emotional climate that encourages children to share their information and feelings.

Activities to Promote Language Development

Conversation   One of the most effective techniques to encourage children's verbal expression is perhaps one of the least used by adults. It is simply to listen quietly and attentively when a child is speaking and to talk *with* him, not *at* him. When an adult has an attitude of respect for the child as an individual who has something interesting to share, the exchange is mutually rewarding and reinforcing.

> *Listen quietly and attentively when a child is speaking and talk with him, not at him.*

Storytime   One of the favorite activities of both teachers and students is reading stories. Each class has its own favorites that it never tires of hearing over and over. Once children become familiar with a story, it can be presented in different ways and with the children becoming more active participants:

- Make puppets from paper bags, paper plates, socks, or mittens to represent the characters in the story.
- Use props that the children can manipulate to act out the story as you tell it or read it.
- Use a cassette recorder to record children as they say the lines of their characters, and then intersperse the recording with the telling of the story. For example, record the Big, Bad Wolf saying "I'll huff and I'll puff and I'll blow your house down," and when you get to that point in the story, let a child push the button to play the recorded dialogue.

If your storytime is *not* successful, ask the following questions:

- Did I preread the book?
- Was it appropriate for the age and interest level of the children?
- Was it too long?
- Did I allow interaction with the children? Did we discuss the illustrations? Did I ask questions? (e.g., What do you think the wolf found when he opened the door?)
- Was the setting appropriate? Were the children comfortable? Could they all see the pictures? Was the room quiet? Were there many distractions?
- Did I paraphrase the language if it was too difficult?
- Did my voice, facial expressions, and body language reflect the mood of the story?

Reading from books is important because it allows children to see how written words are symbols that have specific meanings. It is also important for children to see that we can make up our own interesting stories by using our imaginations.

Other Language Experiences and Activities

Planning Time   One way to encourage children to talk in the group setting is to have a *planning time* at the beginning of the day to discuss the activities for that day. The children may have some ideas the teacher hasn't thought of. At the end of the day, have a *recall time* to talk about what happened that day, both good and bad. Use this time to share memories, ask questions, and express feelings.

Picture Stories   Display several large pictures that have been cut from magazines or calendars and mounted on brightly colored paper. (The *National Geographic* magazine is an excellent source for language stimulation pictures.) Have the children take turns choosing pictures. At first, you should tell a story about the picture. Then gradually encourage the children to help with the story as you ask questions and incorporate their ideas and suggestions. Soon the children will be able to tell a story themselves with little prompting. This is a good language activity for a small group of children.

Field Trips   A field trip not only provides new experiences that can expand children's language, but it also gives them an opportunity to participate in detailed planning before the trip and critical evaluation after the trip.

Promoting Interactions   Provide opportunities for interaction among the children. Give a specific task to two or three children that will involve cooperative planning, such as cleaning and setting the tables for a special snack to welcome a visitor or to celebrate an occasion.

Expressing Feelings   Encourage children to express their feelings. This can be done with older children by using paper plate puppets with expressions of anger, sadness, fright, happiness, surprise, excitement, and so on. Prepare a chart with a slot for each child's name. As each child comes into the classroom in the morning, she may choose to place her name on the chart and beside her name place a circular disc with a face that describes how she feels—happy, sad, angry, and so on. At the end of the day at good-bye circle time, each child is given a chance to change the face beside her name, if her feelings have changed.

My Story   Interview each child using a cassette recorder. Then translate what the child has said about himself into short, simple sentences on a large piece of poster-sized newsprint; leave room at the top for a photograph of the child. Mount the children's stories on the wall so they can be read and reread. This activity can also be done in book form, with the children providing the illustrations.

Building a Classroom Environment
That Promotes Language Development

We cannot compartmentalize language activities. There is no area in the classroom that cannot be used in some way to expand children's vocabulary or engage them in expressive speech. Here are some examples:

172

- The block area is especially effective as children experience words and concepts such as *over*, *under*, *inside*, *outside*, *between*, *around*, *beside*, *on top of*, *smaller*, *larger*, *big*, *little*, *long*, *short*, *fast*, and *slow*. Enhance children's use of blocks in these ways:

  — Expand children's language by encouraging them to build a wide variety of structures and environments—castles, hospitals, factories, farms, zoos, circuses, sports arenas, museums, garages, space stations, and theme parks.

  — Add books, miniature figures, signs, and other props to encourage new ideas. Help children expand their vocabulary as they build by asking questions: "Your zoo is getting so big. But where do the people go if they are hungry? Do you need a refreshment stand?"

  — Encourage children to tell the class about their structures before they knock them down.

- The imaginative play area gives children the opportunity for role-play. Even normally quiet children often become more talkative in a pretend situation. You can vary the area to reflect the current classroom theme or add items that reflect the children's cultures. For example, the imaginative play area can become a Mexican restaurant, a cafeteria, a pet hospital, a grocery store or bodega, part of a fire station, or the galley of a ship.

- Music activities can be used to develop children's ability to listen and to imitate. Songs and finger plays enrich children's language.

- Sensory activities involving smelling, tasting, and especially touching provide wonderful opportunities to extend children's vocabulary. As they play with a variety of interesting materials, you can help them learn words to describe their experiences, such as *salty*, *crunchy*, *squeaky*, *fluffy*, *silky*, *goupy*, *sticky*, *jiggly*, and *crinkly*.

- Even large-muscle activities like climbing and sliding provide opportunities to expand children's vocabulary as you comment on their feats or talk together about how they plan to approach a new challenge.

- Set up a display table or area in the classroom that focuses on a theme (zoo animals, community helpers, etc.) or a question (How do we get milk? Where do letters go?). Give the children active parts in planning and producing the display.

Here are some special tools and props that can be placed in the classroom to foster expressive language:

- Telephones in the house area
- Cassette recorders that the children can operate by themselves
- Puppets, toy animals, dolls, and related props
- Sets of sequence pictures that the children can put together and use to tell stories
- Wordless books
- Mystery objects, such as parts of machines, artifacts from other places or times, unusual plants or plant parts, crystals, natural sponges, pumice stone—anything out of the ordinary that will intrigue children and prompt discussion

173

Simply stated, successful language experiences give children an opportunity to express themselves and their ideas in their own ways. A good teacher can stretch and expand these expressions without stifling creativity and spontaneity.

Educating Young Children in Mixed-Language Classrooms

If you are reading this textbook, you most likely teach in English, even if you speak another language, as well. If you have children in your class whose first language is *not* English, then you have a special challenge—and a special opportunity.

Experts agree that it is important to help each child learn and maintain her home language. The language spoken by a child's family members provides a foundation that helps her learn concepts about the world. It is a valuable part of the child's identity. Fluency in the home language provides the child a base for learning English and for learning to read and write.

At the same time, many parents want their young children to learn English and realize that one of the fastest ways to do that is to be in a group with English-speaking children. For the child, though, the initial experience of entering a classroom in which no one speaks her language can be overwhelming. This is especially true for preschoolers, as words are so central to their pretend play, social interaction, and learning.

What can teachers do to ease the transition? How can they help children learn English? How can they help children maintain their home languages, as well?

First Steps

- Learn to pronounce each child's name correctly. For learning any word in a different language, writing it phonetically—the way it sounds to you—can be helpful. Help the other children learn their friends' names, too.

- Try to arrange for people to help with translation, such as other teachers in your program or family members of the children.

- Check in with each second-language learner's parents or co-workers who speak the home language. Ask them to help you learn words and gestures that are important to interacting with a young child—for instance, to comfort, to show love and acceptance, to encourage effort, and to celebrate accomplishments.

- Find out what the child likes to do and is good at. Let the child teach you—and the other children—some words in her home language related to her favorite toys or activities. With the help of the children, teach the child the English words.

- Help children who are learning English join in pretend play with other children by suggesting roles that don't require speaking, such as cooking, fixing things, and carrying props.

- Help children learn English words for classroom activities and routines by talking about what you and the rest of the children are doing.

Building Fluency

- Help the children who are learning a second language by talking with them a lot. In your conversations, emphasize key words through repetition.

174

- Show interest in what each child has to say. Respond to her verbal and nonverbal questions with words and gestures to develop a foundation of communication between you and the child.

- Actively include children in circle time discussions; encourage them to share in their own languages if they don't know the English words.

- As with any children, expand second-language learners' sentences and restate their words to provide a good model without actually correcting their grammar or pronunciation.

- Encourage children to repeat the new words they are learning and to "use their words" to ask for help, tell stories, and solve problems.

- Ask open-ended questions, and use them to help children think through problems and stretch their knowledge.

- Use picture books and songs to introduce new words and phrases.

Supporting Emergent Literacy

- Read frequently to children in small groups and one on one. Choose books with repeated or predictable text that encourage the children to chime in. Engage the children in conversations about the stories and the pictures.

- Choose books for the whole group that introduce rich, high-interest vocabulary, such as names of animals, transportation vehicles, and the like.

- Use rhymes, hand-clapping games, and tongue-twisters to help children enjoy and appreciate the sounds of words and to recognize their component parts.

- Emphasize features of language, such as particular sounds and word endings, that may be difficult for second-language learners.

- Help children make connections between written and spoken words in both English and their home languages.

Supporting Home Language Development

- Recognize and build on the strengths children have developed through their experiences with their home languages.

- Teach children songs, nursery rhymes, finger plays, and movement games in different languages. Doing so will expand all of the children's cognitive development and show that you value non-English languages.

- Read stories in different languages. Have parents who speak a given language help you with pronunciation before you read aloud a story in that language. (Phonetic notes may help you remember the pronunciations.)

- Make a point of learning some of the basics of each child's home language. Include words in that language in classroom conversations, displays, and play materials.

- Help all of the children and their families to see that knowing two languages is an asset for the individual child and also for the class as a whole.

175

To learn ways of reading to children that encourage active participation and engender a love of books

Carla Caring, the director of the Caring about Children preschool, was supervising a new teacher. In their meeting together, the teacher described several activities she had planned for circle time. The activities sounded appropriate, but Ms. Caring was disturbed about the fact that the teacher had not allotted time for reading to the children.

"What books are you planning to read in circle time?" she asked the teacher. "I have decided not to read to the children," the teacher explained. "The children in my class don't like to be read to. Yesterday when I read them a book, they did everything besides listen." "That's unusual," Ms. Caring commented. "Most children love to be read to. Maybe they just didn't like the book you were reading." Ms. Caring picked up two books with attractive pictures on their covers. "Here, these books just came in. Read them to the children in your morning circle time."

The next day, Ms. Caring made a point of visiting the new teacher's class during circle time. The teacher was sitting in a low chair with the children sitting around her. She was holding the book in her hands and reading to the children word by word, without letting them see the pictures. Ms. Caring was not at all surprised when two of the children started squabbling. "I've got to teach this teacher how to read a book," the director said to herself.

Reading with children is a very special art. Some teachers are like pied pipers: As soon as they pick up a book, the children gather around them. Other teachers need to learn techniques for reading to children that will keep them interested and involved.

> **Reading with children is a very special art.**

That was the case with the new teacher at the Caring about Children preschool. At the next staff meeting, Ms. Caring asked the other teachers to talk about some of the techniques they used when they read to children. Here are some of the suggestions they gave their new colleague:

- Be sure to read the book to yourself before you read it with the children. That way, you can figure out how to introduce the book and how to keep the children engaged in it.

- With some books, you may decide to tell the story in your own words, rather than by reading the text. With other books, you may decide to begin by showing the children the illustrations and asking them to talk about what they notice.

- When you read with children, make sure to position the book so that everyone can see the illustrations. If some children want a closer look, pass the book around.

- It is especially important to read aloud with expression and enthusiasm. Vary your pitch, volume, and inflection to maintain the children's interest. Use different voices when they are appropriate for different characters.

- Don't be in a hurry. Encourage children to ask questions and talk about the story and the illustrations.

- Reread the books that children really enjoy. When a book has a refrain, encourage the children to join in. If some children have memorized the book, give them a chance to "read" along with you. Try hesitating in the middle of a line and seeing if the children can finish it.

- Encourage children to guess how the book will end.

- See if the children can think of a different ending for the story.

- Let the children retell the story in their own words, act out the story, or draw pictures about the story.

- When you finish reading a book, place it on a low shelf where the children can reach it.

- Make books with the children, and encourage them to read those books to you.

- When reading with babies or toddlers, choose a time when you can be with just one or two children and can hold them on your lap. Choose sturdy books with a lot of pictures that the children can point to or with different textures that the children can feel. Stop when the children lose interest.

- Let the children choose the books they would like you to read aloud with them.

To describe early literacy skills and suggest activities that promote them

The following conversation was overheard at the supermarket checkout line:

Parent 1: "Have you heard what they say about that preschool over on Maple Street?"

Parent 2: "No, what about it?"

Parent 1: "Well, they claim that over half of the 4-year-olds are reading by the end of the year and that almost all the children can read before they begin first grade."

Parent 2: "Wow, that sounds terrific! You know, Janie is only 3, but I think I'll call the preschool about enrolling her."

Parent 1: "Good luck! They say the waiting list is so long that parents are filling out applications for admission as soon as their babies are born. I also heard that children who can't keep up with the work are kicked out." ●

Unfortunately, many parents judge the value of a preschool by how much reading is taught there. The philosophy that underlies this book does not support this measure, although it does support parents' belief that reading is important.

After reviewing a large body of research on how children become good readers, a panel of experts commissioned by the National Academy of Sciences concluded that having a preschool language and literacy foundation is important for later reading success (Shonkoff & Phillips, 2000). That foundation involves all kinds of experiences with stories, conversation, word play, books, and other meaningful print (signs, notes, lists, directions, etc.). Its most important component is a rich vocabulary, in whatever language or languages the child speaks. Providing the range of experiences that will build a strong foundation is more important in the long run than simply teaching children to recite the alphabet or to read simple books.

A good preschool, from this point of view, provides children with daily opportunities to "read" or look at books and to sing songs, listen to stories and poems, and tell and act out stories as they play with toys and with their friends. It paves the way for fluent reading by providing experiences that do the following:

- Increase children's use of language
- Increase children's knowledge base
- Promote the enjoyment of books and stories and the motivation to read
- Show children the many different ways that adults use reading and writing in their daily lives
- Encourage children to communicate through "writing" and drawing and to incorporate "reading" and writing into their play
- Help children associate printed and spoken words
- Help children develop specific skills that are related to reading success—namely, *phonological awareness* (recognizing the sounds that make up words), *print concepts* (such as reading left to right and having spaces between words), and *letter naming*
- Help children feel good about themselves and confident that they can learn new things
- Teach children to follow directions
- Help children to attend to a task until they have completed it

The Foundations of Emergent Literacy

There is a great deal of recent research about the components of early literacy and about effective ways to support children's *emergent literacy.* Five major areas have been identified as essential to literacy development:

1. *A meaningful knowledge base* is developed through having many varied experiences with materials, places, and people. Vocabulary building occurs through talking about those experiences.
2. *Oral language* is developed through participating in back and forth communication, individual conversations, and group discussions. Looking at books and having books read aloud to them also promote children's oral language skills.
3. *Phonological awareness* is developed through noticing sounds, playing with the sounds of words, and noticing what sound a word begins with. Children enjoying rhyming words in songs and stories.
4. *Print awareness* is developed as children notice the usefulness of print. This occurs as they experiment with making notes and scribbling and as they find a word in a line of print.
5. *Alphabet knowledge* is developed as children recognize and name letters and name the letter that represents a certain sound.

Let's take a closer look at how we can provide these emergent literacy experiences in early childhood settings. (Promoting self-confidence, the motivation to learn, and the ability to follow directions and complete tasks will be covered in more detail in later chapters.)

Creating an Environment That Supports Literacy

Providing an environment that supports language development goes a long way toward promoting literacy. As mentioned earlier, this language-rich environment should include the following:

> *Providing an environment that supports language development goes a long way toward promoting literacy.*

- Interesting spaces and props that invite sociodramatic play
- Intriguing objects and pictures that invite questions and conversations
- Toys, games, and puzzles that children can use in pairs or small groups
- Blocks, sand, miniature figures, cars and trucks, and other toys that invite children to build things together
- Puppets, sequence cards, a tape recorder, costumes, and other elements that encourage children to tell a story or put on a show

An environment that supports literacy is also rich in meaningful print. It will have these things:

- The children's names on cubbies, artwork, displays of photographs, and charts showing "jobs," like feeding classroom pets and helping with the snack

- Captions for bulletin board displays
- Signs that show where toys go or that provide directions for adults and children to follow
- A calendar or schedule
- Charts related to what the children are learning
- Reminder notes
- Information for parents and classroom visitors
- "Big books" showing the texts of favorite stories so children can read along or point to words as they are spoken

In addition, many teachers use chartpaper and markers to post the following:

- The words to children's favorite songs, chants, poems, and finger plays
- Intriguing things that the children have said
- Recipes
- Children's questions and ideas about a new theme or project
- Each child's contribution to a group story about a field trip or other experience
- Weather reports

> *An environment that supports literacy is also rich in meaningful print.*

Finally, an environment that supports literacy incorporates books, writing materials, and meaningful print into many classroom areas:

- A library or quiet reading corner
- Paper and pencils and even computers in dramatic play areas so that children can "write" shopping lists, prescriptions, menus, tickets, train schedules, office work, checks, notes, secret codes, captains' logs, and e-mail
- Boxes, cans, and other labeled food containers in the "kitchen," "restaurant," or "store"
- Science books, nature guides, and writing materials in the science area so that children can identify found objects, "write" lab reports, make drawings to record their observations, and "do research"
- Story books in the doll corner for reading to the "babies"
- A sign that says "Save" that the children can put on their block constructions to protect them
- Greeting cards, envelopes, letter and picture stamps, and book-making materials in the art area so that the children can create books, letters, cards, notes, props for pretend play, and comic books or cartoons that tell stories
- A computer that the children can use to play reading and writing games and to create books, letters, cards, notes, and props for pretend play
- A "museum" or labeled display related to a theme the children are studying
- Traffic signs for tricycles and miniature vehicles
- A book-making and repair area

Activities for Shared Reading

Shared reading activities should occur every day in every preschool classroom. They provide opportunities for children to enjoy, tell, and retell stories and to expand their language. They also provide opportunities for children to connect the spoken word with the written word, to learn the conventions of print, to develop listening comprehension skills, and to see themselves as part of a community of readers and writers.

> *Shared reading activities should occur every day in every preschool classroom.*

Here are some shared reading activities that preschoolers enjoy:

Storytime Discussions As you read with children, encourage their involvement in the story and their attention to details by asking questions about the following:

- To recall what happened before
- To look at the pictures and predict what will happen next
- What they think a character wants or will do
- To explain or guess the meaning of a word that may be unfamiliar
- How they think the characters feel, what they can do to solve the characters' problems, or why the characters are acting in particular ways
- If they have had experiences like those of the characters in the story
- To repeat or retell their favorite parts

Experience Stories Plan a field trip or nature walk for the children in your class. Take pictures of places or events along the way. Back in class, let the children help you create a picture book by placing the photos in the correct order. Ask the children to talk about each picture so that you can write their words underneath it or on the facing page. Read the experience story with the children.

Choral Reading Print the words to a favorite chant or finger play on a large piece of chartpaper. Point to the words as the children say them with you.

Dictation Let a child dictate a sentence or two, and write down his or her words exactly. Then read them back together.

Activities for Skill Building

Phonological Awareness

Phonological awareness is knowledge of the sounds that make up words. Being able to break words into their component sounds and to put sounds together to make words helps children to sound out and spell new words. Here are some fun activities for developing phonological awareness:

Name Clapping Sing songs using the children's names—for example, "Hello, Costanza. How are you? How are you today?" Have the children clap out the syllables as they say the names: two for *Joey*, three for *Costanza*, four for *Alexander*, and so on.

(continued)

Activities continued

Silly Songs Teach the children songs that involve rhymes and sound play:

- "Ring around the Rosie"
- "The Ants Go Marching"
- "This Old Man"
- "There Was an Old Lady Who Swallowed a Fly"
- "Anna, Anna, Bo-Banna, Banana Fanna, Fo-Fanna, Fi Fie Fo-Fanna, Anna" (substitute each child's name for *Anna*)

The Sound Game Say a compound word—such as *lunchbox, beanbag,* or *playground*—and ask a child to repeat it. Then ask the child to say it again without one of its parts. For example, "Say *lunchbox.* Now, say it again, but this time, don't say *box.*"

Rhyme Cards Make a set of rhyming picture cards—*cat/hat, shell/bell, key/bee.* Color code the backs so that rhyming cards match. Encourage the children to find the rhyming pairs. Four- and five-year-olds can also identify words that have the same beginning or ending sounds.

Invented Spelling Using letter stamps, a computer, or paper and markers, have children write words by writing letters for the sounds that they hear. Some children like to write notes to friends; others like to write captions for their drawings or to make books or journals. If any of the children want you to, you can ask them to read what they wrote "their way" and then write the words underneath "The way I write it."

Print Concepts

By the time they get to preschool, most children already know a lot about print. They may recognize some favorite cereal boxes, store logos, and even books and videos. If they have been read to frequently, they can probably hold a book right side up and turn its pages from front to back. They may even realize that the reader reads the words, rather than the pictures, and they may correct someone who doesn't read every word of a favorite book they have memorized.

Most preschool children are ready to master more advanced print concepts, such as naming letters, recognizing words, and following along.

Letter Naming

By the time they start kindergarten, children should be able to name some letters. Usually, the ones that most interest them are the letters in their names. Here are some fun ways to help children who are interested learn the names of letters:

Name Games Help children identify the letters in their names and find them in different contexts, such as on food labels or on signs in the classroom. Children might also learn to recognize the first letters of each others' names. You might point out the first letter in a book title and ask, "Whose name starts with this?"

Letter Stamping Many children enjoy playing with rubber stamps and stamp pads or with homemade stamps cut from potatoes, sponges, or cucumbers. Use stamps with letters as well as ones with simple shapes. Another fun way to stamp is to roll out a slab of clay or play dough and make impressions with cookie cutters, rubber stamps, plastic letters, and found objects. Encourage children to talk about their stamp pictures. Help them name the letters and shapes they used.

Computers Use any word-processing program with the font size set on 18-point or larger. At first, children will enjoy typing random letters and "reading" back what they have written. Later, they may try to type particular letters, write their names, or ask you to help them write the names of friends and family members.

Letter Books—Beginning Sounds Make individual books for the children by folding and stapling several sheets of paper. Help each child select a letter for the book, and place that letter on the cover. Also talk about different objects that start with that letter. Encourage the child to draw or cut out pictures of things beginning with that letter.

Word Recognition

Children who can recognize familiar signs and logos and who can pick out their own names from a group of words may enjoy some of these word recognition games:

Labels Label objects in the classroom, and read the labels out loud to the children. Every once in a while, take a label away and see if the children can put it back in the correct place.

Lotto Games Buy or make a Lotto game, using pictures of familiar animals or objects on one side of the cards. When you read a Lotto card to the children, show them the word before naming the object or animal.

Word Puzzles Make a series of word puzzles by backing pictures of familiar objects with their names and then cutting them in half to form a two-piece puzzle. Mix the pieces from several of these puzzles in a storage tray. Let the children complete each puzzle on the "word" side. If they select the pieces that go together, they can turn the puzzle over to see the "picture" side.

Word Banks Work individually with children to make cards for words about which they have special interest, such as the names of family members, things they see on the way to school, favorite foods, and so on. When possible, paste a picture on the reverse side of each card. As the children learn to read their words, they can place the cards in their own word banks.

Reading Along

One of the first things a reader needs to know is where to begin. On some occasions when you read with older children, show them where the words begin. Point out the first few words so they can see that printed words correspond to spoken words, that there are spaces between words, and that reading goes from left to right and top to bottom (in English and other languages written with the Roman alphabet).

Some children may want to follow along as the text is being read. They can help you read by pointing to words as you read them aloud.

(continued)

Activities continued

Technology

Technology can be a real boon to beginning readers. Some computer programs highlight the words in a text as they are read aloud. Other programs allow the child to select words or rebuses (pictures that can be changed to words) to use in her writing and will read back what the child has written. You can also make tape recordings of familiar storybooks and encourage the children to read along with the tapes. (Make sure to clap or say "Turn the page" at the end of each page.)

When Do Children Read?

There is no magic age at which children are ready to learn to read. Because each child is a unique individual, the age will vary and will be influenced by the following factors:

- Understanding of and ability to use language effectively
- Development of small- and large-muscle skills
- Social and emotional development
- Background and experiences
- Interest in reading and desire to learn
- Opportunities given to learn to read

Objective 8

To describe the small-muscle skills that are used in writing and suggest activities that develop these skills and provide children with opportunities to practice writing

Even more than reading, *writing* requires the development of skills that are related to physical maturation. Children develop large-muscle skills before they develop small-muscle skills. Even if a 2-year-old knew how to form letters and numbers, he would not likely have the small-muscle skill or eye/hand coordination needed to control a marker and make the appropriate strokes.

Getting Ready to Write

In order to write with a marker, a child must have the strength and muscle control to hold it firmly between her thumb and first two fingers. Just as important, she must be able to swivel her wrist, control the fine movements of her fingers, and coordinate those hand and finger movements with the movement of her eyes.

Activities for Developing Prewriting Skills

The following activities will help children develop and practice prewriting skills:

Dressing Frames or Books Provide dressing frames or "dress myself" books that give children practice in pulling up zippers, doing up snaps, lacing, and buttoning.

Sewing Cards Make sets of sewing cards by cutting up old greeting cards into interesting shapes and punching holes around the outside edges of each card. Use yarn for threading, making sure to put tape around the ends of each piece of yarn to make it easier for the children to thread.

Lockboxes Create lockboxes with different kinds of latches and bolts.

Screw and Bolt Activity Place nuts and bolts in a box, and let the children practice putting them together.

Tweezers Have the children use a large pair of tweezers to transfer items such as cotton balls and rice from one container to another.

Practical Life Activities Children develop strength and coordination by sponging off tables, drying dishes, washing vegetables, and slicing fruit such as bananas.

Spinning Provide the children with spinning toys, like small tops and dreidels.

Bead Stringing Provide the children with opportunities to string increasingly smaller beads.

Clay Encourage the children to mold clay or dough into different forms using rolling pins, cookie cutters, and plastic knives.

Put-Together Toys Provide the children with a variety of small building toys, like pegboards, Tinkertoys, Lock Blocks, Bristle Blocks, and so on.

Puzzles Provide the children with alphabet inset puzzles.

Sand Letters Encourage the children to trace letters with their fingers in sand that has been spread in shallow trays.

Template Activities Provide opportunities for the children to create designs using templates of different shapes.

Tracing Let the children trace their own names by placing see-through paper over their names on a small clipboard.

Creating Initials The children can create the letters of their names using clay or cookie dough.

Sponge Play Let the children use a sponge or an eyedropper to move colored water from one container to another. They can have fun mixing colors to make colors that they like.

Play Writing Encourage children to engage in activities that are related to writing, including making greeting cards, mailing pretend letters, writing birthday invitations, and making signs for the classroom.

To select books that foster empathy, promote prosocial behavior, counteract bias, and support bilingualism

A grandparent was buying books for her 2-year-old grandson. She explained to the salesperson, "My grandson loves the books where pictures pop up, but he tears them up in no time flat. Do you have any of those nice strong cardboard books?" The salesperson showed her a large display of books with cardboard pages. "Did you have any particular books in mind?" she asked the grandmother. "Oh, he's too young to understand what it says in the book," the grandmother explained. "Just find me a couple of nice sturdy books with lots of pictures." ●

Selecting Books

This grandmother is correct in knowing that books with pop-out pictures and movable parts are apt to be torn up if they are left in the hands of a toddler. At the same time, durability is not the only criteria that should be used when selecting books for young children. Here are some other suggestions for selecting books:

- Choose books that are well written, with language that is pleasant to read and repeat. Get in the habit of reading book reviews before you buy a book written by an author you don't know about. Look for books that have won children's book awards and that have been recommended by recognized authorities.

- Choose books with beautiful or playful illustrations, whether drawings, photographs, paintings, or collages. The popularity of some of the all-time favorites—like *Winnie the Pooh*, *Madeleine*, *Goodnight Moon*, and *Curious George*—is due as much to their illustrations as their stories.

- Choose books with antibias themes and books that are representative of different cultures.

- Choose books that show people of different races and ethnicities. If most of the children in your class are white, try to have about half of your people books show people of color. If the majority of your students are nonwhite, try to have about three-quarters of your people books show people of color. Be sure there are some white faces in the books, as well.

- Avoid books with gender and age stereotypes.

- Select different types of books to create a rich and varied library:
  —Animal books
  —Books about everyday events
  —Fantasy books
  —Books about everyday problems

—Books that describe feelings, like love and fear

—Books about mischievous animals or children

—Books about children from faraway places

—Adventure stories

—Silly books

—Books that invite participation

—Books with refrains that are easy to remember

—Rhyming books

—Books with surprise endings

Remember to include a variety of factual books about favorite topics, such as animals, dinosaurs, space, sports, and dance. Studies have revealed that teachers and parents tend to overlook nonfiction books, even though they are very popular with young children. Beautifully illustrated books on a wide variety of topics published for adults can be used effectively with young children, as well.

The books we read to children influence their feelings, their learning, and their actions. Even before children can follow a story line, they are influenced both by the illustrations we show them and by the words that we use to talk about the illustrations. Consider the following:

> *The books we read to children influence their feelings, their learning, and their actions.*

- If we select books in which the doctors are always male and the nurses are always female or in which the grandmothers are always sitting in rocking chairs, we are exposing children to gender and age stereotypes.

- If we talk about feelings as we point to the illustrations—"The puppy is sad; he wants his mommy"—we encourage feelings of empathy.

When children are able to follow a story line, we can select stories with messages we would like to share:

- There are many children's books about children with disabilities, children with different skin colors, and children from different cultures. Reading them can help children respect and appreciate differences.

- There are also many children's books that encourage sharing, being a good friend, helping out, accepting a new baby, using words instead of hitting, and following rules that keep you safe.

- Often, authors of children's books use animal characters so that children can recognize the point of a story while avoiding literal identification with the characters.

Make a list of the kinds of messages you would like to send to the children during the course of the year. Once you have compiled the list, organize it into logical categories. You might want to include books that encourage children to do these things:

- To be kind to each other
- To take care of the environment
- To appreciate their families
- To learn how to share and take turns
- To avoid bias
- To cooperate
- To follow health and safety rules
- To learn about different cultures

Try to find one or more books appropriate for children of different ages from each category you create.

In selecting books to read with the children in your class, also think about whether there is an immediate message you would like to send: Is someone in the class about to get a baby sister or brother? Is a dental hygienist coming to your school to teach the children about toothbrushing? Is there a child in your group who tends to bite? Has a new child come into your class? Have the children been taunting a child in the group because she wears glasses? Some story books effectively help children cope with challenging situations and see things from another person's perspective.

If children in your class hear languages other than English spoken at home, look for books in those languages. You may also find books that are written in two languages, with the text printed in both English and a second language. Invite family members to share songs and nursery rhymes in their home language with the class or to help you make some simple books or tapes in their language. Encourage parents to read to their children in their home language as well as in English. Children may learn sophisticated concepts more easily in their first language. Also, in order to maintain the advantage of knowing two languages, children should hear both informal spoken language and more formal literate language in their home language.

Additional Resources about Communication

Neuman, S., Copple, C., & Bredekamp, S. (2000). *Learning to read and write: Developmentally appropriate practices for young children.* Washington, DC: NAEYC.

Schickedanz, J. (1999). *Much more than the ABCs: The early stages of reading and writing.* Washington, DC: NAEYC.

Shonkoff, J., & Phillips, D. (Eds.). (2000). *From neurons to neighborhoods.* Washington, DC: National Academy Press.

Weitzman, E., & Greenberg, J. (2002). *Learning language and loving it: A guide to promoting children's social, language, and literacy development in early childhood settings* (2nd ed.). Toronto, Ontario, Canada: Hanen Centre.

Creativity

Chapter 7

Overview

Creativity means many things to many people. To some, it means artistic talent. To others, it means having a passion to produce something original, appreciate beauty, discover joy, make a product that is beautiful or inspiring, solve problems, or seek out the unusual.

Creativity and *talent* are not the same thing. *Talent* is the ability to perform easily and well in a particular area. *Creativity* is a more generalized trait that enables individuals to find new ways of arranging materials, asking questions, or solving problems.

It is up to the teacher to structure an environment that nurtures and supports each child's innate creative spark.

Rationale

Whatever its definition, we all recognize that creativity is a highly desirable characteristic that we want to encourage in children. Children who are considered creative are treasured at home and in school. While bright children learn whatever we teach, highly creative children go beyond our teaching and make discoveries on their own.

This chapter focuses on providing opportunities for children to exercise their creative abilities, to appreciate the creativity of others, and to explore and experiment with a variety of media, not only through art, music, and dramatic activities but through all aspects of the program. This chapter demonstrates ways in which teachers can provide children with an array of experiences that stimulate their exploration and ample opportunities to express their creative ideas.

Objectives

1. To use a variety of teaching techniques to encourage children to think and act creatively

2. To recognize ways in which children from birth to age 5 express their creativity at each developmental stage and to identify caregiver behaviors and techniques that foster the development of creativity

3. To describe materials and activities that encourage infants to explore and experiment

4. To describe materials and activities that encourage toddlers to express their creativity

5. To describe materials and activities that encourage preschool children to express their creativity

Supporting Creative Expression

Manuel was a new student at the Magic Years Preschool. The teacher of the 4-year-old group, Miss Try-Hard, had met Manuel's parents when they enrolled him in the school. They described their son as a good kid who "marched to the tune of a different drummer." They were convinced that what he needed was a teacher with a firm hand who would keep him out of trouble.

Miss Try-Hard, who had expected the worst, was surprised to find that Manuel was a delightful child. He had a fantastic imagination, and the other children were drawn to him. One day, he taught the class how to make paper airplanes and they pretended to put on an air show. On another day, he organized a "safari" on the playground. Some children climbed on the jungle gym and pretended they were riding in a swamp buggy. Several others pretended to be wild animals and raced around the playground screeching, roaring, and growling. "Manuel is delightful," Miss Try-Hard told the school director. "Just about every day, he comes up with a creative idea."

Manuel was lucky to have Miss Try-Hard as a teacher. She loved creative ideas and was flexible enough to let the children set their own agenda. She wasn't upset when Manuel rearranged the classroom so that the airplanes had a place to land, and she enjoyed the noise and fun when the children became wild animals racing through the jungle.

190

In this chapter, as we explore the different facets of creativity, we will recognize that a truly creative teacher does not have to be an artist, musician, or star performer. The essential characteristic of a creative teacher is the ability to recognize, value, and support the different ways in which children express their creativity.

To use a variety of teaching techniques to encourage children to think and act creatively

The Funsters were late for their appointment with the director of the Creative Preschool. They wanted to see the school in action before they decided to enroll their twins. They apologized to the director for being late but hoped that they could still see the school. "I would be happy to show you the school," the director responded. "Unfortunately, the children just went home, but you will be able to see how the rooms are set up."

When they went into the toddler room, everything was in perfect order. There was a section with puzzles and manipulative toys; a block area; a child-sized kitchen area equipped with appliances, play food, pots and pans, and dress-up clothes; and a music area with a CD player and a set of rhythm instruments. Mrs. Funster remarked to the director, "This is incredible. This room doesn't look as if even one toddler was in it today, let alone ten. Either your teachers are speed wizards, or the children aren't allowed to play with the toys!"

Mrs. Funster was wrong. In fact, the toddler teachers at Creative Preschool were quite easygoing. A half hour before closing that day, every toy in the room had been out of place. The teachers were also very creative. One had brought out a puppet that she called "Alexander the Great" and had convinced the children that the classroom belonged to Alexander. Alexander loved to share his toys with the children, but he couldn't go to sleep at night unless every toy in his room was put back exactly where it belonged.

Truly creative teachers, in addition to fostering the creativity of children, find creative ways of guiding children's behavior and helping children learn. These teachers invite children to question, like children who are spunky, enjoy humor, and value individuality and diversity. These teachers also have a talent for finding many different ways of getting across new concepts, for recognizing and building on children's interests, and for asking questions and presenting problems that have more than one right answer. Creative teachers invite children to try out new ideas without being afraid of failure.

Think about the activity suggestions in the previous chapters:

- What physical, cognitive, and language activities foster creativity in children?
- Which ones also engage the teacher's creativity?

To recognize ways in which children from birth to age 5 express their creativity at each developmental stage and to identify caregiver behaviors and techniques that foster the development of creativity

Miss Efficiency, the director of the Growing Children Preschool, was developing a curriculum framework for her center. Her goal was to identify the major curriculum categories for each age group so that the school's teachers could develop their own curriculum plans. At a staff meeting, she asked the teachers at what age they felt creativity should be introduced as a curriculum area. While most of the teachers agreed that creativity should be considered as a curriculum area for the 3- and 4-year-olds, one toddler teacher insisted that creativity was a trait that children were born with and that teachers should foster creativity at every age level. As the teachers continued the discussion, they came to the conclusion that if you define creativity *as the push to explore and discover, then creativity begins at birth.* ●

The Developmental Picture that follows provides an overview of how children of different ages express their creativity and what caregivers can do to encourage them.

Developmental Picture

The young infant (0–9 months):

- Is keenly sensitive to sensory information from the moment of birth
- Uses new information to learn about the world
- Distinguishes between new and familiar information and can tune out information that is overwhelming
- Enjoys listening to different kinds of music, experiencing rhythmic movement, and looking at colorful displays and designs

The caregiver:

- Provides a variety of things for the infant to look at, such as mobiles, pictures, and designs, and a variety of experiences with touch and sound
- Enjoys playing with infants and shares their delight in toys, actions, and sounds
- Plays different types of music (cheerful, rhythmic, soothing)
- Dances or sways to the music while carrying the infant; sings to the infant

The older infant (9–14 months):

- Is an active experimenter, trying out new ways of playing and interacting
- Tries out a variety of actions on the same object, such as hitting, banging, shaking, tasting, and dropping
- Tries the same actions on a variety of new objects, noticing the ways that different objects react (some objects bounce when dropped while other objects land with a crash, thud, or splat)

The caregiver:

- Recognizes the ways an infant is playing and exploring and provides toys and objects that support her interests

- Provides infants with different objects and combinations of objects that encourage safe and fun play
- Plays with the infant, sensitively following her interests

The young toddler (14–24 months):

- Experiments with different ways of playing with the same object—drops, rolls, kicks, and squeezes an item like a Nerf ball
- Enjoys using a crayon to make a mark
- Plays with sand and water in a variety of creative ways
- Responds to music with body movements

The caregiver:

- Provides opportunities to play with sand and water using a variety of toys, such as pails, shovels, sieves, plastic containers, pitchers, rakes, and toy boats
- Provides the opportunity to listen and respond to different kinds of music: lyrical, fast, slow, classical, modern
- Provides opportunities for early art experiences, such as finger painting, making marks with crayons, and playing with play dough

The older toddler (2 years):

- Is beginning to understand representation, such as knowing that a doll represents a baby and that a drawing of a dog represents a real dog
- Uses blocks to make a tower, road, or house
- Enjoys things that are beautiful, such as music, flowers, butterflies, and paintings
- Experiments with different scribbles and different ways of finger painting
- Listens to music and invents dances; enjoys marching to music and being part of a rhythm band

The caregiver:

- Provides opportunities for children to look at paintings, hear different kinds of music, and watch different kinds of dancing
- Allows children to play with toys in different ways, such as putting blocks in the frying pan and filling a pail with a variety of small objects
- Provides opportunities for singing, dancing, playing with clay, building with different kinds of blocks, and pretending

The preschool child (3–5 years):

- Enjoys creating with different materials, such as finger paint, water colors, tempera, collage, play dough, and clay
- Is more interested in the process of creating than the product
- Is intensely interested in and committed to her own creations and is unlikely to welcome interference
- Enjoys telling stories and making up songs
- Uses drawing as a way to tell a story
- Enjoys making up rhymes and playing with words
- Enjoys different kinds of dramatic play, including *macro play*, in which he is the actor, and *micro play*, in which he tells a story with miniature objects

(continued)

The caregiver:
- Provides children with opportunities to create in a variety of media
- Gives children the freedom to create in their own ways, rather than directing their productions
- Provides opportunities to participate in different musical experiences, such as singing, dancing, activity records, and rhythm bands
- Encourages individuality but recognizes that children often enjoy copying each other
- Provides opportunities to experience excellent art, music, poetry, and prose
- Provides different kinds of props that encourage pretend play

To describe materials and activities that encourage infants to explore and experiment

Mrs. Kid-Me-Not was observing in the infant room in the Hope County Child Care Center. She nudged one of the caregivers and said, "Hey there, Ms. Kootsey. Do you see what Patsy is doing? You better clean her up. She's got her fingers in Jell-O, and she's spreading it all over the table."

"It's okay," Mrs. Kootsey explained. "Patsy is having fun finger painting with her Jell-O. She likes the feel of it and is particularly interested in the way it looks when she spreads it out on the table. Our little Patsy is an artist in the making!"

Although spreading Jell-O around the table may seem unrelated to any form of art, providing young children with different sensory experiences is the beginning step in encouraging their creativity. When we give infants and toddlers opportunities to experience and experiment with different textures and consistencies and when we allow young children to experience and experiment with rhythm, melody, and movement, we are laying the groundwork for their creative expression.

Using Food in Sensory Experiences

There are differences of opinion in the early childhood field about the practice of using edible food items for sensory play. In this book, we present some sensory activities for babies that use food items like Jell-O, spaghetti, and corn meal. Nonetheless, we recognize some of the reasons that cause other professionals to caution against the practice:

- Food in many communities is scarce and too valuable to play with.
- Young children have to figure out what can be eaten and what cannot be eaten. It is confusing to find out that, for example, one type of finger paint (pudding) can be tasted but another type cannot.

The important thing is to provide a variety of safe sensory experiences for infants and toddlers to enjoy.

Activities That Encourage Sensory Exploration

Because exploration is the wellspring of creativity, an infant curriculum should provide opportunities for a wide variety of sensory experiences. Here are some activities that are appropriate for infants:

Texture Rub Get swatches of different-textured fabrics, and let babies handle them. Play a tickling game, where you rub the material on different parts of the infant's body.

> *Because exploration is the wellspring of creativity, an infant curriculum should provide opportunities for a wide variety of sensory experiences.*

Bubbles Blow bubbles for the infants. The younger babies can watch them move. The older babies can reach for, grasp (pop!), and finally run after them. (Make your own bubble solution by mixing 1 cup of dish-washing liquid soap with 1 cup of water. If you add a tablespoon of glycerin, the bubbles will last longer.)

Cornmeal Play Put some cornmeal out in a large, low basin. Encourage the babies to touch it and play in it. Later, add a variety of implements: spoons, cups, rubber spatulas, toy trucks, and a sieve or funnel.

Spaghetti Pull This is an excellent activity for developing small-muscle skills. Place a tray of cooked wet spaghetti in front of the babies, and let them have fun with it.

Finger Painting Most older infants (9 to 14 months) love to finger paint. Make your own finger paint by mixing some liquid starch with powdered tempera paint. Put the paint in shallow trays, since engaging the children in the process is what matters. (If a product is wanted, press paper onto the tray to pick up the design.)

Sand Play Clean sand can provide older babies with hours of fun.

Paper Fun Provide pieces (1 foot square or bigger) of special crinkly wrapping paper to crush, throw, and so on.

Sound Exploration Provide a variety of sound makers: rattles, squish toys, bells, and musical balls. Let the babies experiment with making similar and different sounds.

Activities for Exploring Music

Setting the Mood Play soothing lullabies during going-to-sleep and feeding times. Play faster, upbeat music when the babies are wide awake. Play all different kinds of music—classical, jazz, reggae, soft rock, and simple folk songs, as well as music written for babies.

Moving to Music Pick the babies up and dance with them. Also encourage them to wave their arms and bounce up and down and to imitate your movements when you play dance music.

(continued)

Activities continued

Music Making Older infants (9 to 14 months) are ready for drum play. At first, they will use their hands to beat a drum. After a while, they will discover that hitting the drum with a stick will make a delightful sound. (A short-handled wooden spoon or a rubber spatula is a safe stick.)

Marching Band Play children's songs, and encourage all the infants to shake a rattle or musical instrument to the music. Put on a marching beat and bang on drums or march in a circle. (Drums made out of oatmeal boxes and coffee cans work just fine.)

Action Songs for Baby Play

Babies need and enjoy one-on-one play with their caregivers. Make the most of this one-on-one time by engaging babies in back-and-forth chants or action songs. Here are some songs and chants that every baby enjoys:

Pat-a-Cake

Pat a cake, pat a cake, baker's man,
Bake me a cake as fast as you can,
Roll it (roll it in the baby's hands), *knead it, and mark it with a B and*
Put it in the oven for baby and me.

How Big Is Baby?

How big is baby?
So big! (Lift up the baby's hands)

Trot Trot to Boston

Trot trot to Boston
Trot trot to Lynn
You better watch out or
You might fall in (Tilt the baby backward and bounce him up)

Bicycle Baby

(Do bicycle exercises with the baby's legs)
Bicycle, bicycle baby
Bicycle, bicycle girl (or boy)

See Saw

See saw up and down, (child's name) *is going to town.*
See saw side to side, (child's name)*'s going for a ride.*
See saw bumpity bump, (child's name)*'s getting ready to jump!*

Objective 4

To describe materials and activities that encourage toddlers to express their creativity

Mrs. Artlover was deciding on a child care placement for her daughter. She described to the director of one center the kind of place she was looking for. "I would like my child to have a creative learning experience," she explained. "I am not hung up on academics. She'll learn to read and write soon enough when she gets to school. But I do want my daughter in a center where she will be immersed in artistic activities. When I read your brochure, I was impressed by the fact that beginning with toddlers, you offer lessons in music, art, ceramics, dancing, and dramatics. Could you talk more about these?"

Although the philosophy of this text recognizes the importance of introducing children to creative arts at an early age, it does not support the introduction of formal artistic lessons. Creativity is not something that you can teach a child. It emerges spontaneously as children play with materials and engage in activities that encourage their observation and self-expression. As such, young children need opportunities to explore and discover their own talents.

Activities That Encourage Sensory Exploration

Sensory activities are usually favorites with young toddlers and 2-year-olds. Such activities provide opportunities for children to heighten their sensory awareness, to practice many small-muscle skills, and to expand their language skills. Additionally, these activities encourage a great deal of social interaction.

Water Play The ideal place for water play is in a water table. To prevent the children from getting too wet, have them wear plastic smocks. If you don't have a water table, use a large dishpan or tub. Add implements like cups of many sizes, pitchers, strainers, and basters. Remember not to crowd the water table or dishpan with these materials.

Cornmeal Play Place cornmeal in a large, low basin. Give the children coffee scoops, cups, and sifters. To vary the activity, add small cars and farm animals and encourage the children to make "roads" and "mountains."

Rice Pouring While playing with rice can get messy, it is very easy to sweep up. The same kinds of implements and activities suggested for cornmeal and water will work well with rice.

Jell-O Play Cut stiff Jell-O into cubes, and let the toddlers have fun picking it up with their fingers and hands.

Smell Jars Use small containers like film canisters and punch tiny holes in the tops. Soak cotton balls in extracts (such as vanilla, peppermint, orange, and almond), perfume, or water mixed with a spice such as cinnamon or ginger. (Be sure not to use any toxic materials, like nail polish!) Stuff a ball in each container and glue or tape the lid shut. Make two sets so you can do matching activities.

Activities for Exploring Music

Toddlers 9 to 14 and 14 to 24 months of age enjoy listening to music, dancing to music, and creating music on their own. Because toddlers are sensitive to the moods that music creates, caregivers often use a record or song to signal a transition. In many child care centers, there is a special song for circle time, for clean-up time, and for saying good-bye at the end of the day. Another common practice is to play soft music at naptime.

> *Toddlers enjoy listening to music, dancing to music, and creating music on their own.*

Also take some breaks from having music playing in your room. Background music that is loud makes it hard to have "conversations" with children and can interfere with their thinking. Vary the volume of music you play, taking care that it does not produce an overall noisy room.

Listening to Music

Toddlers enjoy music most when the tune and the song are familiar. Like a favorite doll or stuffed animal, a favorite song is something you play over and over again and never get tired of listening to. Songs that toddlers enjoy include the following:

"Twinkle, Twinkle Little Star"   "Frére Jacques"

"Happy Birthday"   "Old MacDonald"

"All Around the Mulberry Bush"   "London Bridge"

Dancing to Music

Dancing to music for toddlers means bobbing up and down when the music plays. Because toddlers love what is familiar, it is a good idea to play upbeat music, like disco or rock, that they have heard at home.

Creating Music

Toddlers are not very good at singing words, but they love to clap their hands in time with the music. They also enjoy playing percussion instruments like drums, sticks, and shakers.

Songs, Finger Plays, and Poems

Movement and music activities, like art activities, are expressions of creativity and help children to become more aware of their bodies, to develop their ability to take the initiative, and to learn specific concepts. Performing songs and finger plays gives children the opportunity to hear the structure and rhythm of language and to have fun with words.

If you do not know songs like the classics that follow, use commercial tapes and CDs to learn them. Or ask co-workers to teach you the songs they enjoy singing with young children.

Honey Bunny

(to the tune of "Frére Jacques")
Honey Bunny, Honey Bunny,
Nice and soft, nice and soft (stroke arm),
We love to feed you carrots (pretend to feed carrots), *We love to*
    feed you carrots,
Hop away, hop away. (Put up two fingers and have the children hop)

Raindrop Song

Raindrops fall with a pitter-patter-pat, pitter-patter-pat, pitter-patter-pat,
    (Make your finger go up and down)
Raindrops fall with a pitter-patter-pat,
Making all things grow. (Raise your cupped hands)

Who Has a Nose?

(to the tune of "Frére Jacques")
Who has a nose? I have a nose.
Who has toes? I have toes.
Who has lots of fingers? I have lots of fingers.
Now we know, now we know.

Who can wiggle their nose? I can wiggle my nose.
Who can wiggle their toes? I can wiggle my toes.
Who can shake their fingers? I can shake my fingers.
Now we know, now we know.

(Repeat with mouth, ears, open mouth, wiggle ears, poke belly button. Also
make up other verses.)

Six Little Ducks

Six little ducks that I once knew, (Hold up 6 fingers)
Fat ones, skinny ones, big ones, too. (Use both hands to show size)
But the one little duck with the feather on his back (Put one hand on your back),
He led the others with a quack, quack, quack, (Put the heels of your hands
    together and move your fingers like a beak opening and closing)
Quack, quack, quack.

Down to the river they would go, (Point over your shoulder)
Widdle-waddle, widdle-waddle, to and fro. (Put your hands together
    and move them back and forth)
But the one little duck with the feather on his back,
He led the others with a quack, quack, quack,
Quack, quack, quack.

Variations on Traditional Songs

The Wheels on the Bus Go 'Round and 'Round

After going through the routine verses, sing about a cat on the bus that goes
"meow" and a ghost on the bus that goes "boo." Let the children come up with
new ideas.

199

Old MacDonald Had a Farm

Add variations such as these:

An alarm clock that goes "ding, dong"
A saw that goes "buzz"
A fly that goes "bzzz"
Popcorn that goes "pop"

When You're Happy and You Know It, Clap Your Hands

Try any of the following:

"When you're angry and you know it, stamp your feet."
"When you're sleepy and you know it, start to snore."
"When you're silly and you know it, laugh hee-hee."

This Is the Way We Wash Our Clothes

Try these variations:

"This is the way we wiggle our ears."
"This is the way we tickle our tummies."

Row, Row, Row Your Boat

Here are several variations:

"Pump, pump, pump your bike, gently down the hill,
Merrily, merrily, merrily, do not have a spill."

"Drive, drive, drive your car, gently down the street
Merrily, merrily, merrily, pump it with your feet."

Teddy Bear Poem

Act out the motions to this poem:

Teddy bear, teddy bear, turn around,
Teddy bear, teddy bear, touch the ground.
Teddy bear, teddy bear, go upstairs,
Teddy bear, teddy bear, say your prayers.
Teddy bear, teddy bear, turn off the light,
Teddy bear, teddy bear, say good-night.

For several variations, change "turn around" to "touch your toes" and change "say your prayers" to "wiggle your nose."

Favorite Records for Toddlers

- *Music for One's and Two's*, Tom Glazer
- *And One and Two*, Ella Jenkins
- *Anne Murray Sings for the Sesame Street Generation*
- *Singable Songs for the Very Young*, Sung by Raffi
- *Homemade Band*, Hap Palmer
- *Playtime Parachute Fun for Early Childhood*
- *Getting to Know Myself*, Hap Palmer
- *Early, Early Childhood Songs*, Ella Jenkins

Activities for Exploring Art

By 18 months old, children enjoy arranging blocks in a row and making a pattern in a sandbox by raking the sand with their fingers. By 2 years old, they are intrigued with paint and clay and ready to experiment with paintbrushes and other paint media. Between 2 and 3 years, children begin to arrange objects and materials in an order or array that is pleasing to them. While most children enjoy the sensation of spreading paint with their fingers, other children dislike getting their hands dirty and prefer to paint with a brush.

Materials for Painting

Types of Paint Watercolors, nontoxic tempera paints, finger paints

Surfaces for Painting Young children enjoy variety. Try painting on an easel, painting on individual paper, and painting on a mural (either taped to the table or on the wall).

Paint Media Toddlers can paint with brushes, fingers, sponges, Q-tips, cotton balls, eyedroppers, and string. Stamp painting is also fun: Cut sponges into designs, and dip them into paint in shallow trays. You can cut potatoes in half and etch designs into the tops. Cookie cutters allow children to make familiar designs. On a sunny day, children can enjoy using large paintbrushes to paint with water outside on stone surfaces or concrete walls and sidewalks. It is also fun to paint objects: Let the children collect and paint rocks, shells, pine cones, sticks, and scrap pieces of wood.

Painting and Pasting Activities

Finger Painting Finger painting can be done on a "messy play tray" (commercially available or donated by fast-food restaurants) or directly on the table. When the children create something they want to save, make a print by pressing a piece of paper onto the design.

Shaving Cream Finger Painting Use nonmenthol shaving cream and a smooth surface. Add food coloring to make it even more interesting.

Ivory Snow Flake Finger Painting Add a little water to Ivory Snow Flakes (¼ cup water to 1 cup flakes), and beat the mixture with an egg beater. This makes thick suds that can be used like finger paint. Food coloring can also be added.

Pasting Once children have learned to paste, they can carry out all kinds of craft projects. For very young children, providing large tongue depressors and individual portions of paste placed in baby-food jar lids or on small paper squares works well. Another method of pasting involves watering down Elmer's Glue and painting it on with a brush. Older children can create collages by pasting scraps of paper and other materials on heavy paper or cardboard. They can also draw with paste and then sprinkle on salt, colored sand, rice, or glitter to create interesting effects.

Activities for Sensory Play

Sensory play is a favorite activity for toddlers, who enjoy water play, sandboxes, rice, oatmeal, and cornmeal bins. They are particularly fond of play dough and enjoy a variety of textures.

Play Dough Kneading play dough aids in developing small-muscle skills and is a favorite among younger children. You can make your own play dough with the following recipe:

Use-Again Play Dough

2 cups flour	½ cup salt
2 tablespoons vegetable oil	2 cups cold water
Food coloring (add to the water before mixing with dry ingredients, so the food coloring won't stain your hands)	4 teaspoons cream of tartar

Cook and stir over medium heat until the play dough thickens. Cool and put in a closed container or resealable plastic bag.

Vary the implements presented with the play dough. Try rolling pins and dowels, tongue depressors, small cookie cutters, plastic knives, scissors, and small (nonswallowable) objects such as plastic letters, straws, poker chips, bottle and jar lids, and small toys.

Building with Blocks

Toddlers enjoy creating and experimenting with blocks. They are learning how to carry blocks, line up blocks, stack blocks, balance bigger blocks on smaller blocks, and nest blocks in unique ways. Provide blocks of different sizes, shapes, and textures as well as cardboard blocks, nesting blocks, plastic blocks, and small unit blocks. Avoid large heavy wooden blocks because toddlers like to throw things.

Pretend Play

One of the most exciting aspects of being a teacher of toddlers is to watch the gradual emergence of pretend play. Pretend play begins as imitation. Young toddlers love to imitate grown-up activities. They enjoy babbling into a toy telephone, sweeping the floor with a child-sized broom, and mowing the grass with a bubble-blowing push toy.

> *One of the most exciting aspects of being a teacher of toddlers is to watch the gradual emergence of pretend play.*

With most toddlers, we see a gradual transition from imitative play to pretending at around 2 years old. A little girl may insist on wearing a baseball hat when she pushes her bubble blower. She is not simply imitating the act of pushing a lawnmower; she is pretending to be Daddy mowing the lawn. A boy may stir a pot with a spoon and then put it on a play "stove." He is not just imitating a parent whom he has watched cooking; he is pretending that he is preparing dinner for the family.

Teachers can support the emergence of pretend play by providing the play space, the materials, the dress-up clothes, and the furnishings that allow for the spontaneous emergence of pretend play. Basic props should include kitchen items, a steering wheel, a doctor's kit, dolls, and toy animals.

To describe materials and activities that encourage preschool children to express their creativity

Miss Sue looked around the room sharply, a slight frown creasing her brow. Her glance seemed to rest briefly on each child. "We will not begin until everyone is absolutely quiet and still," she said. A hush fell upon the room. Then suddenly, 20 sets of small eyes turned in unison toward a loud crashing sound coming from the end of one of the long tables.

Miss Sue identified Johnny as the source of the crash and said to him, "Johnny, if you would sit like I told you, with both feet on the floor and both hands folded together on top of the table, you would not keep falling out of your chair."

Miss Sue rolled her eyes up, as if to say "Why me?" and released a long sigh. Then she went on with her talking.

"I am giving each of you a sheet of paper to color. There are five flowers in a pot. Across each flower is written the word that tells you what color that flower should be. If you can't remember what the words say . . ." Miss Sue paused and glanced pointedly toward Johnny. ". . . Then look at the chart on the wall. Remember to work without talking, and try to stay within the lines. When you finish, bring your paper to me to be checked. If you have colored neatly and correctly, you may then go outside to play. If not, you'll have to do the paper over until you get it right. All right, you may begin."

Miss Sue sat down at her desk and checked off "creative activity" on her lesson plan. ●

This story, of course, is an exaggeration of obvious "don'ts" for creative activities. Read through it again and see how many you can pick out. Then continue to learn about some productive ways of encouraging creativity in preschool children.

Creativity in Music

Interestingly enough, when we talk about creativity in arts and crafts, we usually talk about children's involvement in the creative process. But when we talk about creativity in music, we are more apt to think of children as a participating audience that is following the directions of an activity record or singing along with a song written by someone else. In both music and art, children need opportunities to be an appreciative audience *and* opportunities to create on their own.

Singing, dancing, and music making are favorite activities for all preschool children. Music activities provide opportunities for self-expression, creativity, fun, excitement, and comradery. Most important, music activities provide an opportunity for children to experience the joy and sense of power that comes from cooperation.

In this section, we look at three kinds of musical activities that can be used success-fully with preschool children: group singing, rhythm bands, and musical games and movement activities.

Group Singing

Preschool children love to sing. While many preschoolers are not very good at carry-ing a tune or staying on key, most can learn to recognize and repeat the contour and rhythm of a simple song. By limiting the number of different tunes and using the tunes children know in creative ways, preschool teachers can provide children with a delightful repertoire of songs to learn and love.

Favorite Songs and Variations If you do not know songs like the following clas-sics, use commercial tapes and CDs to learn them or ask co-workers to teach you the songs they enjoy singing with young children.

The Wheels on the Bus

The wheels on the bus go round and round,
Round and round, round and round.
The wheels on the bus go round and round,
All through the town.

Variation: For fun, suggest that some farm animals have joined the children on the bus:

The ducks on the bus go quack, quack, quack . . .
The cows on the bus go moo, moo, moo . . .

Old MacDonald

Old MacDonald had a farm, ee-i-ee-i-o.
And on that farm he had a cow, ee-i-ee-i-o.
With a moo, moo here, and a moo, moo there,
Here a moo, there a moo, everywhere a moo, moo.
Old MacDonald had a farm, ee-i-ee-i-o.

Variation: Suggest that Old MacDonald decided to add some things to his farm:

A clock that goes" tick-tock"
A truck that goes "vrum-vrum"
An engine that goes "putt, putt"
A wagon that goes" clappity-clap"

If You're Happy and You Know It, Clap Your Hands

If you're happy and you know it, clap your hands.
If you're happy and you know it, clap your hands.
If you're happy and you know it,
Then you're face will surely show it.
If you're happy and you know it, clap your hands.

Variation 1: Change the first stanza to include different emotions:

If you're silly and you know it, start to giggle . . .
If you're thirsty and you know it, go slurp, slurp . . .
If you're sleepy and you know it, start to snore . . .

204

Variation 2: Change the second stanza:

> *If you're happy and you know it, stick out your tongue . . .*
> *If you're happy and you know it, wiggle your nose . . .*
> *If you're happy and you know it, clap your elbows . . .*

Rhythm Bands

Rhythm bands provide opportunities for creativity, ingenuity, and the development of cognitive skills. They also provide opportunities for making different instruments, for learning about different cultures, for developing listening skills, and for participating in group experience.

Obviously, most children of 3, 4, and 5 do not have the skills to write music or to play standard musical instruments. But this should not discourage a creative teacher.

Rhythm instruments can be created, improvised, and purchased. The simplest instruments to make are shakers, rhythm sticks, and drums. Shakers can be made out of juice cans, coffee cans, and well-washed plastic milk containers filled with pebbles, rice, or beans. (Glue the covers on.) Rhythm sticks can be created from paper towel spindles, chopsticks, and dowels, and drums can be made from coffee cans, oatmeal cartons, and plastic cereal bowls. Another good thing about homemade instruments is that the children can bring their ideas home and their families can create their own rhythm bands.

> *Rhythm bands provide opportunities for creativity, ingenuity, and the development of cognitive skills.*

Also equip your classroom with easy-to-play musical instruments. Montessori bells, xylophones, and kazoos are particularly appropriate.

Once children have created their own instruments or have access to classroom instruments, it is easy to encourage them to create their own rhythms. Try sitting a group of five or six children in a circle and letting each child have a turn being the rhythm leader.

Also encourage children to create their own songs and to make up chants. Provide children with an opportunity to smell a flower, taste a piece of fruit, feel a new texture, or watch a beam of light as it comes through a prism. Then ask them to describe their experience in words. When the children select a descriptive phrase that seems to please them, ask them to say it over and over again. Inevitably, their chant becomes a sing-song, their own original rendition.

Learning about Different Cultures Almost every ethnic group has its own special music. Playing music from different cultures and helping children use instruments to imitate or accent the beat provides a culture-sharing experience.

Developing Listening Skills There are many different ways of teaching listening skills through the use of rhythm instruments. The simplest way, of course, is to buy and use commercial recordings (tapes, CDs) and commercial rhythm instruments. If your program can afford it, this is a good investment because instruments and recordings are unlikely to wear out.

A second way to develop listening skills is to combine the singing of a familiar song with the use of homemade instruments. A good one to try is "Over the Mountain." To begin, sit the children in a circle. Distribute homemade instruments to the group, giving one section shakers, one section sticks, and one section drums. Explain to the group that they all have to watch the conductor so that each section knows when it is their turn to play their instrument.

Have the group sing these words:

The bear went over the mountain,
The bear went over the mountain,
And what do you think he heard?
And what do you think he heard?
He heard the drums all playing, (Have the children with the drums play)
He heard the drums all playing, (Have the children with the drums play)
He heard the drums all playing, (Have the children with the drums play)
That is what he heard.

For the next stanza, have the children sing:

He heard the sticks all playing. (Have the children with the sticks play)

For the third stanza, they should sing:

He heard the shakers all shaking. (Have the children with the shakers play)

For the fourth stanza, sing these words:

He heard the whole band playing. (Have everyone join in)

Musical Games and Movement Activities

Musical games and movement activities are traditional favorites in preschools around the world. They are wonderful opportunities for sharing culture, helping shy children participate, beginning and ending the day, and making productive use of waiting and transition times. Some musical games involve sitting or standing in a circle, while others work best if the children choose partners or line up in two's. Here are some all-time favorites:

Circle Games
- The Farmer in the Dell
- Go In and Out the Window
- Ring Around the Rosie

Dances
- Hokie Pokie
- Little Red Caboose
- Skip to My Lou

Games with Partners
- Row, Row, Row Your Boat
- See Saw, Margery Daw
- London Bridge

- Miss Mary Mack
- Little Brown Jug

Activity records that have the children listen to the words and perform the actions are also common favorites among preschoolers.

Creativity in Art

Preschool children, regardless of their artistic talent, love to engage in art activities. As teachers, we can support this enthusiasm in many different ways. One way is to have art materials available for free choice throughout much of the day. This keeps the focus on the process, rather than the product, and encourages the children to experiment with different kinds of materials. Other guidelines are as follow:

> *Preschool children, regardless of their artistic talent, love to engage in art activities.*

- Encourage the children to be spontaneous. Children's art products should be expressions of their own feelings and their own perceptions. When we give children stencils to color in or examples to follow, we make them dissatisfied with their own creations and stifle their creativity. Unfortunately, even under the best of circumstances, many children lose their spontaneity as they grow older, when their attention turns to copying reality.

- Recognize that the *process* is more important than the *product*. For young children, painting a picture or molding a piece of clay is an ongoing, dynamic activity. They love to watch the paint as it spreads over the paper and to feel the texture of the clay as it slides through their fingers. It doesn't bother young children at all if their multicolored picture turns into a great big glob. The fun is in the doing.

- Give children a chance to talk with you about their artwork, both as they work and after they have finished. They may have questions about technique or materials, they may want to name the objects or colors in a picture, or they may want to share a story. Be sure, however, to follow the child's lead. Even an open-ended question like "What's that?" or a comment like "Tell me about your picture" can be an intrusion, if you insist on getting an answer. No matter how gently you phrase the question, asking a child to tell about a picture suggests that the picture is *about* something. But how can a child explain a painting that is a swoop of his arm, a twist of the brush, and a daring splash of paint, followed by a drip and a dabble?

- Don't insist that a child complete her product. When the child is concerned with the process, not the product, the picture is completed when she has finished the process. Filling up the paper may not be important to the child.

- Try not to be overly exuberant about children's creations. When we tell a child that his picture is beautiful, we are making a value judgment that may not be appropriate. Sometimes, a child will contradict what the teacher says because he wants the teacher to repeat the compliment. At other times, however, the child may not be happy about the picture and the teacher's praise will be distressing. What really matters is the way the *child* feels about his art experience.

- Encourage experimenting with a variety of media. Each medium that the children will use—chalk, crayon, finger paint, watercolor, or poster paint—has its own special characteristics, providing different kinds of opportunities for creative expression. Finger paint is especially good for expressing feelings of exuberance. Poster paint affords an opportunity to express a feeling of power. Crayon or chalk gives children a sense of being in control. By allowing children to explore with a variety of media, we give them a chance to match the media to their moods and to discover the medium that feels best to them.

- Let children decide whether—and if so, how—to display or share their work.

Activities for Planned Art

While process art can be made available to all children at any time, planned art activities require special teacher preparation and/or direction.

Tearing and Pasting Before a child learns to use scissors, tearing is a good small-muscle activity. It can be an end in itself or part of a planned project. For example, as part of a unit on food, the children could tear brightly colored tissue paper and paste the pieces on sheets to fill in large outlines of fruits. The children could then arrange their fruits in a display.

Printing Use sponges that have been cut into various shapes and attached to tongue depressors or Popsicle sticks with rubber bands. Making finger prints, hand prints, and foot prints is also fun for children.

Vegetable Prints Potatoes are especially good for print making.

Puppet Making A variety of puppets can be easily made: paper plate puppets on sticks, finger puppets, sock puppets, and paper bag puppets.

Collages Make collages using any of these materials:

- Materials found outside—leaves, twigs, acorns, small pebbles, shells, sand, bark, feathers
- Things to eat—rice, beans, cereal, macaroni, spaghetti, egg shells, popcorn, seeds
- Scraps of fabrics—lace, rick-rack, ribbons, yarn, buttons, beads, sequins
- Different types and colors of paper—construction paper, tissue paper, napkins, paper towels, cellophane, wallpaper, gummed circles, doilies, confetti
- "Odds and ends"—bottle caps, sponge bits, straws, cotton balls, and the like

Painting and Drawing Again, there are many possibilities:

- Do easel painting on newsprint with large brushes.
- Finger painting—Play a record with a march tempo. Let the children dip their fingers in finger paint and "march" across the paper with their fingers.
- Magic markers—Use nontoxic colors that wash out and do not stain.
- Chalk—Try white chalk on black or dark-blue paper for a nighttime picture or a snow scene.
- Crayons—Dittoed sheets and coloring books are great for teachers but not for children. Coloring within someone else's lines might be a good small-muscle activity (although it is too advanced for 3- and 4-year-olds), but it stifles creativity. It's better to string beads or cut paper to develop small-muscle skills and to let children use crayons to make their own lines, circles, and interesting arrangements with colors and space.

- String painting—Dip a piece of string in paint and lay it on the paper. Or lay it on one side of the paper, fold over the paper, and pull out the string.
- Straw painting—Put a blob of thin tempera paint on a piece of paper, and blow at it with a straw for interesting effects.
- Mirror image—Using a small plastic spoon, drop several blobs of paint on the paper. Fold it over in half, and then unfold it and let dry.
- Sand painting—Drip glue over the paper, and while it is still wet, shake colored sand on the paper.
- Dry tempera painting—Dip cotton balls into dry tempera and rub them on damp paper.
- Paint on a variety of materials to observe different effects: paper towels, tissue paper, rocks, wood, aluminum foil, shells, corrugated cardboard, cloth, and so on.
- Computer art—Many children's software programs enable drawing, stamping, moving or placing pictures, and creating artistic text effects. Computer "coloring books," in which the children select colors to fill in regions of a picture, can also be fun if the children are free to experiment (e.g., changing the sky from blue to black to green).

Creativity with Crafts

Although the product may not be important when the child is involved in an art activity, the exact opposite is true about crafts. Young children love the idea of bringing home a present for their family or making a holiday decoration. Making crafts also can be a wonderful way to teach about the children's own heritage and about other cultures.

Regardless, any craft project can be counterproductive if it is a teacher, rather than a child, activity. No matter how beautiful a product is, it loses some of its value if the teacher has done the bulk of the work.

Here are some guidelines for selecting crafts for 3- and 4-year-olds:

- Select a craft in which the child can do most of the work.
- Choose something that will not be too long or tedious. With few exceptions, it is best to select a craft that can be completed in one sitting.
- Make sure that the craft has meaning for the children. Crafts are most apt to have meaning when they are tied in to a unit of study or associated with a real-life experience.
- Make sure that the craft is not too elaborate or fragile. Children like the idea of taking something home and get frustrated and unhappy if the craft falls apart before it gets there.
- Choose a craft that the children will enjoy doing.
- Choose a craft that allows some leeway for individual ideas.

Activities for Making Crafts

Many good books are on the market that contain ideas and instructions for making interesting objects from throw-away materials. Here are just a few examples:

Egg Carton Garden

Materials: Styrofoam egg cartons, soil, seeds.

Procedure: Punch a hole in the bottom of each small section. Remove the lid and use it as a tray for the "garden." Fill the sections with dirt, and plant a seed in each one.

Fish in the Aquarium

Materials: Styrofoam tray, construction paper, sand, shells, plastic wrap, yarn, Goldfish crackers or cutouts.

Procedure: Have the children glue on the elements of an aquarium scene to the tray and then cover it with plastic wrap.

Paper Plate Faces

Materials: Paper plates, construction paper, glue, yarn (or fabric scraps, buttons, bottle caps, etc.).

Procedure: Have the children glue materials on the plates to create faces. For older children, punch holes around the edge of the plate and thread yarn through for hair.

The Teacher's Responsibilities

- Set up an accessible art center with a variety of materials. Give the children the time, space, and freedom to explore.

- Provide a creative climate. The classroom should be aesthetically pleasing, un-cluttered, and colorful, reflecting the originality and individuality of you and the children.

- Sensitize the children to the beauty and wonder of the world they live in—from a sweeping rainbow to a drop of dew on a blade of grass.

- Integrate art activities into the curriculum as a part of the learning experience, not as something separate and apart. For example, after a field trip, let the children paint a mural to illustrate the things they saw, felt, smelled, and heard.

- Show your own appreciation and enjoyment of creative expression.

- Use creative ways to introduce new concepts. For example, make a "Hungry Lion" paper bag puppet with a slit for its mouth. The lion can "tell" the children that it "only wants to eat triangles today." Have a box of shapes for the children to choose from as they "feed" the lion.

- Clearly define responsibilities and limits. If at all possible, teach the children how to prepare dry tempera paints, wash the brushes they have used, hang their paintings to dry, put away all materials, and clean up any spillage. The children should know what materials they can use, where they are to be used, and when they can use them.

Materials to Encourage Creativity

Materials to Buy Crayons, glue or paste, tempera paint (liquid or powdered), easels, brushes (½- to 1-inch width, 10 to 12 inches long), scissors, magic markers (nontoxic, washable colors), paper (craft, white newsprint, construction paper, and tissue paper in several colors), chalk

Materials to Make Paint containers (baby-food jars set into cut-down milk cartons), play dough or clay, finger paint

Materials to Save

- *Containers:* egg cartons, berry baskets, cardboard food trays, empty cans, oatmeal cartons, milk cartons, plastic jugs, shoeboxes, pie pans, margarine tubs
- *Good to have:* tongue depressors, straws, paper towels, paper towel tubes, toilet tissue tubes, Popsicle sticks, pipe cleaners, toothpicks, cardboard boxes
- *Don't forget:* magazines, newspapers, paper bags, buttons, spoons, bottle caps, stones, shells, coat hangers, clothespins, paper plates, cards, wrapping paper, ribbons

Promoting Imaginative Play

One of the most effective ways to promote creativity in a preschool environment is to encourage pretending. Pretend play allows children to give free reign to their imagination to explore new ideas and invent new situations. In addition to promoting creativity, imaginative play has these benefits:

> *One of the most effective ways to promote creativity in a preschool environment is to encourage pretending.*

- It helps children develop prosocial behavior by providing opportunities to communicate with each other, to plan cooperatively, to share responsibility, and to take a point of view that is different from their own.
- It helps children cope with stress by giving them opportunities to re-create actual life events. Not only can they replay happy experiences, but in the case of frightening and disturbing events, they can assume the roles of powerful people in a safe and new context.
- It encourages creativity as children explore new ideas and invent new situations.
- It benefits children socially, emotionally, and intellectually. It provides children with opportunities to develop representations of reality that provide the basis for symbolic play and abstract thinking.

The Teacher's Role in Promoting Imaginative Play

Teachers encourage imaginative play in the classroom when they do the following:

- Provide the children with a variety of real-world experiences that can be recreated in pretend situations.

- Give the children time and space to develop their pretend play ideas.
- Provide the children with a variety of props that can be used for imaginative play.
- Encourage, model, and join in imaginative play but do not take it over.

In order for imaginative play to flourish, the teacher must be willing to let the children develop and extend their own original play ideas.

Imaginative Play Prop Boxes

In addition to creating a regular area for imaginative play, such as a housekeeping and dress-up area, teachers can greatly expand play opportunities by the use of *prop boxes.* Prop boxes can be created by teachers over time, changed periodically, and even shared by several teachers within a center.

Try these suggestions for creating prop boxes:

"Beach" Play Sunglasses, empty sunblock lotion containers, pails, shovels, beach towels, low beach chairs, swim rings, a picnic basket and thermos, beach balls, flip-flops, sun hats, pretend food, shells

"Doctor" Play Medical bag, sheets, white coats, stethoscopes, play hypodermic needle cases, magic markers, tape, bandages, empty medicine bottles, tongue depressors, hot water bottles, toy thermometers, prescription pads and pencils, toy money

"Firefighter" Play Firehats, hoses, a siren, a bell, lunchboxes, play walkie-talkies, megaphones, first aid kit

"Restaurant" Play Trays, tablecloths, flower vases, menus, cash registers, order pads and pencils, aprons, dishes, glasses, silverware, play food, salt and pepper shakers, creamers and sugar bowls

Other possibilities for prop boxes include those for playing "supermarket," "hairdresser," "post office," "repairperson," "dentist," and "shoe store."

The early childhood years have been called "the magic years" because this is the time when children's pretending is at its height. Take time to enjoy the children's natural creativity as they play with words, music, art materials, toys, found objects, and each other. Let them bring out your creativity and playfulness, as well, as you explore new experiences together.

Additional Resources for Creativity

Althouse, R., Johnson, M., & Mitchell, S. (2003). *The colors of learning: Integrating the visual arts into early childhood curriculum.* Washington, DC: NAEYC. (Co-published with Teachers College Press)

Chenfeld, M. (1993). *Teaching in the key of life.* Washington, DC: NAEYC.

Hirsch, E. (Ed.). (1996). *The block book* (3rd ed.). Washington, DC: NAEYC.

Korelak, D. (Ed.). (2004). *Spotlight on young children and play.* Washington, DC: NAEYC.

The Performers

Supporting Social and Emotional Development and Providing Positive Guidance

Samantha's mother and father were having dinner together after having spent the whole day visiting infant care centers. "We sure got an education today!" Samantha's father remarked. "I knew that finding a good child care center wasn't going to be easy, but I didn't expect it to be this hard. Where do you think we should go from here?"

"Let's go over our notes," Samantha's mother suggested. "There were three places that we didn't put on the blacklist: Gentle Touch, Young People's Paradise, and Kids' Place. We loved the staff at Gentle Touch, but the classrooms were dingy and there didn't seem to be much going on."

"The second school, Young People's Paradise, wasn't too bad," added Samantha's father. "We liked the fact that the rooms were attractive and inviting and that there were plenty of things for the children to do. Our concern was that the caregivers seemed to lack warmth. We never saw a teacher bend down and talk to a child or give a child a hug."

"You're right," commented Samantha's mother. "The third school, Kids' Place, came the closest to meeting our criteria. The teachers were pretty good, the classrooms were well equipped, the children played nicely together, and there were plenty of things to do. The one negative we wrote down was that there seemed to be too many children in each room and too much going on at the same time. We were afraid that Samantha would be completely overwhelmed."

Samantha's father continued the conversation: "Obviously, we're not going to find the school of our dreams, but we've run out of options and it's time to make a choice. If we were choosing a place for my nephew, Mikey, there wouldn't be a problem. Nothing overwhelms that child, and he would do fine in Kids' Place. But with Samantha, it's a different story. She needs to be in a quiet, low-key environment, with a few kids and a loving teacher who has time for every child. I opt for Gentle Touch."

Samantha's mother nodded in agreement. ●

Samantha's parents deserve a lot of credit. Not only did they visit many centers and take careful notes, but they also recognized the importance of selecting a center that would be right for a child like Samantha. Although they preferred the more stimulating setting, they recognized their child's need for a calmer, quieter environment.

In this section, we look at ways of recognizing each child's emotional needs, supporting each child's social and emotional development, and using positive guidance to help children manage their own emotions and respect the rights of others.

Self

Chapter 8

Overview

The *self* refers to the set of inner experiences, thoughts, feelings, sensations, and emotions that constitute each person's unique identity. *Self-concept* is an individual's mental image of his or her own characteristics and capabilities. *Self-esteem* refers to the child's self-evaluation.

Rationale

The feelings that children develop about themselves and about the people around them help to form their emotional makeup and have a direct bearing on their learning in school.

Infants vary in their inborn temperaments. Some are naturally easygoing and easy to soothe. Others are more sensitive, jittery, or feisty. Some quietly take in everything they see and hear; others seem always to be on the go. Some love novelty and look forward to new things; others like predictability and are upset by too much change.

When parents and caregivers respond sensitively, babies learn to calm and arouse themselves appropriately and to experience the joy of mastering new skills. They come to love and trust those around them and to feel good about themselves. They learn eagerly and constantly. However, babies whose cues are missed—who are ignored, overstimulated, or not given individual attention—fail to thrive. They may become depressed and withdrawn or constantly cranky and on edge. They may refuse to try new things or give up quickly, as if they expect to fail. The self is a

215

combination of inborn tendencies and life experiences. Parents, family members, and early childhood teachers and caregivers all play critical roles in shaping whom a child will become.

Most children, regardless of family background, come to school with a sense of security and a rather well-defined concept of self. These activities are developed during their few short years living with a family that is generally giving and supportive. It is the responsibility of the child care center and the individual teacher to provide experiences that continually affirm these positive feelings. Each child must feel love, security, acceptance, and respect from the adults with whom she interacts. The teacher helps each child to know, accept, and appreciate herself as an individual. The teacher also helps each child develop a sense of self-awareness and self-esteem, to express and accept her own feelings—both good and bad—and to develop pride as an individual and as a member of a cultural or ethnic group.

> *The teacher helps each child to know, accept, and appreciate himself or herself as an individual.*

Teachers interact with children many times during the course of a typical day in a child care program. It is critical that teachers be aware of the intimate relationship between self-concept and success in school and indeed success and competence in life. Teachers must know that children who feel incapable of success will not succeed and those who feel unworthy of affection or attention will not thrive. But children who are made to feel special, who are loved and listened to and appreciated, will put forth their best efforts because they experience joy in learning and pride in achievement.

Objectives

1. To recognize the sequence of emotional development from birth to 5 years and the role of the caregiver in supporting this development

2. To recognize ways in which infants develop trust and a sense of security

3. To recognize ways in which young toddlers develop self-awareness and learn to cope with separation

4. To recognize ways in which older toddlers develop a sense of autonomy

5. To recognize ways in which preschool children develop a sense of personal identity and self-worth, recognize and express their feelings, and take pride in their heritage

6. To recognize ways in which caregivers can help young children develop a sense of responsibility

7. To recognize ways in which teachers can create inclusive classrooms where all children are welcome

Supporting Emotional Development

Miss Trying had a difficult day. Although she had only three babies assigned to her in the baby room, there was never enough time to relax and enjoy them. The basic problem was Jesse. "Jesse," Miss Trying explained to the director, "is the most difficult infant I have ever tried to look after. He's as taut as a violin string. If you move too fast or not fast enough, if you get his bottle a little bit too hot or not quite hot enough, he'll start to scream, and it's impossible to soothe him. I wish I knew if he's like this at home, but I never get a chance to talk to his mother."

The director explained that she knew Jesse's mother quite well. As a matter of fact, she was the one who persuaded Jesse's mother to put Jesse in infant care. Jesse had been difficult since the day he was born. He would cry for no obvious reason, and once he started crying, there was no way to calm him down. Just the other day, she had met Jesse's mother in the supermarket. His mother thanked her effusively for keeping Jesse at the center. She was beginning to see some changes in his behavior at home. He was becoming somewhat less irritable and a little bit easier to comfort. She attributed the change both to the fact that Jesse was maturing and to the fact that Jesse's caregivers were so good with him.

All children are born into this world with unique characteristics and temperaments that define their individuality and affect how they relate to other people, cope with stress, and develop self-control and self-confidence. Miss Trying's experience with Jesse demonstrates the importance of recognizing these individual differences. As soon as she realized that Jesse's difficult behavior was a manifestation of temperament and not a reaction to her caregiving, she regained her self-confidence. Jesse, in turn, responded to this new self-assurance, and his difficult behaviors diminished.

> *Recognizing that there are differences in individual temperament can help parents and caregivers be responsive to children's individual needs.*

Temperamental differences are present in infants from the moment of birth. Some babies are even tempered, alert, and predictable in terms of their sleeping and eating cycles. They adapt easily to change and enjoy new experiences. These children are described as having easy temperaments. Other children are irritable, difficult to distract, upset by new experiences, and unpredictable in terms of their sleeping and eating cycles. These children are described as having difficult or feisty temperaments. Because there is always interaction between infants and caregivers, it is difficult to know whether temperamental variables are really enduring or initiate a chain of responses in the caregiving environment that maintains these characteristic behaviors.

Recognizing that there are differences in individual temperament can help parents and caregivers be responsive to children's individual needs. Babies who are temperamentally slow to warm up need to be introduced to new experiences in a gradual way. Babies who are temperamentally irritable need their caregivers to be relaxed, gentle, and especially sensitive to their needs.

In this chapter, we focus on the emotional challenges that every child must face in the first 5 years of life. We discuss ways in which children's success in meeting these challenges depends both on their inborn characteristics, such as temperament and resiliency, and on the kinds of emotional support they receive from loving and caring adults.

Objective 1

To recognize the sequence of emotional development from birth to 5 years and the role of the caregiver in supporting this development

The Developmental Picture that follows discusses children's emotional development and what caregivers can do to support it across various stages.

Developmental Picture

The young infant (0–9 months):

- Is developing a sense of trust and learning to make predictions
- Learns ways of self-comforting
- Demonstrates a variety of emotions, including sadness, anger, surprise, and joy
- Learns to respond to a smile with a smile
- Initiates interactions with parents and caregivers and signals the need for a break
- Shows emerging awareness of self by playing with her own hands or by touching her caregiver's mouth and then her own
- Develops preferences for certain sights, sounds, ways of being held, objects, and activities
- Enjoys active play but can get overstimulated

The caregiver:

- Provides environments and interactions that are interesting without being overwhelming
- Checks with the parents to learn what soothes, engages, and excites their child and what is overwhelming or tiring
- Helps the baby learn to soothe herself by offering a pacifier, a favorite blanket, a change of scene, or a favorite activity
- Engages in back and forth interactions with the baby
- Supports an infant's developing sense of trust by responding to his cries and recognizing and responding to his cues
- Uses words and smiles to let the infant know that he is loveable
- Accommodates the child's preferences for different levels of stimulation
- Recognizes the importance of maintaining a balance between quiet and active play
- Takes into account individual differences and responsively provides each infant with enough stimulation to keep her alert and interested without becoming overwhelmed

The older infant (9–14 months):

- Discovers that she is an agent who can make things happen
- Learns many different ways of getting adults to do her bidding
- Takes the lead in initiating interactions
- Responds to her mirror image by smiling and playing with the mirror

- Forms very special attachments to familiar people
- Shows self-awareness by putting a hat on his head or putting on a necklace
- Demonstrates shyness by hiding behind the caregiver

The caregiver:

- Interacts with the same babies on a consistent basis and with love, caring, and enthusiasm
- Expresses delight when the infant shows off a new accomplishment
- Recognizes when the infant is sad, angry, frustrated, or happy and talks about his feelings with words
- Provides toys that support the infant's body awareness, such as mirrors, soft dolls, and large bead necklaces

The young toddler (14–24 months):

- Is very clear about likes and dislikes
- Recognizes herself in the mirror and wipes her own forehead if she sees a spot in the mirror
- Uses gestures, grunts, and some words to get adults to respond to her wishes
- Enjoys being praised and is upset when scolded
- Shows delight when people clap for her or laugh at what she does
- Shows empathy when someone is hurt
- Expresses a whole range of emotions—happy, thoughtful, worried, frightened, jealous, angry, sad, surprised

The caregiver:

- Lets the toddler know in many ways that he is good and worthy of love
- Expresses delight when the toddler shows off a new accomplishment
- Talks about different feelings, like angry, sad, happy, and worried
- Responds positively when the toddler is playing nicely, supporting the toddler's self-image

The older toddler (2 years):

- Asserts herself in many different ways, insisting on doing things her own way and on getting what she wants
- Is learning to make choices and to say no
- Is emphatic about doing things for himself
- Tests limits by doing what she has been told not to and watching the adult's reaction
- Has temper tantrums when she can't have what she wants
- Can use some words to express feelings
- Recognizes that some things belong to him, resists sharing, and objects if someone takes something that belongs to someone else
- Enjoys being a helper

The caregiver:

- Recognizes that sharing is hard for toddlers and provides more than one of the same toy
- Provides opportunities for children to make choices
- Gives children opportunities to do things for themselves
- Provides opportunities for children to help with tasks and praises them for being helpful

(continued)

- Recognizes that disobedience is a normal way for older toddlers to express their growing independence and selfhood
- Provides safe alternatives when children insist on doing something hurtful or dangerous

The preschool child (3–5 years):

- Is aware of her own individuality and able to express feelings, needs, and desires
- Evaluates his own skills and compares himself to others
- Recognizes her ability to make choices and control her impulsive behavior
- Responds positively to deserved praise and approval

The caregiver:

- Seeks out opportunities to praise children for genuine accomplishments
- Recognizes children who need special encouragement
- Finds ways to help children feel successful
- Offers children love and affection

To recognize ways in which infants develop trust and a sense of security

Amelia, a teen mother, was living with her own mother. Although Amelia felt fortunate that she could live at home and that her mother would help with the baby, she and her mother were always quarreling about what was good for the baby. "You've got to stop picking up that baby every time he lets out a little whimper," her mother insisted. "That baby is already spoiled, and he's not even 3 months old!"

"I am not going to let my baby cry," Amelia insisted. "My teacher at school made it quite clear that you cannot spoil a 3-month-old baby, and I believe her."

"I bet that teacher, whoever she is, never raised a baby of her own," argued Amelia's mother. "Just because she read a book, she thinks she's an authority!"

Although other people may agree with Amelia's mother, Amelia and her teacher are absolutely right. Babies cry because something is bothering them. If you respond to their cries and find a way to comfort them, babies will learn that they can trust you and they will feel safe and secure.

Every baby needs to know that there is at least one person in her life who will always be there for her, who can be counted on to respond to her needs and to find ways to relieve her distress. Through interacting with the responsive people in their lives, babies develop feelings of trust. They know that they are safe as long as one of these special persons is somewhere nearby. They also learn to associate these special people with playfulness and pleasure.

Between 6 and 18 months, when babies are starting to move around on their own, they will not venture very far unless a special person is in sight. They are also likely to become wary of strangers. They know they can trust their special people, but they are not so sure about new people. If a new person tries to pick up a baby, the baby will cling to his special person and turn away from the stranger. If a baby's special person leaves the room, he will stop playing and will likely burst into tears. When the special person returns to

> *Every baby needs to know that there is at least one person in her life who will always be there for her.*

the room, he will greet her with his biggest smile. Infants who develop a strong attachment to at least one special person during their first year will be capable of developing strong and lasting relationships with many people in the years ahead.

A baby who begins child care at 6 months old or later is likely to have some difficulty separating from his parent or primary caregiver. The baby may be perfectly happy in the new setting as long as the parent is in sight, but he does not want his parent to leave. Fortunately, most babies are able to adjust to their new situations, as long as their new caregivers are warm, loving, and attentive. Before long, babies will learn that their parents will always come back and that there are substitute parents in child care who can anticipate and satisfy their needs.

Parents and caregivers can facilitate a baby's adjustment in several ways. Parents can help their baby feel comfortable in the new situation by letting her watch as they talk happily with the caregiver. A baby uses her parents as a social reference. If she feels that her parent is friendly with her new caregiver, the baby will sense that the caregiver can be trusted.

Parents and caregivers can find ways to reduce the difference between the home and the child care center. They can share information about how the baby prefers to be positioned at sleeptime or how the baby likes to be fed. The parents can also bring a favorite blanket or toy to the center.

Caregivers can maintain a homelike atmosphere in the baby room. They can create small spaces, keep the lights relatively dim, and provide soft materials, like cushions and stuffed animals. It is also very important to assign a primary caregiver to every infant. In other words, when two people are working together in the baby room, each should be responsible for a particular group of infants most of the time.

Objective 3 To recognize ways in which young toddlers develop self-awareness and learn to cope with separation

> *Miss Tightface was holding a conference with Melissa's mother. "I am a little concerned about Melissa," Miss Tightface began. "You know she is such a ham. As soon as the music starts, she starts to dance. Then she looks around to make sure everyone is watching. It's the sort of thing that is cute when you are 18 months, but I'd hate to see a child like Melissa growing up to be a show-off."*

Fortunately, Melissa's mother did not agree with Miss Tightface's concerns. She recognized that Melissa's response to an appreciative audience was perfectly age appropriate and did not in any way suggest that Melissa would grow up to be a show-off.

In this section, we will focus on the social/emotional development of young toddlers (14 to 24 months). We will identify the range of emotions they express, their expressions of attachment behavior, and their emerging ability to relate to and make friends with their peers. We will also suggest activities appropriate for toddlers that will enhance their emotional development and emerging social skills.

Emotional Expression

By the time a baby is 1 year old, she is able to exhibit a whole range of emotions, including surprise, pleasure, delight, sadness, wariness, fear, and anger. She is becoming more interested in new people, although she will still react negatively to being picked up by a stranger. It is an age when the baby appears to be saying "Don't come to me. I'll come to you."

While all young toddlers are capable of expressing a range of emotional responses, the intensity of emotional expression is an individual characteristic. Some toddlers are wary by nature. They are slow to warm up in new situations and easily frightened by new sounds, sights, and people. Others are delighted with new situations and respond with exuberance to new and exciting events.

Self-Awareness

Around 18 months old, most toddlers, whether reserved or outgoing, are showing an increased self-awareness. They are developing a sense of identity, an awareness of being a person apart from and different from other people. An 18-month-old will recognize herself in the mirror. If you tape a ribbon to her hair, she will notice the ribbon in the mirror and pull it off her head. It is as if she is saying that she recognizes the image in the mirror as a reflection of a body that belongs to her. Another indication of the baby's newly gained self-awareness is her use of the word *mine* to signify her own possessions. Finally, and most persuasively, the 18-month-old demonstrates a special delight in assuming the role of a performer. If she dances to music and adults applaud the performance, she dances with increased vigor. Recognizing herself as the performer for an appreciative audience is a strong indication of awareness of self as an individual.

Exploration and Self-Control

The explorations of young toddlers inevitably increase the potential of hurting themselves or damaging property. They are continuously learning what kinds of explorations are permitted and what explorations are prohibited. "No, don't touch" and "Hot, don't touch" are familiar words to a busy and inquisitive toddler. Often, we will overhear a child who is about to touch a forbidden object saying "No, no" to himself.

In a home situation, the parents have the option of putting away breakable things or leaving them within a child's reach and teaching him to touch them gently. In a child care situation, this option is not available. Anything that is breakable is also dangerous and must be taken out of the environment. Childproofing an environment for toddlers means not only putting away breakable and sharp things and small parts that can be swallowed; it also means plugging up outlets, eliminating lamp cords, securing outside doors, and removing chests that can topple over if a child stands on a drawer.

The toddler's ability to respond to a "No" is an important development in the second year. It demonstrates the ability to inhibit an action that has been set in motion before it has been completed. Although we like to see children exhibit this control, we do not want to see them inhibited. If the child hears "No" too often or too sharply, he will overgeneralize the prohibition and limit his explorations. The child who is not free to explore is also not free to learn.

> *The toddler's ability to respond to a "No" is an important development in the second year.*

Expressions of Attachment and Coping with Separation

While young toddlers are developing an increased awareness of self, they are also becoming increasingly more discriminatory of the people around them. Their world is no longer divided into only two sorts of people: preferred caregivers and others. Now there are dangerous people (like doctors), harmless people (like their parents' friends), fun people (like teachers and playmates), and special people who take care of them (like Mom, Dad, and other primary caregivers).

While children may enjoy playing with playmates and other fun people, their parents and primary caregivers remain their base of security. As long as they know where Mother is, they are willing to play and explore. Given this, children who begin child care for the first time when they are between 1 and 2 years old may have difficulty separating from their parents and primary caregivers, who are their base of security. The fact that most young children have a limited understanding of language makes it difficult to explain in words the difference between a separation that is temporary and a separation that lasts forever. Keeping this in mind, here are some ways to make separation from a parent more understandable, if not easier, for a child:

- Accept the child's feelings. "You feel sad because your mommy left. We will play for a while, and then Mommy will be back."
- Give parents the option of separating gradually from their children.
- Make sure that parents say good-bye to their children. Once they have said good-bye, they should leave without turning back. The quick look back to make sure the child is all right can destroy the child's confidence.
- Hold the child in your arms and encourage her to wave "bye-bye" when the parent leaves. Then engage her in a favorite activity or in something she finds relaxing, such as rice pouring or playing with play dough.
- Stagger the times and/or days in which new children come to school. A child who is separating from a parent for the first time needs extra attention.

Objective 4

To recognize ways in which older toddlers develop a sense of autonomy

It was the first day of the new school year and all the mothers had left, except for Mrs. Hold-Tight and Mrs. Baby-Lover. Kathleen, Mrs. Hold-Tight's 2½-year-old, was holding on to her mother's shirt and crying softly. Mrs. Baby-Lover was putting Chapstick on her daughter Theresa's lips.

Mrs. Hold-Tight (talking to Kathleen): "I can't believe that a big girl like you would be scared to go to child care. I'll tell you what. Supposing I just stay and watch you while you go into the circle. See, I'll stand in this square and I won't move."

Mrs. Baby-Lover (talking to Theresa): "Okay, sweetheart, go with the other children. Make sure to let Miss Nancy put your sweater on if you go on the playground, and ask your nice teacher to help you get your lunch box open. And remember, if you need help with wiping yourself in the bathroom, you just ask the nice teacher."

Poor Mrs. Hold-Tight and Mrs. Baby-Lover! They were embarrassed about how their children were clinging to them, but they didn't know what to do about it. Mrs. Hold-Tight was giving her daughter mixed messages. She was telling her that she would be okay at child care but also that it was a place where you had to be big and brave. Mrs. Baby-Lover was telling her daughter that the teachers would take care of her if she would tell them what she needed. Obviously, Mrs. Hold-Tight and Mrs. Baby-Lover were having trouble separating from their children.

For older toddlers and preschool children, fear of separation may take several forms. One child may feign illness or succumb to illness in order to avoid separation. A second child may beg, cajole, plead, or have a temper tantrum. A third child may invent all kinds of elaborate manipulations, such as "I'm afraid of my teacher," "I can't go to the bathroom at school," and "I can't go to school because my dinosaur shirt is dirty and it's my favorite shirt."

Ways of Helping Children Separate

The time to prepare a child for separation is before she begins child care. Parents can give children practice with separation by arranging for short visits with family or neighbors, through which the children learn that they can manage without their parents and that their parents always come back. Teachers can help pave the way for a smooth entry into child care by providing different entry options that meet the needs of different families. Here are some options that are used in different child care settings:

- Children visit the center for one or two days with their parents before staying there alone.
- Children become acquainted ahead of time with their teachers through home and/or center visits.

- Entry into child care is staggered so that only one new child enters at a time; this way, teachers can give the new child their full attention.

- During the first week of school, parents can stay with their children until the children are ready to say good-bye.

- Parents are instructed on the importance of saying good-bye cheerfully and then leaving without turning back.

While separation continues to be a major issue for older toddlers and their parents, 2- to 3-year-olds are struggling with another issue: They want desperately to hold on to the secure feeling of being cared for by adoring parents and caregivers. At the same time, they have a strong need to assert their own will and make their own decisions. Their favorite word is "No," and their favorite phrase is "I do it myself." They are torn between their need to hold tight to a protective hand and their need to break away and explore the world in their own ways and on their own terms.

> *Toddlers between 2 and 3 years old are torn between wanting to be coddled and protected and wanting to be autonomous.*

> *Judith and her friend Marsha had decided to take their 2-year-olds to the neighborhood park. When Judith told her son, Butch, that it was time to go home, Butch refused to leave. He pushed his mother away with both hands and ran to the slide with his friend. Marsha agreed to stay in the park for a few more minutes with the two boys. The minute his mother said good-bye and started to turn away, Butch stopped playing, burst into tears, ran to his mother, and jumped into her arms. "He is a typical 2-year-old," Marsha laughed. "That is exactly what my son would do."* ●

Toddlers between 2 and 3 years old are torn between wanting to be coddled and protected and wanting to be autonomous. Although parents and teachers may be exasperated by what appears to be negative behavior, these toddlers are not being ornery. They are working hard to assert their independence and defend their right to make their own decisions and to do things in their own ways. At the same time, they are not ready to give up their dependency on adults, who are the base of their security.

To recognize ways in which preschool children develop a sense of personal identity and self-worth, recognize and express their feelings, and take pride in their heritage

Brian started off the morning in high spirits. He was wearing his beautiful new Spiderman jersey, which Grandma had sent for his birthday. Everything went fine until juice time, when somehow or another, grape juice slipped out of his hand and got all over his jersey.

From that time on, things went from bad to worse. At art time, Brian finished his picture in a hurry so he could go over to the sink and wash the grape juice off Spiderman's face. "Come back to your seat," his teacher called. "I want us all to share our pretty pictures. Oh, look how beautiful Terry's picture looks. Would you like to tell me about it? Oh, Demetria, look at what you've done. You made such a happy picture. I'd like to hear you talk about it." When she came to Brian's picture, the teacher didn't say anything at all.

Then it was circle time, and the teacher asked all the children to put away their crayons and papers and come to the circle. Brian started to put his crayons away, but then he looked at his picture. It really didn't look very pretty, he decided. Maybe he could add a few more strokes. Maybe some black lines going up and down would be a good idea. As Brian was fixing up his drawing, he heard his teacher saying, loud and clear, "What good children I have in my class. I like the way most of you put your crayons away so quickly."

Brian tried to hurry with his picture, but when he went fast with the black crayon, his paper started to tear. He crumpled it up, threw it on the floor, and walked over to the circle. "He threw his paper on the floor," Tommy tattled. "He's bad." "Yes, he's bad," agreed Ben. "He's got juice all over his shirt. His mommy is going to be mad."

The teacher paid no attention to these comments. "Come on now, let's sing in a pretty voice. 'If you're happy and you know it . . .' " At the end of the song, it was dismissal time. All the children asked the teacher to stamp "happy faces" on their hands. "I'm good," Jerry asserted, as he stood in line for his "happy face."

When Brian's mother came to the door, he dashed over to her. "Don't you want to get your 'happy face' before we go?" Brian's mother asked. Brian burst into tears.

All of us, like Brian, have days when one thing leads to another. While we may feel grumpy or out of sorts, we don't think of ourselves as bad people because we've had a bad day. With young children, it may be quite a different story. During the preschool years, children have their own unique way of looking at the world. Because they don't understand the notion of chance, they think that bad things happen for a reason. An accident, in their view, happens to them because they did something or thought something wrong. When a series of bad things happen to children of this age, they begin to think of themselves as bad people.

Brian's bad day was initiated by a minor, accidental spill. This started off a chain of behavior. By the end of the morning, Brian was convinced he was a bad boy, unworthy of a "happy face." Brian's teacher was clearly trying to make the children in her class feel good about themselves, but in Brian's case, her techniques backfired. As she tried to engage the group with upbeat language, she missed Brian's distress over the spilled grape juice and didn't give him the opportunity to finish his picture. She praised the "good" children in a way that made Brian (and probably others) feel "bad."

> *During the preschool years, children are continually making judgments about themselves.*

During the preschool years, children are continually making judgments about themselves. The sum of these judgments constitutes *self-concept*, which is, in essence, each child's value judgment of herself. The preschool teacher can help children develop a healthy self-concept in a variety of ways:

- By helping children develop a sense of personal identity
- By helping children to recognize and express their own feelings
- By helping children cope with separation
- By helping children feel good about their ethnic and cultural traditions

Developing Personal Identity and Self-Worth

All of us get upset when we meet people we know and can't remember their names. We are concerned that these people will interpret our lapse of memory as a sign that we don't think of them as being important. For young children, their own names are especially significant. They expect everyone to know their names and often learn to recognize their names in writing before they can read anything else.

The more opportunities that we find to call each child in class by name, the more we can strengthen this sense of personal identity. But even though we recognize how important this is, we may have problems in the beginning remembering all of the names of the children. Here are some suggestions:

- Become familiar with the class roster in advance. That way, all you will need to do is connect faces with the names on the first day of school.
- Ask the parents to send in photos of their children in advance, or take pictures of all the children on the first day.
- Pin a name card on the back of each child.
- Sing songs in which you repeat the names of the children over and over again.

Learning the names of all the children in the class is a good first step in helping them develop a sense of personal identity. Another way of helping children learn more about themselves is to have each child develop an "All About Me" book, in which he can record personal information about himself. The book should include these pages:

- Table of Contents
- This is my photo.
- This is my handprint.
- This is my family.
- This is my favorite food.
- This is my favorite color.
- This is my favorite animal.
- This is my best drawing of me.

A child's "All About Me" book is both a means of increasing his sense of personal identity and a record of the way he feels about himself.

> *Make time to have a private conversation with each child at least three times each day.*

More important than any activity, however, is on-going personal attention. Make time to have a private conversation with each child at least three times each day. It doesn't have to be formal. You can greet children individually when they arrive and then direct them to interest centers, where you have set up simple and inviting activities. You can write down a child's story for her, admire the caterpillar she found on the playground, let her choose a book for storytime, join her in a block-building project, or converse with her as you put out the snack together. What is important is that you let the child take the lead, that you really listen, and that you show each child you are interested in what she has to say.

Helping Children Recognize and Express Their Feelings

Often, children fail to distinguish between having bad feelings and actually being bad. The concept of feelings is not easy to grasp. Only when children have developed a firm idea of their own identity are they ready to understand what is meant by *feelings*.

> *Once children have learned to express their feelings in words, they are less likely to act them out in ways that are inappropriate.*

Younger children cry when they are sad, strike out when they are angry, and laugh when they are happy. As children grow older, they can use words to go along with these feelings, but it does take time. Once children have learned to express their feelings in words, they are less likely to act them out in ways that are inappropriate. Most important, they learn to recognize that it is good to express their own feelings as long as they respect the feelings of other people.

Activities to Help Children Express Feelings

"Feeling Wheel" Make a "feeling wheel" out of a paper plate. Put a pointer that can spin in the center, and draw happy, sad, angry, and sleepy faces around the perimeter. Give each child an opportunity to use the pointer to show how she is feeling.

Plate Puppets Encourage children to express their feelings by using paper plate puppets that show expressions of anger, sadness, fright, happiness, surprise, excitement, and so forth.

"How I Am Feeling" Chart With older children, prepare a chart that lists all the children's names. As the children come into the classroom in the morning, each places a circular disc next to her name with a face that describes her feelings— happy, sad, angry, and so on. At the end of the day, each child is given a chance to change the disc if her feelings have changed.

Feeling Songs Sing songs about feelings. One of the most appropriate songs is "If You're Happy and You Know It, Clap Your Hands."

Feeling Stories Read stories that describe situations in which a child faces anger, sadness, or jealousy. Talk about the feelings that are aroused in the child.

Drawing to Music Play happy and sad music. Let the children color with crayons along with the music. Talk with them about the differences in their pictures.

Helping Children Cope with Separation

Helping children cope with separation is a joint responsibility of parents and teachers. The techniques used to help with separation vary with the age of the child.

When children are able to understand language, teachers can ease the pain of separation by talking about it:

- Talk about the schedule of the day with older children. Show them where the hands of the clock will be when their parents come to get them. It helps to put up a tagboard clock with the hands set on closing time. The children can compare the real clock time with that shown on the tagboard clock.
- Pretend that a school teddy bear misses its mother or father. Have the children say something nice to the bear during circle time to make it feel better. The children who comfort the bear will begin to feel better themselves.
- Encourage each child to make a picture or "write" (dictate or scribble) a letter to give to his parent at the end of the day.
- Ask the parents to make a book of special people that their child can look at and talk about with you.

Helping Children Feel Good about Their Ethnic and Cultural Heritages

James had just moved from a small southern town to a large city in Connecticut. It was his first week in nursery school. James was happy to be with other children his own age and excited about all the new toys and games in his classroom. At circle time, he was the first one to volunteer to tell a story. "I aksed my mommy where we were," he began.

"James," the teacher stopped him, "you should say 'asked,' not 'aksed.' "

"Asked, not aksed," James repeated. He went on with his story: "And my mommy say we ain't got but a—"

"You don't say 'We ain't got,' " the teacher explained firmly. "You say 'We don't have.' "

James stopped talking. The next day, when it was time to go to school, he told his mother that his tummy hurt. ●

It is easy to understand why James had a stomach ache. Like all preschool children, he wasn't aware of grammar or articulation and so didn't understand why the teacher was correcting him when he was telling the truth. The one thing that he did sense was that the teacher didn't like the way he talked. Was there something bad about his talking? Was there something bad about *him?*

> *Most preschool teachers recognize that it is inappropriate to correct a child's grammar under any circumstances.*

Most preschool teachers recognize that it is inappropriate to correct a child's grammar under any circumstances. It is especially harmful to correct a child's dialect. From the child's point of view, this may be a direct criticism of him and an indirect slur on his family. The best way to destroy a child's self-concept is to make him feel that he comes from a family that doesn't measure up to other families. A child whose ethnic, religious, or language background is different from that of the other children is always vulnerable. Even if the teacher is warm and accepting, the other children, through their words and actions, can make such a child feel different.

Sensitive teachers make a special effort to make children with different backgrounds feel wanted and valued. These teachers check in with the parents to learn what makes the children comfortable and to find out how they are feeling about the classroom. Sensitive teachers learn all they can about each child's heritage and discover ways of helping each child feel proud of who she is.

Here are some ways of helping children appreciate their own ethnic and cultural heritages and the heritages of the other children in the classroom:

- Begin by examining your own feelings very carefully. How do you feel about children from different backgrounds? Do you have any built-in barriers or stereotypes that interfere with your ability to relate in a positive way to any of the children in your class?

- Invite parents from different backgrounds to prepare ethnic snacks for the class and to share folk stories, nursery rhymes, lullabies, and jokes from their own traditions.

- Introduce the children to music, chants, and games from different countries and different traditions.

- Have a multicultural potluck dinner, in which the children are introduced to different foods.

- With the help of the parents, celebrate all of the holidays of the ethnic groups represented in your classroom.

- Select books, picture cards, and picture books that reflect the range of races, cultures, and ethnicities of the children in your class and in the community. Be sure that the children see people of their own races and cultures playing a variety of roles in everyday situations.

- Make sure that children from different races and cultures are represented in the photos and pictures on the walls, as well as the books in the library and the dolls, clothes, and artifacts in the pretend play areas.

- Plan parent/child programs in which the children have an opportunity to meet the parents and grandparents of their classmates and the parents have an opportunity to socialize with each other.

- Plan Show-and-Tell days, on which the children bring in and talk about family artifacts.

- Encourage open conversation in response to children's natural curiosity about differences in skin color, hair texture, language, food preferences, and family type.

- Talk with parents about what you are doing and solicit their ideas, as well.

- Encourage interracial and intercultural friendships, and keep parents informed about their children's friendships.

Objective 6   To recognize ways in which caregivers can help young children develop a sense of responsibility

One of the important ways in which parents and caregivers can prepare children to enter kindergarten is to help them develop a sense of responsibility. Schoolchildren are supposed to keep track of their own possessions. They are also expected to take care of their personal needs, to complete tasks assigned by the teacher, and to follow classroom rules, like taking turns and helping with classroom clean-up. When children have mastered the basic self-help skills and learned to accept responsibility, they are primed for success in school.

> *One of the important ways in which parents and caregivers can prepare children to enter kindergarten is to help them develop a sense of responsibility.*

Families, as well as cultures, differ in their ideas about how much responsibility young children should assume. In some families, the children are fed and dressed by their parents until they are 3 or 4 years old. The parents feel that this gives their children a firm foundation of love and security, upon which to build a sense of responsibility for self and others. In other families, the parents encourage the children to do as much as they can for themselves. They feel that this stretches children's capabilities and makes them feel good about themselves.

Both approaches can lead to happy, well-adjusted children who take responsibility for themselves and for helping others. In both cases, the parent communicates respect for the child and an expectation that the child can and will assume more responsibility as he grows older.

Mastering Self-Help Skills

Listing the self-help skills that children are expected to acquire by the time they are 5 years old is an eye-opener. Helping children acquire and practice self-help skills is a part of the daily routine in child care settings. Many of the self-help skills that can be taught and practiced in school were discussed already in the chapter on health (see Chapter 2). In this section, we will discuss two of the many self-help skills that children need to master in order to be ready for school: independent eating and toileting.

Eating

Often, we think of children as having completed their eating skills when they have learned to drink from a glass or eat with a spoon without spilling. Actually, learning to use utensils is just the beginning. Preschool children are expected to learn a host of customs and rules that have to do with eating. Often, we scold children for having poor manners without realizing all there is to learn and remember. Let us look at some of the eating rules that children have to learn:

- Use the right kind of utensil for the food you are eating. Some food is eaten with the fingers, some with a spoon, and some with a fork.
- Some foods can be eaten directly, and some foods can be eaten only if they are put on other foods (butter, sugar, jam, ketchup, gravy, salt, pepper).
- You should wipe your mouth with a napkin whenever it gets dirty.
- If you want food that is across the table, you say "Please pass . . ."
- Chewing has to be done quietly and with your mouth closed.
- It's all right to talk at the table but not while you have food in your mouth.

Obviously, there are too many rules to expect children to learn at one time and too many for children to remember at the same time. To teach children good table manners, do these things:

- Make sure that mealtimes are happy times.
- Model good table manners.
- Explain the reasons for certain prohibitions. "Eating a spoonful of salt is unhealthy for your body."

Toileting

At some child care centers, the requirement for entry into the preschool program is being out of diapers. Although this is understandable from the point of view of the director, it may not always be in the best interest of either the center or the child. Parents who know that their children must be toilet trained in order to enter a child care program may become so tense about the process that their efforts at such training will be counterproductive.

Although children who have not learned to use the toilet may learn easily at the child care center, it is also common for children who have good control at home to have accidents at the center. A critical rule for all child care centers is to make sure that each child has an extra set of name-tagged clothing in his cubby. When a child does have an accident, he should be changed in a matter-of-fact way. No child, under any circumstances, should ever be shamed about having an accident.

One of the questions that often comes up about toileting in child care programs is whether there should be a special time when all children go to the bathroom or whether children should simply have access to the bathroom whenever they need it. In some situations, such as when the bathroom is not adjacent to the classroom, the teacher must take the children to the bathroom as a group. In other situations, when the bathroom is easily accessible, the teacher has a choice. Although it seems to be more reasonable and certainly more natural to let children go on demand, there are several advantages to having bathroom times scheduled:

- The teacher has an excellent opportunity to enforce sanitary rules, such as using toilet paper, flushing the toilet, and washing hands after toileting.
- The teacher can watch the children as they practice appropriate handwashing.
- Other routines, such as lunchtime and naptime, are less apt to be interrupted if a set bathroom time has been scheduled.
- Children who are very busy playing or working may forget to use the bathroom.

In most cases, teachers can schedule bathroom times but still encourage children to use the bathroom when they need to.

Assuming Responsibility for One's Own Behavior

Adolph arrived in preschool with a note to his teacher pinned to his shirt. The note, which was from Adolph's mother, said, "Please make sure that Adolph puts his sweater on when he goes out to the playground. If he does not eat all his lunch, put anything he did not eat back in the lunch box. Please find the tubby toy that he left in school yesterday and put it inside the lunch box. Thank you."

"No wonder Adolph won't do anything for himself," his teacher grumbled, as she reminded Adolph to take his lunch box off the table and put it in his cubby. ●

We cannot find fault with Adolph's teacher for grumbling. Children cannot be expected to be responsible unless they are given responsibilities. At the same time, if we give children responsibilities they are not ready or able to assume, they will not learn to be responsible. They will either feel guilty because they let someone down, or they will become very adept at finding alibis that explain away their lapses.

Mrs. Neatnik gave her daughter, Candy, strict instructions not to get her party dress messed up in school. They were going to visit Grandma right after school, and Candy had to look very pretty. Candy was very careful about putting on her smock before she finger painted, and she remembered to wash her hands so she wouldn't get the red paint on her dress. But then the class went out on the playground. Some of the children were digging in the mud, searching for dinosaur bones. There was no way that Candy could resist the temptation to join the diggers. ●

233

If we want children to assume responsibility for their own behavior, we need to be realistic in the demands we place on them. Mercer Mayer's book *Just for You* (1998)

> *If we want children to assume responsibility for their own behavior, we need to be realistic in the demands we place on them.*

captures the dilemma of the preschool child who wants to be good and helpful but can't quite pull it off. In the book, Little Monster keeps trying to do something special to help her mother. Unfortunately, she keeps taking on tasks that are beyond her capabilities. When she tries to carry the groceries, the bag breaks. When she tries to wash the dishes, she gets soap all over the floor. When she tries not to splash in her bath, there is a "storm." Finally, she solves the problem by giving her mother something she really wants—a kiss.

Other Self-Help Skills

Other self-help skills that may or may not be taught or used in child care settings include dressing, brushing teeth, falling asleep, and keeping track of personal possessions.

Dressing Skills For children living in cold climates, putting on sweaters, jackets, boots, mittens, and hats in preparation for outdoor play can be a major chore. Most children 5 and under will need some help in putting on their outside clothes, but there are parts of the task that they can learn to do by themselves. Children as young as 2 years old can go to their cubbies and gather up their outdoor clothes. At 3 and even younger, children can learn to lay out their jacket or sweater in front of them, put in their arms, and flip the garment over their head. Doing up buttons, snaps, and zippers can be more or less of a problem, depending on the child's age and dexterity and the size and type of the closure. Dressing boards can provide children with practice with zippers, snaps, and buttons, but it is always more difficult to do up a closure when you are wearing the garment than when you are manipulating a dressing frame.

Brushing Teeth Some child care centers include brushing teeth as part of the daily schedule. Children who resist brushing their teeth at home are likely to enjoy brushing their teeth in a group at school.

Falling Asleep When naptime is a part of the daily schedule, most children under 5 will fall asleep on their cots or mats when the lights are dimmed and soft music is played. A few children may need to have their backs rubbed. Allowing children to look at picture books or do puzzles may help them rest quietly even if they don't fall asleep.

Keeping Track of Personal Possessions By at least 3 years old, children can assume the responsibility of putting their possessions into their cubbies and of taking their things out of their cubbies when it is time to go home. Problems are likely to arise when children are allowed to bring toys and other "treasures" from home. Some schools insist that children come to school with empty hands and empty pockets. Other schools take a compromise position: Items may be brought to school and shared with the group at circle time, but they must be left in the cubby for the rest of the day. Still others, especially centers and family child care homes that work to build a sense of family, encourage children to share their personal items with the group and to help each other find clothing, special blankets, and stuffed animals that need to be taken home.

Helping Others

Tammy was in tears. Her mother insisted that she stay home, just because she had a fever. "But Mommy, I got to go to school," she whimpered. "It's my turn to pass out the crackers."

Beginning in the toddler years, young children vie for opportunities to help out their parents and teachers. Helping out gives children a chance to feel grown up and powerful. At home, children love to help clean, sort the laundry, wash the car, rake the leaves, and even empty the trash. At school, coveted chores may include passing out the crackers, feeding the goldfish, turning the dial on the weather chart, putting an "X" on the calendar to mark off the day, and leading the line out to the playground.

> *Beginning in the toddler years, young children vie for opportunities to help their parents and teachers. Helping out gives children a chance to feel grown up and powerful.*

When children are told to do chores—like putting their jackets in their cubbies, cleaning up a spill they have made, or putting together a puzzle they have just tossed on the floor—the same children who loved to do the "teacher helper" chores may resist the chores they have been asked to do. Helping the teacher makes you feel grown up; being told what to do makes you feel like a baby. With a change of tone and a little finesse, this kind of resistance is easy to overcome. "Please, hurry and pick up the puzzle, Hal. It's time for us to go outside and play some games on the playground."

Helping Children Learn to Care for Each Other

Karina, the new child in the Play Together Preschool, was totally vision impaired. Miss Show-Me, the preschool teacher, was initially skeptical about accepting such a child into the classroom. "I am afraid she might get hurt," Miss Show-Me explained to her director. "Besides, the other children might tease her, and she might feel bad if the other children are doing things she can't do." The director was sympathetic but firm. "I understand your concerns, but I would like you to give Karina a chance."

Miss Show-Me had a prior appointment the next morning, so the director took over her class. When she arrived, Miss Show-Me was amazed. Karina was sitting at the table with the other children, drawing in her daybook. José was holding her hand, helping her draw a circle for a face. Next, he helped her make dots for eyes and a line for the mouth. "I made a face," Karina announced proudly, as she felt the crayon marks with her finger.

For the rest of the day, Karina joined in all the activities. When the class went outside, one of the children held her hand and told her when to step down. When they played catch in a circle, the children told Karina to hold her arms out before they threw her the ball. When the ball hit her in the face at one point, Karina responded cheerfully, "I'll catch the ball next time."

At the end of the day, Miss Show-Me went into the director's office and said, "It's hard to believe. How did you ever do it? Karina had a great day. The kids let her join in their play. They were amazing in the way they helped Karina without making a big deal."

"I didn't do anything," the director insisted. "You did it. You have helped your class learn to help each other. The nice thing about it is that your kids didn't make Karina feel as if she was different and they let her do as much for herself as she could. You have done a fine job."

The director of the Play Together Preschool was right in praising Miss Show-Me. The children in her class knew without being told how to welcome a child with a disability and make her feel accepted.

The climate in a classroom is a reflection of the values promoted by the teacher, the example she has set, and the subtle messages she has sent to the children by respecting their individual needs. Miss Show-Me had always respected each child in her class, emphasized the importance of cooperation, and modeled trust, courtesy, and caring. She did not have to worry about including a special-needs child in her classroom because her students had already learned to value differences and to care for and about each other.

To recognize ways in which teachers can create inclusive classrooms where all children are welcome

Prior to bringing her daughter, Sunshine, to the school, Mrs. Fairchild requested an opportunity to talk to her teacher:

Mrs. Fairchild: "You know, this is Sunshine's first experience with any kind of child care. Even since I found out about her cerebral palsy, I have stayed at home and devoted full time to her. But now, my husband isn't well, and I have no choice—I have to go to work."

Mr. Upbeat: "I know that this is a difficult step for you. What can I do to make it easier?"

Mrs. Fairchild: "I guess what I really want to know is what you will do to help Sunshine make the adjustment."

Mr. Upbeat: "I have always worked in settings where children with special needs are included in the class. Over the years, I have developed four guidelines that have worked well for me. First, I always begin by talking to the parents, just as I'm talking to you now. I ask what they would like their child to experience in the course of the year and what they can tell me about their child that would help me do a good job. Second, I try to determine the child's strengths and teach through those strengths. Third, through modeling and through talking, I help the children recognize how lucky we are to be in a class where every child feels welcome. Finally, I use every resource I have, including, of course, the parents, to find out ways of helping the child have a productive year."

Mrs. Fairchild: "I feel better already. Let me tell you about Sunshine."

Mr. Upbeat has had many positive experiences with including children with special needs in preschool programs for typically developing children. He recognizes that children with special needs are, above all else, *children*. Like all children, they need to be nurtured, to learn, and to be accepted as part of the community. Like all children, they also have their own sets of needs and strengths.

An inclusive early childhood environment that is designed to meet individual needs and build on individual strengths is appropriate for *all* children. Children with special needs benefit from being with other children, who can serve as appropriate role models and can include them in their play. Children with special needs gain opportunities to stretch their capabilities in multiple realms of development and to just "be kids." Children without disabilities learn to be compassionate, helpful, and comfortable with all types of people and to see strengths as well as deficits. All children can learn from one another when they spend time together in a program that meets their individual developmental needs and supports their social interaction.

Welcoming the Family

The parents of children with special needs have the same needs that other parents do. They want their children to be in a safe, stimulating, and caring environment, where they can learn, have fun, and make friends. If possible, the parents would like that environment to be in the same place where they bring their other children. Above all, the parents want their children to be accepted and treated with respect.

Although many parents hope that their children will catch up to others of the same age in terms of development, others recognize that this is an unrealistic goal. Their main hope for their children's child care or school experience is that their children will play with same-aged peers and have the happy experiences that all children enjoy. At the same time, they want to see their children make steady gains in physical, social/emotional, language, and cognitive development. They want their children to feel competent, confident, and proud of their accomplishments, whatever they may be.

Talking to the parents of a special-needs child about their hopes, dreams, and realistic expectations for that child, as well as about the child's strengths, preferences, and characteristic learning style, can help you plan. And as with any parents, maintaining open, two-way communication about what is happening in the classroom and at home will enable you to work as partners in fostering the child's development and providing a satisfying experience.

Many parents who have a child with special needs have their own special needs for support. They often feel that they are being judged by society because their child does not look or behave the way other children do. These parents can grow from being around other parents who know their child as an individual and can support them and their family. Because these parents have had to fight harder than most to get their child's needs recognized and met, they can also be strong supports for each other and for parents whose children are developing more typically.

Modeling Inclusiveness and Helping Children Appreciate Each Other's Strengths

The teacher is the deciding figure when it comes to the attitudes in the classroom. The way the teacher handles herself around the children in the classroom will be reflected in the way the other children react in the room. Given this, the teacher needs to think about the way she uses language, including body language:

- If she shows that she considers each child to be equally important and worthy of respect, the children will follow her lead.
- If she models kindness, good humor, a spirit of adventure, and a lust for learning, the children who look up to her will emulate these qualities.
- If she seeks creative ways to enable every child to participate, the children will get the message that no one should be left out.

238

- If she cheers children on as they struggle to master new skills, the children will join her in cheering on their friends.

- If her attitude toward difference and disability is one of matter-of-fact acceptance, the children will come to see these as facts of life, not as impediments to friendship.

The teacher is also in a position to highlight each child's strengths, both for that child and for his peers. The teacher can choose a mix of activities that give different children chances to excel. She can introduce cooperative activities that give every child an important role, such as playing parachute games, making murals, cooking, and having a group of children act out a story that another child has told or written. She can praise and display work that children are proud of, noting each child's progress without comparing different children's products. She can enable a child who has difficulty to take his turn at helping and then thank him for his efforts.

Providing the Right Amount of Help and Protection

Every child has her own set of strengths and needs. Through observing the special-needs child in various situations, you can determine the areas that should be addressed, just as you would look at any child in your care who needs more experiences with handling scissors or more opportunities to use language. By recognizing what a child with special needs can do, you can make tasks easier for her without actually doing them for her. Like any child, a child with special needs must be able to fail on occasion if she is to taste the joy of success. If you let the special-needs child try something challenging, she may surprise you with a new ability. If you provide help only when she asks, she will learn to trust you to provide help when she needs it but also that you trust her to do things independently. Above all, every child needs to feel successful and to develop self-esteem.

> *Like any child, a child with special needs must be able to fail on occasion if she is to taste the joy of success.*

Many caregivers are afraid that children with special needs may get hurt in their care. Be cautioned that being overprotective can be damaging to these children. Children should be allowed to try activities, as long as they are safe, and encouraged to participate as fully as they are able. Most likely, if the activities are safe for typically developing children, then they also will be safe for children with special needs.

There may be a few occasions on which you need to pay closer attention to certain children. For example, a child who uses crutches may need a few seconds to get up and move to the next activity, so that the other children do not accidentally knock her over in the rush to be first.

When children ask questions about a child's disability, it is important to be open and honest with them. Remember that children are naturally curious and that noticing a difference is not the same as making a negative judgment.

Available Resources

The best resource available is the parents, who have lived with the child and know her best. The parents have probably been successful in trying many ways of adapting the child's environment and dealing with her behaviors. If the child is receiving early intervention services, her therapists may also be able to offer suggestions as to how to best work with her. The child's pediatrician may be able to provide you with background information on her particular disability and with a list of local resources and support groups.

Individualized Education Plans

A child with special needs may have an *individualized education plan (IEP)* in effect that states the goals that the family wants to accomplish with him. An IEP summarizes the recommendations of an interdisciplinary team of specialists—including the child's parents and teachers—who have evaluated the child in key developmental areas. It states the services the child is receiving, the duration and amount of those services, how the child was assessed to determine the need for services, how the child will be evaluated to determine if progress is being made, and the goals that the child will be working on.

Knowing some of this information can help in the classroom. For example, if a goal for the child is to use two to three words when speaking, then you will know that if the child just points to a toy car and grunts that it is especially important to encourage him to say "car" and to use the word in a sentence, such as "Want car." Along with the goal, the IEP may state how the goal will be accomplished. If the goal states that the child will learn to use language in social situations, he will need to be around other children and have opportunities to practice this skill.

The Americans with Disabilities Act (ADA) entitles all young children to an evaluation and, if warranted, early intervention services so that they can receive a free and appropriate education.

Additional Resources about Self-Development

Derman-Sparks, L. (1989). *The anti-bias curriculum: Tools for empowering young children.* Washington, DC: NAEYC.

Heart Start: The emotional foundation of school readiness. (1992). Washington, DC: Zero to Three.

Honig, A. (2002). *Secure relationships: Nurturing infant–toddler attachment in early care settings.* Washington, DC: NAEYC.

Hyson, M. (Ed.). (2003). *The emotional development of young children: Building an emotion-centered curriculum* (2nd ed.). New York: Teachers College Press.

Jervis, K. (Ed.). (2000). *Separation: Strategies for helping two- to four-year olds.* Washington, DC: NAEYC.

Lieberman, A. (1993). *The emotional life of the toddler.* New York: Free Press.

Mayer, M. (1998). *Just for You.* New York: Golden Books.

Social Development

Chapter 9

Overview

Social development refers to the growth of the child's ability to make and maintain friends and to develop mutually supportive relationships with adults and children. It also includes learning to work and play cooperatively with children and adults and to assume the role of either leader or follower.

Rationale

Preschool children are egocentric. They see the world from their own point of view and have difficulty understanding points of view that are different from their own. A typical example of this is the 2-year-old who holds a finger painting up to the phone and asks her Nana to admire it. Children's inability to recognize others' points of view does not mean, however, that they are unable to be kind, cooperative, and empathetic. Children are natural mimics and talented actors. They can imitate the behavior of a kind and nurturant model and play the role of another person. Adults who are concerned with the development of social skills in young children must serve as positive models and at the same time structure an environment in which children have opportunities to learn how other people act and feel.

Objectives

1. To recognize the sequence of social skill development from birth to 5 years and the role of the caregiver in supporting this development

2. To recognize ways in which infants and toddlers develop meaningful relationships with parents, caregivers, and other children

3. To recognize ways of encouraging preschool children to make friends and engage in social play

4. To help children build on their strengths and overcome their difficulties

5. To describe ways in which caregivers can encourage helping, sharing, and caring behaviors among children

6. To design a classroom environment and curriculum that support cooperative behavior

Supporting Social Development

It was Tina's first day at We-Are-Pals Country Day School. Mrs. Pusher, Tina's mother, gave her some last-minute advice when she dropped her off at school: "Now, Tina, I don't want you to be shy. You go right up to the children and ask them to play with you. You have to let the children know that you're friendly and you want to play."

Tina said good-bye to her mother and went out to the playground. A group of children were climbing on the jungle gym. "May I play with you?" asked Tina. "No," said a big boy with a Ninja Turtle sweatshirt. "No girls allowed."

Next, Tina walked over to the sandbox. Three boys were busily building something in the sand. Tina dug a small hole on the other side of the box. "This is a neat fort," one boy announced. "We got to put guns in it." Tina handed him a stick and said, "Here, take this. It's a machine gun." The boy took it and gave Tina further instructions. "Okay, it'll do. Now, find us some ammunition."

Tina played with the boys in the sandbox for several minutes. Then she slid down the slide by herself, joined a bug hunt, and finally climbed to the top of the jungle gym with a group of new pals. Despite her early rejection by the group of children on the jungle gym, Tina had a fine first day at We-Are-Pals.

Tina was a better authority than her mother on 4-year-old group-entry techniques. She knew that it was appropriate to shrug off the first rejection and try a different method. She also knew how to participate in pretending without waiting for an invitation. ●

In this chapter, we focus on the development of social skills. We look at ways of helping children make friends, respect the feelings of others, and play cooperatively with other children.

Objective 1 To recognize the sequence of social skill development from birth to 5 years and the role of the caregiver in supporting this development

The Developmental Picture that follows presents the sequence of children's social skill development and ways in which caregivers can support it.

Developmental Picture

The young infant (0–9 months):

- Maintains eye contact from the moment of birth
- Cries contagiously when another infant cries
- Enjoys watching another baby
- Engages in back and forth conversations with parents and other caregivers
- At 6 or 7 months, may show anxiety when approached by a stranger

The caregiver:

- Uses a low voice to quiet and comfort the baby and a higher voice to engage the baby in playful interactions
- Sings and plays interactive games with the infant, like Peek-a-Boo and Patty-Cake
- Provides infants with opportunities to look at and babble with each other

The older infant (9–14 months):

- Recognizes several different relatives and caregivers and reacts to them in different ways
- Can play alone for very brief periods
- May still show anxiety when approached by a stranger
- Enjoys being with other children and imitating what they are doing
- Forms attachments to transitional objects, like blankets and play animals
- Is distressed when a special person, such as a parent or favorite caregiver, leaves the room and gives her a special welcome upon her return

The caregiver:

- Provides many opportunities for social interaction with children as well as adults
- Plays back and forth games that include opportunities for the infant to imitate actions and enjoy interactions
- Engages babies in two-person and group games that involve music and movement

The young toddler (14–24 months):

- Enjoys being with other children but does not understand taking turns or sharing
- Enjoys playing Follow-the-Leader games and may join others in throwing toys off shelves and making a mess
- Is likely to select one or two special friends
- May bite another child as an experiment, a way of getting attention, or an expression of anger and frustration
- May join a friend in beginning pretending, such as making "vroom-vroom" sounds with a toy car or feeding a pretend cookie to a stuffed animal

(continued)

The caregiver:

- Develops special relationships with four or five toddlers
- Demonstrates affection by hugging, holding, rocking, and spending special time with each toddler
- Recognizes and reinforces early friend making
- Recognizes that toddlers may seek to spend some time in solitary play
- Pays particular attention to a child who bites and takes note of what was taking place before the biting episode
- Recognizes that the young child does not have the concept of sharing and, when possible, gives him a matching or similar object

The older toddler (2 years):

- May find a special friend
- Is likely to get into a quarrel with a friend over who gets to play with a particular toy
- Uses pretend play as a way of initiating friendship
- Uses transitional objects, such as dolls and toy animals, to overcome fears
- Enjoys playing running and chasing games with others
- Is learning to use words in pretend play and to converse with peers

The caregiver:

- Watches for and encourages the development of special relationships
- Uses pretend play as a way of enhancing empathy
- Provides duplicates of popular toys

The preschool child (3–5 years):

- Forms special friendships
- Initiates play and figures out ways of joining established groups
- Is learning to assume the roles of leader and follower, even though she may have a preferred role
- Is learning to settle conflicts and disputes with words
- Engages in increasingly more complex games with peers
- Makes plans with friends

The caregiver:

- Recognizes that preschool children have their own play styles and that they need opportunities to engage in the play they most enjoy
- Provides children with opportunities to be alone as well as to join groups
- Gives special help to children who are shy or fearful of joining groups
- Gives special help to children whose aggressive, impulsive, or bossy behavior causes them to be rejected by peers or is hurtful to other children
- Encourages cooperative play
- Helps children negotiate with each other and work out solutions to conflicts
- Models consideration, helpfulness, friendliness, and concern for others and for the environment

To recognize ways in which infants and toddlers develop meaningful relationships with parents, caregivers, and other children

Noreen had just given birth to a baby girl, Lisa, and she and her husband, Daren, were in the hospital room. Daren called his mother to tell her she was a grandmother. Full of emotion, he said, "I can't even tell you in words what it was like. When the doctor handed Lisa to me just seconds after she was born, my knees turned to rubber. I know you won't believe it, but she opened her eyes, looked up at me, and stared directly into my eyes. It was an awesome experience. I know that as a father, I will never be free again, but I wouldn't want it any other way." ●

Infants are born into this world primed to seek out social contact. Immediately after birth, an infant experiences a period of alertness. The baby searches for her mother's eyes, and for a few magic moments, mother and infant gaze lovingly at one another. The bond between the mother and infant is strengthened during the early months through every caregiving moment. As the mother responds to the child's cries, holds her close in her arms, speaks to her softly, and strokes her cheek, the bond between the two is strengthened. Soon, the baby will learn that other people, too, can be trusted to meet her needs—a father, a grandparent or other consistent caregiver, and even older siblings. The baby will develop a special bond with each caregiver who is in tune with her needs.

> *Babies who have developed secure relationships with adults in the first 2 or 3 months become quite social.*

Babies who have developed secure relationships with adults in the first two or three months become quite social. They smile in response to smiling adults and are ready to carry on cooing conversations. Around 3 months old, a well-loved and cared for baby will smile spontaneously when she sees a new face and will engage in interactive vocalizations.

By 6 or 7 months, caregivers may notice a change in the infant's social behavior. Rather than smile spontaneously at every new face, the infant at this stage may be wary of new people who approach her. She may stiffen up, cling to her caregiver, and turn her head away when a new person tries to talk to her. While caregivers may be concerned that their nice, friendly baby is becoming antisocial, the emergence of *stranger anxiety* is a healthy developmental sign. The baby has learned to recognize her primary caregivers, even from a distance. She knows that they will play with her and respond to her needs, but she is not so sure about people who are not familiar.

By 8 months old, most babies will demonstrate *attachment behavior*. They will feel free to play with toys and explore new territory as long as their special person is in sight. The minute that person disappears, the babies will become sober or even distressed. Depending on their temperament, some babies will resume play in a few minutes and tolerate the presence of a new person. Babies who are temperamentally wary may continue to show distress until their attachment figure returns and will resist the overtures of an unfamiliar person. But regardless of temperament, all babies

245

who are securely attached to a special caregiver will give that person an enthusiastic greeting when she returns to the room.

At 12 months old, patterns of attachment are firmly established. Children who are securely attached to one or more caregivers are ready to move away from their attachment figure. In a new situation, they will leave their caregiver's side and explore their surroundings, looking back from time to time to make sure their caregiver is watching. With one reassuring smile from their caregiver, they renew their exploration with gusto.

The relationships that an infant establishes with his primary caregivers provides the prototype for all the relationships he will make throughout his life. The baby who learns to trust and to love in his first year of life will have the capacity to make other meaningful relationships as his social world expands.

> *The baby who learns to trust and to love in his year of life will have the capacity to make other meaningful relationships as his social world expands.*

Between 1 and 3 years old, there is a dramatic increase in the number of social relationships that children form. Toddlers make friends with members of their extended family, friends of the family, and friends of older siblings. Toddlers who are placed in child care develop close relationships with their caregivers and make friends with other children in their group.

Making Friends with Siblings and Peers

Infants as young as 3 months old love to watch other children. An older sibling saying "Boo" in the baby's face or jumping up and down will quite likely elicit the baby's first genuine laugh. During the course of the first year, the baby will engage in reciprocal play with an older sibling, knocking down a tower that the sibling has built or creeping after a wheel toy that the sibling is pulling around the room.

Although some authorities insist that babies and young toddlers are not ready to make friends, caregivers who work with groups of youngsters attest to the fact that older infants and young toddlers are quite likely to select a favorite playmate. As soon as they arrive in the morning, some toddlers are likely to pair off and continue playing with each other for a good part of the day.

As we would expect, toddlers who spend a good part of every day playing with each other are quite likely to get into hassles, most of which are over toys. A hassle over a toy can begin as a shouting match—"My bear!" "No, my bear!"—and escalate into a battle, with shoving, grabbing, kicking, and hitting. Often, this type of confrontation is short lived. Before the teacher can intervene, the toddlers have dropped the toy and are off playing with something else. At other times, the quarrel escalates and the caregiver has to step in. Consider this example:

> *Nathaniel and Rosia loved to play together and were usually quite compatible. One day, they were playing with the class mascot, a threadbare, lanky monkey called Mimi. They were taking turns tossing Mimi into the air and trying to catch her. Nathaniel tossed Mimi a bit too high, and she fell on the*

floor. Rosia and Nathaniel picked her up at the same time and started a tug of war. "My turn," shouted Nathaniel. "I get to catch her." "No, my turn," shouted Rosia in an even louder voice, " 'cause you just threw her." Recognizing that the quarrel was escalating, the teacher decided to intervene. "I think Mimi is very tired," the teacher insisted. "It's time for Mimi to rest." Rosia and Nathaniel ran to put Mimi in the doll's crib. They forgot about their quarrel and went off to play in the block corner. ●

The very fact that toddler twosomes get into hassles underscores the importance of encouraging early friendships. From the toddler's point of view, "It is mine if I am playing with it, and it is also mine if I want to play with it." Through interactions with a favorite friend and skillful interventions from a caregiver, toddlers gradually learn about sharing and taking turns. They come to recognize that the fun of playing with another child makes sharing and taking turns worthwhile.

Suggestions for Encouraging Friendships

- Because their play is largely imitative, provide toddlers with matching toys. Playing together for toddlers means playing side by side with the same toy.
- When you notice a friendship emerging, place the children together at mealtime and naptime. Budding friendships should be encouraged.
- Provide equipment that encourages children to play together, like climbing structures, see-saws, big balls, and rocking boats.
- Tell the parents about it when their children begin developing a friendship. The parents may wish to provide additional opportunities for the friends to play together.
- Accept the fact that toddlers who play together are going to get into hassles. Before you intervene, give the toddlers an opportunity to resolve a problem on their own.
- When a hassle gets out of hand and requires intervention, do *not* try to find out which toddler is in the wrong. Make the assumption that what is wrong is the particular situation, and redirect the children to a different activity.
- Set up the classroom in a way that encourages friend making. Make sure that there are plenty of opportunities in each section of the classroom for children to play together in groups of two, three, or four.

Activities for Encouraging Friendships

Block Area Provide enough of the same sorts of blocks to allow children to work together. Add props like miniature animals, cars, and trucks and miniature characters so that toddlers can play with the block structures they create.

Imaginative Play Area Make sure that there are props in the imaginative play area that appeal to both girls and boys. Include props for playing "doctor" or "rescue" and for "cooking" and "pet care."

(continued)

Activities continued

Art Area Put up double easels so that two children can paint beside each other. Provide materials that encourage side-by-side play, like water play, sand play, and play dough.

Reading Corner Make sure there are cozy spots where two children can read together.

Manipulative Play Area Include large floor puzzles that two or more toddlers can complete together. Introduce some simple cooperative games that the whole group can play together.

Circle Time During circle time, play very small group games, such as dancing with a partner, playing Farmer-in-the-Dell (where the children choose friends), and Ring-Around-the-Rosie. Encourage the children to have fun together.

Parachute Play Seat the toddlers around a parachute or a bed sheet, and have each child grasp its edge. Play slow and then faster music, letting the children move the parachute up and down in time with the music. With older toddlers, place a beach ball in the center of the parachute and see if the children can make it bounce up and down without rolling off.

Egg Hunt Before the children go outdoors, hide a dozen plastic eggs around the playground. At playground time, bring out an egg carton and a stuffed animal. Ask the children to help their animal friend find all of the eggs that go in the carton. Encourage them to hunt in pairs or small groups. Use prompts such as "Why don't you three look in the sandbox? I think some eggs might be hiding there."

Punchinello Have the children form a circle, and then have one child go into the center. This child becomes *Punchinello*. The whole group sings "What can you do, Punchinello, funny fellow? What can you do, Punchinello, funny you?" Punchinello then performs a simple trick, such as spinning around, putting his hands on his head, or walking like a duck. The whole group then imitates Punchinello as they sing "Well, we can do it, too, Punchinello, funny fellow. We can do it, too, Punchinello, funny you." Give each child who wants a turn the chance to be Punchinello.

To recognize ways of encouraging preschool children to make friends and engage in social play

Collegiate Preschool was located in a suburban area, where the population was predominantly white and middle class. When Bartholomew, a recent Haitian immigrant, was enrolled in the school, the director was both delighted and concerned. She wondered, "How will this child get along with the other children when he doesn't know English? Will the other children reject him because his skin is a different color? Will he be behind the other children because he has had no experience in a preschool?"

When Bartholomew arrived at the preschool two days later, the director was upset with herself. She had not told the mother to dress Bartholomew in play clothes, and Bartholomew was wearing a shirt with a collar and a tie. "How many strikes can one child have against him?" the director thought to herself.

As soon as she had dealt with the business of the day, the director went into Bartholomew's classroom. Bartholomew and another child were passing a truck back and forth underneath a tunnel made out of blocks. The director asked the classroom teacher if he had had any problems with Bartholomew. "Why should I have problems?" the teacher asked. "He's a fine kid. The only thing I did was to give him a tee-shirt to change into. He was wearing a dress shirt, and I didn't want him to worry about getting it dirty. I hope his mother won't mind." ●

When parents are asked what they would like their children to achieve in preschool, making new friends is always a top priority. Most parents recognize the importance of group acceptance. Some children, like Bartholomew, have a natural talent for making friends and can fit quite easily into a group. Other children, for a whole variety of reasons, including temperament, experience, and self-confidence, need some extra help. There is clear evidence in the research literature that preschool children who get along well with their peers tend to be well adjusted when they enter elementary school, whereas children who are consistently rejected by their peers in preschool are at risk for later problems. Unquestionably, helping children make friends needs to be a top priority for teachers as well as parents.

The Teacher's Role in Helping Children Make Friends

Teachers play a critical role in helping children make friends. Effective early childhood teachers create a climate and initiate activities that encourage the development of social skills.

Creating a Classroom Climate That Encourages Social Skill Development

A primary way in which teachers and caregivers can create a friendly environment is by setting a good example. Teachers who are warm and friendly with parents, visitors, and fellow staff members model good social skills. When visitors are expected, make sure that the children help you prepare for the visit. You could help the children make a "welcome" poster, prepare a snack, or practice a "welcome" song that they could sing to the visitors. Other ways to encourage strong social skills include setting up an environment that encourages social interaction, planning a schedule that provides time for free play and for socialization, and planning activities that encourage social skill development.

Setting Up an Environment That Fosters Social Skill Development

An environment that fosters social skill development provides space and equipment that encourage different types of social interaction. Sensory bins filled with sand, water, shaving cream, or unusual materials like "oobleck" (cornstarch and water) encourage small groups of children to carry on conversations as they play side by side or together in a noncompetitive situation. Semienclosed areas, such as book corners and

playhouses, also provide opportunities for intimate play. Open spaces, indoors and on the playground, provide opportunities for children to play in larger groups.

Planning a Daily Schedule That Allows Time for Social Interaction

A daily schedule that provides large chunks of time for free play affords children ongoing opportunities to learn and practice social skills. During free play, children have the opportunity to play together in groups. This is the time when children are most likely to play out favorite pretend scenarios with their old friends and also to make new friends as they join new groups.

Activities That Encourage Social Skill Development

In preparing a curriculum for a preschool classroom, the teacher should make social skill development a priority goal. Activities that encourage social skill development include puppet play, cooperative art projects, book reading, cooperative games, and pretend play.

> *In preparing a curriculum for a preschool classroom, the teacher should make social skill development a priority goal.*

Puppet Play Teachers can use puppet play in several different ways to encourage social skill development. Teachers can use puppets who talk to each other or to the children to suggest ways of making friends and resolving conflicts. Teachers can also encourage children to use puppets to build friendships and talk about troublesome issues.

Consider the following exchange between Irene and Theodore, who wanted to play together but could not agree on what they wanted to play with. The teacher suggested that they use the class puppets to talk about different ideas:

> *Theodore* (talking for his puppet): "I wanna play with the clay and make a birthday cake for my uncle."
>
> *Irene* (talking for her puppet): "I don't wanna play with clay. It gets my hands all dirty, and I don't even know your uncle! I wanna play in the housekeeping corner."
>
> *Theodore:* "That's dumb. Housekeeping corners are for girls, and I'm a boy."
>
> *Irene:* "My daddy's a boy, and he makes blueberry pancakes every Sunday morning."
>
> *Theodore:* "I know how to make blueberry pancakes. You mix all the stuff in a bowl, stick in the blueberries, and put it on the stove."

Theodore and Irene continued to talk back and forth with their puppets until it was time to go outside.

Cooperative Art Projects Although we often think about art projects as individual activities, a creative teacher can find different ways to encourage cooperative art projects that allow for individuality. Favorite cooperative art projects include making collages and murals, building a "city" out of different-sized boxes, and making a "museum display." The children could make a science museum display by creating a planetarium with stars, moons, and planets or a natural history museum with arrangements of rocks or shells.

Book Reading Book reading is a favorite activity in most preschool classrooms, and books that encourage social skills are easy to find. Children particularly enjoy books about animals that have problems with making friends, sharing toys, taking turns, or doing a fair share of the work. Traditional favorites include the *Frances* books by Lillian and Russell Hoban, the *Little Monster* books by Mercer Mayer, the *Arthur* books by Marc Brown, and for younger children, books by Rosemary Wells. Books about real children are equally helpful and provide opportunities to show a range of families and neighborhoods and to address a wide range of issues. Ezra Jack Keats, Maurice Sendak, Stephen Kellogg, Alma Flor Ada, and Eloise Greenfield are among the authors who convey just what it feels like to be a young child.

Cooperative Games Although older children are attracted to games that are competitive, preschool children are less concerned with winning than they are with having fun. From the point of view of most preschool children, the best games are those in which everybody is the winner. (More ways for children to cooperate are described later in this chapter in the section on Objective 6.)

Pretend Play Pretend play provides children with special opportunities to assume the roles of important people and to see the world from the perspectives of others. Children who have good play ideas are very desirable companions. Teachers can encourage pretending by scheduling the day so that there is plenty of time for this activity, by joining in pretend play, and by arranging and equipping the classroom and the playground to maximize pretend play. One classroom arrangement that encourages boys and girls to pretend together is setting up two pretend play spaces: a housekeeping area and a neighborhood place. The neighborhood place could be a pretend convenience store, fix-it shop, doctor's office, post office, camera shop, or restaurant. Encourage children in the housekeeping area to visit the "store," and let the children working at the store make a "home delivery."

> *Children with good play ideas are very desirable companions.*

Objective 4

To help children build on their strengths and overcome their difficulties

Children, like adults, have different social styles. Some children are outgoing while others are shy. Some children are leaders, some children are followers, and some children can assume the role of either leader or follower. Some children enjoy being part of a large group, some children like to be part of a small group, and some children prefer having one or two intimate friends. Some children enjoy engaging in active physical activities. Other children enjoy quiet play, creating an art product or carrying on a conversation. Some children love to stir up a controversy; others enjoy being the peacemaker. Some children have strong preferences for group size and social role; others are happy to "go with the flow."

Natural Leaders in the Social Structure of a Preschool Classroom

If you watch any preschool classroom over time, you will notice that there seems to be a distinct social structure. It is not exactly a "pecking order," nor is it like the set of "in" and "out" groups or cliques that are often found among adolescents. Rather, some children naturally take a leadership role, and some children are happy following others' leads in play. This is visible as they engage in dramas such as the following:

Melissa: "OK, children. I'm gonna make your breakfast. Gimmie those eggs, Cassandra. I gotta make an omelet."

Cassandra: "I don't want an omelet. I want regular eggs."

Melissa: "I told you—I am making an omelet."

Alexis: "May I mix the eggs, Mother?"

Melissa: "No, you may not. Your hands are dirty."

Shalimar (pretending to be a baby): "Wawa-wawa! I want breakfast!"

Melissa: "Be quiet, baby. I gotta make it first."

Shalimar: "Wawa-wawa!"

Melissa: "Alexis, take that baby out of here. Who's got the garlic? I need it right now."

Cassandra: "We don't got no garlic."

Alexis: "Here is your garlic, Mother."

Shalimar: "Wa-wa-wa!"

Melissa: "Cassandra, how many times do I got to tell you? Alexis, you take the baby out of here."

Some children, like Melissa, are the leaders of groups. They may be benevolent and easygoing, or they may be bossy and domineering. Melissa was rather domineering, directing her playmates with an iron hand. Many children, like Alexis, are perfectly happy doing as the leader suggests. Others, like Cassandra and Shalimar, are somewhat rebellious and disgruntled.

Children's social patterns are interesting to observe, but what should teachers do with the information? Whether a teacher should intervene, and if so, how, depends on how the children are feeling. If they all seem happy in their roles and are able to resolve conflicts among themselves in their play scenarios, then it is best to stay out of their way. Children who seem obnoxiously bossy may also be full of fun ideas; in the give and take of group play, they will learn to also incorporate the ideas of others. The children who willingly comply with others' ideas, as well as those who cheerfully insist on being contrary within the boundaries of the game, are learning how to cooperate to keep a project going. When things are working well, all the children contribute to their joint project and all the children, including the leader, learn to listen to each other's ideas.

Knowing When to Intervene

But what if all is *not* well in the social structure of the classroom? What if some children end up as victims or are rejected altogether? What if a child wants to join a group but doesn't know where to begin? What if a child is too aggressive or socially inept to find a comfortable place within a group? What if a child is cruel to others? In these situations, it is essential for the teacher to intervene.

Helping Children Who Are Victims

A teacher's natural inclination is to protect children who are victims. There are generally three ways to do this effectively: prevent or minimize the problem, modify the victim's behavior, and/or modify the behavior of the victimizer.

Prevention is the strategy of first resort. Keeping a running record of where and when problems occur can help you identify ways to prevent them. You may find that children are restless or cranky at certain times of the day, that some classroom areas get too crowded or invite wild play, or that some groups of children have become stuck in patterns that are overly controlling or otherwise hurtful. Once you have recognized such a problem, you may then be able to eliminate it simply by reconfiguring the schedule or the classroom space. Changing play props or introducing new themes may encourage children to form different groups. A cooperative curriculum (see Objective 6) helps create a classroom climate that prevents problems.

> **Prevention** *is the strategy of first resort. Keeping a running record of where and when problems occur can help you identify ways to prevent them.*

Despite teachers' best efforts at prevention, there are one or two children in almost every preschool classroom who tend to be victimized repeatedly. Other children hit or push them, call them names, and say "We don't want you to play with us." Victims may be smaller children who cannot defend themselves or children who stand out as being different. Most frequently, the victim is a child who is timid and fearful and who cries and runs to the teacher whenever he is touched. An effective way to help the victim is to step in before the tears start (or simply to ignore them if they have started) and, deliberately ignoring the victimizer, give the child words with which to defend himself. "I know it made you really mad when John pushed you. I hope John remembers our 'No pushing' rule. If he forgets again, tell him to stop. Nobody likes to be pushed." Focusing attention on the victim while preventing his tears is also an effective way to modify the victimizer's behavior.

Helping Children Who Are Victimizers

Miss Right-Things was concerned about Adam, who often hit and kicked smaller children. She sensed that this victimizing was the only way that Adam knew of getting the other children to notice him. Miss Right-Things decided to use a class puppet, Pinocchio, as a way of helping Adam. During circle time, she had a conversation with the puppet. "Now, Pinocchio," she said, "if you want the children to like you, you have to stop hitting and kicking. What? They wouldn't let you play in the sandbox? Okay, I'll tell you what to do. If you find out that the children in the sandbox are baking a cake, bring them over some sand that they can use for icing. The children will see that you are a good helper and will let you join their play."

> *The victimizer needs help in gaining group acceptance without resorting to negative behavior.*

Very often, children who victimize other children are concerned about being accepted by the peer group. Because the victimizer lacks adequate social skills, he plagues the other children as a way of gaining prestige. The victimizer needs help in gaining group acceptance without resorting to negative behavior.

Helping Children Who Are Loners

Before seeking ways of helping the loner find a friend, it is important to know whether that child is happy being alone. Some children are easily accepted when they choose to join a group but like to spend time pursuing their own interests. Other children are unhappy with their loner status. They may not be as socially mature as other children, or they may be temperamentally slow to warm up. These children would like to have friends but don't how to go about getting them. You might try pairing such a child with a more socially adept partner for a task like giving out the snack or cleaning up the block area. Or you can help the child find a role that connects his talents and interests with what other children are doing. For example, you might ask a group of children who are building a block "city" if they need a police station, and if the idea is accepted, help the loner child get started in building it.

Helping Children Who Are Actively Rejected

The child who is actively rejected by other children is likely to be unhappy. Quite often, the rejected child has tried too hard for group acceptance and has been labeled by the group as a pest. Unfortunately, preschool children do not want to befriend a low-status child. The best solution in this case is usually to help the child find another group that will be more accepting. Another tactic is to include the low-status child in a fun game or activity that you engage in with a small group. Try to choose a cooperative activity—such as putting together a floor puzzle, setting up a "restaurant," or building a miniature "zoo"—in which each child's contributions will be valued. It is best, too, if the activity is one that the children can then do on their own.

Other children are rejected because they really are difficult to play with. They may be impulsive or destructive, or they may insist on having their own way. These children need positive guidance (see Chapter 10) to help them modify unacceptable behav-

254

iors and learn good social skills. When the problem is not within the child's control—for example, when a child who is clumsy or visually impaired tends to bump into others or knock down their constructions—you may also need to engage the other children in helping to solve the problem.

To describe ways in which caregivers can encourage helping, sharing, and caring behaviors among children

Mr. Greene was eavesdropping in the dress-up corner when he heard a dialogue between Mary and Ernest:

Mary: "I be the mommy, and you be the daddy. You want some orange juice?"

Ernest: "Okay—I'm the daddy. No orange juice. I got to work. Where's my lunch box?"

Mary: "No, you can't work. The baby's sick. He's got the chicken pops!"

Ernest: "No, he don't got chicken pops. He's just sick."

Mary: "I'm the doctor. Open your mouth, baby. You want a lollipop? Now you're all better."

Ernest: "No, poor baby. He's still sick. I give him medicine—okay?"

Mr. Greene was glad he had eavesdropped. He had been worried about Ernest for a while because Ernest seemed to be unconcerned about the feelings of other people. Now Mr. Greene recognized that at least in his pretending, Ernest could express empathy and concern and play a helping role.

Respecting the Personal Feelings of Others

One of the qualities that we associate with social competence is the ability to express our own feelings and appreciate the feelings of others. It can be quite difficult for young children to recognize and differentiate their own feelings. A child who is wound up and irritable may not realize that the real problem is that he is feeling tired. A child who becomes aggressive may not recognize that he is feeling frustrated and inadequate. A child who is exuberant and wild may not recognize that he is seeking an outlet for his happy feelings. Here are some suggestions for helping children recognize and describe their feelings:

> *One of the qualities that we associate with social competence is the ability to express our own feelings and appreciate the feelings of others.*

- Talk about happy, sad, and angry feelings, and ask the children to think about times when they have these different types of feelings.
- Read a story like *Today I Feel Silly: And Other Moods That Make My Day*, by Jamie Lee Curtis (1998), and ask the children how each character feels when something good or bad happens. Remember to include angry feelings and to give children opportunities to talk about a range of feelings.

255

- Play short tracks of different types of music, and ask the children to tell you when the music is happy or sad.

- Ask the children to make pictures with colors that make them feel sad. Ask the children to make pictures with colors that make them feel happy.

- Use puppets to act out situations similar to those that the children have experienced. Encourage the children to talk about how the puppets are feeling and how they should respond.

- Acknowledge children's negative feelings by reading books like *Alexander and the Terrible, Horrible, No Good, Very Bad Day* (Viorst, 1972) and referring to characters like *Sesame Street's* Oscar the Grouch.

- Act out simple tales that involve strong emotions, such as "Goldilocks and the Three Bears" and "The Three Little Pigs."

- Redirect negative behaviors by giving children acceptable ways of expressing their feelings.

Supporting Pretend Play

Pretend play provides children with many opportunities to initiate and develop friendships and helps them develop understanding of others' points of view. Moreover, pretend play is downright fun and gives many opportunities to initiate and join in group play situations. Pretend play provides the chance to use imagination and creativity. It also provides a way to replay events that might have been scary, thereby helping children come to terms with difficult events.

To design a classroom environment and curriculum that support cooperative behavior

Mrs. Go-Getter was the first mother to sign up for a teacher's conference. Here's how the conference went:

Teacher: "I am so glad you have come. Your son, Ulysses, is a real joy. I have been looking forward to meeting you."

Mrs. Go-Getter: "I'm glad to be here. Ulysses absolutely loves coming to school. The one problem I have is that he doesn't tell me much about what he does in school."

Teacher: "That's true of many of our children. At this age, children think about parents as knowing everything. Ulysses probably figures that you know what he's doing at school. At any rate, what would you like to know about?"

Mrs. Go-Gettter: "Well, how exactly is he doing? Is he keeping up with the other children? Would you say he's at the bottom of the class, top of the class, or somewhere in the middle?"

Teacher: *"Well, you know, at this age we don't give grades and we don't compare the children with each other. As a matter of fact, we try to downplay competition. We encourage the children to cooperate, to work together, and to help each other succeed."*

Mrs. Go-Getter: *"That sounds all very good for right now, but what will happen to Ulysses when he gets out in the real world? You know, out there, it's dog-eat-dog and every man for himself."*

Teacher: *"I understand your concern, but you know it's a changing world. Young people who can work well with other people will be at an advantage in whatever they undertake."* ●

The Nature of a Cooperative Classroom

When they talk about *cooperation*, early childhood teachers are likely to refer to a children's developmental sequence. Children begin with *parallel play*, where they play side by side; move to *associative play*, where there is a sharing of play ideas; and eventually progress to *cooperative play*, where they work toward a common goal.

The philosophy that underlies this book provides a much broader view. Namely, *cooperation* is any social exchange in which children take into account each other's point of view. Cooperation includes cooperative play, as traditionally defined, but it also takes place when children talk to each other in the art corner, negotiate turns on a tricycle or swing, and take part in a teacher-directed group activity. The essence of cooperation is sharing perspectives, and the outcome of cooperation is making friends.

Cooperative Play

Cooperative play, in the traditional sense, is most likely to occur in pretend play. Whether the children are acting out an exotic theme, like being an astronaut in a space ship, or a more commonplace theme, like eating dinner or going shopping, they are working toward a shared goal. Plans are made, roles are assigned, ideas are exchanged, and conflicts are negotiated. The most common role-play theme for promoting cooperation is "family" play. This kind of pretending creates strong feelings of intimacy and group interdependence. Other themes, like "monster" play and "superhero" play, are more likely to create feelings of excitement and exuberance. Whatever form it takes, pretend play generates cooperation that is emotionally intense.

At the other extreme, cooperative play can be quiet and relaxing and emotional expression can be muted. This kind of cooperative play occurs most often in manipulative play

activities, as when children are rolling out play dough, shaping sand, or pouring water. A group of acquaintances can casually share such sensory experiences. Their play is largely imitative, but as they play, the children watch each other and converse periodically.

> *Whatever form it takes, pretend play generates cooperation that is emotionally intense.*

Then there are activities in which the natural outcome is a tangible product. Block building, artwork, and cooking all fall into this category. Cooperation in these instances depends on having good leadership, and it is frequently necessary for the teacher to take an active role in organizing a group effort. Despite the fact that the cooperation is directed by the teacher, the final product can give young children a strong feeling of pride and group achievement.

Working Cooperatively

In the same vein yet somewhat distinct are those activities that emphasize group discussion and an exchange of ideas. When successful, these activities also foster a feeling of group identity, a feeling of being at home in a familiar classroom. Typically, the teacher encourages this kind of cooperation during circle time. For example, the children might cooperate in writing a story about a recent field trip, predict what will happen next in a story they are reading, decide what to put in the "science museum" they are making, or simply reflect on the high points of their day. Movement activities that require partners also promote this type of cooperation.

A cooperative curriculum can extend to every part of the classroom. Each time of the day and each setting in which the children work and play has its own possibilities for increased interaction and caring. Teachers who make a commitment to fostering cooperation and friendship in the classroom will want to explore all these different forms of cooperative interaction. They also will want to encourage social experiences that range from intimate to exciting to relaxing.

Additional Resources for Social Development

Curtis, J. L. (1998). *Today I feel silly: And other moods that make my day.* New York: Harper-Collins.

Katz, L., & McClennan, D. (1997). *Fostering children's social competence: The teacher's role.* Washington, DC: NAEYC.

Rice, J. (1995). *The kindness curriculum: Introducing young children to loving values.* St. Paul, MN: Redleaf Press.

Stone, J. (2001). *Building classroom community: The early childhood teacher's role.* Washington, DC: NAEYC.

Viorst, J. (1972). *Alexander and the terrible, horrible, no good, very bad day.* New York: Atheneum.

Guidance

Chapter 10

Overview

Guidance involves helping children learn and practice appropriate behaviors that contribute to their own well-being and the well-being of others.

Rationale

One of the major challenges that teachers face is to create and maintain a climate within the child care setting where children are happy and productive and where stress and confrontation are limited. Teachers seek to achieve this goal in many different ways, depending on the ages and characteristics of the children and the number of children they are responsible for. Infant caregivers recognize the importance of creating an environment that is basically quiet and soothing. Toddler caregivers recognize the importance of arranging and equipping the classroom to invite cooperative play and minimize disputes over toys. Preschool teachers find it helpful to develop classroom rules that emphasize responsibility and define acceptable behaviors.

A second challenge that all teachers face is to identify ways of redirecting behaviors that are negative and nonproductive. Again, the techniques that teachers use depend on the ages and characteristics of the children. The one rule of thumb for all child caregivers is that the guidance techniques they use must be *positive*. The goal of guidance is not to punish bad behavior but to help children learn ways of achieving their own goals while respecting the rights of others.

New research has shown that *emotional intelligence* is the most important predictor of school readiness and of life success. Emotional intelligence involves the ability to handle stress without falling apart, to know right from wrong, to control impulses and exert self-discipline, to keep working in the face of challenge, to recognize one's own feelings and those of others, and to empathize with and take care of others. These abilities begin to take shape in the first year of life. Teachers and caregivers of infants, toddlers, and preschoolers play a critical role in guiding their development.

Objectives

1. To identify ways of helping infants achieve self-regulation and develop coping skills

2. To identify ways of helping young toddlers explore their world and make new discoveries without being destructive or wasteful and without causing injury to themselves and others

3. To help older toddlers cope with fear, anger, and frustration and strike a balance between their longing for nurturance and desire to be independent

4. To learn ways of helping preschool children recognize and value differences, resolve conflicts, express their feelings in words, and accept reasonable limits

5. To recognize ways of using positive guidance techniques to reduce children's unwanted behaviors

6. To recognize ways of providing positive guidance for children whose families use styles of discipline that are different from those the teacher has been taught

Providing Guidance

Mrs. Toe-the-Line was interviewing for a job at the Heart Smart Preschool. The director asked her about the discipline techniques she uses. "I never have problems with discipline," Mrs. Toe-the-Line assured the director. "The kids in my class recognize that they can have lots of fun as long as they obey the rules."

Next, the director asked, "And if the children forget to follow the rules, what do you do?" Mrs. Toe-the-Line explained, "First, I talk to them and restate the rule in a firm voice. If they continue to act up after that, then the kids all know you have to pay the consequences."

"Do you use physical punishment?" the director asked. "If you mean paddling," Mrs. Toe-the-Line replied, "I would never do that! I just give the child a good smack on the back of his or her hand. Children need to know that when I say something, I mean it." ●

Mrs. Toe-the-Line did not get the job at the Heart Smart Preschool. Her punitive approach to discipline didn't fit with the positive guidance approach followed at the school. The director was dismayed at the thought of hitting a child to discourage him from misbehavior.

In this chapter, we focus on positive guidance as a way of enhancing desirable behavior and reducing behavior that is nonproductive or disruptive. We emphasize the fact that guidance is a *constructive* way of teaching that does not require punishment. Caregivers who maintain a climate that encourages self-regulation, coping, and cooperation and who help children accept reasonable limits and respect the rights of others are practicing positive guidance. They are helping children to develop skills and character traits that they will use their entire lives.

> *Guidance is a* constructive *way of teaching that does not require punishment.*

Objective 1

To identify ways of helping infants achieve self-regulation and develop coping skills

Mary, a teen mother, brought her 4-month-old baby, Tina, to a family child care provider. The provider, Mrs. Totlove, asked her to stay for a while so that they could talk about Tina. "She's a sensitive little girl," Mary explained, "and she gets really upset if she is left alone in the crib. I don't know if this is OK, but I put her in my bed at night. I let her sleep in her crib during the day, but the minute she wakes up, she starts crying." Mrs. Totlove asked, "What do you do when she cries?" "If my mother isn't there," answered Mary, "I pick Tina up right away and she stops crying." "What happens when your mother is there?" asked Mrs. Totlove. "Well, my mother keeps telling me that if I pick Tina up every time she cries, I will spoil her," Mary explained. "So I try not to go to her too quickly when my mother is watching."

Mrs. Totlove thought for a moment before she responded. She knew that research had made it quite clear that when caregivers respond quickly and consistently to an infant's crying, the infant develops feelings of security and trust. You can't spoil a baby by responding to her needs. Later, perhaps, when she knew Mary better, she would talk to her about different child-rearing beliefs and help her find ways of talking about these differences with her mother.

After a pause, Mrs. Totlove responded to Mary sympathetically without talking about spoiling. "I see that you feel badly when Tina cries. I'm like you— I don't feel comfortable letting a baby cry. What else would you like to tell me about Tina? You know your baby so well, and the more I can learn from you about Tina, the more responsive I can be to her needs." ●

Mary, although still a teenager, is tuned in to her baby's individual needs. And while she does not want to contradict her mother, she feels instinctively that being responsive to her baby's needs will not spoil her. She feels her baby is especially sensitive and needs constant reassurance that she is loved and her needs will always be met. (See the Developmental Picture on the next page for more about the needs of infants.)

Developmental Picture

The young infant (0–9 months):

- Is fully dependent on the caregiver for meeting all his needs
- Is learning ways of self-comforting, initiating interactions, and eliciting responses
- Has an individual schedule of sleeping, waking, and eating; for some infants, this schedule is consistent, and for others, it is irregular

The caregiver:

- Learns to interpret an infant's particular cues
- Responds to the infant's signals promptly and appropriately
- Recognizes that infants can be soothed in different ways, by holding, rocking, singing, patting or stroking, or by placing a thumb or pacifier in their mouth
- Adjusts caregiving routines to conform to the unique schedule of each infant

The older infant (9–14 months):

- Experiments with interesting things—for example, tosses food or toys off the feeding table to watch them fall or watch an adult pick them up
- May insist on being carried even when he has learned to walk
- Stops doing something when she hears "No" but is likely to continue after a brief pause

The caregiver:

- Provides opportunities for infants to learn by experimenting in ways that do not require adult interference
- Recognizes the importance of being flexible in responding to infants' demands
- Recognizes that babies can be demanding when they are tired or out of sorts
- Reserves "No" for times when the infant is doing something that is dangerous, destructive, or hurtful and makes sure the infant stops what he is doing

The young toddler (14–24 months):

- Is developing an awareness of what behaviors are OK and not OK but continues to experiment or tease with not-OK behaviors, like throwing blocks and touching fragile things
- May get busy playing and not recognize that she is tired or hungry
- Recognizes when adults are pleased or displeased with his behavior
- Has difficulty settling down or controlling herself when she is excited or wound up
- Enjoys doing things that please beloved adults

The caregiver:

- Praises a child's good behavior and limits opportunities for behavior that is not OK
- Redirects the young toddler when she is doing something that is not OK and provides a substitute toy when the toddler wants something she cannot have
- Recognizes the importance of introducing a different activity when the toddler is getting too excited or wound up
- Recognizes that toddlers may not realize when they are hungry or tired and maintains a regular schedule for mealtimes and resting times

Caregiver Responsibilities

Caregivers of infants are charged with an awesome range of responsibilities. They must recognize the unique characteristics of all of the children in their care. They must modify each infant's environment in response to subtle cues from her, providing all infants with assurance that their needs will be met and that they can trust their caregivers. Caregivers also must recognize that each infant has his own threshold for stimulation and then provide enough stimulation to keep each infant alert and interested. At the same time, caregivers must recognize that too much stimulation is stressful for babies and look for telltale signs of overload, like changes in color, hiccups, body tension, and rapid breathing (see the following box on overstimulation).

> *Caregivers must recognize that while some babies are disturbed by too much stimulation, others are not responsive unless the stimulation is intense and persistent.*

Signs of Overstimulation

An infant is likely overstimulated if she displays these signs:

- Persists in avoiding the stimulation (whether sight, sound, or interaction) by turning her head away or falling asleep
- Shifts suddenly from laughing out loud to whining or crying
- Purses her lips and turns white around her mouth.
- Hiccups, has a bowel movement, or spits up in response to a caregiver's overtures
- Tightens her muscles and curls her toes

Caregivers must recognize that while some babies are disturbed by too much stimulation, others are not responsive unless the stimulation is intense and persistent. Caregivers must persist in their efforts to interact with nonresponsive infants by providing different kinds of stimulation. They must not assume that nonresponsive infants don't like them and give up their efforts to provide stimulation (see the following box on understimulation).

Signs of Understimulation

An infant is likely understimulated if he displays these signs:

- Stares blankly into space
- Seldom smiles or vocalizes
- Spends more time asleep than other babies his age
- Does not engage in a back and forth cooing conversation
- Bangs his head against the crib, as if seeking self-stimulation

Like all relationships, the relationship between a caregiver and a baby is interactive. That means that the way the baby behaves with the caregiver is influenced by the baby, the caregiver, and the history of their relationship. A baby who is nonresponsive may become more receptive to stimulation as his nervous system matures, but his caregiver may not be emotionally available if she has learned not to expect much of a response. By the same token, if the caregiver is emotionally unavailable during a baby's early attempts at interaction, the baby may be emotionally unavailable to the caregiver at a later time, when the caregiver is ready and eager to interact with the baby.

> *The way the baby behaves with the caregiver is influenced by the baby, the caregiver, and the history of their relationship.*

Self-Regulation and Coping Behaviors

Two of the most important behaviors that babies acquire in the first year are self-regulation and coping. *Self-regulation* is the ability to maintain equilibrium when exposed to stressors. *Coping* is the process of developing strategies to overcome and manage stress. In the early months, babies learn to calm themselves, or self-regulate, by putting their thumbs in or near their mouths or by relaxing their muscles and cuddling with their caregivers. A baby who is cared for by responsive caregivers will continue to develop new techniques for self-regulation, such as sucking on a pacifier or her fingers, fingering a favorite blanket, or simply being still. As she learns new cognitive and physical skills, she will develop new ways of coping with new stressors. A hungry infant will stop crying when her caregiver approaches. A 6-month-old will search for the toy that she has dropped in the crib. A 10-month-old will seek comfort from a new caregiver when her favorite person disappears.

Here are some ways of helping infants achieve self-regulation and develop coping skills:

- Learn about the temperamental characteristics of each infant in your care by observing the infant intensely and over time.

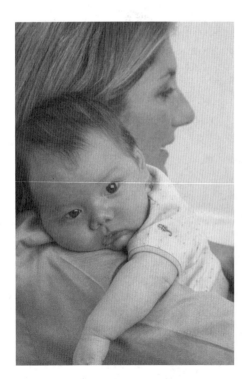

  - As each new infant enters your program, ask the parents to describe their baby's characteristics, preferences, and special needs.
  - For babies that are overactive and excitable, use a quiet voice and soothing gestures to help them calm themselves and control their impulses.
  - For babies that are usually inactive and lethargic, gradually introduce them to new experiences that are stimulating and engaging.
  - For babies that are unusually sensitive or jumpy, try using only one or two senses at a time. Talk to these babies in a soft voice, without making eye contact, or hold them close and silently show them a toy.
  - Increase babies' ability to cope with novel situations by introducing them to new experiences when they are physically healthy and cheerful.
  - For babies that appear to be withdrawn, observe them carefully and search for subtle cues that are indicative of their needs.

- Keep track of the kinds of stimuli that are either aversive (unpleasant) or pleasurable for each of the infants in your care.
- Keep track of the changing amount of activity and excitement that each infant can handle before becoming overwhelmed.
- Get to know each baby's cycles of sleep, quiet alertness, feeding, and crying.
- Help babies to achieve a quiet, alert state—a prime time for play and learning.
- Slow down or stop interaction when a baby signals a need for a break or seems tired, before overload occurs.
- Help babies learn calming and coping skills. You might give a young baby a pacifier to suck or a favorite blanket to finger when she is mildly distressed, or you might help an older baby recover from a bump by playing with an interesting toy.

To identify ways of helping young toddlers explore their world and make new discoveries without being destructive or wasteful and without causing injury to themselves and others

There is no special magic in a baby's first birthday, but somewhere between 10 and 15 months, a remarkable change takes place. When a baby goes from creeping or scooting to walking, she sees the world from a new perspective. She can see more things, reach more things, and explore more places. Her emerging abilities provide new opportunities for investigation and, at the same time, make her world somewhat more hazardous.

> *Young toddlers, as a group, are fun, affectionate, curious, eager to please, and excited about learning new things.*

Young toddlers, as a group, are fun, affectionate, curious, eager to please, and excited about learning new things. They can also keep you on your toes and exhaust the most energetic caregiver. Young toddlers can mess up a room in two minutes flat. They waste crayons, pads of paper, tissues, Band-Aids, and bottles of ketchup or paste. Before you can catch them, they will dirty their clothes, overwater a plant, or overfeed the goldfish, as they try to do the things they have seen older people do. Young toddlers can stick beans up their noses or in their ears, pull the pictures off the wall, climb up things that are not meant for climbing, and take a bite of another child who happens to be in their way. For the most part, toddlers are not malicious or even trying to be naughty. They just require constant watching.

In infancy, caregivers provide guidance by recognizing and meeting infants' needs, by helping them learn how to calm themselves, and by teaching them to cope with new stressors and challenges. With young toddlers, the guidance role of caregivers takes on a new dimension. They must not only maintain an environment that provides toddlers with opportunities to engage in a variety of safe and fun activities, but they must also limit toddlers' opportunities of engaging in inappropriate behaviors and redirect those behaviors when they do occur.

Situations That Require Intervention

Situation 1: Pedro is an exuberant child who loves to make other children laugh. One day during lunch, he opened his tuna salad sandwich and smeared tuna salad all over his face and hair.

Caregiver's Response: Before the other children can imitate Pedro's antics, the teacher takes him by the hand, tells him in a firm but calm voice that tuna salad sandwiches are to eat, and cleans him up in the bathroom.

Situation 2: Rasheed has pulled all the tissues out of the box, torn them into small pieces, and thrown the pieces into the air. "Snowing, snowing," he shouts out gleefully.

Caregiver's Response: "Rasheed, I know you are having fun making snow. Here is one more tissue. The rest of the box is going up on the shelf. I will help you find something else that is fun to do."

Situation 3: Bartholomew has discovered the light switch and continues to turn the lights on and off.

Caregiver's Response: The teacher takes Bartholomew's hand and says, calmly and firmly, "The light switch is not a toy. Would you like to build a tower with the blocks or go up and down the slide with Patrick?"

Situation 4: Henrietta has pulled the tray of crackers off the table, dumped them on the floor, and stomped on them.

Caregiver's Response: "The tray of crackers belongs on the table. Here is the broom. We have to sweep up the crumbs so that our room stays nice and clean."

Situation 5: Kayla will not lie quietly on her mat; she keeps rolling around and getting up to bother her friend, who is sleeping nearby.

Caregiver's Response: The teacher explains to Kayla that it is quiet time and the children need to rest on their mats. "If you are not sleepy, you may choose to read three books or do a puzzle quietly on your mat." (If Kayla is a very active child who does not need the nap, the caregiver might take her to another space, where she can play quietly without disturbing anyone.)

Situation 6: Joey is playing near Jane when he suddenly takes a bite out of her arm.

Caregiver's Response: The teacher first gives attention to Jane, putting ice on the bite and comforting her. Then the teacher says to Joey, "It hurts when you bite your friend. You can't bite other children. Here, you can bite this teether." (If Joey is having problems with biting, the teacher should record the time and situation for reflecting on what seems to lead up to a biting incident.)

To help older toddlers cope with fear, anger, and frustration and strike a balance between their longing for nurturance and desire to be independent

Jeremy and Alicia were playing together in the park. Alicia's mother offered each of the children an animal cracker. "I want a 'yion,'" Alicia stated emphatically. "I want a lion first," Jeremy insisted as he pushed in front of

Alicia. "Watch your manners," Jeremy's mother cautioned. "I am sure that there are two lions in the box." Alicia's mother pulled two lions out of the animal cracker box and gave each child a lion. "I don't want this 'yion.' It's broken," Alicia whined as she handed the cookie back to her mother. Jeremy's mother tried to help. "Jeremy, why don't you trade like a big boy?" "No way," Jeremy growled, shoving the cookie in his mouth.

By now, Alicia was crying loudly. After dumping out all the cookies, Alicia's mother victoriously pulled out another lion and gave it to Alicia. "I don't want a 'yion;' I want a tiger!" Alicia screeched as she threw the lion on the ground. ●

Older toddlers can be stubborn, baffling, and sometimes downright infuriating. Their sudden bursts of language allow them to be quite explicit about what they want. At the same time, their wants can be totally irrational and impossible to meet. These children are trying out the limits of their power. Parents and teachers are faced with the challenge of helping toddlers understand their limits without destroying their spirit or dampening their desire to do things on their own.

> *Parents and teachers are faced with the challenge of helping toddlers understand their limits without destroying their spirit or dampening their desire to do things on their own.*

A favorite word for most 2-year-olds is "No." Saying "No" is not simply a way of expressing "I don't want it" or "I won't do it." It's also a way of declaring their right to make decisions. Two-year-olds want to do things by themselves, even when that may not be in their best interest.

While "No" may be older toddlers' favorite word to say, it is their least favorite word to hear. From toddlers' point of view, "No" is more than a simple prohibition. It is an attempt by a grown-up to limit their power. Their immediate reaction to hearing "No" is to throw a temper tantrum.

For the most part, the tantrums of a 2-year-old will disappear as long as they are ignored. After all, it is not really worth having a tantrum if no one is going to pay attention. A few children at this age, however, have tantrums as a reaction to being tired, and leaving them alone does not change the behavior. For these children, it is usually a good idea to take them out of the situation, hold them quietly but firmly, remind them they will regain their composure soon, and invite them back to play when their screaming stops. It's especially important to stay calm yourself while a child has a tantrum.

While 2-year-olds are adamant about wanting what they want and will go to great lengths to get their own way, they are not always convinced that growing up is desirable. They want their parents and caregivers to recognize that they need to be grown up and independent, but they also want their parents and caregivers to know that they need to be cared for, cuddled, and treated like babies. When a new baby arrives, the same toddler who has been insisting that he can do everything by himself may curl up in his mother's lap and ask her to nurse him or give him a bottle. (See the Developmental Picture below for an overview of 2-year-olds' divergent needs.)

Having exaggerated fears can also be an issue for 2-year-olds:

> *One day, Hans, who always enjoyed his lunch, strongly resisted when his teacher asked him to open his lunch box. "You always open your lunch box by yourself, Hans. Why don't you want to open it today?" his teacher asked. "There is a dinosaur in my lunch box," Hans explained, and then he immediately burst into tears. "I'll tell you what," said the teacher in a soothing voice as soon as the tears began to subside. "I'll take the dinosaur outside and put him in a cage so he can't hurt anyone, and then you can eat your lunch. OK?"* ●

Although she handled the situation expertly, Hans's teacher was surprised by his sudden fear of his lunch box. Hans appeared to be a self-confident and independent toddler. Had something happened to Hans that could account for this change in behavior? In actuality, Hans's sudden demonstration of fear is not atypical. Many toddlers develop fears that adults might interpret as illogical or ridiculous. Lions and tigers may lurk in the closet, or a big bad monster might have established residence under the bed. Interestingly enough, the exaggerated fears of toddlers go along with their

Developmental Picture

The older toddler (2 years):

- Is curious and active and loves exploring
- Is aware of what he wants and has difficulty accepting a "No"
- Has difficulty recognizing and accepting limits
- May have temper tantrums
- Gets frustrated and may bite another child
- Enjoys routines and follows simple rules
- Is able to use words to express his wants and needs

The caregiver:

- Respects the child's need to explore, act, and experiment
- Uses creative ways of managing and redirecting behavior
- Finds creative ways of controlling behavior, such as using humor, and does not get into power struggles
- Does not use time-out as a way of managing inappropriate behavior
- Manages difficult behavior such as biting by preventing it from happening and by helping the child learn acceptable ways of expressing frustration and anger

developing an expanded view of the world. Not only might things exist even if they disappear from toddlers' sight, but things can exist that are not a part of their everyday experience and may be figments of their active imagination.

> *The exaggerated fears of toddlers go along with their developing an expanded view of the world.*

To learn ways of helping preschool children recognize and value differences, resolve conflicts, express their feelings in words, and accept reasonable limits

Teresa entered the All Faiths Preschool in the middle of the year. On her first day, she seemed to be settling in nicely with the group until snacktime. Then, Angelica, an African American child, asked Teresa to sit beside her. "No, I can't," Teresa said politely. "Your skin is brown and I don't want to get dirty." At first, their teacher, Miss Right-It, was taken aback, but then she recognized that she had to intervene without being punitive. "You can sit beside Angelica," she told Teresa in an upbeat tone. "Angelica's skin is a different color than yours, but it's not dirty. Skin comes in lots of different colors." With this, Teresa was reassured and sat down beside Angelica. ●

Young children like Teresa are not "color blind," but noticing differences among people is very different from being biased against them. Miss Right-It quickly recognized that Teresa didn't want to insult Angelica. It was just that Teresa had never seen a child with dark skin and assumed that *dark* meant *dirty*.

During circle time that day, Miss Right-It introduced a game. Each child was given a turn to hold hands with the person on his right and talk about one way he was like that person and one way he was different. "Do you know what this game is called?" she asked the children. "It is called 'We Are All Alike and We Are All Different.' " (See the Developmental Picture on page 270 for more information on caregivers' interactions with preschoolers.)

Helping Children Use Words to Express Their Feelings

A common problem among preschool children is the inability to find appropriate words to express their feelings. When someone knocks down a preschooler's block tower, his first instinct may be to lash out with his fists or express his anger in a negative way. "You're a stupid dumbhead and I hate you!" is a common response. In such a situation, the teacher can only make matters worse by scolding the child who knocked down the tower or berating the child whose tower was knocked down for using his fists or saying something nasty. The appropriate solution is to empathize with the child's feelings and model appropriate language: "You are angry because your block tower fell down. You worked hard to make it big. Tell Manuel that it makes you mad when your block tower gets knocked down, and ask him to help you fix it."

Developmental Picture

The preschool child (3–5 years):

- Is learning to follow simple directions and play cooperatively with other children
- May be fearful when there is no danger and fearless when there is danger
- Is sometimes impulsive, whiny, demanding, or willful
- Enjoys rules and accepts rules without questioning them
- Acts impulsively without thinking about consequences
- Is learning about turn taking, sharing, and using words, not hands, to express displeasure
- Is learning to negotiate with other children and to settle disputes with conversation

The caregiver:

- Clarifies classroom rules and reminds the children to comply
- Helps the children take turns, share, and help with classroom tasks
- Reinforces appropriate behaviors
- Helps the children find ways to resolve conflicts before stepping in as an arbitrator
- Models appropriate behaviors
- Recognizes the importance of having a balanced schedule, in which active activities are rotated with quiet activities
- Never uses physical punishment as a way of maintaining good behavior
- Uses time-out sparingly and only as a way to provide a child with a cooling-off time

Let's look at some other situations in which children need to find the right words to express their feelings.

Situation 1: Sally is an attractive child with long blond hair that everyone likes to touch. But she hates it when anyone strokes her hair. One day, all the children were playing "family" in the housekeeping area. Sally was assigned the role of "little girl." When the mommy stroked her hair, Sally ran out of the housekeeping area and refused to go back.

Caregiver's Response: The next day in circle time, the teacher enacted a similar scene using the class puppets:

> *Puppet 1:* "I am going to stroke your hair. It's pretty."
>
> *Puppet 2:* "I am glad you like it, but don't touch me. I hate to have my hair stroked."

Situation 2: Bobby came to school in a terrible mood. He stomped on the daffodils that the children had planted in the garden, gave one of the girls a kick when she asked for a turn on the bike, and then came inside and knocked down a shelf full of blocks.

Caregiver's Response: Bobby's teacher walked with him to the quiet area. "You are having a bad day," she said. "First, you need a few minutes by yourself to calm down. Then, you need to find words to talk about how you feel." Bobby plopped himself down on a beanbag chair and said in an angry voice, "Go away! I hate you and I hate everybody and I hate my baby brother." The teacher responded in a calm voice, "You are feeling sad and left out. It's hard having a new baby brother who takes up so much of your mommy's time." Now sulking, Bobby answered, "I'm going to throw him in the garbage and get him dead and send him back to the hospital." Still calm and patient, the teacher replied, "You are going to say to your mommy, 'I don't like you spending so much time with that baby. I need you to spend time with me.'"

Situation 3: Melissa wanted to be first in line and tried to push her way ahead of Donald. Donald poked her very hard in the ribs, and Melissa started crying.

Caregiver's Response: Their teacher spoke firmly to Donald. "Donald, I know you didn't want Melissa to get ahead of you, but next time, tell her with words that you are the leader instead of hitting her."

To recognize ways of using positive guidance techniques to reduce children's unwanted behaviors

Mrs. Coattails was irate when she called her son's preschool teacher. "This is the third time that a child in your class has picked on my little Percy," she said angrily. "On Tuesday, somebody got red finger paint all over his 'Mommy's Little Angel' shirt. On Wednesday, somebody ate half of his heart-shaped cookie. And today, he came home with tears streaming down his cheeks because some nasty kid called him 'Mommy's boy!' What are you going to do about these children?" ●

Fortunately, Percy's teacher was a master of diplomacy. She talked about Percy's creative artwork and his storytelling talents before she discussed Percy's need to develop coping skills. By the end of the conference, Mrs. Coattails recognized that her son needed practice solving his problems and resolving his conflicts without adult intervention.

Positive Ways of Resolving Problems

When preschool children come to us with a tale of woe—somebody knocked down their block tower or scribbled on their Halloween picture—our first instinct is to feel sorry and rush in to solve the problem. At times, our efforts to rescue children are more hurtful than helpful. We need to make a practice of helping children learn coping strategies and negotiation skills. In this section, we look at some common problems that are likely to emerge in preschool settings and describe positive strategies for preventing problems, redirecting negative behaviors, and helping children develop social skills.

Reminding Children of the Rules

One of the first tenets of positive discipline is *prevention.* Most problems can be avoided by practicing sound classroom management techniques. A particularly effective technique is the development of classroom rules. For young children, rules have very special meaning. Rules are part of the order of things and must be obeyed.

Because children accept rules without question, the classroom teacher can use a set of simple rules as the backbone of classroom discipline. When these rules are simple, clear, and understood by the class, many potential problems can be averted by

reminding children about the classroom rules. Here is a set of rules that has stood the test of time:

1. We are kind to each other.
2. We take good care of our classroom.
3. We share toys and take turns.

Simply referring to a rule is often all that's needed to avoid potential problems:

> "Sue, please pick up that paper. Remember the rule: 'We take good care of our classroom.' "
>
> "Roger, give Enrique some of your clay. Remember the rule about sharing."

Also consider the following conversation between Anthony and Patrick, who were in the middle of a hassle:

Anthony: "Don't put your hands on me. You're dirty."

Patrick: "I am not dirty. You're dirty. And your mother has yucky yellow hair."

Anthony: "She does not. Your mother and your daddy have yucky hair and . . ."

Mrs. Comfort (interrupting): "Oops, you two boys are forgetting the rule: 'We are always kind to each other.' "

Because Anthony and Patrick were good friends, the quarrel ended with no further repercussions.

Reinforcing Positive Behaviors

Another tried and true technique for changing children's behaviors is the use of *positive reinforcement*. Children are likely to enjoy praise and covet attention. If we can catch them being good and give them praise, they are less likely to seek attention in negative ways. Here's how one teacher provided positive reinforcement:

> *Lorenzo was not very good about putting materials back on the shelves. Polite requests to help with clean-up time had not been successful. Miss Coper had an idea. She put Lorenzo's favorite puzzle out on the table and as he put the pieces back, she praised him for "putting the pieces away so nicely." As Miss Coper found more and more opportunities to praise Lorenzo for putting things away, his refusals to help clean up became extremely rare.* ●

Helping Children Resolve Their Own Conflicts

Although preschool teachers may feel that they spend a lot of their time arbitrating quarrels, the truth is that most preschool children try to solve their own problems directly without going to the teacher. In the following conversations, try to identify the strategies the children use to resolve a potential conflict:

272

Conversation 1

   Nathan: "I want the red crayon."

   Alicia: "You can't have it because I'm using it and I got it first."

   Nathan: "I'll be your best friend."

   Alicia: "Okay, but give it right back."

Conversation 2

   Mavis: "I'm the mother, and I'm making pesghetty and brownies for dinner."

   Siri: "No fair, you always get to be the mother".

   Mavis: "Well, you can be the other mother."

Conversation 3

   Kent: "Ha, ha, I got here first. I'm the leader."

   Dennis: "You're too short. You can't be the leader."

   Kent: "Can so!"

   Dennis: "Cannot!"

   Kent: "Well, I'll be the leader going frontwards and you be the leader
         backing up."

The strategies that children use to solve their conflicts are not very sophisticated, but they do seem to work. Children enjoy playing with each other and are not about to let quarrels interfere with their play. When children ask for help in settling a squabble, the teacher has a good opportunity to strengthen their social skills. Rather than arbitrate the quarrel and build up the children's dependency, the teacher can express confidence in their ability to find their own solution. Here's an example:

> *When children ask for help in a squabble, the teacher has a good opportunity to strengthen their social skills.*

> *Olivia and Harry were building with blocks and fighting over who should get the long block:*

> *Olivia: "I got it first!"*

> *Harry: "You got it last time. It's my turn."*

> *Olivia: "That's no fair. I'm telling the teacher."*

> *At this point, the teacher interrupted, "You two are good block builders. See if you can figure out a way of settling the problem. I will come back again when you have found a really good solution."*

Another time when preschool children can solve their own problems is when they have spilled or broken something. For example, when a child spills milk at the lunch table, the best way to handle the situation is to matter of factly help him get a sponge to wipe it up. Additionally, it is helpful to teach how to pour milk and how to hold the cup so that it is unlikely the children will spill.

Focusing Attention on the Victim, Not the Aggressor

Despite their best efforts to teach children to express their feelings with words, classroom teachers recognize that some acting out is inevitable. When an aggressive incident occurs, the inexperienced teacher is likely to focus attention on the child who did the aggressing. But in fact, that doesn't work very well. The child who acts out is reinforced both by the attention he is receiving and by the fact that his victim is being temporarily ignored. Focusing attention on the victim while letting the aggressor eavesdrop is more likely to be effective, as shown in this scenario:

> *Annette had an unfortunate habit of hitting children with her fist when she felt that they were in her way. The more Miss Henrietta talked to her about how it was wrong to hurt other children, the more likely Annette was to punch and hit and shove. Miss Henrietta decided to change her tactics. When Annette gave Gwendolyn a shove, Miss Henrietta arrived on the scene before the crying began. She said, "Gwendolyn, you are such a big girl. You didn't even cry when Annette pushed you. I hope Annette remembers next time that we don't push other people." Annette was surprised about being left out of the conversation. She discovered that pushing other children wasn't much fun when she didn't get a lot of attention.* ●

Redirecting the Activity

In some instances, when children are quarreling or exhibiting other negative behaviors, intervening with words is not very effective. This is particularly true with most children under 3 and when the negative behavior is associated with boredom, hunger, or fatigue. Rather than focusing on the problem in these situations, distracting the child or refocusing his attention is both wise and effective:

> *Alonzo and Matthew had been chasing each other around the playground on their tricycles. As their excitement mounted, so did their speed and the inevitable crash occurred. Although neither of the boys was hurt, they immediately accused each other of being stupid and not watching out. Miss Corvette intervened: "The bikes are tired. Hurry and put the bikes in their parking place so you can have a turn with the swings."* ●

A related technique is allowing a child to save face by taking a break. This works especially well when a child is refusing to comply with a request from you:

> *When Yung Jin didn't want to pick up his toys before playground time, his teacher gave him another choice. "OK," the teacher said. "You can go put on your jacket and then come back and help me." By the time Yung Jin had put his jacket on, he had forgotten that he was refusing to pick up toys. "Let's see how fast you can pick up three toys so we can hurry and get out to the playground," his teacher called out in a cheery voice. Yung Jin quickly picked up the three toys and rushed to the door.* ●

Handling Transitions

Any time the action in the classroom changes, there is the chance of upset. It is important to prepare children for *transitions*. Having a regular daily routine helps set the tone of things happening in a predictable order. The children get used to having a snack after playing outdoors and taking a nap after lunch and stories. A special song can signal clean-up time, and another song can mean it's time to get ready for lunch.

Giving notice helps the children be ready for the transition: "In a few minutes, we'll be putting our toys away so we can go outside." It's best to have two teachers with each group so one can move the main group and the other can follow behind with the stragglers.

Routines for arriving and departing also can lessen the distress. Children can use a good-bye ritual until they feel comfortable, like a kiss and a wave good-bye. Having an object from home or a photo of Mom and Dad to carry around might help, as well. (Parents also sometimes need help saying a quicker and more confident good-bye.)

Special Words to Use with Children

Putting Specifics with the Message "Good Job!"

Some teachers' tendency simply to say "Good job" wastes the opportunity of reinforcing specific actions. Phrases to try include the following:

- "I like the way you colored your picture."
- "You look so nice when you smile like that."
- "You are a very good helper with cleaning the table."
- "Thank-you for sharing such a good idea about using chalk outside."
- "You are very good at cleaning up the block area."
- "You are a super jumper off the biggest step outside."
- "You washed your hands all by yourself. That's fantastic!"

Ways of Encouraging Just a Little Bit More

Use these phrases to encourage more of a positive behavior:

- "That was a good start. Let me see you do some more."
- "I know you can figure out how to finish that puzzle."
- "The room will look better when you pick up all the toys."
- "Let's put away the blocks quickly so we can go outside."
- "Oops, don't forget the 'No standing on the table' rule."
- "That's a hard puzzle, but I think you can do it."
- "Terrance is sad because you hit him. Make him feel better."
- "I really hear you better when you talk in your inside voice."
- "Whining makes me feel cross. Could you say that in your grown-up voice?"
- "I know you are feeling angry, but hitting is not allowed."
- "Clara did not want her house knocked over. Help her build it back up."

Responding to Challenging Behaviors

Mrs. Contrite requested a conference with her son's teacher, Miss Knowing. Several neighborhood parents had approached her angrily, complaining that 2-year-old Dennis had bitten their children.

Mrs. Contrite: *"I really don't know what to tell these parents. I don't blame them for being so upset, but I don't know what to say to them."*

275

Miss Knowing: "Biting is a common problem with 2-year-olds. It may be that some 2-year-olds are still teething and like to bite down on something soft. More likely, 2-year-olds bite because they are angry or frustrated and can't express their wants or feelings with words. Also, 2-year-olds are likely to bite children who get very upset when they're bitten."

Mrs. Contrite: "I know that biting is a common problem, but I don't know how to stop it. Is there anything that we're doing wrong at home or anything that we could do differently that could stop Dennis's biting?"

Miss Knowing: "Unfortunately, biting is a difficult behavior to control. I often think that the best way to handle biting is to wait for the child to grow out of it. Of course, in a preschool, that's not a practical solution."

Mrs. Contrite: "Well, how do you deal with biting at school?"

Miss Knowing: "We observe the child carefully so that we can identify the times or situations when he is most likely to bite. Then, during these times or situations, we watch the child closely and try to redirect him before he gets a chance to bite. If the child bites when we're not expecting it, we say firmly, 'No biting! Biting hurts!' Then we sit the child down in a quiet spot and ask him to chew on a teething ring."

Mrs. Contrite: "I appreciate the way you handle Dennis, but how can I explain his biting to other parents?"

Miss Knowing: "Just tell them that you are also very upset about his biting, that you have talked to me about it, and that we are hoping that we can get it under control." ●

No matter how hard teachers try to reduce troublesome behaviors and no matter how cooperative parents are, young children do exhibit challenging behaviors that have to be managed. Those behaviors include spitting, biting, kicking, punching, using foul language, running away, destroying property and other children's work, and engaging in self-injurious behaviors, such as head banging.

> *There is no one right way to manage challenging behaviors.*

Observing Children's Behavior

Unfortunately, there is no one right way to manage challenging behaviors. What works well in one situation may not work at all in a similar situation. Before deciding on a course of action, the classroom teacher needs to ask another teacher or administrator to observe the problematic child on several occasions and share her observations. The classroom teacher should also speak with the child's parents and then ponder the following questions:

- Is the behavior typical for the child's age?
- Does the behavior occur frequently or just once in a while?
- What happens just before and just after the behavior? What does the target child do? What does the victim do? How do I react?

- When I spoke to the parents, did they describe any stressors at home that could explain the behavior? Does the child demonstrate this or other challenging behaviors at home? What techniques have the parents used to reduce her challenging behaviors?
- Does the child demonstrate any other challenging behaviors?
- Does the child have any friends or siblings who model this behavior?
- How well does the child get along with the other children in the class?
- Does the child recognize that this behavior is not acceptable?
- Does the child show empathy when other children are hurt or unhappy?

Developing an Action Plan

Once you have answered these questions, write up your impressions and a potential course of action in a short paragraph. After you have written up the paragraph, develop an *action plan*. Here are some examples:

Impressions of José: The destructive behaviors José is demonstrating may be a reaction to some stressors at home. He did not destroy his own and other children's work until quite recently, when his parents adopted a baby. Most of the time, he gets along quite well with the other children and appears remorseful when he realizes that he has upset one of his buddies. Time, extra attention, and positive reinforcement may be all that José needs. It may also be a good idea to encourage him to talk about his feelings and to read books in circle time about children's reactions to the arrival of a new baby.

Action Plan

- Provide José with extra attention so that he feels wanted and loved
- Use positive guidance techniques when José destroys his own work, the work of other children, or classroom property.
- Find books to read in circle time about getting new sisters and brothers.
- Share the books I find with José's parents, and encourage them to read to him at home.
- Keep a daily log of José's destructive behaviors.
- Reassess my plan in two weeks, and make necessary changes or additions.

Impressions of Janet: Janet has never really been a happy child. She craves attention from other children, and when they don't give her attention or invite her to play, she responds by spitting and pinching. Her parents are very concerned about her behavior and feel as I do that she will respond well to social training. I would like to refer this child to the neighborhood center, where they have an excellent social training program for preschool children.

Action Plan

- Get a pamphlet from the neighborhood center for Janet's parents.
- Once Janet's parents have set up an appointment at the center, request their permission to discuss Janet's progress with the social training instructors.
- Use positive guidance techniques to help reduce Janet's undesirable behaviors.

- Ask Janet to help me with simple chores. Use this as an opportunity to engage Janet in conversation and to praise her for being helpful.
- Pair Janet with Gail, an unusually gentle and socially adept child, for some chores and partner games.
- Keep a weekly log of Janet's behaviors.
- Reevaluate in six weeks and change the approach, if necessary.

Impressions of Alfred: Alfred has been a concern ever since he came to the classroom. He is constantly punching other kids, grabbing things away from them, and using swear words. I have tried all the usual techniques: I praise him when he does something right, I reason with him, and I have even tried time-out, which I almost never use. His parents are not at all concerned. They told me quite bluntly that it's a tough world out there, and they want their son "to have guts." On the one hand, I believe that I should respect the child-rearing beliefs and values of Alfred's family, but on the other hand, I don't want him hurting someone or setting a bad example for the other kids. I am also concerned that Alfred is caught in a bind because he is getting mixed messages. I would like to bring this up at the next teacher's meeting. I know that the problem with Alfred is not unique and that we need to develop a strategy for dealing with this kind of student.

Action Plan

- Continue to use positive guidance to help Alfred manage his behavior.
- Introduce some active, cooperative games and activities that will allow Alfred to be successful without having to prove his toughness.
- Discuss my next steps with my director, co-workers, and/or a consultant in accordance with the director's suggestions.

Impressions of Nadra: Nadra is a bright child and a joy to have in class, except when she starts to whine, which happens every time she wants something from me. I have always let her know that if she will just use her words, I will be happy to listen to what she is saying. But that doesn't work. She continues to whine and I continue to ignore her, until she bursts into a full-fledged temper tantrum. I spoke to Nadra's mother about the whining, and she told me Nadra used to whine at home until a friend gave her a good idea. When Nadra starts to whine at home, her mother says in a calm voice, "I can't hear you because I am wearing my antiwhine ear plugs." I tried Nadra's mother's strategy at school, and she was right. It really works. After only two days, I think Nadra has just about given up whining.

Action Plan

- Use the "antiwhine ear plugs" technique suggested by Nadra's mother to help Nadra control her whining.
- Keep a weekly log of Nadra's whining.
- In two weeks, if the whining continues to lessen, call Nadra's mother and tell her of Nadra's progress.
- If there is no permanent change in Nadra's whining, continue to ignore it and try to decrease my own negative reactions to whining.

There is no one way to manage challenging behaviors. When a child's challenging behaviors persist or increase in either frequency or intensity, it is important to focus your attention on the target child and craft a well thought out plan to help her. While it is tempting to look for a resource that lists each challenging behavior and how to deal with it, there is never a "one-size-fits-all" solution. If we are concerned with individualization and with helping each child be the best that she can be, we need to give special attention to the children who need us the most.

To recognize ways of providing positive guidance for children whose families use styles of discipline that are different from those the teacher has been taught

Ms. Can-Do-It was frustrated. All of the 3-year-olds in her class were learning to put on their own coats and boots—all, that is, except Rosita. Rosita, who was usually a sweet and cooperative child, wouldn't even take her own coat off the hook. If Ms. Can-Do-It insisted that she try to put it on, Rosita was likely to burst into tears.

At her wit's end, Ms. Can-Do-It called Rosita's mother and explained the situation. Rosita's mother was startled. "But I always dress Rosita," she explained. "She's much too young to have to do this for herself. How will she know I love her if I don't take care of her when she's little?"

The disciplining of children is one area in which parents and professionals are likely to disagree. While some parents routinely use the techniques suggested earlier in this chapter and others are eager to learn these techniques when they see how well they work in the classroom, still other parents are convinced that the way they were brought up is the best way to bring up their own children. Their style may not be yours, or it may be one that you used before you studied teaching. Regardless, you must recognize that the parents are the child's first and most important teachers, and the discipline and positive guidance techniques they use are the ones the child is used to.

> *When parents' beliefs about discipline are very different from your own, and especially if you come from different cultures, forging a partnership can be challenging.*

How can you develop an effective partnership with parents that is respectful of their beliefs and their relationship with their own child and at the same time not violate your own ethical code? When parents' beliefs about discipline are very different from your own, and especially if you come from different cultures, forging a partnership can be challenging. Here are some pointers that can help you be successful:

- Remember that children vary temperamentally in their responses to discipline and positive guidance. Some children may fall apart when they "run out of calories," and no amount of redirection or reminding of rules will help until they have been fed. Some children, even at 2, will respond better to a long explanation, such as "Please don't do that. I'm worried that you might fall and hurt your-self," than to a simple "No!" which is likely to send them into tears or provoke resistance. Others, of course, do better with the "No!" and will already have got-ten in trouble by the time you finish the long explanation. Although you may be the expert on children in general, parents are the experts on their own children.

- Be a good listener and a good communicator. Ask parents about the techniques that they find work well with their children. Ask not only what they do but why. Share your own observations about the child's coping skills, the situations she finds difficult, and the kinds of things that seem to help her.

- Engage parents in frank discussions about your expectations for the child and theirs. Explore any differences together in a spirit of curiosity and respect, rather than judgment.

- When a child comes from a culture different from your own, seek advice from colleagues from that culture. They may be able to explain the fine points of ap-proach, phrasing, body language, and intonation that will make the child more receptive to your suggestions.

- Pick your battles. You can agree to put on a coat for a child like Rosita until she feels comfortable doing it herself. But you can't violate your center's policy by spanking a child, no matter how much the parents might insist that that is the only way to make him mind.

- Explain your positions to the child's parents. "Thank-you for explaining what you do at home. It helps me understand Jack better. But when I'm working with a group, I find that a bit of humor works best because the children tend to copy each other."

- Although it is important always to be respectful and supportive of parents, you may, at times, need to take a contrary stand. If you suspect a parent of neglect or abuse, for example, you are required by law to report it.

Additional Resources about Guidance

Bailey, B. (1997). *Conscious discipline: Seven basic skills for brain smart classroom man-agement.* Oviedo, FL: Loving Guidance.

Gartrell, D. (2004). *The power of guidance: Teaching social–emotional skills in early child-hood classrooms.* Clifton Park, NY: Delmar Learning and NAEYC.

Greenman, J., & Stonehouse, A. (1996). *Prime times: A handbook for excellence in infant and toddler programs.* St. Paul, MN: Redleaf Press.

Kaiser, B., & Rasminsky, J. (1999). *Meeting the challenge: Effective strategies for challenging behaviours in early childhood environments.* Ottawa, Ontario, Canada: Canadian Child Care Federation and NAEYC.

Section V

Behind the Scenes

Working As a Professional with Families and in Child Care Programs

Mrs. Many-Hats was volunteering at a booth on career options in early childhood at the county jobs fair. The first person to approach her booth introduced himself as Mr. Undecided.

Mr. Undecided: "I have always been interested in becoming a preschool teacher, but I'm just not sure that it would be a good career choice. I love kids, and if I do say so myself, kids love me. But I do have some concerns."

Mrs. Many-Hats: "Tell me about your concerns. I have been a preschool teacher for the last seven years, and I know the profession like the back of my hand."

Mr. Undecided: "Well, the first thing that concerns me is that teaching can get you in a rut. You do the same things every day, and you don't have an opportunity to assume new responsibilities and explore and expand your own capacities."

Mrs. Many-Hats: "No, teaching children is never routine. I was just thinking about what I've done besides teach in the last two weeks. Last week, at the request of our director, I mentored a new teacher who was having difficulty managing her classroom. Then after school, I met with a parent who was worried about her son's short attention span. We shared some ideas and came up with a good plan that we can work on together. This week, I took the children on a field trip to three different ethnic grocery stores. I learned as much as the kids did. I also took part in a panel discussion on the importance of play that was sponsored by our local early childhood association. Then just yesterday, I took part in a staff meeting at our center to plan our self-study for accreditation."

Mr. Undecided: "Well, you have certainly addressed my concern about getting into a rut. But here's one other concern: Suppose I want to advance my career in early childhood. What are the opportunities?"

Mrs. Many-Hats: "Early childhood is a growing profession. As long as you have the motivation and the commitment, the opportunities will be waiting for you. You could direct your own center, become a teacher trainer, an accreditation validator, a college professor . . ."

Mr. Undecided: "Enough already! I'm sold! Just call me Mr. Decided from now on." ●

Mrs. Many-Hats is perfectly right. Early childhood is a growing field that has come into its own. Across the United States, people have gradually come to recognize that if children are our future, then their teachers—and especially the teachers of very young children—are our most important resource.

In this section, we talk about some of the behind-the-scenes work that Mrs. Many-Hats described: the critical connections with families, the individual and team planning, and the commitment to professionalism that supports the high-quality child care and early education that prime children for later success.

Families

Chapter 11

Overview

In the context of child care, the *family* can be defined as the person or people who have primary responsibility for the care, nurturing, and upbringing of the child. The family is the crucible for transmitting culture, heritage, and traditions across the generations.

Today's families come in many forms: one or two parents and their children; adoptive, blended, step-, and foster families; families with two fathers or two mothers; and multigenerational extended families. When the word *parent* is used in this chapter, it means anyone who fills this role. When we talk about *families*, we mean to embrace their diversity. We recognize that in many cultures, parents, grandparents, and other relatives are all involved in making decisions about children's welfare. It is important for teachers and caregivers to get to know the whole family, however it is defined.

Rationale

It is widely believed that parents are and generally should be the single most important influence on the education and development of a child. It is the role of the teacher to maximize the impact of the educational experience by involving the parents and family in the life of the school or center. By encouraging involvement, by communicating frequently, by offering opportunities for input, and by exchanging information, the teacher can create an atmosphere of cooperation, which benefits the child, her family, and the school or center.

283

Objectives

1. To understand the many purposes of establishing good communication with parents

2. To learn how to set up a parent/school partnership

3. To learn strategies for keeping parents informed about center activities and encouraging participation in parent meetings and volunteer opportunities

4. To learn strategies for serving as a resource for families and building a community that supports families

5. To learn strategies for engaging parents in decision making and advocacy

Supporting Parents and Families

Jim: *"Want to come outside and play a game of catch?"*

Dad: *"No Jim, not right now."*

Jim: *"How 'bout a quick game of Nintendo?"*

Dad: *"Look, I said not now. Now bug off!"*

Jim (to Mother): *"Did I do something wrong or something?"*

Mother: *"No, it's nothing you did. Dad just had a bad day at work. He'll be okay in a few minutes if we just leave him alone."*

Like Jim, many young children are confused by their parents' behavior. They don't understand why a bad day at the office or a stack of unpaid bills should make their parents cross with them. From the point of view of a child, adults have only one role to play: that of a parent. Likewise, if you are a teacher, you can't also be a mother, and if you are a father, you can't also be a carpenter. The fact that adults function in many roles, both within and outside the family, is beyond the understanding of many young children.

In this chapter, our focus is on *families*. Recognizing that the well-being of every child is intimately associated with the well-being of her family, we identify ways in which caregivers can establish partnerships with parents. We describe ways of enhancing communication between families and caregivers, of fostering parents' participation in their children's schools, of recognizing and meeting parents' needs, and of promoting parent advocacy.

To understand the many purposes of establishing good communication with parents

Establishing good communication with parents is vital for many reasons:

- Parents have the right and the duty to be involved in the educational lives of their children. We must never forget that the ultimate responsibility for the child's welfare rests with his parents. A major thrust of our efforts in a sound educational program is to support the parents' role.

- Parents can provide information that aids our understanding of many aspects of their child's behavior in school. Learning that a child does not play with other children at home, for instance, helps us to understand her quiet, withdrawn manner at school. A sensitive teacher will work toward building this child's social skills by drawing her gently into interaction with other children.

- By sharing our knowledge of child development, we help parents establish reasonable expectations and goals for their children. A parent who is concerned about her 4-year-old's regression to babyish behavior since the birth of a new sister can be reassured by the knowledge that this is a perfectly normal response.

- Regular contact with parents helps us to discover their talents. A wise teacher is always on the lookout for people with special talents or abilities or whose occupations or hobbies will be of interest to the children. Although we must be sure to communicate that *all* parents have the skills necessary to assist in regular classroom activities, we can recognize that a few can serve as special resources for the children.

- The unique perspective that parents can offer is an important ingredient in program development and evaluation. We must provide a system of input for parental thoughts, feelings, ideas, and reactions. Keeping a record of parent input can also help us understand parental needs and thus benefit the center's program.

- A healthy relationship with parents creates the best possible public relations and advertising program for the child care program. Satisfied parents who are knowledgeable about the program will be amazingly supportive.

- Parents are in an excellent position to assist our educational efforts at home. When they are aware of the goals and purposes of school activities, they can learn to recognize and then reinforce their children's emerging skills.

- Many problems can be solved better at home than at the center. By establishing healthy channels of communication, we can ensure that parents will understand and support our requests for cooperation.

- Parents benefit by developing the knowledge and self-confidence necessary to function as advocates for their children.

- Children benefit from seeing their parents and teachers working together on their behalf.

To learn how to set up a parent/school partnership

The parents are the child's first and most important teachers. They are responsible not only for what a child knows but also for what he believes and values. From the beginning, children's feelings about themselves and the amount of confidence they have in their own abilities are an outgrowth of the experiences they have had at home. Children learn from a very young age the kinds of behaviors their parents value and the things they disapprove of. Children judge their self-worth by the kinds of feedback they receive at home as they meet or fall short of their parents' expectations.

The teacher who develops a close relationship with a child's family can share information and perceptions of the child with the family. This shared knowledge can provide the basis of a school/parent partnership with long-term benefits for the child.

Whether parents come to the child care setting on a regular basis or only on special occasions, a responsible early childhood teacher makes a special point of getting to know each one. Again, the parents can give us insights into a child's feelings and concerns that cannot be derived from other sources. The parents also set the tone for how a child approaches child care. Although we may not be able to reach every child's family, the more effort we, as teachers, make to establish a home/school partnership, the more likely we are to succeed.

Strategies for Getting to Know a Child's Family

Teacher: "Does anyone have something special to tell us about his or her family?

Xavier: "Me! Me! Me!"

Teacher: "Xavier would like to tell us something about his family."

Xavier: "Maria got losted and she was all dirty and Mommy said she gots to stay outside."

Teacher (sounding incredulous): "Maria had to stay outside?"

Xavier: "Yes, but then she meowed real loud and Mommy let her in."

Teacher: "Oh, Maria is your cat, not your sister!"

Xavier is confused. If he knows Maria is a cat, why doesn't his teacher know that, too? ●

The more familiar a teacher is with a child's home and family life, the safer and more comfortable the child will feel in the child care setting.

Preschool teachers recognize that young children expect them to know their families and understand their stories. The more familiar a teacher is with a child's home and family life, the safer and more comfortable the child will feel in the child care setting. The following sections provide suggestions for getting to know the families of the children in your class.

Visit with Each Family

Having an individual visit with the family, whether at the child care program or at the child's home, is the ideal. Doing so gives parents the opportunity to share their intimate knowledge of their child as well as their hopes and concerns for him. The more you learn about a child in advance, the easier it will be to help him adjust to school. Something as simple as knowing the name of a favorite teddy bear or family pet can comfort a frightened child.

For two years before his family had moved, Germaine had been in a family child care home with the same provider. Now, his mother, Mrs. Handholder, was concerned about taking him to a new child care center. "I'm worried about putting Germaine in Tots-R-Ours," she told her husband. "He is not used to being with a whole group of children and with more than one unfamiliar adult."

When Mrs. Handholder brought Germaine to Tots-R-Ours, she was pleasantly surprised. Germaine's teacher asked if she could visit Germaine at home before he joined the group, so that she could have an opportunity to get to know him.

The teacher's transition plan for the family was successful. The home visit had worked out fine. At first, Germaine hid behind his father's leg, but when his teacher asked about his dog, Bootie, Germaine joined the conversation. His teacher asked him if he would like to bring a picture of Bootie to the center and show it to his new friends. Germaine immediately asked his mother to find a picture. He had no difficulty separating from his mother on the first day.

At circle time, Germaine showed the children his picture of Bootie. The teacher suggested that the other children should also bring pictures of their pets to school and that they would create a pet gallery on the bulletin board. "I don't got a pet," one child complained. "But you have a stuffed panda bear," the teacher reminded him. "Bring a picture of Panny the Panda to school." For the rest of the day, Germaine played happily with the other children. ●

Have Parents Fill Out a Developmental Questionnaire

The information needed by the teaching staff can be collected through parent responses on a *developmental questionnaire* (see the example on page 288). The items on this questionnaire should serve as the basis for a parent interview by the center director or teacher prior to the child's participation in the program. Additional comments for the clarification of any parent responses also can be recorded on the questionnaire by the center director or the child's teacher. The purpose of a developmental questionnaire is to introduce the child to his teachers. It should be reviewed yearly for possible revision.

After the parents have completed the developmental questionnaire, it is a good idea to read it over and then meet with them to review the information. Meeting also gives the parents an opportunity to talk further about concerns they might have about their child prior to enrollment.

Sample Developmental Questionnaire

Child's Name _____   Birthdate _____

Father's Name _____   Occupation _____

Mother's Name _____   Occupation _____

Marital Status of Parents _____

Custody/Visiting Arrangements _____

If child is adopted, list age at adoption: _____   Is child aware of adoption? _____

Give names and ages of other children in family and names and relationships of other family members who live with you:

_____

_____

Is any language other than English spoken at home? _____   If so, describe: _____

Is your child toilet trained? _____   Describe toilet assistance needed and list words used: _____

What are your child's napping needs? _____

What are your child's favorite activities? _____

Does your child have any special fears? _____

At the present time, do you have special concerns about your child's development (i.e., speech, motor development, etc.)?

If so, describe: _____

List the age at which your child (if applicable):

Crawled on hands and knees _____   Named simple objects _____   Sat alone _____   Was toilet trained _____

Spoke in complete sentences _____   Slept through the night _____   Walked _____

Does your child have any health problems, including allergies, that we should be aware of? _____

If so, describe: _____

Has your child had any serious accidents or operations? If so, describe: _____

_____

List illnesses your child has had: _____

Does your child take any medication regularly? If so, describe: _____

Do you restrict your child's diet in any way? If so, describe: _____

Has your child participated in a child care program before? _____

If so, describe previous experience(s): _____

Has your child ever been cared for by someone besides the family? _____

If so, describe: _____

Why have you selected this program for your child? _____

_____

As a parent, how might you participate in the program (i.e., by attending parent meetings, volunteering in the classroom)?

_____

Please use the back of the form to tell us anything else you think we should know about your child or your family.

Parents' Signatures _____   Date _____

_____   Date _____

Build Bridges with the Family as Well as with the Child

The process of enrolling a child in a child care center or home provides many opportunities to build bridges:

- Completing registration forms can give parents the opportunity to share information about what is important to them and their family, such as hopes for the child care experience, family holidays and traditions, and ways in which they would like to be involved with the center and with other parents.
- Holding an open house can give families an opportunity to visit the classroom and meet their children's teachers informally and individually.
- Giving tours of the center to prospective enrollees can include an opportunity for teachers and parents to meet.
- The parents and teachers can get to know each other as they work together on a transition plan for a newly enrolled child.
- Parents who have the time can stay with their child for a while, getting to know the caregiver and helping the caregiver and child get to know each other.
- Having a pizza party or potluck supper for the families and staff can help everyone get to know each other in an informal setting.
- Parents can put family pictures on the child's cubby.

Strategies for Sharing Information about a Child

Getting to know a child's family is certainly a critical component of establishing a parent/school partnership. A second and equally critical component is sharing information about the child with the parents. Of the many strategies that classroom teachers can use to keep the family informed, holding parent/teacher conferences is certainly the most effective.

> *A carefully planned conference with the child's parents is the most effective vehicle for sharing information about her.*

Parent/Teacher Conferences

Father: "Before we begin this conference, I would like you to get one thing straight. I do not want a wimp for a son. If you are here to tell me that my son is a bully and I should do something about it, then you are barking up the wrong tree."

Mother: "Herman, give the teacher a chance. Maybe he has something worthwhile to say about Dennis."

Mr. Wiseman (Dennis's teacher): "I am glad you were able to come today. It sounds as if you are both very interested in Dennis and the progress he is making."

Father: "Okay, get on with it. I have exactly 15 minutes."

Mother: "Herman, take it easy."

Mr. Wiseman: "Dennis is a lot like you, Mr. Blowhard. He is an energetic child who loves to keep busy and get things accomplished." ●

Although parent conferences may not always start off smoothly, an empathetic teacher like Mr. Wiseman can find a way to make almost every conference a genuine sharing opportunity. Unquestionably, a carefully planned conference with the child's parents is the most effective vehicle for sharing information about her.

Strategies for Effective Parent Conferences

1. Know the objective of the conference. If you have initiated the conference, be clear about your agenda. What are your objectives? If the parents have initiated the conference, think about their potential objectives.

2. Be certain that you and the parents have agreed on the time and place, and then confirm the conference the day before by telephone or written notice.

3. Help the parents arrange for child care so you will not be in the position of talking about a child with her present.

4. Gather all relevant materials, including anecdotal reports and other records that are available. Contact other people within your organization who work with the child. You may want to invite other staff to join you in the conference.

5. Set up a meeting space where adults can sit comfortably. Don't sit behind a desk, creating a barrier between you and the parents.

6. Be on time for the meeting and be ready. Any papers that are to be used in the conference should be in a folder with the child's name on it.

7. Unless there is an emergency, do not accept telephone calls during a conference.

8. Begin the conference by introducing yourself and your staff. Use people's full names.

9. Following the introductions, whoever initiated the conference should present the objectives. If the parents initiated the conference, you may want to open with a statement like "I am glad we are able to get together. Tell me what you would like to discuss."

10. Assume the role of listener. To be a good listener, do the following:
    - Maintain eye contact and show interest through your facial expressions and body positions.
    - Respect the parents' ideas, whether or not you agree.
    - Resist the temptation to become defensive or get into a debate.
    - Recognize that the real message may not be the same as the surface message.

11. Also assume the role of facilitator:
    - Create a positive climate by emphasizing the child's strengths and good qualities.
    - Provide the parents with *alternatives*, rather than *solutions*.
    - Describe the ramifications of or problems associated with the different alternatives.
    - Allow the parents to construct or help in the construction of an action plan (if indicated).

12. End the conference on a positive note:
    - Repeat the objectives of the conference.
    - Summarize any actions that were decided on, and detail everyone's post-conference assignments.

13. Make plans, if appropriate, for a follow-up conference.
14. Do your homework after the conference:
    - Immediately write a summary of the conference and the proposed plan.
    - Write a brief note to the parents, thanking them for attending.
    - Note on your calendar your own assignments and due dates.

Other Strategies for Information Sharing

You can also use many other strategies for keeping the family informed, as described in the following sections.

Home Visits So much information can be learned by visiting the child's home. In addition to what we learn by making a home visit, we are demonstrating our concern in a concrete, tangible way. A home visit brings center staff to the family's turf and provides an opportunity to make friends. This useful strategy should not be overlooked.

Telephone Calls Although a telephone call is not nearly as effective as a conference for sharing information about a child, it can be used as an alternative when neither a scheduled conference nor a home visit can be arranged. When possible, make an appointment for a telephone conference at a time that is convenient for both you and the parents.

Class Parent If one parent in each group will assume the responsibility to contact and coordinate the other parents of children in that group, the teacher's burden will be reduced significantly. The additional advantage of this strategy is that those parents who are reluctant to share real concerns with the teacher may feel more comfortable doing so with another parent.

Classroom Observation Inviting parents to spend a day in the classroom is one of the best ways to create a strong bond between the child care setting and home. Parents learn about the program and develop an increased understanding of the difficult tasks faced by the teacher daily. The teacher can prepare for an observation by getting the children ready for visitors and by creating a system of feedback for parents in order to answer questions generated by the visit.

Send Home Notes Contact each family at least twice a month (daily for infants) to share something positive about their child. You may use a brief telephone call or send home a note, like one of these:

Sample Notes

"Becky had a wonderful day. She and her friend Alisa did a collage together, and we put it up on the wall. "

"Jimmy is becoming much more confident about participating in circle time. Today, he told us all about how much fun he had riding in the truck with his father."

"I know that you have been worrying about Carlos, but he is doing very well. He cries when you leave in the morning, but then he settles down and starts playing in about two minutes. All the children love him."

Send Home Work Samples Another way to keep the family informed about their child is to send home a drawing or a craft or a photo of an activity the child engaged in

291

that day. If the parents take an interest in their child's daily work (a point to emphasize at parent meetings and in your newsletter), they will learn more about the program and have an opportunity to talk with their child about things that happen at the center.

Create a "Post Office" Set up a file with a folder for each child and one for each teacher, in which parents can receive and leave messages.

Create a Family Poster Have each child bring in a photo of his family, and then lay out all the children's photos on a poster. Be sure to label each photo. In circle time, you can talk about how there are different kinds of families and that every family is special.

Keep Family Records When you learn something important about a child's family—for example, that a new baby is expected or that a grandparent is going to visit—make a note of it in your "Family Album." This will help you and the children anticipate events before they happen.

To learn strategies for keeping parents informed about center activities and encouraging participation in parent meetings and volunteer opportunities

> Teacher 1: *"I have tried so many times to get Gary's mother to come to the center. I just don't know what to do anymore."*
>
> Teacher 2: *"Yes. It seems that it is most difficult to see those parents whose children have the greatest need. Sometimes, I feel it is a lost cause. So many parents don't seem to care about their children."* ●

This is one example of how teachers become discouraged with parents. This discouragement often leads to cynicism and the belief that attempts at parent involvement are doomed to fail.

While it is easy to understand how this attitude develops, most of us know intuitively that the majority of parents care very deeply about their children. Many factors totally unrelated to the parents' degree of concern play a role in their involvement in the child care center:

- Some parents are consumed with problems of more immediate concern and do not have time or energy to devote to the center.

- Many parents have negative impressions about school due to their own school experiences and are reluctant to become involved.

- Many parents feel unequipped to deal with teachers. They may feel inferior educationally and/or financially, and they may feel that they have nothing to contribute.

- Some parents feel that they are going to be blamed for their child's shortcomings and that difficulties are a reflection of their own knowledge, integrity, or ability as parents.

- Some parents are kept away by difficulties with transportation, arranging substitute care for younger siblings or disabled family members, inflexible work schedules, and language barriers.
- The people in some cultures consider being involved with a child care center or school as interfering in a realm that is best left to professionals.

Understanding parents' schedules, expectations for involvement, and concerns, as well as the ways in which they can and want to be helpful, will help you to design policies and strategies that welcome every family.

Strategies for Keeping Parents Informed

Sharing information about the program with parents is the responsibility of the program director and of every member of the staff. The responsibility begins before the child enters the center and continues as long as the child is enrolled. With today's busy lifestyles and multicultural communities, many programs find that they need to use several different approaches to keep parents informed and engaged.

Making Families Feel Welcome

Parents should feel welcome in the center at all times. They might linger at drop-off or pick-up time, come regularly to nurse a baby, join their child for lunch, stop in for a quick visit, or volunteer in the classroom. Whether they feel wanted will depend not only on the center's policies

> *Centers that are especially welcoming to families find families to be an enormous asset.*

but also on how those policies are implemented and communicated. Centers that are especially welcoming to families find families to be an enormous asset.

Here are some strategies that can make diverse families feel comfortable:

- Welcome fathers as well as mothers. Introduce them to the other parents as well as to the children. Keep them informed, encourage their participation, and seek their advice.
- Make sure the center or family child care home reflects the families it serves. Parents should see representations of their cultures, dominant languages, and neighborhoods, as well as their child's work, photographs, and family mementos.
- Provide appropriate seating for adult guests.
- Provide a parent room, family corner, or family bulletin board.
- First greet parents by their formal names, and then ask them how they would like to be addressed and introduced.
- Let parents know that you will be available for individual conferences, if they would like to set up an appointment.

Parent Handbook

Providing a parent handbook is a good way to answer parents' questions and address common concerns. Items to include in a parent handbook are the following:

- The history of the center and its educational philosophy
- Information on policies, hours, fees, enrollment procedures, lunches, snacks, late arrival and pick-up, sick child and bad weather policies, and the like

293

- Lists of supplies and clothing the parents must purchase or bring to the center
- Frequency of reporting to parents, parent/teacher conferences, phone conversations, home visits, and so on
- A schedule of parent meetings and other activities
- A section with frequently asked questions and concise answers based on the center's philosophy and policies
- A sample daily schedule for each age group
- Volunteer opportunities and parent committees
- Important phone numbers and e-mail addresses (Some centers also include parent contact information with the parents' permission)

Newsletters

Regularly distributing a newsletter is another excellent way to communicate with parents. It demonstrates the center's concern for sharing information and reaches those parents who might otherwise have little direct contact with the center. Items to be included in the newsletter are as follow:

- Information on field trips and special events
- Notification of meetings
- Requests for donations of useable materials
- Requests for volunteers and expressions of recognition and gratitude to those parents who have assisted in the program
- Craft suggestions
- Reports on school "happenings"
- Introductions of new staff members
- Tips for teaching skills at home
- Recipes for nutritious snacks
- Weekly menus so that parents can plan complementary home meals
- A special "Parent" section with articles provided by parents
- Information about community events, issues, and campaigns affecting young children

Parent Meetings

Large-group parent or family meetings should be held on a regular basis. These meetings provide opportunities for parents to meet, share ideas, discuss problems, and learn from each other. They also serve as a vehicle for communicating effectively with many people at one time. Here are some suggestions for organizing group meetings:

- Notify parents and include an RSVP card that can be mailed back or dropped in a box at the center. This way, you will have an idea of the number of people who will attend, and you can follow up on those who don't respond.
- Survey the parents for the best times to meet. Schedule evening as well as daytime meetings to ensure maximum attendance. Some centers find that breakfast or Saturday meetings work best.

- Provide child care for all the children who might come with the parents.
- Provide refreshments.
- Develop the program according to the needs of the parents, and involve parents in the planning:
  — Offer information about the center's program.
  — Provide hands-on experiences of things children might enjoy at the center.
  — Present speakers on child development, toilet training, sibling rivalry, eating habits, discipline, and so on.
  — Offer fun activities, like "Movie Night" or a potluck supper.
- Evaluate meetings formally using an anonymous questionnaire that parents submit at the end of the meeting and informally through the "grapevine."
- Use the information gained from the evaluations to plan the content of subsequent meetings.

Parents as Volunteers

The use of parent volunteers has an impact in two important areas: It can supply an extra pair of hands for center activities, and it can provide a systematic way to involve those parents who have special skills or talents or who enjoy donating their time and working with children.

You can recruit volunteers at the time of initial enrollment, through regular contact with parents, and by using a parent activity chart. Place a simple sign-up list on the bulletin board, enlisting parents' help as volunteers and offering them a choice of dates, times, and types of contributions.

Parents can help by doing any of the following:

- Sharing something from their work or cultural heritage
- Arranging for other visitors whose work is related to something the children are investigating
- Reading to the children
- Introducing special activities
- Helping with activities like cooking, woodworking, and field trips that require extra supervision
- Making educational games and toys for the classroom
- Fundraising
- Acting as substitute teachers
- Serving on parent committees, such as long-range planning, diversity, fundraising, evaluation, and policy committees
- Coordinating parent/teacher activities and classroom celebrations
- Helping with the newsletter and other communications
- Translating for other families
- Bringing in recycled materials and items that can be used for art projects and pretend play or to make toys and games
- Preparing meals and snacks

- Sharing family photos
- Loaning books, toys, and other materials
- Helping to repair books, toys, and other materials
- Helping with clean-up days, gardening, and playground repair
- Sharing special talents
- Recruiting, interviewing, and evaluating teachers
- Planning the curriculum and special projects
- Ensuring that the center's policies are family friendly
- Letting others know about the program's special strengths
- Completing parent surveys that provide program feedback (such as those required for accreditation)
- Serving as liaisons to other parents
- Letting teachers know about their children's interests, friendships, concerns, and perceptions of school experiences
- Informing the school about community events of interest to families with young children
- Participating in advocacy
- Letting teachers know when they have done an especially good job

Parents are almost always helpful. Occasionally, however, their involvement can create problems. This can be minimized with planning:

- If you are counting on a parent to come in for a special activity or field trip, confirm it the previous day or evening.
- Remind parents who plan to help in the classroom or office that all information about children and families is confidential.
- Resolve any disagreements over educational philosophy or classroom management in private, not in front of the children.
- If a parent's presence in the classroom is disruptive or her child is unduly upset when she leaves, hold a parent conference to discuss the pattern and work out a solution.

To learn strategies for serving as a resource for families and building a community that supports families

Teacher: "*I am so pleased with Cornelius. He's doing so many things for himself these days. You know, he's my best helper at clean-up time.*"

Parent: "*I'm glad he's being good at the center, but you know, I'm still having problems with him at home. When he makes his bed, it looks worse than when he began, and if I depended on him to feed the dog, Rover would be dead from hunger.*"

Teacher: "*Many parents of 4-year-olds share your concerns about helping children learn responsibility. As a matter of fact, we are having a workshop on responsibility that you may want to attend.*" ●

Strategies for Serving as a Resource for Parents

In addition to involving parents in the program and sharing information about their children, a family-oriented child care program seeks ways of meeting the needs of parents. Parents may need information on child growth and development, guidance in child-rearing issues, or leads on community services and resources to help their families.

In situations where parents express or demonstrate a need for increased knowledge of child development, it is important for the classroom teacher to follow up by discussing that need with the director and other staff members. Setting up a family education program can be a benefit to the teachers as well as the parents.

A good way to identify parental needs and interests is to send home a parent survey like the one shown below. Then, once you have identified the parents' needs and interests, you can use creative strategies to meet those needs. Strategies that have been used successfully in many centers are discussed in the next several sections.

Parent Workshops

Parent workshops are most successful when they focus on topics that parents have identified as being important to them. For example, child management issues are a prime concern for most families. Other topics that can be suggested

Parent workshops are most successful when they focus on topics that parents have identified as being important to them.

to parents include using the community as a resource; children's health, safety, and nutrition; and preparing children for kindergarten and beyond.

Sample Parent Survey

Name _____ Date _____

I would be interested in attending parent workshops: Yes   No

I would be able to come to a talk on: (Please check available times)

_____ Weekday evening (circle best days: M   T   W   T   F   )

_____ Saturday morning

The following topics would be interesting to me:

_____ Sleeping problems and solutions

_____ Bad dreams and other fears

_____ Selecting and reading good books with my children

_____ Ways of handling biting

_____ Sibling rivalry

Other ideas: _____

I will need child care if the workshop is scheduled on the weekend or in the evening: Yes   No

---

Parent Resource Center

Although space is often a priority in a child care setting, devoting a shelf or section of a room to materials for parents is always a good investment. This section could include brochures and books on child development and positive guidance, informational pamphlets on community resources, and materials on health, safety, and nutrition. In many cities, free magazines on issues related to child care are available for distribution.

You will also want to provide parents with information about other services for which they may be eligible. You may be able to arrange with the appropriate agencies to distribute their application forms. Such services may include the following:

- WIC (Women, Infants, and Children): a nutritional supplement program for pregnant women, infants, and new mothers
- CHIP (the Children's Health Insurance Program): this program goes by different names in some states
- Food stamps: food-purchasing assistance for low-income families
- Medicaid: health care for low-income families
- Earned income tax credit: a tax credit or refund for low-income working families with children
- Dependent care tax credit: a tax credit for some child care expenditures
- Section 8 housing: housing assistance for low-income families
- Parents as Teachers and other home-visiting programs: provide parenting education and support
- Early intervention screening and services
- Health and dental screening and other services provided by the local public health department
- Kindergarten enrollment and transition services
- Voter registration

Contact your local resource and referral agency, public library, school district, Department of Public Health, or licensing agency for information on these and other family-service programs.

Family Bulletin Board

A good place for a family bulletin board is near the entrance to the center or the entrance of your classroom. You may want to include these items:

- The center calendar and notices of upcoming events
- Copies of flyers and newsletters
- Pictures of the children at work and play
- Notices of community events
- Advertisements by individual parents
- Requests for volunteers
- Interesting articles from newspapers and magazines

- Weekly menus
- Information on family or center charitable projects, such as a food drive, fundraiser, or toy and clothing drive

Parents may also want to use this bulletin board to sell or exchange infant equipment or clothing and to exchange information related to babysitting, carpooling, or providing child care to children with mental illnesses.

Community-Building and Parent Empowerment Strategies

When Dawn, 4-year-old Rachel's mother, was suddenly diagnosed with a brain tumor, the parents at Rachel's child care program organized themselves to help. They agreed to provide dinners for the family during Dawn's hospitalization and chemotherapy. A schedule was posted in the center, and families signed up for days when they could provide meals. The meals were brought to the center and sent home with Rachel. Five months later, when Dawn was feeling much better, everyone celebrated with a family potluck supper.

Parents look to professionals for child-rearing advice, but they also look to each other for advice and support. Who is the best local children's dentist, and how far in advance do you need to make appointments? Where can you get bargains on children's clothing? What are the strengths and weaknesses of different kindergarten programs and teachers? These are the kinds of questions that other parents are best equipped to answer.

The kind of community in which parents know and trust each other enough to ask for and receive help doesn't just happen, however. It needs to be built.

> *Parents look to professionals for child-rearing advice, but they also look to each other for advice and support.*

Parent support programs, based on a model developed by PSP (Parent Services Project, Inc., in Fairfax, California), are parent-to-parent programs that use the child care center as their base of operations. The child care center provides organizational leadership, meeting space, and child care while the parents organize recreational and educational programs based on the interests of their families. These PSP programs are likely to sponsor holiday celebrations and outings. In addition, they can sponsor stress management and parenting workshops, vocational education, revolving loan funds, and respite care.

Other community-building activities include the following:

- Holding informal get-togethers for parents and staff, with or without children
- Designating parent work days, on which some parents volunteer to provide child care in their homes while others work in teams to give the center a thorough cleaning, build new playground equipment, create materials for classrooms, or make needed repairs
- Developing babysitting co-ops and other barter and mutual assistance programs, such as shopping clubs and exchange banks, where parents exchange toys and furniture for money or services

- Conducting fundraising and center beautification projects that reflect families' talents and traditions

Another benefit of community building is that parents and teachers get to know each other. Then, when a special need arises—such as the birth of a new baby or a parent's unexpected hospitalization—a support system will already be in place. The parents will be less likely to feel isolated or depressed and more likely to feel empowered as they help each other in usually small but occasionally large ways.

Objective 5 To learn strategies for engaging parents in decision making and advocacy

> *Gina's mother was upset about the fact that Gina was having toileting accidents at school. When she discussed the problem with Gina's teacher, they were both convinced that Gina would get so engrossed in her play that she would wait too long before going to the bathroom. The teacher agreed to arrange the schedule so that Gina would go to the bathroom before going out to the playground.* ●

> *Although Timothy had never been identified as having a hearing problem, his mother felt that he had difficulty hearing when there was any kind of background noise. She discussed the problem with his teacher, who agreed that Timothy should be referred to Child Find for a full evaluation of his speech and hearing. Next, the teacher arranged for a follow-up conference to discuss the outcome of the evaluation.* ●

Helping Parents Advocate for Their Own Children

Parents need to feel that when they have concerns about their children, those concerns will be taken seriously and actions will be taken to address them. As shown in the previous examples, the first step in helping parents become advocates for their own children is to endorse their role as advocate.

> *The first step in helping parents become advocates for their own children is to endorse their role as advocate.*

Providing an open channel of communication, as previously discussed, will help make parents comfortable in sharing concerns about their children and becoming partners in solving their problems. It is important to recognize, however, that some parents look to the teacher as the expert and expect her to solve problems independently, while others want very much to be involved.

Parents who defer to teachers may hesitate to be critical, especially in public. Teachers need to find tactful, culturally appropriate ways of soliciting those parents' input. If you are unfamiliar with a parent's culture, try to find a colleague from that culture who can give you advice.

Encouraging Parent Participation in Center Governance and Advisory Groups

Just as it is essential to involve parents in decisions that affect primarily their own children, it is also important to involve them in decision making that affects the program as a whole. The more parents know about the program's curriculum, policies, finances, long-range plans, dreams, and challenges, the more helpful they can be.

A parent/teacher advisory council or board of directors can meet monthly and take responsibility for center governance. This elected group can solicit the opinions of other parents through surveys, informal get-togethers, and "phone trees" when controversial issues need to be decided. A committee structure allows many parents to contribute in their areas of interest and expertise. The leadership and advocacy skills that parents develop through these kinds of involvement will serve them and their children well for years to come.

Some parents will need little prodding to join advisory and decision-making groups. They have clear ideas about what they want for their children and are eager to have a hand in anything that affects their children's education and upbringing. Other parents may need more encouragement. In order to get a representative group and to make every family feel that their input is valued, you and the parents you are working with can try some of these techniques:

- Provide information about governing and advisory boards and committees in the parent handbook and at the first parent meeting. Encourage current board and committee members to share why their work is important, what they have learned, how much time is involved, and what challenges and opportunities are currently at the top of the agenda.
- Seek out the natural leaders. These are not necessarily the most vocal or educated parents; rather, they are the ones who are looked to by others for information and guidance, who have strong opinions but are willing to listen to those who disagree with them, and who have a talent for building bridges and smoothing over differences.
- Try to ensure diversity of opinion, gender, race/ethnicity, income level, and age of children, as appropriate.
- Create a nominating committee to recruit new board members.
- Hold meetings that are open to all. Publish the agenda in advance, and print the minutes of the meeting in your newsletter.
- Be sure to provide child care, food, transportation, and translation services when needed and to hold meetings at times that are convenient for families.
- Use the committee structure to nurture next year's leaders.

Empowering Parents as Advocates for All Children

Once parents have become comfortable serving as advocates for their own children, they are ready to broaden their horizons and become advocates for all children. Recognizing that the critical tool for a child advocate is *information*, teachers can play

301

an important role in keeping parents informed about issues related to children. Here are some ways to keep parents informed and committed:

- Maintain a bulletin board that includes updated pamphlets, periodicals, and news releases that focus on children's issues at the federal, state, and local levels.
- Inform parents of upcoming television specials related to children's issues.
- Invite parents to participate in workshops and study sessions devoted to issues that are relevant to your center.
- Post reminders to vote as election day approaches.
- Invite elected officials to visit your center when an issue affecting young children is on the agenda. Ask parents to join you in highlighting how the issue affects their families.
- Invite candidates for local office to speak at a parent meeting.
- Get involved yourself! Work with your local child care provider association, a state or local child advocacy group, or a national group, such as Stand for Children.

Parent involvement is an effort toward establishing common aims and goals, so that the labors of home and school are consistent. The greater the congruence between the values and objectives of home and school, the greater the influence of each and the greater the benefit to the child.

> *Once parents have become comfortable serving as advocates for their own children, they are ready to broaden their horizons and become advocates for all children.*

Finally and perhaps most important, realize that you are the child's teacher for only one or two years. The effect that you have during that time, however great, cannot match that of the parents, who will influence the child throughout her formative years. The parents are the child's real teachers. We professionals have the greatest impact when we share our knowledge and ability with the child's family, extending our influence into the child's future.

Additional Resources about Families

Diffly, D., & Morrison, K. (Eds.). (1996). *Family-friendly communication for early childhood programs.* Washington, DC: NAEYC.

Drawing strength from diversity: Effective services for children, youth, and families. (no date). San Francisco: California Tomorrow.

Greenman, J., & Stonehouse, A. (1996). *Prime times: A handbook for excellence in infant and toddler programs.* St. Paul, MN: Redleaf Press.

Seiderman, E., Lee, L., & Leinfelder, J. (1996). *Sharing the vision.* Fairfax, CA: Parent Services Project.

Stand for Children. www.childrensdefense.org.

Program Management

Chapter 12

Overview

Program management in center-based child care refers to the role of the teacher in promoting the smooth running of the program. It includes observing, recording, and tracking the development and behavior of each child; following administrative policies and procedures set by the center; working as a team with other members of the staff in program and curriculum planning; and participating with the director and other staff members in evaluating the strengths and needs of the center. In family child care, program management includes curriculum planning, record keeping, business management, and other administrative duties.

Rationale

The level of cooperation evidenced by staff members is a critical component in the development of a healthy, productive center. In the best of circumstances, staff members share resources, materials, and ideas. In addition, time is set aside for joint planning and problem solving. Staff meetings are devoted to discussing problems and identifying opportunities.

Being a good program manager requires both interpersonal skills and managerial skills. The teacher with program management skills can work cooperatively with other adults, sharing ideas, resources, and expertise. In addition, a good program manager maintains individual records on all of the children in her class or home and uses these records as the basis for program planning and curriculum development.

303

Objectives

1. To work cooperatively as a member of a team

2. To follow the policies and procedures set down by the center

3. To maintain a record-keeping system that serves as the basis for individual and group program planning

4. To manage a classroom efficiently so that most of the teacher's time can be devoted to working directly with the children

Understanding Program Management

The director of We-R-Caring Nursery was having a conference with one of her teachers.

Director: "*I am pleased with the way you are interacting with the children. The one thing I would like to work on is improving your management skills.*"

Teacher: "*Oh, that's no problem. I don't ever plan to go into management. If there is any managing to do in the school, I'll leave that up to you.*" ●

This new teacher's lack of concern reflects a lack of experience, as program management is part of every teacher's job. Classroom teachers are responsible for participating with other teachers in program planning. They are responsible, too, for tracking the progress of the children in their classrooms, for knowing the policies and procedures developed for their center, and for evaluating their own performance as a classroom manager. All of these duties are addressed in this chapter.

To work cooperatively as a member of a team

During a staff meeting, Miss Spontaneity made her position quite clear: "I am happy to cooperate in any way I can, but I am very much against the idea of a shared monthly calendar. How can I possibly know now what kind of field trip I am going to plan for next month? I like to plan field trips that either emerge from the spontaneous interests of the children or that take advantage of some unplanned event going on in town, like last year when we found out two days before it happened that there was going to be a parade of old and new fire engines or the time when the new yogurt store had its opening and they passed out mini-cones with frozen yogurt to all the kids."

The director praised Miss Spontaneity for recognizing the importance of expanding on the children's interests and taking advantage of unplanned events. The monthly calendar, he assured her, is not a document written in stone. Rather, it is a way of identifying events that affect some or all of the classes, a way of knowing in advance when there is a need to get permission slips or arrange for transportation, a way of coordinating open houses so that parents with more than one child do not run into conflicts, and a way for teachers to share their good ideas.

Miss Spontaneity had to agree that having a monthly calendar wasn't such a bad idea. ●

Planning as a Team

> The most effective sharing comes about when teachers plan together on a regular basis.

While a director can create the right climate for team building through her leadership style and the policies she promotes, it is up to the rest of the staff to make team building happen. The ingredients of a successful staff team include a shared philosophy about children and how they learn, mutual trust and respect, and an ongoing commitment to planning together and sharing ideas and resources. Although some sharing of information can come about informally, as teachers eat lunch together or meet after school, the most effective sharing comes about when teachers plan together on a regular basis.

An incredible group energy can develop when a group of early childhood teachers plans together. Ideas are generated that bring out the best of the team's knowledge and experience. Much more creativity is shown when groups of teachers plan parts of the program together than when individual teachers plan in isolation from their colleagues.

The Yearly Calendar

A yearly calendar describes the major events that will take place during the year that affect the whole center. While teachers may feel pressure in the beginning of the year to get their rooms set up and their individual curricula planned, spending time before classes start to set up the yearly calendar will set the tone for cooperation throughout the rest of the year. In addition to regularly scheduled holidays and vacations, the yearly calendar should include major centerwide events, like parent nights, parent conferences, field trips, community events, health-related activities, and annual fundraisers and food drives.

Monthly Plans

While the yearly calendar alerts classroom teachers to the major scheduled events, monthly planning meetings provide the opportunity to outline tasks and divide the responsibilities associated with these events. Monthly planning meetings also give teachers a chance to talk about new opportunities for joint projects and events. For instance, two classes may decide to get together for a Mother's Day breakfast, or one of the teachers may suggest a centerwide recycling project.

Sharing Ideas with Other Teachers

Once teachers discover the advantages of joining forces, sharing will take place on a spontaneous basis. Some effective ways of sharing include the following:

- Participating in weekly or bi-weekly staff meetings
- Having regular times set aside for group planning
- Designating a special topic for discussion at a staff meeting
- Asking a teacher to offer a special presentation for the staff
- Having a special time designated to discuss the progress the children are making
- Going together with one or more teachers on a special outing or field trip
- Making up activity boxes (with a lesson plan, directions, and all of the necessary materials for an activity) that can be rotated through the classrooms
- Sharing materials for special projects
- Developing a library schedule in which the teachers take turns checking out library books for the center
- Placing a large carton in the storage area where teachers can put leftover scraps and craft materials that can be shared with others
- Inviting another class to share a celebration or performance
- Having the children from two classes exchange greeting cards that they make
- Sharing ideas, lesson plans, and useful websites via e-mail
- Writing brief articles for the center newsletter

To follow the policies and procedures set down by the center

Mother: *"I am sorry about Bruce acting up in class. You know, I always say, 'Spare the rod and spoil the child.' If you would give him a rap on the knuckles now and then, you wouldn't have any more problems."*

Mrs. Toe-the-Mark: *"I agree with you, but you know we're not allowed to hit kids. It's a stupid rule, but I have to follow it or I will lose my job."*

Mrs. Toe-the-Mark was quite pleased with herself. She had managed to placate this mother without violating the policies of the center. Or had she?

> *A teacher is responsible for supporting the policies of her center in word as well as in deed.*

Obviously, Mrs. Toe-the-Mark did not understand her responsibility for following the policies and procedures of the center at which she taught. Even when a teacher is not in agreement with a center policy, she is responsible for supporting that policy in word as well as in deed.

This does not mean, however, that a teacher should simply follow policy without question. If a teacher understands the reason for a policy and still disagrees with it, it is important to talk over the policy with the director.

Almost inevitably, an open discussion of a policy will lead to a modification that everyone can accept. If a teacher feels she cannot support a center policy after a thorough discussion, then she really needs to find another position.

Types of Policies

A child care teacher who supports the policies and procedures of a child care center is thoroughly familiar with its written and unwritten policies and procedures and is conscientious in their implementation. The policies and procedures operational in a child care center fall into three categories: personnel, families and children, and the center.

Policies Related to Personnel

All child care programs should have written policies and procedures related to personnel. Typically, a personnel handbook describes the rights and responsibilities of employees and includes sections on salary and benefits, evaluation procedures, release time, liability, and termination. In the absence of a written document, it is important for every staff member to be familiar with her job description and to discuss job-related benefits and responsibilities with the director.

Policies Related to Families and Children

Centers that have a personnel handbook are also likely to have a parent handbook. As noted in Chapter 11, a parent handbook may describe policies for parents related to fees and service charges, health safeguards, drop-off and pick-up times, class visitation, insurance, field trips, and clothing.

Some personnel policies, both written and unwritten, are related to children, including those regarding maintenance of child-related records; accident, late arrival, and absentee procedures; and procedures to follow in cases of suspected abuse and neglect. Personnel policies related to discipline, safety, use of facilities, curriculum and lesson planning, television watching, and inclusion of children with special needs are also child related. Personnel policies that concern families may include the number and types of contacts the teacher must initiate, the maintenance of confidentiality, policies related to minor illness, and procedures to follow when a noncustodial parent attempts to take a child from the center.

Policies Related to the Center

Policies related to the center fall into two categories: health and safety and inventory and maintenance. Policies for health and safety address fire drill practice, emergency procedures, and upkeep of health records. Policies for inventory and maintenance address consumables used, furniture and equipment that needs repair, and the like.

From Knowledge to Implementation

While being knowledgeable about policies and procedures is extremely important, it is equally important to know how and when to implement them. It is helpful to practice filling out forms like inventory time sheets, accident reports, and contagious disease exposure forms before having to do it for real. It is also helpful to mark down on the yearly calendar the dates for turning in reports and evaluations.

To maintain a record-keeping system that serves as the basis for individual and group program planning

Mrs. Carefree was surprised to find a note in her box from Yvonne's parents. It said, "We would like to set up a conference with you in order to find out how Yvonne is progressing."

"That's the most ridiculous thing I ever heard of," Mrs. Carefree remarked to another teacher. "Yvonne is a perfectly okay kid. She's not having any problems, as far as I can tell, but her parents keep wanting to know how she is doing."

Yvonne's parents' request is not unreasonable. Classroom teachers with good management skills monitor the progress of their children on an ongoing basis. They maintain checklists based on curriculum objectives as well as anecdotal reports to keep track of individual progress. They may also use behavioral observations when children exhibit special needs or problems.

Maintaining records that tell you about each child's progress is a very good idea. Doing so will help you know if each child is making appropriate progress. It will also help you recognize the types of activities each child enjoys. You will be able to check the progress of children who need special help and identify the types of activities in which children need special practice.

Such record keeping also provides information for making regular weekly plans and guides yearly planning. And it makes communication with parents much easier and more beneficial, since you can tell parents exactly what activities a certain child enjoys and suggest some things they could work on at home.

Checklists

The use of a *checklist* developed by the teacher and based on the curriculum objectives is the simplest way of tracking the progress of all children in the class. A checklists should be age specific and should include a place for the date, the child's name, and his age and date of birth (see the sample on page 309).

The specificity of the checklist will depend on the curriculum used in the classroom. A classroom with a highly structured curriculum and sequenced behavioral objectives will require an elaborate checklist. A more simple checklist will be appropriate for a curriculum that is relatively flexible and developmentally oriented. Checklists should be filled out at least three and preferably four times a year.

Anecdotal Records

Throughout the year, the teacher should record observations that yield an in-depth understanding of each child. Written observations can be used to plan a curriculum that capitalizes on children's interests. These observations also provide rich examples to share with parents and document children's experiences in the program.

Sample Developmental Checklist: Birth–6 months

Child's name _____ Age _____

Date of birth _____ Date form completed _____

Name of person completing form _____

Behavioral Objective	Yes	At times	No
1. Follows a moving rattle with eyes for short distance	☐	☐	☐
2. Turns head toward source of sound	☐	☐	☐
3. Smiles in response to smile	☐	☐	☐
4. Brings thumb to mouth	☐	☐	☐
5. Watches own hands	☐	☐	☐
6. Engages with caregivers in back and forth babbling	☐	☐	☐
7. Holds own head up when being carried	☐	☐	☐
8. Reaches and grasps rattle	☐	☐	☐
9. Lifts head and chest when on stomach	☐	☐	☐
10. Rolls over	☐	☐	☐
11. Picks up toy	☐	☐	☐
12. Crawls	☐	☐	☐
13. Chuckles out loud	☐	☐	☐
14. Transfers toy from one hand to other	☐	☐	☐
15. Sits with support	☐	☐	☐
16. Sits without support	☐	☐	☐

In sum, there are three reasons to record observations:

1. To get to know each child deeply; to have a rich knowledge of what interests and motivates the child, what bothers and upsets the child; to fully understand the child; to answer a question you are pondering about a child and be able to say, "I have just learned something about this child"
2. To have material to back up the assessment ratings you may be recording on a developmental checklist
3. To be able to share meaningful anecdotes with parents—wonderful moments that the parents have missed while their child is with you

Observations may be recorded on a formal observation form to be kept in the child's portfolio. They may also be collected on scraps of paper, stick-on notes, and the like for teacher planning use.

An *anecdotal record* should be short and precise, describing what the child is saying or doing. It should not include the teacher's impression or analysis of the behavior. It

---

Sample Anecdotal Record

Date: February 12

Time: 9:30 a.m.

Setting: Block corner

Situation: Betty was building a block tower. Jonathan has knocked it down.

What happened: Betty said to Jonathan in a firm voice, "You knocked down my chocolate factory. Help me build it up." Jonathan sat down beside Betty, and the two children rebuilt the block structure.

---

is especially important to record the date, time, and setting for each anecdotal record, as shown in the sample above.

Creating anecdotal records is the most effective way of personalizing a record-keeping system and providing parents with a real picture of how their child functions in typical class situations. For instance, an anecdote such as the one shown above can be very useful for sharing with parents the good things that their child is doing. Betty's parents were concerned about her tendency to let other children take advantage of her. By sharing this anecdote, Betty's teacher was able to show how Betty could be appropriately assertive without being confrontational or stepping out of her role as peacemaker. Anecdotal records can also be used to discuss behaviors that may be of concern. It is important, however, that when we share worrisome anecdotes with parents, we also share anecdotes that demonstrate their child's strengths.

> *Creating anecdotal records is the most effective way of personalizing a record-keeping system and providing parents with a real picture of how their child functions in typical class situations.*

Anecdotal records are also useful for developing an *anecdotal portfolio*, which serves as an ongoing assessment of the child's progress. The portfolio should include anecdotes that demonstrate a child's salient characteristics and performance and understanding in various areas. If areas of concern are identified in the beginning of the year, anecdotal reports can describe incidents in which the child has shown progress in those targeted areas.

Objective 4

To manage a classroom efficiently so that most of the teacher's time can be devoted to working directly with the children

At the suggestion of the director, Miss Wing-It was visiting Mrs. Got-It-Together's classroom. In the morning, the children all went to circle time. They listened to a story about spiders and sang some songs, including "There's a Spider on My Leg." After circle time, the children selected tokens

from the choice board. Each token represented an interest center, and each child took a turn to choose a token. One of the children explained to Miss Wing-It that each token was an admission ticket to an interest center. When Miss Wing-It asked what happened if there were no tokens left for the interest center she wanted, the child answered matter of factly, "You just choose a different interest center."

During the course of the day, the children went out to the playground, completed a collaborative art project, made Jell-O, put on a puppet show, had snacks and lunch, napped, acted out a story, met with their teacher in small groups, picked up their toys, and joined in a circle to talk about the day. There were no incidents, and Mrs. Got-It-Together seemed perfectly relaxed.

Miss Wing-It was incredulous. "How do you manage 10 children by yourself and keep them all busy and happy without getting frazzled? You must have a magic formula."

"No, it's not magic," Mrs. Got-It-Together explained. "I just have a routine for everything, so I don't spend time looking for things. I also plan each day in advance, so I don't have to scramble around getting things ready at the last minute."

Organizing the Classroom

Although Mrs. Got-It-Together makes managing a classroom seem simple, it takes a while for every teacher to develop classroom management skills.

Following Miss Wing-It's visit to Mrs. Got-It-Together's classroom, the director asked Mrs. Got-It-Together to visit Miss Wing-It's classroom.

Miss Wing-It began the day with circle time. She read a story to the children, and they seemed to really enjoy it. After the story, the children asked her if she would play the "Hokey-Pokey" tape. Miss Wing-It agreed, but she had to get the tape recorder from the other side of the room and then she couldn't find the tape. When she finally found it and returned to the circle, two of the children were engaged in a wrestling match and three others had left the circle and were racing across the room. Miss Wing-It called everyone back to the circle and put on the "Hokey-Pokey" tape. After two rounds of "Hokey-Pokey," Miss Wing-It told the children that she had a special surprise. "Find a chair and sit down at a table and see if you can guess what it is."

Miss Wing-It showed the children a bag of flour. "I know," Cecile shouted out, "we're going to bake cookies!" "Maybe later," Miss Wing-It responded, "but right now, we are going to do something else."

After a few more guesses and a lot of laughter, Miss Wing-It told the children that they were going to make play dough. She put a big bowl on the table and started to set out the ingredients. "Okay, now get ready to work," she told the children. "Oh dear," Miss Wing-It interrupted herself, "I seem to have forgotten the salt!"

At that moment, the director summoned Mrs. Got-It-Together to come into her office. "So, what do you think of Miss Wing-It?" the director asked.

"Oh, she's a great teacher," Mrs. Got-It-Together responded. "She is full of fun, and the children seem to love her. The only thing is that she is a little bit disorganized."

"You mean she can't seem to get it together?" asked the director. "Do you think she'll ever learn?"

"Of course she will," Mrs. Got-It-Together replied. "She just needs a little help with organization. I'll be happy to help her." ●

Some teachers are by nature more organized than others. Even so, caregivers and teachers in child care settings need to know where to find things when they need them. A good way to think about how you would like to reorganize your classroom is to think back over the last two weeks and make a note of each item that you needed but couldn't find without a search.

Well-organized teachers offer the following suggestions:

Teacher Materials

- Place the things that you use on a daily basis on one shelf. This should include items such as scissors, stapler, hole puncher, paper clips, note pad, pens, tissues, first aid kit, and planning book. Also keep a notebook that includes children's birthdays, a list of children with allergies, parent contact information, and any other vital information that you need to keep at hand.

- Place the special items you are planning to use for the week on a second shelf. This should include your activity plans, books and tapes you will use, and materials for crafts and other special activities.

Record Keeping

- Keep a folder for each child. Include anecdotal records and observations, work samples, notes and follow-up plans from parent meetings, and any observations or recommendations by consultants.

- Keep a file with all the blank forms you use on a regular basis. Place them in manila folders, labeled and organized alphabetically.

Classroom

- Give the children visual clues so that they can help maintain classroom organization. You might post the daily schedule, make a job chart that shows who's turn it is to pass out the snack or feed the pets, use pictures and labels to show what belongs on specific shelves or in certain bins, and put stickers on the wall or floor to show how many children can be in each interest center.

- Look at your classroom from a child's point of view. Does everything have a logical home? Are items placed near where they will be used?

Planning

- Strike a balance between following your plans to the letter and going with the flow. Remember that you can accommodate children's wishes without granting them immediately. For example, you can keep a list of books the children want you to read, and read one or two at naptime or circle time each day.

- Balance activities that require a lot of preparation with ones that you can do on a moment's notice. Introduce only as much variety as you and the children can comfortably handle.

- Plan some activities that evolve over time. For example, you and the children could build a "store" in the classroom, adding new items each day. Later, you can introduce play money, add a new department, or even invite visitors from another class.

- Keep a "to do" list in the back of your plan book. Check off items when you finish them.

Remember to schedule time for yourself. Give yourself time for planning, collecting materials, arranging, and just thinking.

Share the work and share the fun. Ask other teachers and parents to help you with big projects. Celebrate your success by doing something fun and relaxing together.

Weekly Plans

Weekly plans provide a way of mapping out the daily activities that take place in the classroom. An effective weekly plan for preschool children describes the theme of the week (if applicable), the special learning activities planned, new materials to be added, and the changes needed to activity centers to develop specific concepts. The plan should also provide a place to outline the preparation needed in order to carry out an activity. In addition, the weekly plan can describe special activities designed for children who have special needs.

> *Weekly plans provide a way of mapping out the daily activities that take place in the classroom.*

The weekly plan does not need to include the events that take place every day, such as breakfast, washing up, rest time, closing time, and the like, as they are already on your daily schedule. On a simplified planning form, you should have spaces each day for the following:

- Group times (songs, stories, games, special topics)
- Storytimes (books to be read and activities to extend the story)
- Small-group learning activities (special activities offered by the teacher during activity center time)
- Outdoor activities (special activities to enrich outdoor time)
- Special planned activities (classroom visitors, field trips, etc.)

Also have a space for each of the following classroom activity centers and the materials you want to add to it:

- Books
- Blocks
- Imaginative play
- Art
- Manipulatives/construction
- Science/discovery
- Sensory

Resource Files

Keeping a well-organized and up-to-date resource file is a great timesaver. Although it is quite possible to use a carton to store your individual resource files, it will be easier to keep your files organized if you use a file case with large hanging files.

A resource file should contain two kinds of resources: information and lesson ideas. The information should be organized according to topic: for instance, field trips, parent programs, classroom visitors, articles about special-needs children, and advocacy material. Resource files for lesson plans and activity ideas should include health and safety activities, creative art projects, science activities, and so on. If you use themes in your classroom, you may want to organize your files of lesson plans and activities by theme.

Volunteers in the Classroom

Having volunteers in the classroom can be either a great help or a real bother. When volunteers are prepared and willing to take on jobs that need to be done, they can be quite useful. But when volunteers either take on jobs that were not requested or continually ask how to do each task and what they should do next, they can be a burden.

The most willing and most useful volunteers in the class are the children. Children love to be helpful and may vie to wash the tables, sort out puzzle parts, and pass out snacks.

Your next best volunteers can be parents. They have a stake in what happens in the classroom and have experience with young children. They often bring special skills and talents and can share their family and cultural heritages. Occasionally, however, parents overstep their bounds. They may usurp the teacher's role in disciplining children, introduce an unplanned activity, make a promise that can't be kept, or hover over their own children. They may also find out information about another child or family and forget to keep it confidential. Unfortunately, concerns over these types of excesses have prompted some centers to limit the use of parent volunteers.

Whether your volunteers are parents, college students, or seniors, it is always helpful to orient them ahead of time.

Whether your volunteers are parents, college students, or seniors, it is always helpful to orient them ahead of time. Find out about their skills, their time commitment, and the tasks they enjoy doing. It often helps volunteers when they are given a list of tasks that need to be done, such as updating bulletin boards. That list could include any of the following:

- Writing down the words children use to describe their pictures
- Reading to the class, to a small group, or to an individual child
- Arranging the children's artwork on the wall
- Helping individual children with tasks they are having difficulty with, like cutting with scissors
- Playing informally with children in an activity area
- Helping children put on outer garments when they go out to the playground
- Giving extra attention to a child who needs it
- Working with a small group of children to prepare a meal or snack
- Teaching a song or game

Before inviting volunteers into the classroom, check your center's policies. Some centers require every volunteer to be fingerprinted and go through a background check.

Behind the Scenes

Organization and preparation may take a lot of work, but they save time in the long run. Over time, you will find that a well-managed classroom tends to run itself.

> *A well-managed classroom tends to run itself.*

As the children learn the routines, they will need less direction, leaving you more time for real communication and teaching. With a well-organized set of resources at your fingertips, you will be prepared to build on the children's emerging interests and spontaneous questions. As you read over your well-kept records, you will most likely be delighted with what you and the children have accomplished.

Additional Resources about Program Management

Bredekamp, S., & Copple, C. (1997). *Developmentally appropriate practice in early childhood programs* (Rev. ed.). Washington, DC: NAEYC.

Curtis, D., & Carter, M. (1996). *Reflecting children's lives: A handbook for planning child-centered curriculum.* St. Paul, MN: Redleaf Press.

Dodge, D., Colker, L., & Heroman, C. (2002). *The creative curriculum for preschool* (4th ed.). Washington, DC: Teaching Strategies.

Greenman, J., & Stonehouse, A. (1996). *Prime times: A handbook for excellence in infant and toddler programs.* St. Paul, MN: Redleaf Press.

McAfee, O., Leong, D., & Bodrova, E. (2004). *Basics of assessment: A primer for early childhood educators.* Washington, DC: NAEYC.

Professionalism

Chapter 13

Overview

A *professional* is defined in the *American Heritage Dictionary* as "one who has an assured competence in a particular field or occupation." The professional early childhood teacher/caregiver has a strong knowledge of early childhood theories and effective practices. This ever-growing knowledge base informs her judgment and guides her daily activities.

Rationale

Because children's development is determined in large part by their early experiences, caregivers and teachers of young children play a critical role in shaping the future. Recognizing the importance of this professional role, we must not only follow best practices and maintain the highest ethics of the profession, but we must also continually strive to increase and share our own knowledge and serve as advocates for children.

Objectives

1. To seek opportunities to increase professional knowledge and improve professional skills
2. To serve as an advocate for children and families
3. To maintain the ethics of the early childhood profession
4. To build a professional support system

Developing Professionalism

Angelica had just graduated from high school and was talking with a girl-friend about what she would like to do with the rest of her life. "One thing is for sure," she started off, "I am not *going to college. I hate studying. I tried waitressing for a while, but I didn't like it. Too much work, and some of those people are real nasty. Last summer, I had a pretty good job in a department store selling cosmetics. I would have stayed with it, but they gave me all this boring stuff I was supposed to learn. You know what I think I would really like? Working in a child care center. I love kids! Besides, when you work with children, you don't have to keep learning stuff."*

Obviously, Angelica needs some career guidance. It takes more than a love for children to be successful in child care. Taking care of children is a professional commitment. It requires energy, dedication, and a commitment to professional growth. In this chapter, we identify four components of professionalism: continuing to gain knowledge and skills, serving as an advocate for children, maintaining the ethics of the profession, and creating a system or network to provide professional support.

To seek opportunities to increase professional knowledge and improve professional skills

Early childhood is a growing profession, in several respects. It is growing in terms of the amount of material there is to learn, the status of the early childhood professional, and the career opportunities that are opening up. The increased recognition that is being given to early childhood professionals stems from a growing awareness of the importance of children's early years and the increased demand for quality child care as mothers enter the workforce.

> *Every early childhood professional has an obligation to seek self-improvement.*

Every early childhood professional has an obligation to seek self-improvement. The basis of quality child care is a well-trained and competent staff. As the field grows in knowledge and expertise, all staff must keep current with new knowledge and continually upgrade their skills. This process of self-improvement requires you to take five critical steps:

1. Assess your strengths and weaknesses.
2. Identify your goals.
3. Identify available educational resources.
4. Implement a self-improvement plan.
5. Share your new expertise with others.

We'll look at each step in one of the following sections.

Step 1: Assess your strengths and weaknesses

Miss Driven had just spent an hour talking with Michael's parents. Michael had been diagnosed as mildly autistic. The psychologist who tested him felt that he should be placed in a classroom with typically developing children. Based on the psychologist's recommendation, Michael's parents had decided to enroll their son in the Wee Care Preschool.

Michael's parents were extremely satisfied with the progress Michael had made. Miss Driven's toilet-learning routine had been successful, and Michael seldom had an accident. Also, he had completely stopped biting his hand and had learned to say several new words.

Following the conference with Michael's parents, Miss Driven scheduled a conference with her director. Despite the fact that Michael's parents were pleased with their son's progress, Miss Driven was convinced that she was not helping Michael enough. "He is such a nice kid," she complained to the director, "but he is still a loner. There must be something I can do to help him play with the other children."

Miss Driven is being too hard on herself. She is so focused on what she hasn't accomplished that she hasn't taken credit for all that she has accomplished. Some practitioners, like Miss Driven, are not very good at self-evaluation. They are either so focused on their areas of weakness that they lose sight of their strengths, or they are so focused on their strengths that they overlook their areas of weakness. Fortunately, most practitioners are quite accurate in their self-assessments.

The *Trainee's Manual* that accompanies this textbook includes a self-assessment in every chapter, providing a comprehensive way to evaluate your areas of strength and weakness. Doing this self-assessment asks students to make plans for growth and to evaluate their accomplishments throughout the Child Development Associate (CDA) training program in all 13 Functional Areas. The checklist on page 319 looks at the whole range of expertise needed by early care professionals.

Back up your self-assessment with a portfolio of photographs, lesson plans, and notes from parents, supervisors, and colleagues that demonstrate your strengths and your teaching philosophy. Then share your self-evaluation with supportive professional colleagues who can give you a "reality check." If everyone agrees with your assessment of your competencies, you are ready to take the next step: to identify your career goals.

Step 2: Identify your goals

As you look at your self-assessment, you will see areas of strength and areas in which you need to improve your skills. At this point, you can set two kinds of goals: goals for improving the skills related to your current position and goals for improving the skills needed for career advancement.

Sample Self-Assessment Checklist

	Always	Sometimes	Desired Growth Area
1. I follow the policies and procedures of my child care program, including work ethics and curriculum planning.	☐	☐	☐
2. I work cooperatively with all members of the staff and am willing to assume additional tasks when called on.	☐	☐	☐
3. I have the knowledge and skills to work effectively with children with special needs and with children from different cultural backgrounds.	☐	☐	☐
4. I am competent in the areas of classroom management and curriculum development and implementation.	☐	☐	☐
5. I have excellent relationships with the families of the children in my class, and I find creative ways of involving them in the program.	☐	☐	☐
6. I reflect on my practice and consult with others to improve my professional knowledge and skills.	☐	☐	☐
7. I am an advocate for children and families and for my profession.	☐	☐	☐
8. I am committed to sharing my knowledge and skills and assuming an active role in my center and my community.	☐	☐	☐
9. I am familiar with the options for careers in early childhood and am either comfortable with my current role or open to pursuing another option.	☐	☐	☐

If your self-report indicates room for improvement, you may want to search out workshops, readings, mentorships, and other learning opportunities that will help you in the necessary areas. It is best to start with just one or two goals that you can achieve within a year. Your success in meeting these self-selected goals will likely fuel your desire for further learning.

If your self-assessment indicates that you are at the top of your form, you may want to stay in your current position but take on new challenges, such as mentoring others and sharing your expertise through facilitating conferences and workshops. Or you might decide that it is time to move on.

As the number of early childhood programs has continued to grow in the twenty-first century, the supply of child care personnel has not kept up with the demand. The United States is desperately short of child care providers who have the knowledge and skills to fill the job vacancies in infant and toddler care, in preschool programs, in public and private prekindergarten and kindergarten programs, and in programs for young children with special needs. Perhaps even more serious is the desperate shortage of personnel who can manage and direct new programs, train personnel, train the trainers of personnel, license child care facilities, mentor family providers and relative caregivers, provide specialized coaching in areas such as literacy promotion and child assessment, and provide technical assistance to new child care programs and to programs seeking accreditation or self-improvement.

Not too long ago, child care was considered a dead-end profession. At this point, however, the career ladder offers a range of options. Moreover, the quality of child care in the United States depends on our ability to find personnel who are ready to ascend the ladder.

Step 3: Identify available educational resources

Mrs. Here-to-Stay was attending an in-service session required by her center. A consultant had been invited to the session to describe educational opportunities for child care providers. Mrs. Here-to-Stay had no interest in the topic. She sat herself down in the back of the room and pulled out her knitting. Unfortunately, her knitting needles made a clicking sound that caught the director's attention. During a break, the director approached Mrs. Here-to-Stay and suggested that she put her knitting away.

As soon as the director left, Mrs. Here-to-Stay whispered to a co-worker, "I don't know why we had to come to this stupid meeting. I have been taking care of babies for 27 years, and the last thing I need is an education." ●

While no one can quarrel over the value of experience, being experienced does not necessarily mean being well informed. Mrs. Here-to-Stay had some valuable skills. She could change a baby's diaper faster than any one in the center, and she knew exactly what to do when it came to quieting a crying baby. Unfortunately, Mrs. Here-to-Stay knew nothing about new research about the brain, refused to look at books with babies, and continued to give parents misinformation about nutrition, immunization, and developmental screening. Even if Mrs. Here-to-Stay had no interest in seeking a degree or in ascending a career ladder, her refusal to keep informed was interfering with her ability to provide quality care.

Educational Resources

Early childhood personnel interested in furthering their education have many different options:

- Reading newsletters, articles, chapters, and books
- Attending conferences, lectures, and workshops
- Watching videotapes and listening to audiotapes
- Networking with other personnel through meetings, telephone calls, e-mail, and Internet bulletin boards, listservs, and chat rooms
- Accessing information from Internet websites
- Visiting other early childhood programs
- Participating in leadership training and fellowship programs

Professional Organizations

Early childhood professional organizations provide many valuable resources in the forms of workshops, conferences, magazines and journals, websites, videotapes, colleagues, and mentors. Here is a partial list of these organizations:

National Association for the Education of Young Children (NAEYC)

1509 16th Street NW

Washington, DC 20036-1426

www.naeyc.org

NAEYC is the largest professional organization of early childhood professionals in the country. It has 100,000 members and 360 affiliate groups located in different states and regions. In addition to sponsoring an annual conference, NAEYC publishes a bi-monthly journal, *Young Children*, and many other excellent publications on early childhood issues.

National Association for Family Child Care

5202 Pinemont Drive

Salt Lake City, UT 84123

www.nafcc.org

NAFCC seeks to promote quality in family child care and advance the family child care profession. It advocates for family child care providers, provides technical assistance to local provider associations, runs a national conference, and promotes family child care accreditation.

National Black Child Development Institute (NBCDI)

1101 15th Street NW, Suite 900

Washington, DC 20005

www.nbcdi.org

NBCDI is an early childhood organization that supports the healthy growth and development of black children and motivates positive social change. It sponsors an annual conference and disseminates a variety of publications.

National Head Start Association (NHSA)

1651 Prince Street

Alexandria, VA 22314

www.nhsa.org

NHSA is a membership organization representing 835,000 children, some 170,000 staff, and 2,050 federally funded Head Start programs. It runs training conferences, provides distance education via satellite TV, promulgates new research, and publishes *Children and Families*, *NHSA Dialog*, and other resources for teachers.

National Council of La Raza (NCLR)

1126 16th Street NW

Washington, DC 20036

www.nclr.org

La Raza is the largest Hispanic child care organization and a leading advocate for Hispanic children. It has a national office and seven regional offices and provides a variety of publications and training conferences.

Zero to Three: National Center for Infants, Toddlers and Families

2000 M Street NW, Suite 200

Washington, DC 20036

www.zerotothree.org

Zero to Three is the nation's leading resource on the first three years of life. It provides information to professionals in many disciplines, as well as to parents, through its website, an annual conference, the *Zero to Three Bulletin*, growth chart posters, and other publications.

Early Childhood Education Courses

Formal coursework on early childhood education is available online from sources such as Pacific Oaks College (www.pacificoaks.edu) and Nova Southeastern University (www.nova.edu). Courses may also be available at your local community college or university, through your local resource and referral agency, or through Head Start, military base child care programs, and other federal and state programs. Try to choose courses that will help you climb the early childhood career ladder.

Child Development Associate (CDA) Credential

One way to improve your educational status is through the Child Development Associate program. A CDA is a professional who has been assessed by the CDA national credentialing program and judged to be competent as an early childhood teacher. To get more information from the Council for Professional Recognition, go to www.cdacouncil.org.

Associate's, Bachelor's, and Advanced Degree Programs

Your local community college may offer an Associate of Science (AS) degree in early childhood education and/or an Associate of Arts (AA) degree in general education. Some AA degrees have a special emphasis in early childhood education. In most community colleges, an AS is a vocational degree, whereas an AA articulates with a Bachelor of Arts (BA) degree in early childhood education (allowing you to receive full credit for the first two years of the bachelor's program). In other words, students with an AS degree may have to take additional coursework in the process of completing a bachelor's degree. Students who complete a bachelor's degree in early childhood or a related field may pursue a graduate degree in early childhood development or education on a master's or doctoral level. Many bachelors' programs in early childhood education offer college credit to candidates who have received a CDA or have documented life experiences. Also, because an increasing number of colleges are currently offering courses at night and on the weekend, along with distance education degrees, it is now possible for early childhood personnel to earn an advanced degree without giving up their jobs.

Continuing Education Units (CEUs)

Whether you are teaching in a licensed early childhood setting or hold an advanced degree and are teaching in a public or private school, most states require that you renew your skills within a prescribed period by receiving a set number of continuing education units (CEUs). CEUs are also required to maintain your status as a CDA or certified teacher. Some CEU courses count toward undergraduate or graduate credit if you complete extra assignments and pay an additional fee.

Certification

Career opportunities in early childhood are not automatically available to people who hold an undergraduate or graduate degree in early childhood. Every state has a system for certifying early childhood educators. To be certified as an early childhood teacher via the state Department of Education for public school employment, it is necessary to meet the standards of the state where you are seeking employment. In most states, you must be certified in early childhood education to be eligible for a prekindergarten or kindergarten position within the public schools.

Financial Support

Financial support for furthering your education through courses or conferences may be available from several sources:

- TEACH (Teacher Education And Compensation Helps) scholarships in several states underwrite educational costs and provide stipends for graduates who agree to stay in the field.
- Pell grants support college education for students of modest income.
- Many resource and referral agencies provide free courses and administer scholarship programs.
- Professional conferences are often partially underwritten by corporate or foundation sponsors, who provide scholarships for some attendees.
- Many centers will pay all or part of your tuition for work-related study.

Step 4: Implement a self-improvement plan

> *Mr. Coolit:* *"What are you doing now? Can't you for once in your life leave work at school so that we can spend some time together?"*
>
> *Mrs. Coolit:* *"Don't worry. This won't take more than five minutes. My evaluation is tomorrow, and the director and I have plans to write these professional improvement plans."*
>
> *Mr. Coolit:* *"That's stupid. I like you just the way you are."*
>
> *Mrs. Coolit:* *"I know it's silly. We go through this every year. These plans are like New Year's resolutions: You make these great plans, stick them in the drawer, and promptly forget about them."*

Mrs. Coolit has described exactly what a professional plan should not be and what you should not do with it. A meaningful professional plan is based on a self-evaluation and describes the resources you will use to reach your self-improvement goals. Look at the sample professional plan below. It states a goal and lists steps toward achieving it. Notice that the plan includes both learning experiences (readings and a workshop) and initial ideas for applying the learning in the classroom and in work with parents.

> *A meaningful professional plan is based on a self-evaluation and describes the resources you will use to reach your self-improvement goals.*

Sample Self-Improvement Plan

Goal: To expand the curriculum to include a greater focus on multicultural and antibias education

June: Order materials for the classroom that are culturally appropriate: multiethnic dolls, play foods from different cultures, and multicultural books.

July and August: Read materials on antibias and cultural responsiveness:

Roots and Wings: Affirming Culture in Early Childhood Programs (York, 2003)

Anti-Bias Curriculum (Derman-Sparks, 1989)

In Our Own Way—How Anti-Bias Work Shapes Our Lives (Alvarado et al., 1999)

September: Redo the curriculum for the year, including one activity per month that teaches children to value diversity.

October: With the children and parents, develop a showcase in the classroom with artifacts from all of the different cultures represented in our classroom.

November: Meet with families to discuss how to approach holidays. Do parents want their children to learn holiday songs and games from their own and other traditions in school? Do they have special family or cultural traditions that they would like to share with the children and each other? Or would they prefer that religious holidays not be a part of the school curriculum?

March: Participate in a professional workshop on celebrating diversity.

April and May: Gather recipes from the different families in the class. Reproduce them and bind them to create a class cookbook. Have the children make cookbook covers in class and then give their mothers the cookbooks for Mother's Day.

Step 5: Share your new expertise with others

Whether you have researched an area, made changes in your classroom, or qualified for a new career, you should look for opportunities to share what you have learned:

- Share what you have learned informally with colleagues.
- Invite other teachers to visit your classroom.
- Share a book or videotape that you found valuable with parents and colleagues.
- Plan a presentation or discussion for a staff or parent meeting.
- Contribute an article to a newsletter or journal.
- Join with colleagues to present at a workshop or conference.
- Mentor a colleague.
- Assume an office in a professional organization.

To serve as an advocate for children and families

When the director of the Growing Together School asked the staff if they would attend a legislative hearing supporting an increase in funds for child care subsidies, Miss Not-Me, a new teacher, was annoyed. "Why should we spend our time supporting child care?" she asked. "It is bad enough that we have to take care of kids for the kind of money they pay us. If parents want the government to pay for their child care, let them attend the hearings!"

The director of Growing Together was taken aback by Miss Not-Me's attitude. She had assumed that all *teachers were concerned about the welfare of children and would seek opportunities to serve as child advocates.*

Although the director of Growing Together may be expecting a lot of a brand-new teacher, she is certainly right in stressing the importance of early childhood teachers becoming involved in advocacy issues. Teachers of young children have firsthand knowledge of the needs of children and their families. When teachers share this knowledge with legislators and government officials, they will likely be listened to. Just as important, teachers are in a good position to share their knowledge with parents and associates, who can in turn become child advocates.

Miss Not-Me needs to do some thinking. She is absolutely right when she complains about the poor wages paid in the field. She is also right when she asserts that parents should advocate for child care subsidies. But instead of sitting on the sidelines, she should argue that having an underpaid child care workforce and having a scarcity of parent advocates both point out the need for change. Caregivers know the importance, as well as the cost, of quality care for young children and are in a prime position to educate policymakers. Those child care givers who have earned the trust of parents are also in a prime position to help parents advocate for their children.

Many caregivers, like Miss Not-Me, would rather stand on the sidelines and complain than join the ranks of the advocates. Before discussing how to change their view, let us look at some of the reasons caregivers give for shying away from being advocates:

"I get up at 5:00 in the morning, get the kids off to school, get home at 6:00, make dinner, clean the house, and help the kids with their homework. I don't have time to breathe, let alone do this advocacy stuff."

"I am not one for mixing into politics. I don't care which party they belong to: They're a bunch of crooks, and I wouldn't give them the time of day."

"I never was much of a reader, and I don't know one candidate from the other. If I start giving them advice about what they should vote for, I'll sound like a bumbling idiot. I once went to one of those political open houses, and I was supposed to tell a candidate about why he should vote for a children's board. I turned red and stuttered so much that I'm sure he didn't listen to a word I said."

"They told me I should write this letter about market rates and that I should use my own words. I really tried, but I get tongue tied when I have to write something. By the time I have my letter written, the legislative session will be over."

"I think voting should be private. I'm not going to tell anybody what or whom they should vote for."

"Legislators get hundreds of calls. One little call for me is not going to make a difference." ●

Ways of Overcoming Concerns about Being an Advocate

As we read through the reasons caregivers offer for shying away from advocacy, it is relatively easy to identify the issues that underlie their reluctance: feel overextended, lacking confidence and experience, worrying about being uninformed, lacking motivation, feeling ineffective, and having a distrust of government. If we want child care givers to assume an advocacy role, we need to find ways of overcoming these concerns.

The director of Growing Together, Miss The-Buck-Stops-Here, discovered several different ways of inspiring reluctant caregivers to become committed advocates:

"When teachers tell me that they don't have time for advocacy, I make the time for them. I take over their class for five minutes while they make their advocacy calls. I also pass around postcards at teachers meetings, explain the cause we need to support, and write several short sample notes on the board. At the end of the meeting, I collect and mail the postcards."

"When teachers lack confidence and/or experience with advocating, I invite them to accompany me to a public hearing, a rally, a visit to a legislator, or a school board meeting. One year during spring break, I used the school bus and took several staff members up to the state capital. We walked the halls and talked to several legislators about the need for subsidized child care slots. Not only did we have a blast, but we also became part of a larger group that got more money than had been originally earmarked for child care subsidies from the legislature."

"When teachers are fearful about being uninformed, I write out short summaries about issues that affect children and we discuss them at our Friday teachers meeting."

"When teachers seem to lack motivation, I find an issue that hits home for them and we talk about it. One approach I use all the time is to find an issue that relates to our own school, like the need for a stop sign on the corner. Then we plan an advocacy campaign together. I even encourage my staff to advocate against me for more vacation days and better classroom supplies."

"When teachers tell me that their one call to a legislator or their one vote won't count for anything, I remind them that we wouldn't be living in a democracy if everyone thought the way they did."

"When teachers tell me about their distrust of government, I remind them that our government is no better than the people we put in office. If people don't get interested in supporting good candidates, the government will not become any better." ●

To maintain the ethics of the early childhood profession

Mrs. Quickreader was visiting with a child care provider, Mrs. Lean-on-Me, to learn about her center:

Mrs. Quickreader: "As I told you on the phone, I am looking for a family child care home where I can place my son Jason, who is now 6 months old."

Mrs. Lean-on-Me: "I am glad you have come here. We do have an opening for a 6-month-old. Talk to me a little bit about your son."

Mrs. Quickreader: "He's a wonderful baby—social, outgoing, and full of smiles and laughs. I am sure he will make a good adjustment wherever I put him, but I am especially interested in finding a caregiver with whom I can build rapport."

Mrs. Lean-on-Me: "Again, you have come to the right place. I make a practice of keeping the parents informed about everything their baby is doing, and I listen carefully when parents have concerns. As a matter of fact, the reason I have an opening is that Mrs. Yellow-Tail, who also has a 6-month-old boy, is moving to Arizona. The last day her baby was with me, she gave me a hug and told me that she felt as if she was losing more than a caregiver—she was losing her best friend. I feel so sorry for Mrs. Yellow-Tail. Her husband never helps her with their son, and when she moves to Arizona, she'll have no support system at all."

Mrs. Quickreader thanked Mrs. Lean-on-Me and went to another interview. She decided not to place her son in Mrs. Lean-on-Me's home. ●

As you may have recognized, when Mrs. Lean-on-Me divulged personal information about another client, she was violating an important ethical principle. Maintaining the ethics of one's field is important to being a professional.

The Principles of Ethical Practice

A *code of ethics* is a set of principles that describe the behavior expected of a professional in a given field. In some situations that occur in the child care setting, ethical behavior can be clearly identified. For instance, it is not ethical to share confidential information, to misrepresent one's credentials, to put extra hours on a timesheet, to talk to one parent about problems with another parent, or to withhold information on an accident report that may be incriminating. In other situations, the ethical course is harder to determine. Should we report a parent for abusing a child when we are pretty sure (but not positive) that the abuse occurred? Should you tell a nervous parent that her child fell down on the playground when the child wasn't even hurt?

> *A code of ethics is a set of principles that describe the behavior expected of a professional in a given field.*

Many different codes of ethics have been written. However, these five principles are inherent in the code of ethics for early childhood professionals:

1. Professionals always maintain the confidentiality of the parents and co-workers in the child care setting.

2. Professionals are honest, dependable, and reliable in performing all of the duties related to the center. This includes following all procedures related to the health, safety, and well-being of the children and adhering to the program's philosophy.

3. Professionals are truthful with children, parents, co-workers, and directors. They do not make promises that they cannot keep, and they do not commit to a course of action that they cannot follow.

4. Professionals treat all children and families with respect, regardless of gender, race/ethnicity, culture, sexual orientation, and economic status. Being respectful to parents includes respecting differences in beliefs and child-rearing philosophies and maintaining your calm even when you are attacked unfairly.

5. Professionals treat each child as an individual. They recognize the importance of building on each child's strengths, of providing realistic challenges, and of providing opportunities for each child to be successful. They are concerned with making each child in their group feel wanted, welcome, and successful, regardless of the child's level of competency.

The NAEYC Code of Ethical Conduct

The National Association for the Education of Young Children has established a Code of Ethical Conduct and Statement of Commitment (NAEYC, 2005). (Both can be found at the NAEYC website: www.naeyc.org.) Each person who earns the national CDA credential is asked to attest that she will follow the NAEYC Code of Ethical Conduct and Statement of Commitment.

In the its Code of Ethical Conduct, the NAEYC uses ideals and principles to define responsibilities in four basic areas. The following are a few key ideas from each of the four areas:

1. *"Ethical responsibilities to children"*
   - Not to harm children, above all else
   - To provide appropriate programming for children
   - To promote and protect children's well-being
2. *"Ethical responsibilities to families"*
   - To develop relationships of mutual trust
   - To respect families' cultures and values
   - To keep families informed about the program and about their children's experiences in it
   - To connect families with community resources
3. *"Ethical responsibilities to colleagues"*
   - To develop relationships of respect, trust, and cooperation with co-workers
   - To attempt to resolve differences collegially
   - To assist the program in providing high-quality services
4. *"Ethical responsibilities to community and society"*
   - To serve as a voice for children everywhere
   - To provide high-quality services
   - To advocate for all children to have access to high-quality services

The NAEYC's Statement of Commitment is reprinted in the box on page 329.

Applying Principles to Practice

As you read through the following vignettes, identify the ones in which there is a clear violation of an ethical principle and the ones in which the ethical course of action is difficult to determine. Think about how you would handle each situation.

Situation 1

Mrs. Yellow-Belly was a newly hired teacher assistant assigned to a seasoned teacher, Mrs. Do-It-My-Way. One of the first things that Mrs. Do-It-My-Way told her assistant was not to let a child named Dorothea play on the playground. "One of the parents," she explained, "told me confidentially that Dorothea was exposed to AIDS. If she happened to get scratched on the playground, her blood might get on another child, and it could start an epidemic." ●

Situation 2

Mr. Corner was telling his co-worker about the telephone call he had received from Naomi's mother. "I know you won't believe it, but Naomi's mother told me that Naomi is not allowed to participate in the Christmas pageant because her family doesn't celebrate Christmas. Well, her mother can keep her home on the day of the pageant, but I'm certainly not going to keep Naomi from taking part in the rehearsals!" ●

Statement of Commitment*

As an individual who works with young children, I commit myself to furthering the values of early childhood education as they are reflected in the ideals and principles of the NAEYC Code of Ethical Conduct.

To the best of my ability I will

- Never harm children.
- Ensure that programs for young children are based on current knowledge and research of child development and early childhood education.
- Respect and support families in their task of nurturing children.
- Respect colleagues in early childhood care and education and support them in maintaining the NAEYC Code of Ethical Conduct.
- Serve as an advocate for children, their families, and their teachers in community and society.
- Stay informed of and maintain high standards of professional conduct.
- Engage in an ongoing process of self-reflection, realizing that personal characteristics, biases, and beliefs have an impact on children and families.
- Be open to new ideas and be willing to learn from the suggestions of others.
- Continue to learn, grow, and contribute as a professional.
- Honor the ideals and principles of the NAEYC Code of Ethical Conduct.

*This Statement of Commitment is not part of the Code but is a personal acknowledgement of the individual's willingness to embrace the distinctive values and moral obligations of the field of early childhood care and education. It is recognition of the moral obligations that lead to an individual becoming part of the profession.

Source: Reprinted, by permission, from the National Association for the Education of Young Children, Code of Ethical Conduct and Statement of Commitment, 2005 Revision (Washington, DC: NAEYC, 2005). The Code of Ethical Conduct is available online at www.naeyc.org.

Situation 3

Mrs. Cantelli had requested a conference with her daughter's teacher, Mrs. Carter, to discuss the reading curriculum. "I know that it doesn't hurt to expose children to reading and writing," she said, "but I don't think you should be teaching phonics to preschoolers. Do you really think these children are ready to learn phonics?" *Ms. Carter didn't know how to respond. She felt that Mrs. Cantelli was right, but the director of the school had made it quite clear that everyone had to teach phonics.* ●

Situation 4

Cuddle Care is the only licensed child care facility available in the camp of migrant workers. That means that during harvesting, Cuddle Care is often overenrolled. The director has realized that if she does not take the children into her center, many of the infants might be left in the care of their young brothers and sisters. She's also worried about losing her license. When someone from the health department arrived unexpectedly one day, the director was afraid that she might be shut down for overcrowding. She asked one of the teachers to take 10 of the children on a walk so the health department wouldn't find out how many children were in the center. The teacher was not sure whether she should follow the director's instructions, but she did. ●

To build a professional support system

Being a professional means that, to some extent, you operate independently. You make judgments and decisions every day and are responsible for their consequences. While this can be empowering, it can also feel lonely and even, at times, intimidating. That is why teachers, like all professionals, need to reflect on their practice, find colleagues with whom they can discuss new ideas and "tough calls," and build a network for personal and professional support.

Making Time for Reflection and Discussion

In addition to planning and preparation time, early childhood teachers and caregivers need time to think: to reflect on what they are doing and what is and isn't working, to puzzle out what is happening with individual children and why, to read about new research and explore what it might mean for their classrooms, and to dream up new ideas. Some of this thinking is best done alone, and some is best done through conversations with colleagues, parents, supervisors, and consultants.

With all of the demands on your time, how can you make time for reflection and discussion?

- Set aside at least 15 minutes each day for "kidwatching." Use this time to observe individual children and make notes about behaviors that impress, intrigue, and puzzle you. Some teachers like to keep a journal on each child, including observations, photographs, and samples of the child's work. This journal can be shared with the child's parents, who may also make entries.

- Set aside at least an hour each week for learning. Read early childhood journals, attend a class or workshop, search out early childhood Internet sites, exchange e-mail with colleagues, and browse through catalogs and activity books to get ideas and research topics you are studying with the children.

- Insist on having regular staff meetings and breaks. Use these times to discuss issues and ideas with your colleagues, as well as to relax and socialize.

- Arrange with colleagues to visit each other's classrooms.
- Use professional days to visit other centers, attend conferences, and participate in advocacy events.
- Meet regularly and as needed with your supervisor or with a colleague who can support you. Bring your own goals, issues, and questions to these meetings.
- Find a mentor—a more experienced colleague who can share her experience, answer your questions, and help you think through plans and ideas.
- Enlist parents as partners. They can help you understand their children, their families, and their cultures. They may also have special skills and ideas that can enrich your classroom.
- Look at your classroom through the eyes of a child and through the eyes of a parent. What new things do you notice?

Building Relationships

The staff at the We're a Family Center were proud and elated. They had just put on a very successful conference for parents and professionals in their community. Teachers and directors from other centers had joined them to hear about the latest research on language development and to see some of the things they were doing in their classrooms. Once the conference was over, the staff went out for dinner to celebrate. They were each other's best friends, and they didn't want this day to end too soon.

Relationships like those at We're a Family don't happen overnight. The teachers there had been working together for more than 10 years. They knew each other's dreams and foibles, joys and burdens. They had spent time with each other's families and had supported each other through challenges and triumphs. They shared inside jokes and memories. They had gone together to professional conferences, both as learners and as presenters. They had worked together to improve wages and working conditions, to earn accreditation for their center, and to figure out how to meet the needs of new immigrant families and several children with challenging disabilities. Through shared work and shared play, the teachers had become a team.

Whether you are working in a family child care home, in a small center, or in a large organization, you need to form adult, work-based relationships. Here are some things you can do to build supportive relationships:

> *Whether you are working in a family child care home, in a small center, or in a large organization, you need to form adult, work-based relationships.*

- If you are working alone or with few colleagues, take advantage of community resources and events. Bring your group to the library, playground, or local drop-in center, where you can meet other colleagues.
- Plan parties, potluck dinners, and other social events. These can be for staff only, staff and parents, or staff and professionals in the field.
- Visit each other's classrooms. Share lesson plans, craft ideas, and materials.
- Work together to make things for your classrooms.

- Meet regularly with colleagues to plan joint activities and field trips.
- Plan special days when you can all have fun together. You might put on a carnival as a fundraiser, celebrate Halloween with costumes (no masks) and special treats, have a family picnic, or go on a field trip together.
- Celebrate accomplishments and milestones: birthdays, graduations, and both individual and center achievements.
- Invite a celebrity to visit the school.
- Enroll in courses or workshops together.
- Start a learning circle or peer-mentorship relationship. Meet regularly in person or on the phone with a few colleagues to discuss your work.
- Spend some time with colleagues when work is *not* on the agenda. Just have fun together.
- Advocate for your needs. You may wish to join a union (directors can join, too) or form a task force within your center to investigate ways to improve communication, working conditions, or wages and benefits.

You and your local colleagues may want to join a professional organization together or even found your own chapter. Joining a professional early childhood organization provides you with access to current publications as well as opportunities to attend conferences and conventions, network with other professionals, and join working committees and plan workshops.

As you take your place within the ever-widening circle of early childhood professionals, remember that you not only have a lot to learn and live up to. You also have a lot to contribute.

Additional Resources about Professionalism

Alvarado, C., Burnley, L., Derman-Sparks, L., Hoffman, E., Jimenez, L. I., Labyzon, J., Ramsey, P., Unten, A., Wallace, B., & Yasui, B. (1999). *In our own way: How anti-bias work shapes our lives.* St. Paul, MN: Redleaf Press.

Bloom, P. (1997). *A great place to work: Improving conditions for staff in young children's programs* (Rev. ed.). Washington, DC: NAEYC.

Brunson-Day, C. (Ed.). (2004). *Essentials for child development associates working with young children* (2nd ed.). Washington, DC: Council for Professional Recognition.

Derman-Sparks, L., & ABC Task Force. (1989). *Anti-bias curriculum: Tools for empowering young children.* Washington, DC: NAEYC.

Feeney, S., & Freeman, N. (1999). *Ethics and the early childhood educator: Using the NAEYC Code.* Washington, DC: NAEYC.

Jones, E. (Ed.). (1993). *Growing teachers: Partnerships in staff development.* Washington, DC: NAEYC.

National Association for the Education of Young Children. (2005). *Code of ethical conduct and statement of commitment.* Washington, DC:Author.

York, S. (2003). *Roots and wings: Affirming culture in early childhood programs* (Rev. ed.). St. Paul, MN: Redleaf Press.